U.S. Flotilla Service in the War of 1812

Heritage Books by Eric Eugene Johnson:

Transcribed by Eric Eugene Johnson

American Prisoners of War during the War of 1812: Birth, Death, and Parole Records

American Prisoners of War Held at Chatham During the War of 1812

American Prisoners of War Held at Dartmoor During the War of 1812

American Prisoners of War Held in Montreal and Quebec During the War of 1812

American Prisoners of War Held at Plymouth During the War of 1812

American Prisoners of War Held at Portsmouth, Stapleton, Gibraltar and Malta during the War of 1812

American Prisoners of War Held at Quebec During the War of 1812, 8 June 1813–11 December 1814

American Prisoners of War Paroled at Dartmouth, Halifax, Jamaica and Odiham During the War of 1812

American Sea Fencibles in the War of 1812: United States Sea Fencibles, State Sea Fencibles

Black American Prisoners of War Held by the British Royal Navy during the War of 1812

Black Regulars in the War of 1812

Black Regulars and Militiamen in the War of 1812

Forgotten Americans Who Served in the War of 1812

Maryland Regulars in the War of 1812

Transcribed by Eric Eugene Johnson; Foreword by Christos Christou

Ohio and the War of 1812: A Collection of Lists, Musters and Essays

Ohio's Regulars in the War of 1812

Roster and History of the 15th U.S. Infantry, Mexican-American War, 1846–1848

Rosters of Ohio Militia in the War of 1812

Tennessee Regulars in the War of 1812

The Men of the Lake Erie Squadron: 1813–1825

The Ultimate Guide in Researching War of 1812 Veterans

U. S. Flotilla Service in the War of 1812

U. S. Flotilla Service in the War of 1812

Eric Eugene Johnson

Society of the War of 1812
in the
State of Ohio

HERITAGE BOOKS
2025

HERITAGE BOOKS
AN IMPRINT OF HERITAGE BOOKS, INC.

Books, CDs, and more—Worldwide

For our listing of thousands of titles see our website
at
www.HeritageBooks.com

Published 2025 by
HERITAGE BOOKS, INC.
Publishing Division
5810 Ruatan Street
Berwyn Heights, Md. 20740

International Standard Book Number
Paperbound: 978-0-7884-4644-3

- Table of Contents -

Introduction

One of the most unique naval services of the United States during the War of 1812 was the U.S. Flotilla Service, which was created by the U.S. Congress on 16 April 1814. It was the brainchild of privateer captain Joshua Barney of Baltimore, Maryland, who on 4 July 1813 proposed a 'flying squadron' to the Secretary of the Navy William Jones in order to protect Baltimore's harbor.

The U.S. Navy operated a gunboat service throughout the War of 1812, which protected our harbors from British attacks. Most of the gunboats were old, heavy, and very clumsy to sail. They were a defensive weapon, better used as floating gun batteries. Offensively, they were of little value in this conflict. Barney's idea of creating a 'flying squadron' made perfect sense. These gunboats would be lighter and easier to sail. They could defend a harbor, and at the same time, be used to attack the British vessels before they entered our harbors.

Barney's 'flying squadron' would be formed to replace the Navy's gunboat squadron at Baltimore. He originally had proposed his plan for this squadron to the Maryland State Assembly. This state's House of Delegates rejected this plan, but the state's Senate approved the proposal. The plan called for twenty barges, 1,000 naval officers and men, and 500 marines. Nothing further happened to his plan at the State Assembly, so Barney wrote his letter to the Secretary of the Navy.

Secretary William Jones embraced Barney's plan and expanded his original idea. In a letter to Senator John Gaillard, the chairman of the Naval Committee of the U.S. Senate, Jones proposed to create a new naval service to replace some of the squadrons of the U.S. Navy's gunboat Service. Four captains and twelve lieutenants would be commissioned for this new service. The new service would take over the duties of the Navy's gunboats serving in the Chesapeake Bay and New York City.

The justification for this new service was that it would free up U.S. naval officers and seamen for duty on the Great Lakes, and to man the new ships being built for the U.S. Navy on the east coast. This service would be made up of men who wanted to serve but didn't want sea duty. Local men, protecting their own harbors, seemed to be a perfectly logical idea.

The U.S. Congress created the U.S. Flotilla Service on 16 April 1814 as a separate military service. The service was not a part of the U.S. Navy, but it was still under the direct control of the Secretary of the Navy. The President appointed all of the commissioned officers with the approval of the U.S. Senate.

The gunboats and barges of the Baltimore Gunboat Squadron, the Potomac Gunboat Squadron, and the New York Gunboat Squadron, operated by the U.S. Navy, were turned over to the U.S. Flotilla Service. Barney was commissioned as a captain and he took command of the Chesapeake Bay Flotilla Squadron, which was made up of the former Baltimore and Potomac squadrons, while Jacob M. Lewis was commissioned as a captain, and he commanded the New York Flotilla Squadron.

The Chesapeake Bay Flotilla Squadron fought in three naval battles and one land battle during the War of 1812. This squadron was the only American unit along with a U.S Marine Corps detachment, which stood their grounds, and fought the British during the Battle of Bladensburg on 24 August 1814. The New York Flotilla Squadron saw minor action during this war. Approximately 2,500 men served in the U.S. Flotilla Service. The Chesapeake Bay Flotilla Squadron had 1,003 officers and men on its muster rolls, while the New York Flotilla Squadron had over 1,000 officers and men.

On 27 February 1815, the U.S. Flotilla Service was disbanded and its gunboats and barges were either sold or laid up. All of the men in the service were discharged and given four months extra pay. Had the War of 1812 continued, at least two more squadrons of the U.S. Flotilla Service would probably have been created.

The success of the Chesapeake Bay Flotilla Squadron proved that Barney's plan for a 'flying squadron' was the correct one. Had the British attacked New York City, Captain Lewis' flotilla squadron would have probably obtained the same glory as Captain Barney.

Little has been written on the U.S. Flotilla Service and its accomplishments during the War of 1812. The purpose of this work is to give the reader a short history of this forgotten naval service and to identify the men who served within its ranks.

U.S. Flotilla Service

Upon taking office in 1801, President Thomas Jefferson vowed to reduce the national debt. One area of the government which he felt needed to be reduced was the military, both the U.S. Army and the U.S. Navy. In 1802, the U.S. Army was reduced to a defensive force, with the understanding that the militia could always be called up to defend this nation.

Prior to 1801, President John Adams had increased the size of the U.S. Navy to a force of fifty-four ships during the Quasi-War (1798-1800) with France, and then this service was down-sized to twenty ships during the First Barbary War (1801-1805) under Jefferson. After 1805, Jefferson further down-sized the navy leaving America's merchant ships to deal with the British Royal Navy and the north African privates on their own.

Thomas Jefferson and his Democratic-Republican Party pushed through Congress a number of bills creating a naval gunboat service in order to protect the ports and harbors of the United States. This turned the majority of the U.S. Navy into a defensive force.

On 28 February 1803, Congress passed the first bill, appropriating $50,000 to build fifteen gunboats.[1] The money was used to build, man, and outfit these vessels. The second bill was approved on 21 April 1806.[2] This bill allocated $250,000 to build fifty more gunboats, and another $20,000 to man and equip these vessels. An additional $150,000 was allocated to fortify and to protect the nation's ports and harbors.

The final bill, under the Jefferson administration, was approved on 18 December 1807, and it authorized the building of 188 gunboats.[3] This bill appropriated $852,500 to build or purchased gunboats, and to man and equip these vessels.

A total of 278 gunboats were authorized, but only 166 were completed prior to the War of 1812. They were all given a numeric designation. Many of these gunboats had been laid up before the war, while the older gunboats have been dismantled due to their age.

The next president, James Madison, had to increase both the U.S. Army and the U.S. Navy in 1808 on the eve of the War of 1812. Despite Madison's efforts, the nation was still unprepared to fight another war with Great Britain.

During the War of 1812, most of the U.S. Navy's warships were tied up in ports due to the British blockade of our eastern and southern coasts. The ship's crews were either sent to Lake Erie, to Lake Ontario, to Lake Champlain, or to the navy's gunboat squadrons. Most seaman did not want to be transferred to the gunboats, where they would have to man the oars. Sea or lake duty was desired by most officers and seamen.

The only success of the U.S. Navy's Gunboat Service during the War of 1812 was Master Commandant Thomas McDonough's defense of Plattsburgh, New York in September 1814. He properly used his ten gunboats during the Battle of Lake Champlain. If he had more brigs and frigates, instead of gunboats, the Battle of Lake Champlain could have been fought on the open lake and not in a bay at Plattsburg.

If Master Commandant Oliver Hazard Perry had four gunboats instead of the four schooners, that were built at Erie, Pennsylvania, he would have been forced to battle the British within the 'safe harbor' at Put-in-Bay or possibly in Sandusky Bay, both in the state of Ohio. The British would have had the advantage over Perry, if Pery had gunboats in his squadron instead of the more 'sea worthy' lake schooners.

Lieutenant Thomas ap Catesby Jones lost his naval gunboat squadron of two sloops and five gunboats to the British in 1814 during the Battle of Lake Borgne in Louisiana. This was a delaying tactic, which gave Major General Andrew Jackson time to prepare for the Battle of New Orleans.

The U.S. Congress passed the last act to strengthen the U.S. Navy's Gunboat Service on 5 July 1813 when it gave the President the authority to build barges for the defense of the ports and harbors of the United States.[4] These barges could be no longer the forty-five feet in length and could carry only heavy guns. The bill appropriated only $250,000 to build, supply, and man these barges. Normally, barges were not self-propelled, and they had to be towed into position and anchored. They were floating gun batteries, and could easily be overrun and captured.

Jefferson's gunboat navy was a total failure! The $947,500 allocated before the War of 1812, and the other moneys during the war, could have been better spent on building frigates and ships-of-the-line.

Gunboat types

During this period in history, gunboats were small, defensive warships carrying one or two heavy cannons, which were designed to attack coastal targets or to protect harbors. They were not intended to be used on the open seas. Many of these gunboats were actually galleys, row galleys, or barges. These terms were interchangeable but there is a difference in these types of gunboats.

The standard gunboat during the War of 1812 was either 75-foot in length or 50-foot in length, but the older gunboat types were at least 40-foot in length. Most of these types of gunboats did not have decks, and the cannons were placed of platforms at the bow and at the stern of the vessels.

The larger gunboats were armed with two cannons or cannonades. The smaller gunboats may have had only one cannon. A cannon was a long-range weapon while the cannonades were a short-range weapon. The bow cannon was larger than the stern cannon or cannonade, and some gunboats carried smaller cannons amounted on the sides or on swivels in the middle of the vessel. The main propulsion were one or two sails, while the secondary propulsion were large oars, called sweeps. The sails were normally lateen sails, which were triangular in shape.

A galley used oars for propulsion but still could rig a sail when needed. Row galleys only used oars instead of sails. Barges (also called floating batteries) had no propulsion and they had to either be towed into place or poled by the men.

Gunboats primarily used 24-pound, 32-pound, or 42-pound cannons and/or cannonades. The numbers are the weight of the cannon balls. These vessels also used small caliber weapons when the larger weapons were not available.

Gunboats also were small merchant ships, usually sloops or schooners, which were modified to carry one or two heavy cannons. These vessels were mostly used as mother ships for the gunboat squadrons. These sloops and schooners had decks and larger sails, while the other types of gunboats did not have decks and used smaller sails.

The standard armed sloops and schooners used 9-pound, 12-pound, 18-pound, and sometimes, 24-pound cannons or cannonades. These vessels were not gunboats and they were used by the U.S. Navy on the high seas.

Creating the U.S. Flotilla Service

Before the war, Joshua Barney was an established sea captain and during the first part of the War of 1812, he was a very successful privateer captain. His idea of a 'flying squadron' failed to pass the Maryland state legislature, so on 4 July 1813, he wrote a letter to the Secretary of the Navy William Jones outlining the need for his flying squadron to protect the harbor at Baltimore, Maryland.[5]

Barney started his letter to the Jones by stating that the two U.S. frigates stationed at Baltimore could not leave the harbor due to the British blockade of the Chesapeake Bay. The current gunboats were too heavy and too clumsy to sail, and they were only fit to lay moored to protect the Baltimore harbor.

His flying squadron would consist of twenty small-draft gunboats, armed with a single 24-pound cannon, and manned by fifty officers and men plus twenty-five soldiers. The gunboats would be propelled by light sails and oars. It was a type of gunboats currently being used in Denmark, Sweden, and Spain.

He would need 1,000 officers and men to operate the gunboats, and another 500 officers and soldiers to act as marines on these vessels. Also, he would need from three to four sailing vessels to support his squadron. He ended by stating that his plan was rejected by the Maryland House of Delegates but it was passed by the Maryland Senate.

It is safe to say that the Secretary Jones loved the idea of a flying squadron, and he further expanded Barney's idea, which he brough forth in a letter to U.S. Senator John Gaillard:

> Communicated to the U.S. Senate on 18 March 1814 to the Honorable John Gaillard, Chairman of the Naval Committee of the Senate from Secretary of the Navy William Jones, Navy Department, 22 February 1814, Condition of the Navy, and the Progress made in Providing Materials and Building Ships. [6]
>
> We have a right, sir, to anticipate, during the ensuing summer, the most urgent occasion for the vigorous employment of the flotilla for the defense of the waters of the United States; and it has become a very interesting question how that force is to be commanded with the best effect. That service is, at best, unpopular with the regular officers of the navy; and the services of those officers who are qualified for separate commands are required to meet the increased demand for the regular naval force, particularly on the lakes, which is very pressing. Those officers who are deficient in experience are justly averse to the flotilla service, because they can acquire but very little useful professional knowledge; and indeed, it is a service in which those who are to form the officers for the ships of war ought not to be engaged.
>
> There are other intrinsic difficulties in this service, which are unknown onboard ships of war. The temptations to insubordination and vice are much greater in this scattered and amphibious kind of force; and the rigors of naval discipline, unless tempered with judgment and great moderation, discourage the recruiting for this service.

> Bay and river craftsmen, seaman, ordinary seamen, who have families, riggers, and naval mechanics out of employ, will engage in this service, under a local commander of capacity and influence, when they will not engage for the regular naval service.
>
> As rank, in our naval service, can only be attained by regular gradation, commanders of talents, local knowledge, influence, and distinguished courage, cannot be commissioned for this service under the present regulations. The necessity of the case, from the reasons which I have assigned, has induced the employment of a few acting officers, with command, but without rank, in two of the most important situations, viz: New York harbor and the Chesapeake Bay. These appointments appear to have given great confidence in these districts, and the success in recruiting for the service on these stations, considering the unequal competition of the military and private service, has been favorable.
>
> I would, therefore, take the liberty of suggesting the utility of providing by law for the appointing of four captains, with the same relative rank and authority in the flotilla service, and the same pay and emoluments as captains in the navy; and twelve lieutenants, with the same relative rank and authority in the flotilla service, and the same pay and emoluments as lieutenants in the navy, but limited to the temporary employment of the flotilla, without rank in the navy other than in the flotilla in which they may serve, and subject only to the orders of the President of the United States. In all other respects, to be governed by the rules and regulations provided for the government of the navy.
>
> W. Jones

The U.S. Congress created the U.S. Flotilla Service on 16 April 1814 as a separate military service. The service was not a part of the U.S. Navy, but it was still under the direct control of the Secretary of the Navy. Four captains and twelve lieutenant positions were authorized for this service with the same relative rank and authority as the same grade in the U.S. Navy. Captains received the same pay of a captain in the navy who was commanding a ship of twenty guns and less than thirty-two guns. Lieutenants received the same pay and subsistence as their counterparts in the navy. The President appointed all of the officers with the approval of the U.S. Senate.

An act authorizing the appointment of certain officers for the flotilla service [7]
16 April 1814

> Section 1 – The president may appoint with the approval of the Senate four captains and twelve lieutenants for the Flotilla Service of the United States. They do not have rank within the Navy but they will have the same relative rank and authority in the Flotilla Service of the same grade that is entitled in the Navy.
>
> Section 2 – The captain shall receive the same pay and subsistence of a captain in the Navy who is commanding a ship of twenty and under thirty-two guns. Lieutenants will receive the same pay and subsistence of a lieutenant in the Navy.
>
> Section 3 - The president may appoint officers in the Flotilla Service during a recess of the Senate but the appointments must be approved during the next session.

In a letter to the U.S. Senate outlining the condition of the navy and the progress of the naval construction for 1814, the Secretary of the Navy William Jones said that the purpose of the U.S. Flotilla Service was to replace the officers and seamen in the naval gunboat service with local family men who wanted to serve in the navy but who did not want sea duty. Experienced naval officers were badly needed for the new warships being built on the east coast and at our naval squadrons on the Great Lakes. Most officers and seamen in the naval flotilla service wanted sea duty. Secretary Jones further stated that the new service would be governed by the same rules and regulations provided for the U.S. Navy.

The gunboats and barges of the Baltimore Gunboat Squadron, the Potomac Gunboat Squadron, and the New York Gunboat Squadron, operated by the U.S. Navy, were turned over to the U.S. Flotilla Service. Captain Joshua Barney took command of the Chesapeake Bay Flotilla Squadron, which was made up of the former Baltimore and Potomac gunboat squadrons, [8] while Captain Jacob M. Lewis commanded the New York Flotilla Squadron.[9]

Early in the war, Jacob Lewis was the captain of the privateer *Bunker Hill* out of New York City.[10] He was commissioned as a master commandant (now the rank of commander) in the U.S. Navy on 27 November 1812.[11] Lewis was given command of the naval gunboat squadron at New York City. This squadron had thirty-eight gunboats protecting the New York harbor.[12] After the squadron at New York City was transferred to the U.S. Flotilla Service, Lewis was promoted to captain on 26 April 1814.[13]

Joshua Barney was also a privateer captain early in the war. He was the master of the schooner *Rossie*, homeported at Baltimore.[14] He was commissioned as an acting master commandant in the U.S. Navy on 20 August 1813, and he was given the command of the new Chesapeake Bay Flotilla Squadron.[15] On 4 March 1814, the flotilla had one gunboat, a pilot boat, and thirteen barges, with ten more barges under construction. Barney was promoted to captain in the U.S. Flotilla Service on 25 April 1814.[16]

Captain Barney was never a commodore during the War of 1812. There was no authorization of this rank for the U.S. Flotilla Service, and there would not be a rank of commodore in the U.S Navy until 1862. Commodore was a title bestowed on Barney, probably by himself or by his men, since he commanded a squadron of small vessels. It was common during this time period of American history to use the title 'commodore' if an officer commanded more than one ship, vessel, or gunboat.

The Secretaries of the Navy did bestow the title of commodore on senior captains who commanded naval shipyards, which built warships, or to senior captains who commanded a squadron of warships before 1862. These captains were permitted to wear the epaulet of a commodore (with a star on the epaulet), and to fly a commodore's pennate on a warship in which he commanded. Commodore was actually a brevet rank which placed these officers as equals to the U.S. Army's brigadier generals. Even though they were treated as a commodore, these officers still received the pay of a senior captain.

Solomon Rutter and Solomon Frazier both were commissioned as lieutenants in the U.S. Flotilla Service: Rutter on 25 April 1814 and Frazier on 26 April 1814.[17] Both men were assigned to the Chesapeake Bay Flotilla Squadron. Although the U.S. Flotilla Service was authorized four captains and twelve lieutenants, no other commissioned officers are known to have been appointed. A number of sailing masters (also called masters), surgeons, pursers, and midshipmen were appointed in both squadrons. These last officers were warrant officers and not commissioned officers, and their appointments did not need approval of the U.S. Senate.

A bill was introduced in the U.S. House of Representative in October 1814 to reimburse the men of the flotilla for lost personal items resulting from the battles in Maryland.[18] It was suggested to give these men three months extra pay to compensate for their losses. The bill was tabled by a vote of 66 to 59. However, after the ratification of the Treaty of Ghent on 17 February 1815 ending the War of 1812, the U.S. Flotilla Service was disbanded on 27 February 1815, and its barges were either sold or laid up. All of the men in the service were discharged and given four months extra pay.

An act to repeal certain acts concerning the flotilla service, and for other purposes [19]
27 February 1815

Section 1 – The act of 5 July 1813, chapter 6, for building barges is repealed. The act of 16 April 1814, chapter 59, creating the flotilla service is repealed.

Section 2 – The barges of the flotilla establishment are to be sold or laid up after their guns and stores have been removed. The moneys shall be paid into the treasury.

Section 3 – The officers, warrant officers, and privates shall be discharged with four months extra pay.

Section 4 – The president is authorized to sell or lay up the vessels on the lakes except what is necessary to enforce and revenue laws. The armament and stores are to be removed before the vessels are laid up or sold.

Section 5 – The act of 15 November 1814, chapter 3, is repealed. The vessels that were built or purchased under this act are to be sold with the moneys paid into the treasury.

Section 6 – The president may sell as many gunboats that are no longer needed for public safety after the guns and stores have been removed. The warrant officers and privates from these gunboats are to be discharged and then given four months extra pay.

The Chesapeake Bay Flotilla Squadron was discharged on 15 April 1815, with the officers and men receiving four months extra pay. The New York Flotilla Squadron began discharging men who have been transferred from the idle warships at the New York Navy Yard back to their ships starting in mid-January 1815. The last of this flotilla men were discharged in mid-July 1815.

The U.S. Navy's gunboat service also was called the U.S. Navy flotilla service, but in this work the service will always be referred to as the U.S. Navy's gunboat service. This is to help prevent any confusions for the readers. Also, the U.S. Navy had gunboat squadrons, while the U.S. Flotilla Service had flotilla squadrons.

Chesapeake Bay Flotilla Squadron muster rolls [20]

There are two payroll reports and two partial muster rolls for the Chesapeake Bay Flotilla Squadron under Captain Joshua Barney at the National Archives. Each man was given a unique payroll number which matches each man's muster roll number. This avoids the problem of identifying and paying men with the same name, such as, John Smith.

The first payroll report covers the period from 23 August 1813 to 6 April 1814, and it contains the names of 359 officers and men. The second payroll report covers the period from 7 April 1814 to 15 April 1815, and it contains the names of 1,003 officers and men. The second report includes the 359 men from the first report, and it updates the information on these men after 6 April 1814.

The two payroll reports cover the time period when the Chesapeake Bay Flotilla Squadron was first created and when it was officially disbanded. Therefore, the figure of 1,003 personnel serving in this flotilla is extremely actuate. But, of the 1,003 men listed on the payroll reports, fifty-five men had been entered twice, leaving 948 officers and enlisted men who actually served in the U.S. Flotilla Service in the Chesapeake Bay Flotilla Squadron under Captain Barney.

Not all of the men listed on the payroll reports served during the flotilla's naval battles in southern Maryland and at the Battle of Bladensburg. Some of the men had died before the battles, deserted, or deserted and then came back. The men who deserted and came back were re-entered on the rolls with a new payroll number. Also, some of the men were promoted and then re-entered on the rolls with a new number.

The men with payroll numbers 446 through 924 came from the U.S. Frigate *United States*. They had the same payroll numbers on this ship as in the flotilla. Numbers 1 through 329 appears to be the men who Barney had enlisted in the Baltimore area. Many of the men from numbers 360 through 445, and from numbers 925 through 1003, appears to have come from the U.S. Navy's Potomac Gunboat Squadron. These men from this squadron had originally come from the U.S. Frigate *Adams*.

The two muster rolls are very incomplete because of missing pages. The first muster roll has the names of the men from numbers 1 to 52 and from numbers 925 to 1,002. The second muster roll only has the men whose numbers were from 40 to 78.

The formation of the Chesapeake Bay Flotilla Squadron

On 4 March 1814, the U.S. Navy had 126 gunboats, thirty-two barges, and eleven armed vessels, with fifty-nine barges being built, in its gunboat service.[21] This service had sixteen gunboat squadrons located at New Orleans, Georgia, Charleston (SC), Wilmington (NC), Norfolk, Potomac (Washington, DC), Baltimore, Delaware (Philadelphia), New York, Lake Champlain, New London, Newport (RI), New Bedford, Boston, Newburyport, and Portsmouth (NH). The Baltimore gunboat squadron had been reassigned to the U.S. Flotilla Service's Chesapeake Bay Flotilla Squadron, but the Potomac gunboat squadron was still with the U.S. Naval Gunboat Service on this report. The New York gunboat squadron had been reassigned to the U.S. Flotilla Service.

Prior to the War of 1812, the U.S. Navy numbered their gunboats and did not assigned names to them, although the crews would 'nickname' their gunboats. This practice seems to have fallen by the wayside during the war, since gunboats built on Lake Erie, Lake Champlain, and other places, were given names and not numbers.

The Sailing Navy 1775-1854 [22] lists 176 gunboats built for the U.S. Navy prior to the War of 1812. The book has no information on numbers 169 through 176 (the last eight gunboats). In *The U.S. Brig Oneida: A Design & Operational History,*[23] it is stated that three gunboats were authorized on the lakes, one on Lake Ontario and two on Lake Champlain. However, the gunboat on Lake Ontario was built from the keel up as the U.S. Brig *Oneida*, and it was a warship and not a gunboat.

It is not known if the two gunboats on Lake Champlain were going to be gunboats number 169 and 170. They were completed as the U.S. Gunboats *Ludlow* and *Wilmer*. The other gunboats on this lake that were built during the war also were given names, and not numbers.

Six gunboats were authorized to be built at the Black Rock Naval Station near Buffalo, New York early in the war. Only four were laid down, and none were completed. They were actually 40-foot row galleys. If they had been completed, then they would have probably been numbered from 171 through 176. Four 50-foot gunboats were laid down at Erie, Pennsylvania, but they were completed as schooners for Master Commandant Oliver Hazard Perry's

Lake Erie Squadron. Although still classified as gunboats, they were more 'sea worthy' than if they had been completed as originally designed.

After the War of 1812 started, it appears that the U.S. Navy's system of numbering the gunboats fell by the way side. The gunboat builders at the various naval stations and private boatyards simply numbered their new builds starting with the number one at each location, or the gunboats were given names.

The 166 gunboats commissioned by the U.S. Navy prior to the War of 1812 came in all shapes and sizes. Many of the early gunboats were purchased from European counties for use during the Barbary Wars (1801-1805) in north Africa, while other gunboats were built in the United States and then towed to Europe. Many of the early gunboats that were built were experimental in design, and were laid up after a few years.

Chief Naval Contractor James Doughty designed a 40-foot row galley before the war. The row galleys were poor sailors and normally had to be towed into position. Baltimore City constructed six of these row galleys for their own defense. Commodore James Barron designed a better gunboat in 1806 but these gunboats were also poor sailors.

Doughty came up with two gunboat designs early in the war, which was the basis for nearly all gunboat construction during this war. His 1st class gunboat was 75-feet in length while the 2nd class gunboat was 50-feet in length. These vessels could protect a harbor and also attack enemy warships.

The new-built gunboats for Barney's flotilla squadron were of these new two designs while the gunboats on Lake Champlain also used these designs. Fifteen gunboats were being built on Lake Ontario but were unfinished by the end of the war. Nearly all new-built gunboats in 1814 and 1815 were either 1st class or 2nd class gunboats. Contractors had a habit of modifying the basic gunboat designs. A 1st class gunboat built at one city may look different from a 1st class gunboat built at another city.

Gunboat types in 1814

	1st Class	**2nd Class**	**Row Galley**	**1806 Design**
	2 sails	1 sail	(no sails)	Lateen sail and jib
Length	75 feet	50 feet	40 feet	64' 5"
Wide	15 feet	10 feet	10 feet	16' 10"
Depth	4 feet	3.5 feet	3 feet	
Cannons	2	2	2	1

Manning the new-built gunboats

1st Class	**2nd Class**
1 Sailing Master (commanding)	1 Sailing Master (commanding)
1 Master's Mate	1 Master's Mate
1 Gunner	1 Gunner
1 Boatswain	1 Boatswain
1 Steward	1 Steward
1 Cook	1 Cook
10 Seaman	8 Seaman
34 Ordinary Seaman	26 Ordinary Seaman
50 Total	**40 Total**

The Potomac Gunboat Squadron (U.S. Navy)

The Potomac Gunboat Squadron had three gunboats, three barges (with one being built), and the armed vessels: the U.S. Schooner *Scorpion*, the U.S. Schooner *Hornet*, and the U.S. Cutter *Asp*. The squadron was established on 17 Feb 1813 with Master Commandant Arthur Sinclair as its commander.[24] He would become the commander of the Lake Erie Squadron after Captain Oliver Hazard Perry was reassigned to the east coast after the Battle of Lake Erie on 10 September 1813. The Lake Erie Squadron also had a schooner named *Scorpion.*

By the time that this squadron was transferred to the Chesapeake Bay Flotilla Squadron, Lieutenant Edward Kennedy was the new commander. The squadron was manned by the officers and sailors from the U.S. Frigate *Adams*. The *Scorpion* had been transferred from the Norfolk Squadron in February 1813.

The *Asp* was a sloop, armed with one 12-pound cannon and two 12-pound cannonade.[25] The *Scorpion* was a block ship measuring 48'8" x 18'2" x 4'6", and armed with one 24-pound cannon, one 18-pound canon, and two 12-pound cannonades. Gunboats 70 and 71 had been built at the Washington Naval Yard, while Gunboat 137 had been built at Baltimore. The 137 measured 60' x 16'6" x 6'6".

The Washington Naval Yard starting building one 1st class gunboat and two 2nd class gunboats in 1814. These gunboats were completed by the time of the British invasion of Maryland, but they were prevented from joining Barney's flotilla squadron. The 1st class gunboat was at Alexandria, DC (now Virginia) and it was captured by the British when this city fell during the attack on Washington, DC. The other two gunboats survived the burning of the Washington Naval Yard.

The Baltimore Gunboat Squadron (U.S. Navy)

The Baltimore Gunboat Squadron had one gunboat, thirteen barges (with ten being built), and one pilot boat.[26] As one of the major ports in the United States, Baltimore had the smallest gunboat squadron, but it was supplemented with four contract vessels serving as gunboats.

Gunboat 138 was the only active gunboat at Baltimore. She was built in Baltimore, measuring 60' x 16'6" x 6'6", and armed with one 24-pound cannon and two 12-pound cannonades. Nine of the gunboats assigned to this squadron were at Annapolis, Maryland being repaired.

The U.S. Navy had leased four schooners (privateers) from owners in Baltimore. They were the *Comet*, the *Patapsco*, the *Revenge*, and the *Fox*. The *Comet* was unmanned, while the *Revenge* and *Patapsco* were half manned and the *Fox* fully manned. The City of Baltimore also had one row galley and six barges in its squadron.

The Norfolk Gunboat Squadron (U.S. Navy)

The Norfolk Gunboat Squadron at Norfolk, Virginia had twenty-three gunboats, one barge (with ten being built), and one bomb vessel. Since the Norfolk Gunboat Squadron was not transferred to the Chesapeake Bay Flotilla Squadron under Captain Barney, it has to be assumed that Barney's squadron would protect the northern areas of the Chesapeake Bay, while Captain Joseph Tarbell, commander of the Norfolk gunboat squadron, would protect the southern areas of the bay.

The gunboat squadron had seven gunboats in commission.[27] They were gunboats 60, 61, 67, 149, 152, 154, and 155. The station also had two tenders: the *Franklin* and the *Dispatch*. The Norfolk Gunboat Squadron was tied up protecting the port of Norfolk and the Gosport Naval Station during the British blockade for most of the war.

The Chesapeake Bay Flotilla Squadron [28]

The Chesapeake Bay Flotilla Squadron was a combination of old and new designs of gunboats. U.S. Navy purchased the row galley *Vigilant* and barges 4, 5, and 6 from the City of Baltimore. Three gunboats were being built at Washington, DC, ten gunboats were being built at St. Michael's, MD, and eight gunboats were being built at Baltimore, MD. Of the eight gunboats being built at Baltimore, four were 1st class gunboats while the other four were 2nd class gunboats. Nine of the other gunboats assigned to this flotilla squadron were at Annapolis, Maryland being repaired. Not all of the gunboats were ready by the time Barney left Baltimore to engage the British.

From the U.S. Naval gunboat squadrons, Barney received gunboats 70, 71, 137, and 138, plus the vessels *Scorpion, Hornet*, and *Asp*. Gunboats 70 and 71 had been built at Washington, DC, while Gunboats 137 and 138 had been built at Baltimore. Gunboats 137 and 138 were 60-feet in length and had been built between 1806 and 1808.

Gunboat 137 and the *Asp* had been refitted as storeships. The *Asp* was armed with one 12-pound cannon and two 12-pound cannonades. The *Scorpion* was originally the Gunboat 59, built at Hampton, Virginia, and converted to a sloop. She was 48-feet in length and armed with two 12-pound cannons, one 18-pound cannon, and one 24-pound cannon.

When Barney left Baltimore with his flotilla squadron, he had the following gunboats and vessels:

3 - 1st Class gunboats with one 24-pound cannon and one 42-pound cannonade [29]
4 - 1st Class gunboats with one 18-pound cannon and one 32-pound cannonade
2 - 2nd Class gunboats with one 18-pound cannon and one 24-pound cannonade
4 - 2nd Class gunboats with one 12-pound cannon and one 24-pound cannonade
1 - Row galley (*Vigilant*) with one 18-pound cannon
2 - Gunboats (*Numbers 137 and 138*) with one 24-pound cannon
1 - Sloop (*Scorpion*) with one 24-pound cannon, one 18-pound cannon, and two 12-pound cannonade
1 – Lookout boat with one 18-pound cannon (*not named, possibly the Shark*)

The lookout boat may have been the U.S. Schooner *Shark*. The twenty-six men of the *Shark* were transferred from the Potomac Gunboat Squadron to the Chesapeake Bay Flotilla Squadron on 20 April 1814, and the vessel may have also been transferred.[30] A small sloop or a small schooner would have been an ideal vessel to serve as a lookout boat.

Captain Barney left behind at Baltimore eleven gunboats and the *Asp*, all without crews. These vessels would be used during the Battle of Baltimore as floating batteries in the harbor.

Manning the Chesapeake Bay Flotilla Squadron

Captain Joshua Barney's squadron of gunboats were used as a delaying tactic to give the defenders of Baltimore time to prepare to fight the British. Half of Barney's gunboats were left behind at Baltimore and they were used to defend this port. These gunboats were far too slow to be used against the British in Chesapeake Bay. Had the British been able to sail near Fort McHenry, these gunboats would have been used to defend this fort and Baltimore.

The Chesapeake Bay Flotilla Squadron fought in three naval battles and one land battle during the War of 1812. The flotilla engaged the enemy's gunboats during the Battle of Cedar Point on 1 June 1814 and in the Battle of St. Leonard's Creek on 10 June 1814, and again at this creek on 26 June 1814. They were successful in tying up the British naval forces in southern Maryland during the summer months of 1814. After the final engagement, Captain Barney was forced to order the destruction of his flotilla. The men then joined the American forces defending the national capital. The Chesapeake Bay Flotilla Squadron of the U.S. Flotilla Service was the only American unit (along with a U.S. Marine Corps detachment), which stood their grounds and fought the British during the Battle of Bladensburg on 24 August 1814.

The number of men and vessels that Captain Barney took with him to the fight the British, and the number of men and vessels he left behind at Baltimore has been in dispute with a number of books written on the U.S. Flotilla Service. Barney, in a letter to the U.S. House of Representatives, dated 30 October 1814, stated that he had upwards of 400 men with him during the naval campaigns in southern Maryland.[31] A bill had been introduced in the House of Representatives to compensate for the loss of personal clothing and equipment of the flotilla men serving under Barney. It is known that many more men had volunteered to serve with Barney, but they had not enlisted in the flotilla service.

In Weller's *Commodore Joshua Barney: The Hero of the Battle of Bladensburg,* Weller states that Barney took 503 men with thirteen barges and the sloop *Scorpion* with him to southern Maryland, and he left behind thirteen barges and 500 men at Baltimore.[32] Shomette's *Flotilla: The Patuxent Naval Campaign in the War of 1812* seems to have listed the most accurate number of gunboats and vessels in Barney's flotilla. He took with him eighteen gunboats and vessels, and he left behind eleven gunboats and one vessel at Baltimore. He also states that Barney took all of his men with him to southern Maryland and he left no one in Baltimore. *Flotilla* is probably the best written book on the battles of the Chesapeake Bay Flotilla Squadron.

The *Naval War of 1812: A Documented History*, volume three, states that Barney split his forces. Lieutenant Rutter, with thirteen barges and 500 men, stayed in Baltimore to defend the city while Barney and Lieutenant Frazier, with the *Scorpion*, thirteen barges, and 503 men headed south.

The payroll report for the flotilla squadron lists 1,003 men but when you delete the duplicates, Barney had 948 men in the flotilla. Prior to the battles, six men had died, twenty-five men had deserted, five men had enlisted but they never mustered, and two men were discharged early. This leaves 910 officers and men in the flotilla squadron. It is not known how many men were sick or were disabled, and could not serve with the squadron and they were left behind in Baltimore.

To man his flotilla, Barney could have needed 590 officers and men to operate the thirteen 1st class and 2nd class gunboats, and upwards to forty men each for the remaining vessels, for a total of approximately 830 officers and men. He would have needed nearly all of his men to man his gunboats and vessels and not 400 men as he stated to Congress. It appears that he had under-manned gunboats. He left behind at Baltimore only the sick men and a few others to watch over the remaining vessels of the squadron.

There were other men who were volunteers and who had not enlisted into the flotilla service. These men were not placed on the muster rolls, and it is doubtful that they were paid for their service. Last minute volunteers from the U.S. Navy in Baltimore, plus civilian seaman and slaves help fill the positions on each of the gunboats. It will never be known how many men actually served with the flotilla squadron over and beyond those listed on the muster and payroll reports.

Five men claimed to have served with Barney when they applied for military land bounties in 1855, and these men were not listed on the payroll report. Another eight men were wounded and they were listed on the hospital report for the Washington Naval Hospital after the Battle of Bladensburg.[33] They claim to have served with Barney. Four men were listed on the prisoner of war records for the Halifax Prison Depot in Canada, who claim to have served with the flotilla service.[34] They were captured by the British. Many other men simply showed up and volunteered to serve at the last minute in Baltimore and others volunteered in southern Maryland. Barney would not have said no to them. He needed all of these men. Most of these new men probably served as rowers or cooks.

One volunteer was a runaway slave, Charles Ball, who wrote his biography after the war in 1837. He stated that he did serve with Barney. There were probably many slaves in this service who served as cooks, gun crew, rowers, or servants to the officers and warrant officers, and who were not listed on the rolls. Ball states in his book, *Slavery in the United States: A Narrative of the Life and Adventures of Charles Ball, a Black Man*: [35]

> When Commodore Barney came into the Patuxent with his flotilla, I enlisted on board one of his barges, and was employed sometimes in the capacity of a seaman, and sometimes as cook of the barge.
>
> I had been on board, only a few days, when the British fleet entered the Patuxent, and forced our flotilla high up the river. I was present when the flotilla was blown up, and assisted in the performance of that operation upon the barge that I was in. The guns and the principal part of the armament of the flotilla, were sunk in the river and lost.
>
> I marched with the troops of Barney, from Benedict to Bladensburg. When we reached Bladensburg, and the flotilla men were drawn up in line, to work at their cannon, armed with their cutlasses, I volunteered to assist in working the cannon, that occupied the first place, on the left of the Commodore.
>
> I stood at my gun, until the Commodore was shot down, when he ordered us to retreat, as I was told by the officer who commanded our gun.

Charles Ball has been depicted in the picture to the right as serving in the U.S. Flotilla Service, and he is wearing the uniform of a flotillaman. Although the uniform of the flotilla service may be totally accurate in this picture, it is doubtful that Ball would have been issued the uniform of this service.

Having 'joined' the flotilla at the Patuxent River in southern Maryland, his name was not added to the muster rolls and he probably wasn't paid for his service, especially as a runaway slave. It is also doubtful that extra uniforms were loaded onto the two supply vessels in the squadron, since water, food, and ammunition were more important to be transported. All of the volunteeers probably wore their own clothes, unless some of the flotillamen had extra uniform parts that could be given to these men.

Nothing is known of Ball after 1837. He did not apply for a pension or a military land bounty. A lawyer, Issac Fisher, helped Ball write his book. It is also not known if he was married at the time of this death.

Charles Ball - Wikipedia

Chesapeake Bay Flotilla Squadron in action

On 24 May 1814, Captain Barney's flotilla squadron set sail from Baltimore and headed south towards the Patuxent River in southern Maryland. The squadron engaged the British squadron at the Battle of St. Jerome Creek on 1 June 1814. The creek was a tributary of the Patuxent River. The Americans were outnumbered and outgunned by the British forces, and the squadron was forced to retreat up the creek. The creek was too shallow for the British vessels to enter.

The squadron remained in the St. Jerome Creek until 26 June 1814, when U.S. Army troops and a detachment of marines under the command of Captain Samuel Miller, set up artillery batteries along the shores of the Patuxent River, which forced the British vessels to retreat from the mouth of the creek, and the American squadron was then able to move up to St. Leonard's Creek. Gunboats 137 and 138 had to be scuttled. The rest of the squadron sailed further up the Patuxent River. This skirmish is known as the Battle of St. Leonard's Creek.

Barney left eight men with each gunboat in order to destroy them and to sink the cannons and ammunition in the river. Several men were taken as prisoners by the British. He took 400 men with him and headed towards Washington, DC. Many of the men left behind would later rejoin Barney.

On August 24th, Barney and his squadron participated in the Battle of Bladensburg. The squadron stood their ground and the British suffered heavy casualties at the hands of Barney's cannoneers. Barney received a serious wound to his thigh from a musket ball and since they were about to be overwhelmed by British regulars, ordered the flotilla squadron to retreat. The squadron, along with a detachment of U.S marines under the command of Captain Samuel Miller, were the last two American units to leave the battlefield.

Barney and a number of men were taken prisoners by the British. Lieutenant Rutter, now commanding the squadron, headed towards Baltimore with the marines. Had Barney and Miller not stood their grounds during this battle, the American causalities would have been far greater in this battle.

U.S. Marine Corps detachment

Captain Barney's flotilla squadron was blessed with the addition of a U.S. Marine Corps detachment under the command of Captain Samuel Miller. This detachment was formed in May of 1814, under the orders of the Secretary of the Navy William Jones, and then placed under the command of Captain Barney. Secretary Jones had the foresight to supply Barney with field cannons, which were operated by the marines.

Barney and his men did not have time to build carriages for the cannons of his squadron, and when the squadron was scuttled, the cannons of the gunboats were thrown into the river. Without Miller, Barney would not have had cannons at Bladensburg and the flotilla squadron would have had to retreat with the militia.

This marine detachment constructed field carriages for two 18-pound and three 12-pound cannons at the Washington Naval Yard, and they began training in using these mobile cannons. No surviving muster rolls for this detachment has been discovered. These rolls may not have survived the burning of the naval yard or they were never completed.

Only one muster roll is known for the marine detachment at the Washington Naval Yard during the War of 1812 and it is dated 1 July 1813, thirteen months before the Battle of Bladensburg.[36] The detachment was under the command of Captain Robert D. Wainwright and it lists forty-six enlisted men. The other officers of this detachment were not listed. Wainwright would be transferred to the Lake Ontario Squadron prior to 1 September 1813 when First Lieutenant Samuel Miller, the Marine Corps adjutant, completed the *Monthly Detail of the Officers of the Marine Corps*.[37]

The Marine Corps was under the command of Lieutenant Colonel Franklin Wharton. The other officers stationed at the Washington Naval Yard in September 1813 were First Lieutenant John Crabb, the paymaster of the Marine Corps, First Lieutenant Joseph Woodson, First Lieutenant Charles S. Hanna, First Lieutenant Alexander Sevier, First Lieutenant Alfred Grayson, First Lieutenant John Heath, First Lieutenant Samuel Bacon, the quartermaster of the Marine Corps, and First Lieutenant John Contee. Many of these men had been reassigned to other naval stations or to ships by August 1814.

It is not known how many marines were stationed at the Washington Naval Yard in August 1814, but it appears that there were over 110 officers and men. Based on the July 1813 muster roll, approximately fifty officers and men were assigned to this station on a permanent basis. An additional 100 officers and men were waiting for the completion of the U.S. Frigate *Essex* which was being built at the naval yard. This 44-gun frigate was the newest sister ship to the U.S. Frigate *Constitution*, and it was destroyed by naval personnel to prevent its captured by the British as they stormed Washington, DC. The 100 officers and men would have been assigned duty on the *Essex* after the ship was commissioned into naval service. Some of these marines may have also been waiting for assignment on the U.S Brig *Argus*, which also was being built at the naval yard. The *Argus* also was destroyed to prevent its capture.

Four marine officers and thirteen enlisted men have been identified as participating in the Battle of Bladensburg. Eight men were listed as wounded on the *Register of Patients* for the Washington Naval Hospital.[38] Other sources, including pension papers, military land bounties papers, books, and other printed material, identified the other men. These marine officers and men are included in the list of men in the chapter on the men of the U.S. Flotilla Service's Chesapeake Flotilla Squadron.

The U.S. Marine Corps officer promotion list was released on 18 June 1814.[39] Samuel Miller was promoted to captain, Alfred Grayson was breveted as a captain (but he was still paid as a first lieutenant), Alexander Sevier was promoted to captain, and Richard Benjamin was promoted to first lieutenant. Miller also was the adjutant and inspector general of the Marine Corps, while Grayson was the quartermaster and Sevier was the paymaster. Captain Miller was the senior captain at the naval yard since he had the earliest commissioning date of the four officers. The staff of Lieutenant Colonel Wharton was in command of this marine detachment.

Secretary Jones stated in a letter to Congressman Richard M. Johnson on 3 October 1814, that he sent about 110 marines and five cannons to Captain Barney under the command of Captain Miller.[40] He also stated that he ordered Captain Grayson and his team to load the three gunboats at the Washington Naval Yard with provisions and powder, and to move these boats up the Potomac River to the Little Falls so that these gunboats would not be captured by the British. It is not known how many men were in Grayson's team.

After completing his task, Grayson volunteered his team to go to defend Baltimore, but first they served at Bladensburg where two of his men were killed.[41] Captain Miller and his detachment participated in the Second Battle of St. Leonard's Creek on 26 June 1814 in support of Barney's flotilla.[42] Shead in his book, *The Chesapeake Campaigns 1813-15,* states that both Captains Miller and Grayson were at this battle along with 100 men and three 12-pound cannons.[43]

Waterhouse's, *Marines in the Frigate Navy,* says that there were 103 marines at the Battle of Bladensburg and that Miller received a sever wound to his left arm while Captain Sevier was slightly wounded in the neck.[44] First Lieutenant Benjamin Richardson and Sergeant Hilliday (possibility Sergeant William Holliday) were also listed as being in this battle. According to Donald Shomette in this book, *Flotilla: The Patuxent Naval Campaign in the War of 1812,* the marines suffered eleven dead and sixteen wounded men during the battle.[45]

The Battle of Fort McHenry

Lieutenant Solomon Rutter and 439 men of the flotilla men then marched to Baltimore and they participated in the Battle of Fort McHenry, 13-14 September 1814. Sailing Master John Webster and fifty men operated the cannons at Fort Babcock. This was a small fort just east of Fort McHenry (actually it was an artillery battery).

Lieutenant Rutter and 338 men manned the thirteen gunboats and barges in front of Fort McHenry on the Patapsco River. Across this river from Fort McHenry, Lieutenant Solomon Frazier and forty-five men operated the cannons of the Lazaretto Battery. On the grounds of Fort McHenry, Sailing Master Solomon Rodman and sixty men operated the cannons of the Water Battery.

The flotilla men manned these positions throughout the Battle of Fort McHenry. Sailing Master Webster and his men turned back on attempted night assault on Fort Babcock by a Royal Marine landing party. One flotilla man was killed in action at the Water Battery, and three others were wounded.

The marine detachment left Bladensburg and participated in the Battle of Baltimore on 12-13 September 1814. This detachment and a detachment of U.S. Navy personnel took up defenses at Hampstead Hill, on the east side of Baltimore, under the command of Commodore John Rodgers.

New York Flotilla Squadron

The Acting Secretary of the Navy Benjamin Homans notified Master Commandant Jacob M. Lewis on 7 January 1813 that his commission as captain in the U.S. Flotilla Service had been confirmed by the U.S. Senate.[46] He had been commissioned as a master commandant in the U.S. Navy on 27 Nov 1812.[47] After the U.S. Flotilla Service was disbanded, Secretary Benjamin W. Crowinshield on 28 April 1815 notified Jacob Lewis that the U.S. Senate had confirmed his appointment as the U.S. Consul for the Island of Malta in the Mediterranean Sea.[48]

On 26 February 1813, Secretary of the Navy Jacob Jones ordered Lewis to reduce the number of gunboats to fifteen vessels at the New York Station.[49] At this time, the New York Gunboat Squadron had thirty-eight gunboats, which was the largest gunboat squadron in the U.S. Navy. [50] Thirty-one gunboats were in commission, while the other seven were laid up. It appears that Lewis kept in commission only the newest and most-fit gunboats.

The payroll report shows only thirteen gunboats active on 30 September 1814. These were Gunboats 6, 8, 29, 30, A, B, 40, 103, 105, 109, 112, 113, and 114. The report shows two gunboats without numbers and they are listed here as Gunboats A and B. Sailing Master Samuel Wares was in command of Gunboat A, while Sailing Master Thomas Hardwick commanded B. There were a total of 430 warrant officers and men listed on the payroll report.

New York Flotilla Squadron	
Vessel	**Officers and men**
Gunboat No. 6	62
Gunboat No. 8	54
Gunboat No. 29	20
Gunboat No. 30	28
Gunboat No. A	29
Gunboat No. B	30
Gunboat No. 40	38
Gunboat No. 103	30
Gunboat No. 105	28
Gunboat No. 109	28
Gunboat No. 112	28
Gunboat No. 113	29
Gunboat No. 114	26

The table to the left shows the number of warrant officers and men assigned to each of the active gunboats on 30 September 1814 as taken from the payroll reports.

Gunboats 6 and 8 appears to be fully manned, but the other gunboats seem to be short of a full complement of men.

At this time, the size of these gunboats and the number of men needed to operate these vessels is not known.

Total	430

Silvertone's *The Sailing Navy 1775-1854* states that Gunboats 46 through 57 were built in 1806.[51] Twenty-three gunboats, numbered 93 through 115, were built in New York City, but Silverton does not give a date for their construction. Of the thirty-eight gunboats at New York City, Lewis kept the best gunboats in service, and when he had the man-power, he used more than fifteen gunboats in his operations against the British.

New York Flotilla Squadron muster rolls [52]

None of the naval reports from the New York Naval Station indicate when the U.S. Navy's New York Gunboat Squadron became the U.S. Flotilla Service's New York Flotilla Squadron. Since Jacob Lewis was promoted to captain on 26 April 1814, it is assumed that this also is the date of the transfer.

Captain Lewis did not order new records started when the U.S. Flotilla Service was created, but he continued to use the muster rolls and payroll reports belonging to the U.S. Navy. This makes it very difficult to determine how many men actually served with the U.S. Flotilla Service in New York City. The records for each man had to be examined. The New York Flotilla began discharging men who have been transferred from the idle warships at the New York Navy Yard back to their ships starting in mid-January 1815. The last of the flotilla men were discharged in mid-July 1815.

The muster rolls for the New York Flotilla Squadron have not been found with the records of the U.S. Flotilla Service, however, parts of three U.S. Navy payroll reports, one U.S. Navy promotion list, and a U.S. Navy statement of amounts are with the naval records at the National Archives. The payroll reports have missing pages and they are not complete.

The three payroll reports are for the U.S. Navy's New York Naval Yard with the flotilla men under Captain Lewis imbedded in these pages. The first payroll report lists 168 warrant officers and men starting with payroll number 1 and ending with payroll number 168.[53] How many pages are missing cannot be determined after payroll number 168. The last page would have had the signatures of the commander (Master Commandant Jacob Lewis) and the purser. The men were entered on this roll on either 26 September 1813 or 3 October 1813. There is no date as to when this payroll report was completed.

The second payroll report contains the names of 501 warrant officers and men from payroll numbers 123 to 2,753, with many pages missing.[54] These men were entered on the forms between 5 October 1813 to 14 July 1815. The final page is missing, which would have had the signatures of the commander and the purser. There is no date as to when this report was completed, but it appears that over the two-year period, 2,753 men were assigned to the New York Naval Yard including the men from the U.S. Flotilla Service.

A third payroll report lists 224 warrant officers and men from payroll number 933 to 1,156.[55] The first 932 men's names are missing and it is not known how many men would have been listed after payroll number 1,156. The names of the men and their payroll numbers from this report does not match the names and numbers from the first two reports. It is signed by Jacob Lewis and George S. Wise, the purser from the New York Naval Station. It has to be assumed that this report is an earlier report from the U.S. Navy's New York Naval Station prior to the formation of the U.S. Flotilla Service. Lewis would have been a master commandant at this time. No payroll date is listed on these forms.

The U.S. Flotilla Service's New York Flotilla Squadron did not have 2,753 officers and men assigned to the squadron. This figure represents all of the warrant officers and men assigned to the New York Naval Station. Officers would have had their own payroll reports. Captain Lewis had thirty-eight gunboats but only thirteen were manned during daily operations. Some operations used around eleven gunboats and others as high as twenty-five. If these were the smaller gunboats, each with forty officers and men, then Lewis had around 520 flotilla men assigned to him. The larger and newer gunboats had seventy-five officers and men, for a total of 650 men. Both figures are based on thirteen gunboats in service.

The Statement of Amounts is the only complete payroll report for the New York Naval Station.[56] It contains the payroll record for each man as to what he was paid, what he was owed, and what was deducted from his pay. It lists the warrant officers and men from payroll numbers 1 through 1476 between 1 October 1813 and 30 September 1814. Nine men from the Gunboat 30 are not listed with a payroll number, their names were added after payroll number 1476. The form was signed on 30 September 1814 by Jacob Lewis and George S. Wise, the purser from the New York Naval Station.

The first 223 men are listed by their gunboat assignments. Five gunboats are listed: 6, 8, 29, 30, and two without numbers. The men assigned to Gunboats 103, 105, 109, 112, 113, and 114 are imbedded in other areas of this report. A second statemen of amounts would have been completed after 30 September 1814 but it is missing from the naval station's records. Jacob Lewis is not listed on these reports, except his approving signatures. It appears that all reports pertaining to commissioned officers at the naval station are missing.

This report lists only 439 flotilla men by their gunboat assignments. Since the report stops at 30 September 1814 and the flotilla squadron was disbanded in July 1815, there has to be another Statemen of Amounts to account for the missing months. There may have been a total of 1,000 men in the flotilla squadron at New York City under Captain Lewis.

A list of promotions and demotions containing the names of sixty warrant officers and men are included in the records of the New York Naval Yard.[57] The entry dates are between 2 October 1813 through 16 Dec 1814. There are no muster roll\payroll numbers on this report, nor is the signature of Jacob Lewis.

History of the New York Flotilla Squadron

Guernsey's *New York City and Vicinity during the War of 1812-15* has the history of the New York Flotilla Squadron.[58] Master Commandant Jacob Lewis was appointed the commander of the U.S. Navy's New York Gunboat Squadron in December 1812, after the former commander, Captain Isaac Hull, was transferred to the Boston Naval Yard. This squadron would become the U.S. Flotilla Services' New York Flotilla Squadron in April 1814.

The squadron was headquartered at the New York Naval Station, which would eventually become the Brooklyn Naval Yard. The station was on the Brooklyn side of the East River, across from Manhattan Island. The gunboats could head east on the river to the Long Island Sound or south to the entrance of the New York harbor. At the mouth of the New York harbor was Sandy Hook, a huge sandbar which was connected to New Jersey. There were military installations on this sandbar which protected the entrance to the harbor.

In the fall of 1812, a New York state sea fencible company was attached to Captain Lewis' command. This was a one-year marine militia unit. In early January 1813, a British squadron appeared off Sandy Hook. Lewis tried to send his gunboats to Sandy Hook but the ice in the harbor prevented this from happening, so the gunboats returned to the naval station. By the spring of 1813, Lewis had over 1,000 men in his flotilla. In March, he received orders to reduce the squadron from forty to fifteen gunboats, and many men were discharged.

On 5 September 1813, Lewis engaged the British blockading squadron off New London, Connecticut. He had brought twenty-five gunboats from New York, and both squadrons exchanged cannon fire. The British withdrew from this engagement and Lewis sent his gunboats to Sandy Hook. Although, Lewis had been ordered to downsize the gunboat squadron to fifteen vessels, he kept most of them and if he had the man-power, he used them. Also, most of the American gunboats were armed with at least one 24- or 32-pound cannon, while the British preferred smaller caliber cannons on most of their ships. One American gunboat could inflect great damage on a British frigate.

The H.M.S. *Plantagenet*, a 74-gun ship-of-the-line, on 3 November 1813 forced an American vessel, the *Sparrow*, to ground off Sandy Hook. The British captain then sent a boarding party to capture the *Sparrow*. A detachment of 100 flotilla men recaptured the *Sparrow*, saving the ship and its cargo. One flotilla man, Seaman William Mitchell, was killed in this action.

At the beginning of 1814, the New York Gunboat Squadron had about 1,000 men on its rosters. On 8 March 1814, the British drove another American schooner onto the shore near Sandy Hook. A detachment of flotilla men, with a small field piece (cannon), fought off a British landing party and saved the schooner. The schooner was refloated and brought safety into the Port of New York.

On 7 Apr 1814, Captain Lewis once again headed for New London with thirteen gunboats but this time to chase off the British privateer *Liverpool Packet*. The gunboats then escorted over fifty American vessels up the Thames River to New London, and then they engaged the British blockading squadron with hot cannon balls, disabling a sloop and maiming a frigate.

A British warship attacked the American brig *Regent* off Sandy Hook on 29 May 1814. Eleven gunboats drove off the enemy, and the *Regent* was able entered the New York harbor. The brig had come from France with a valuable cargo. On 23 May 1814, the gunboat squadron fought a three-hour battle with three British ship-of-the-lines, four frigates, and several smaller vessels. The squadron drove off the British and let forty American coastal vessels to escape from New London.

In August 1814, the New York Station was the home port for the U.S. Frigate *President*, the U.S. Storeship *Alert*, thirty-eight gunboats, and 1,300 men. On 1 Oct 1814, Captain Lewis took nineteen gunboats and two bomb ketches from the station, up the East River through Hell's Gate to Long Island Sound in order to attack the British squadron which had traveled down the Long Island Sound towards New York City. The British squadron had left the area by the time the gunboat squadron had entered the Long Island Sound.

On 9 March 1815, the Secretary of the Navy Benjamin W. Crowninshield ordered Captain Jacob Lewis to demobilize the New York Flotilla Squadron.[59] All of the gunboats, except Gunboats 6 and 8, which were retained in service, were stripped of all cannons, ammunitions, and naval stores, and they were sold in a public auction. These were Gunboats 37, 42, 43, 44, 57, 97 and 100. Gunboats 6 and 8 were armed with two 32-pound cannons. Forty-seven other gunboat hulks were also sold in auctions. These old gunboats had been decommissioned prior to Crowninshield's order on March 9th.

Although the gunboat squadron at New York City was engaged in no major battles, the squadron kept at bay the British blockading squadron off New York City and at New London. The gunboats protected these ports and assisted the American costal vessels and privateers throughout the War of 1812.

Summing up the U.S. Flotilla Service

In a way, the U.S. Flotilla Service was a failure but it did serve a vital purpose during the War of 1812. Not all of the U.S. Navy's gunboat squadrons were transferred to the Flotilla Service, only three squadrons. Only two flotilla squadrons were created, even though the service could have had four captains commanding flotilla squadrons. Smaller flotilla squadrons could have been commanded by lieutenants. It is not known why the rank of master commandant was not authorized for this service. This is a naval rank between a captain and a lieutenant.

The majority of the men who served in the Flotilla Service were not local seaman who did not want sea duty, but instead, they were U.S. Navy personnel who were transferred to the Flotilla Service and when this service was disbanded, these men were transferred back to the U.S. Navy.

Captain Lewis' flotilla squadron was no different than the U.S. Naval gunboat squadron he commanded prior to the formation of the Flotilla Service. No new gunboats were built for this squadron, and Lewis operated the flotilla squadron in the same way he operated the gunboat squadron. The flotilla squadron did very good service in protecting both the New York harbor and the Long Island Sound, but this could have been achieved with the gunboat squadron.

On the other hand, Captain Barney operated his flotilla squadron separate from the U.S Navy's gunboat squadrons. He was given the fund to build eight new gunboats (galleys), which were larger and more powerful than the gunboats authorized before the war. He took the war to the British in southern Maryland, which gave Baltimore time to prepare their defenses. Sadly, the City of Washington did not prepare for a British invasion. Baltimore was considered the main target of any British intrusion.

The highlight of the U.S. Flotilla Service was the Battle of Bladensburg when Barney's squadron and a detachment of U.S. marines held up the advancing British army, letting the militia and some regular army unit time to flee the battlefield. Had this not happened, the causality rate for the U.S. forces would have been far greater.

Finally, with Captain Barney as a wounded prisoner of war, Lieutenant Solomon Rutter took the flotilla squadron and the marine detachment to Baltimore harbor, where they manned the remaining gunboats and some of the land batteries during the Battle of Fort McHenry. Captain Barney will always be known as Commodore Barney and for his role in defending Maryland during the War of 1812.

---

[1] *Public Statutes at Large of the United States of America*, (Charles C. Little and James Brown: Boston 1845), volume II, Seventh Congress, session II, chapter XI, page 206, 28 February 1803, an act to provide an additional armament for the protection of seamen and commerce of the United States.

[2] Ibid., Ninth Congress, session I, chapter XLVII, page 402, 21 April 1806, an act for fortifying the ports and harbors of the United States, and for building gun boats.

[3] Ibid., Tenth Congress, session I, chapter IV, page 451, 18 December 1807, an act to appropriate money for the providing of an additional number of gun boats.

[4] *Public Statutes at Large of the United States of America,* (Charles C. Little and James Brown, Boston 1846), volume III, Thirteenth Congress, session I, chapter VI, page 3, 5 July 1813, an act authorizing the President of the United States to cause to be built barges for the defense of the ports and harbors of the United States.

[5] Dudley, William S., *The Naval War of 1812, A Documentary History*, volume 2 1813, (Washington, DC: Naval Historical Center, Department of the Navy, 1992), page 373-375, Chesapeake Bay Theater, Joshua Barney's letter of 4 July 1813 to the Secretary of the Navy William Jones.

[6] *American State Papers*, (Gales and Seaton: Washington, DC 1834), Naval Affairs, volume 1, number 111, 22 February 1814, Condition of the Navy, and the Progress made in Providing Materials and Building Ships, pp. 305-309.

---

[7] *Public Statutes*, volume III, Thirteenth Congress, Session II, Chapter 59, 16 April 1814, page 125, An act authorizing the appointment of certain officers for the flotilla service.

[8] Crawford, Michael J., *The Naval War of 1812, A Documentary History*, volume III 1814-1815, (Washington, DC: Naval Historical Center, Department of the Navy), pp. 33-37, Barney's Flying Squadron Takes Shape.

[9] Hughes, Christine F. and Charles E. Brodine, Jr., *The Naval War of 1812: A Documentary History,* Volume IV, *1814-1815, Atlantic Ocean and Gulf of Mexico,* (Washington, DC: Naval Historical Center, 2023), pp. 159-168, The New York Flotilla – A Manning Tug of War.

[10] Dudley, *The Naval War of 1812*, volume 2 1813, (Washington, DC: Naval Historical Center, Department of the Navy, 1992), page 39, Jacob Lewis and the New York Flotilla.

[11] Callahan, Edward W., *List of Officers of the Navy of the United States and of the Marine Corps from 1775 to 1900,* (New York, New York: L. R. Hamersley & Company, 1901), page 331, Jacob M. Lewis, Commander.

[12] *American State Papers*, number 111, 22 February 1814, Condition of the Navy, and the Progress made in Providing Materials and Building Ships, pp. 305-309.

[13] Naval Records Collection of the Office of Naval Records and Library, General Records of the Office of the Secretary of the Navy, Record Group 45.2.1, Letters sent 1798-1886, Roll 453, *Letter from Secretary of the Navy Jones to Captains Barney and Lewis*, 26 April 1814, pp. 164-165, National Archives and Records Administration, Washington, D.C.

[14] Weller, M. I., *Commodore Joshua Barney: The Hero of the Battle of Bladensburg*, Records of the Columbia Historical Society (Washington, DC), volume XIV, pp. 140-141.

[15] Naval Records, Record Group 45.2.1, Letters sent 1798-1886, Roll 453, *Letter from Secretary of the Navy Jones to Joshua Barney*, 20 August 1813, pp. 38-39, National Archives and Records Administration, Washington, D.C.

[16] Ibid., Letters sent 1798-1886, Roll 453, *Letter from Secretary of the Navy Jones to Captains Barney and Lewis*, 26 April 1814, pp. 164-165, National Archives and Records Administration, Washington, D.C.

[17] Ibid., Letters sent 1798-1886, Roll 453, *Letter from Secretary of the Navy Jones to Lieutenants Rutter & Frazier*, 26 April 1814, page 165, National Archives and Records Administration, Washington, D.C.

[18] The Debates and Proceedings in the Congress of the United States, Thirteenth Congress, Third Session 19 Sep 1814 to 3 March 1815, (Gales and Seaton: Washington, DC 1854), October 1814, House of Representatives, Relief of Commodore Barney, pp. 414-416.

[19] *Public Statutes*, volume III, Thirteenth Congress, Session III, Chapter 62, 27 February 1815, pages 217-218, An act to repeal certain acts concerning the flotilla service, and for other purposes.

[20] Naval Records, Record Group 45.2.3 Personnel records, Muster rolls and payrolls 1798-1859.

[21] *American State Papers*, number 111, 22 February 1814, Condition of the Navy, and the progress made in providing materials and building ships, 4 March 1814, page 309, List of the Naval Force of the United States.

[22] Silverstone, Paul H., *The Sailing Navy 1775-1854*, (Naval Institute Press: Annapolis, MD 2001), pp. 56-58, Gunboats built in the United States.

[23] Gibson, Gary M., *The U.S. Brig Oneida: A Design & Operational History*, The War of 1812 Magazine, Issue 19, December 2012.

[24] Dudley, *The Naval War of 1812*, volume 2 1813, (Washington, DC: Naval Historical Center, Department of the Navy, 1992), pages 333 and 335, Potomac Squadron.

[25] Silverstone, *The Sailing Navy*, pp. 55 and 59

[26] Dudley, *The Naval War of 1812*, (Washington, DC: Naval Historical Center, Department of the Navy, 1992), pp, 331, 350-352, Baltimore Squadron.

[27] Ibid., page 316, 2 March 1813, Norfolk Squadron.

[28] Shomette, Donald G., *Flotilla: The Patuxent Naval Campaign in the War of 1812*, (The Johns Hopkins University Press: Baltimore, MD 2009), page 90, Pen the Flotilla Within.

[29] Cannons were long range weapons while cannonades were short range weapons.

[30] *Abstract pay roll of twenty-six men transferred from the Potomac to the Chesapeake Flotilla (U.S. Schooner Shark)*, Naval Records Collection of the Office of Naval Records and Library, Record Group 45.2.3, Roll 203, 20 April 1814, page 7; National Archives and Records Administration, Washington, D.C.

[31] The Debates and Proceedings in the Congress of the United States, Thirteenth Congress, Third Session 19 Sep 1814 to 3 March 1815, (Gales and Seaton: Washington, DC 1854), November 1814, House of Representatives, The Flotilla Men, page 517.

[32] Weller, *Commodore Joshua Barney*, pp. 141-165.

[33] National Archives and Records Administration, Record Group 52, Records of the Bureau of Medicine and Surgery, Field Records Case Files for Patients at Naval Hospitals and Registers, Entry 45, *The Register of Patients Naval Hospitals 1812 -1934* Volume 45, Washington Naval Hospital, Register of Patients from the Battle of Bladensburg entries 1-90.

[34] *Records relating to American Prisoners of War 1812-1815*, British Admiralty, Microfilm BRRAM ADM 103 series, reel 5, volumes 167 through 173, Halifax Depot, Public Records Office, London, Great Britain.

[35] Ball, Charles, *Slavery in the United States: A Narrative of the Life and Adventures of Charles Ball, a Black Man*, (John S. Taylor, publisher: New York, NY 1837), pp. 467-468.

[36] *Muster Rolls of the U.S. Marine Corps, 1798-1892*; (National Archives and Records Administration, Washington, D.C.), National Archives Microfilm Publication T1118; Records of the U.S. Marine Corps, Record Group 127, page 80, Muster Roll of a Detachment of Non-Commissioned Officers, Music, and Privates of the United States Marines stationed at the Washington Naval Yard, June 1812.

[37] Ibid., page, 136, Monthly Detail of the Officers of the Marine Corps stationed at the Washington Naval Yard, September 1813.

[38] National Archives, Record Group 52, Records of the Bureau of Medicine and Surgery, Field Records Case Files for Patients at Naval Hospitals and Registers, Entry 45, *The Register of Patients Naval Hospitals 1812 -1934* Volume 45, Washington Naval Hospital, Register of Patients from the Battle of Bladensburg entries 1-90.

[39] Callahan, *List of Officers*, pp. 681, 687, 694, and 697.

[40] Crawford, *The Naval War of 1812*, page 313, Secretary of the Navy Jones to Congressman Richard M. Johnson, Navy Department, 3 October 1814.

[41] Ibid., Captain David Porter to Secretary of the Navy Jones, Washington, 7 September 1814, page. 255.

[42] Ibid, Captain Joshua Barney, Flotilla Service, to Louis Barney, with flotilla, 27 June 1814, page 123.

[43] Sheads, Scott S., *The Chesapeake Campaigns 1813-15*, (Osprey Publishing Ltd.: New York, NY 2014), Second Battle of St. Leonard's Creek, 26 June 1814, page 22.

[44] Waterhouse, Charles H., *Marines in the Frigate Navy*, (History Division, U.S. Marine Corps: Washington, DC 2006), The Final Stand at Bladensburg, Maryland 24 August 1814.

[45] Shomette, *Flotilla*, pp. 323-324, I told you it was the Flotillamen.

[46] Naval Records Collection of the Office of Naval Records and Library, General Records of the Office of the Secretary of the Navy, Record Group 45.2.1, Letters sent 1798-1886, Roll 382, *Letter from Acting Secretary of the Navy Homans to Captain Lewis,* 7 January 1814, page 266, National Archives and Records Administration, Washington, D.C.

[47] Callahan, *List of Officers*, Jacob M. Lewis, Commander, page 331.

[48] Naval Records, Letters sent 1798-1886, Roll 212, *Letter from Secretary of the Navy Crowninshield to Captain Lewis,* 28 April 1815, page 313, National Archives and Records Administration, Washington, D.C.

[49] Dudley, *The Naval War of 1812*, volume 2 1813, (Washington, DC: Naval Historical Center, Department of the Navy, 1992), page 39, 26 February 1813, Jacob Lewis and the New York Flotilla.

[50] *American State Papers*, number 111, 22 February 1814, Condition of the Navy, and the Progress made in Providing Materials and Building Ships, pp. 305-309.

[51] Silverstone, *The Sailing Navy*, pp. 56-58, Gunboats built in the United States.

[52] Naval Records, Record Group 45.2.3 Personnel records, Muster rolls and payrolls 1798-1859.

[53] *Pay roll of the U.S. Flotilla, Jacob Lewis, Esquire, Commanding*, Naval Records Collection of the Office of Naval Records and Library, Record Group 45, Roll 202, 3 October 1813, pp. 160-166; National Archives and Records Administration, Washington, D.C.

[54] *Pay roll report of the U.S. Flotilla*, Naval Records Collection of the Office of Naval Records and Library, Record Group 45, Roll 194, 7 January 1814 - 30 September 1814, pp. 210-221; National Archives and Records Administration, Washington, D.C.

[55] Ibid, Roll 154, pp. 87-94; National Archives and Records Administration, Washington, D.C.

[56] *Statement of amount advanced to officers and men attached to the New York Station from 1 October 1813 to 30 September 1814 inclusive*, Naval Records Collection of the Office of Naval Records and Library, Record Group 45.2.3, Roll 155, 12 December 1814, pp. 178-243 National Archives and Records Administration, Washington, D.C.

[57] *List of petty officers, seaman, ordinary seaman, landsmen, and boys promoted and reduced by order of Jacob Lewis, Esquire, commanding U.S. Flotilla New York*, 2 October 1813 through 16 December 1814, Naval Records Collection of the Office of Naval Records and Library, Record Group 45.2.3, Roll 154, pp. 57-58; National Archives and Records Administration, Washington, D.C.

[58] Guernsey, R. S., *New York City and Vicinity during the War of 1812-15*, 2 volumes, (Charles L. Woodward: New York, NY 1895).

[59] Hughes, *The Naval War of 1812*, page 776, Captain Jacob Lewis, Flotilla Service, to Secretary of the Navy Crowninshield, New York, 19 March 1815.

The Scorecard

This section will explain the data fields and terms used in recreating the rosters of the officers and men of the U.S. Flotilla Service.

Data Field	Explanation	
Rank	The highest known military rank is listed for each serviceman.	
	U.S. Flotilla Service	
	Officer ranks:	
	Captain	Lieutenant
	Warrant officer ranks:	
	Sailing Master (or Master)	Chaplain
	Midshipman	Boatswain
	Surgeon	Gunner
	Surgeon's Mate	Sailmaker
	Purser	Carpenter
	Mate ranks	
	Master's Mate	Carpenter's Mate
	Boatswain's Mate	Sailmaker's Mate
	Gunner's Mate	
	Enlisted ranks	
	Quarter Gunner	Cooper
	Quartermaster	Ship's Corporal
	Master-at-Arms	Steward
	Armorer	Cook
	Yeoman	Coxswain
	Able Seaman	Landsman
	Ordinary Seaman	Boy
	U.S. Marine Corps	
	Officer ranks	
	Lieutenant Colonel Commandant	First Lieutenant
	Major	Second Lieutenant
	Captain	
	Sergeant ranks	
	Sergeant Major	Sergeant
	Quartermaster Sergeant	
	Fife Major	Drum Major
	Enlisted ranks	
	Corporal	Drummer
	Fifer	Private
Documents	Muster, Roster, Transfer, or Ship's documents	
Number	Muster, roster, etc. numbers for each man	

Data Field	Explanation
Entry Date	Date that the information on a flotilla man was entered onto a document
Naval Pension	SC-9999 – Survivor's Certificate SO-9999 – Survivor's Original WC-9999 – Widow's Certificate WO-9999 – Widow's Original Navy IF - Invalid File Navy WF - Widow File
Military Land Bounty (Bounty land warrant)	BLW 999999-999-99 999999 = Bounty land warrant number -999- = number of acres issued for the warrant -12 or -14 or -42 or -50 or -55 = Years of the Land Bounty Acts, that is, 1812, 1814, 1852, 1850, or 1855

Terms and phases

Ran

The term 'ran' denotes a serviceman who left his ship without permission, and who did not return to duty, same as deserted. These men were not entitled to their enlistment benefits.

Prisoner of War

Information taken from the *General Entry Books of American Prisoners of War*, British Admiralty, Public Record Office, London, Great Britain.

Chesapeake Bay Flotilla Squadron Roster

with the U.S. Marine Corps detachment

Abbit, Lambert - Seaman - Payroll 1 - Number: 256 - Entry Date: 2 Mar 1814 - Payroll ended on 6 Apr 1814 - Payroll 2 - Number: 256 - Entry Date: 2 Mar 1814 - Discharged on 1 Apr 1815

Abbot, John - Seaman - Payroll 2 - Number: 897 - Entry Date: 1 Jan 1814 - Ran on 19 Dec 1814 - BLW 2222-160-55 - U.S. Sloop-of-War Ontario - Number: 76 - Entry Date: 14 Jan 1814 - Discharged on 17 Apr 1814 to the flotilla (ran) - U.S. Frigate United States - Number: 897 - Entry Date: 7 Apr 1814 - Ran on 29 Sep 1814 from U.S. Sloop-of-War Ontario

Abbot, Thomas - Ordinary Seaman - Payroll 2 - Number: 921 - Entry Date: 11 Aug 1814 - Seaman -Payroll 2 - Number: 862 - Entry Date: 15 Aug 1814 - Discharged on 1 Apr 1815

Abrams, William - Master's Mate - Payroll 1 - Number: 297 - Entry Date: 11 Mar 1814 - Payroll ended on 6 Apr 1814 - Payroll 2 - Number: 297 - Entry Date: 11 Mar 1814 - Discharged on 1 Apr 1815

Adams, Moses - Ordinary Seaman - Payroll 1 - Number: 227 - Entry Date: 3 Feb 1814 - Payroll ended on 6 Apr 1814 - Payroll 2 - Number: 227 - Entry Date: 3 Feb 1814 - Discharged on 24 Aug 1814

Adams, Robert - Seaman - Payroll 1 - Number: 271 - Entry Date: 12 Mar 1814 – Payroll ended on 6 Apr 1814 - Payroll 2 - Number: 271 - Entry Date: 12 Mar 1814 - Discharged on 1 Apr 1815 -

Adams, Samuel - Seaman - Payroll 2 - Number: 253 - Entry Date: 25 Feb 1814 - Discharged on 25 Feb 1815 - Payroll 1 - Number: 253 - Entry Date: 25 Feb 1814 - Payroll ended on 6 Apr 1814

Adkinson, William - Master's Mate - Payroll 1 - Number: 293 - Entry Date: 10 Mar 1814 - Payroll ended on 6 Apr 1814 - Payroll 2 - Number: 987 - Entry Date: 10 Mar 1814 - Discharged on 7 Jul 1814 - Sailing Master - Payroll 2 - Number: 987 - Entry Date: 8 Jul 1814 - Discharged on 1 Apr 1815 - Muster - Number: 293 - Entry Date: 8 Jul 1814 - Discharged on 1 Apr 1815

Aimes, William - Ordinary Seaman - Payroll 2 - Number: 753 - Entry Date: 18 Jun 1814 - Discharged on 1 Apr 1815

Allen, Asia - Seaman - Payroll 1 - Number: 186 - Entry Date: 3 Jan 1814 - Discharged on 28 Feb 1814 - Payroll 2 - Number: 186 - Entry Date: 3 Jan 1814 - Ran on 28 Feb 1814

Allen, Nathan - Ordinary Seaman - U.S. Frigate United States - Number: 608 - Entry Date: 7 Apr 1814 - Discharged on 6 Dec 1814 to U.S. Sloop-of-War Ontario - Payroll 2 - Number: 608 - Entry Date: 5 Apr 1814 - Discharged on 6 Dec 1814 to U.S. Sloop-of-War Ontario - U.S. Sloop-of-War Ontario - Number: 159 - Entry Date: 16 Mar 1814 - Discharged on 5 Apr 1814 to the flotilla - Transfers - Number: 38 - Entry Date: 6 Apr 1814 - Discharged on 6 Dec 1814 - U.S. Sloop-of-War Ontario - Number: 242 - Entry Date: 7 Dec 1814 - Discharged on 5 Mar 1815 from the flotilla

Amby, Henry - Cook - Payroll 2 - Number: 915 - Entry Date: 12 Mar 1814 - Discharged on 1 Apr 1815

Amos, John - Cook - Payroll 1 - Number: 97 - Entry Date: 20 Sep 1813 - Payroll ended on 6 Apr 1814 - Payroll 2 - Number: 97 - Entry Date: 20 Sep 1813 - Discharged on 27 Sep 1814

Amsden, Ira - Ordinary Seaman - Payroll 2 - Number: 471 - Entry Date: 18 Apr 1812 - Discharged on 1 Apr 1815

Anderson, Andrew - Seaman - Payroll 1 - Number: 209 - Entry Date: 17 Jan 1814 - Payroll ended on 6 Apr 1814 - Payroll 2 - Number: 209 - Entry Date: 17 Jan 1814 - Discharged on 17 Jan 1815

Anderson, John - Seaman - Payroll 1 - Number: 308 - Entry Date: 10 Mar 1814 - Payroll ended on 6 Apr 1814 - Payroll 2 - Number: 308 - Entry Date: 10 Mar 1814 - Discharged on 1 Apr 1815

Anderson, William - Landsman - Payroll 2 - Number: 847 - Entry Date: 7 Aug 1814 - Discharged on 1 Apr 1815 - BLW 6198-160-55

Andrews, Thomas K. - Midshipman - Payroll 2 - Number: 784 - Entry Date: 20 Jul 1814 - Discharged on 16 Dec 1814

Armstrong, James C. - Clerk - Payroll 1 - Number: 13 - Entry Date: 16 Dec 1813 - Payroll ended on 6 Apr 1814 - Payroll 2 - Number: 13 - Entry Date: 16 Dec 1813 - Discharged on 7 Apr 1815 - Muster - Number: 13 - Entry Date: 16 Dec 1813 - Muster ended on 6 Apr 1814

Armstrong, John - Ordinary Seaman - Payroll 1 - Number: 188 - Entry Date: 3 Jan 1814 - Discharged on 20 Feb 1814 - Payroll 2 - Number: 188 - Entry Date: 3 Jan 1814 - Discharged on 20 Feb 1814

Arnamel, John - Seaman - Muster - Number: 966 - Entry Date: 9 Feb 1814 - Discharged on 1 Apr 1815 - Payroll 2 - Number: 966 - Entry Date: 9 Jul 1814 - Discharged on 1 Apr 1815

Artus, Burril - Landsman - Payroll 1 - Number: 119 - Entry Date: 25 Sep 1813 - Payroll ended on 6 Apr 1814 - Payroll 2 - Number: 119 - Entry Date: 25 Sep 1813 - Discharged on 7 Oct 1814

Ash, George W. - Landsman - Payroll 2 - Number: 583 - Entry Date: 23 Apr 1814 - Discharged on 29 Dec 1814 - BLW 3060-160-55

Assrayders, William - Ordinary Seaman - Payroll 2 - Number: 432 - Entry Date: 13 Apr 1814 - Discharged on 1 Apr 1815

Atwell, Benjamin - Ordinary Seaman - Payroll 1 - Number: 237 - Entry Date: 26 Feb 1814 - Payroll ended on 6 Apr 1814 - Payroll 2 - Number: 237 - Entry Date: 26 Feb 1814 - Discharged on 26 Feb 1815

Auld, Thomas - Landsman - Payroll 2 - Number: 376 - Entry Date: 7 Apr 1814 - Discharged on 1 Apr 1815

Ausward, John C. - Seaman - Payroll 1 - Number: 157 - Entry Date: 27 Sep 1813 - Discharged on 24 Dec 1813 - Payroll 2 - Number: 157 - Entry Date: 27 Sep 1813 - Ran on 24 Dec 1813

Auterbridge, David - Seaman - U.S. Sloop-of-War Ontario - Number: 74 - Entry Date: 14 Jan 1814 - Discharged on 13 Apr 1814 to the flotilla - Transfers - Number: 25 - Entry Date: 15 Apr 1814 - Discharged on 6 Dec 1814 - Payroll 2 - Number: 900 - Entry Date: 1 Jan 1814 - Discharged on 6 Dec 1814 to U.S. Sloop-of-War Ontario - U.S. Frigate United States - Number: 900 - Entry Date: 7 Apr 1814 - Discharged on 6 Dec 1814 to U.S. Sloop-of-War Ontario - U.S. Sloop-of-War Ontario - Number: 210 - Entry Date: 7 Dec 1814 - Discharged on 5 Mar 1815 from the flotilla

Averill, Joseph - Seaman - Payroll 2 - Number: 516 - Entry Date: 12 Feb 1812 - Discharged on 28 Jan 1815 to U.S. Frigate United States - Number: 516 - Entry Date: 12 Feb 1814 - Discharged on 28 Jan 1815 from U.S. Battery Scorpion - BLW 11111-160-55

Averill, William - Seaman - U.S. Frigate Adams Muster - Number: 347 - Entry Date: 4 Apr 1813 - Discharged on 10 Nov 1813 to U.S. Galley Shark - U.S. Frigate Adams Payroll - Number: 347 - Entry Date: 4 Apr 1813 - Discharged on 10 Nov 1813 to U.S. Galley Shark - U.S. Frigate United States - Number: 460 - Entry Date: 11 Apr 1814 - Discharged on 23 Feb 1815 to U.S. Gunboat 137 - U.S. Gunboat 137 - Number: 9 - Entry Date: 23 Feb 1813 - Payroll ended on 4 Mar 1814 - Payroll 2 - Number: 460 - Entry Date: 28 Feb 1813 - Discharged on 23 Feb 1815

Avery, Joseph - Seaman - U.S. Sloop Scorpion - Number: 22 - Entry Date: 21 Jan 1813 - Payroll ended on 11 Feb 1814 - U.S. Frigate Adams Payroll - Number: 151 - Entry Date: 22 Feb 1813 - Discharged on 10 Nov 1813 to U.S. Gunboat 137 - U.S. Frigate Adams Muster - Number: 151 - Entry Date: 22 Feb 1813 - Discharged on 10 Nov 1813 to U.S. Gunboat 137

Aysgarth, George - Midshipman - Payroll 2 - Number: 807 - Entry Date: 16 Jun 1814 - Killed on 26 Jun 1814 at St. Leonard's Creek - U.S. Frigate United States - Number: 807 - Entry Date: 17 Apr 1814 - Killed on 26 Jun 1814 at St. Leonard's Creek

Baggott, John - Seaman - Payroll 2 - Number: 690 - Payroll 2 - Number: 948 - Entry Date: 4 May 1814 - Ran on 19 Oct 1814 - Wounded on 11 Jun 1814 at St. Leonard's - Pension: Navy IF-134 - Muster - Number: 690

Bailey, Joseph - Quarter Gunner - Payroll 2 - Number: 538 Entry Date: 29 Dec 1813 - Discharged on 6 Dec 1814 to U.S. Sloop-of-War Ontario - U.S. Sloop-of-War Ontario - Number: 71 - Entry Date: 14 Jan 1814 - Discharged on 13 Apr 1814 to the flotilla - U.S. Frigate United States - Number: 538 - Entry Date: 7 Apr 1814 - Discharged on 6 Dec 1814 to U.S. Sloop-of-War Ontario - Transfers - Number: 6 - Entry Date: 15 Apr 1814 - Discharged on 6 Dec 1814 - U.S. Sloop-of-War Ontario - Number: 208 - Entry Date: 7 Dec 1814 - Discharged on 5 Mar 1815 from the flotilla

Baker, Robert - Ordinary Seaman - Payroll 2 - Number: 819 - Entry Date: 21 Jul 1814 - Ran on 21 Nov 1814

Barker, Thomas - Seaman - Muster - Number: 49 - Entry Date: 14 Sep 1813 - Died on 6 Oct 1814 - Payroll 1 - Number: 49 - Entry Date: 14 Sep 1813 - Payroll ended on 6 Apr 1814 - Payroll 1a - Number: 49 - Entry Date: 14 Sep 1813 - Payroll 2 - Number: 49 - Entry Date: 14 Sep 1813 - Died on 6 Oct 1814

Barling, William - Gunner - Muster - Number: 44 - Entry Date: 28 Sep 1813 - Discharged on 28 Sep 1814 - Payroll 1a - Number: 44 - Entry Date: 28 Sep 1813 - Payroll 1 - Number: 44 - Entry Date: 28 Oct 1813 - Payroll ended on 6 Apr 1814 - BLW 5161-160-55 - Payroll 2 - Number: 44 - Entry Date: 28 Oct 1813 - Discharged on 28 Sep 1814

Barnard, William - Seaman - Payroll 1 - Number: 141 - Entry Date: 12 Oct 1813 - Discharged on 18 Dec 1813 - Payroll 2 - Number: 141 - Entry Date: 12 Oct 1813 - Died on 19 Dec 1813

Barnes, Jonathan - Ordinary Seaman - U.S. Frigate Adams Payroll - Number: 348 - Entry Date: 4 Apr 1813 - Discharged on 10 Nov 1813 to U.S. Gunboat 137 - U.S. Schooner Shark - Number: 7 - Entry Date: 11 Nov 1813 - Discharged on 29 Mar 1814 - U.S. Frigate United States - Number: 546 - Entry Date: 7 Apr 1814 - Ran on 11 Oct 1814 from U.S. Galley Shark - Payroll 2 - Number: 546 - Entry Date: 2 Mar 1813 - Ran on 11 Oct 1814

Barney, Joshua - Commander - Payroll 1 - Number: 1 - Entry Date: 23 Aug 1813 - Payroll ended on 6 Apr 1814 - Revolutionary War pension - Payroll 2 - Number: 1 - Entry Date: 23 Aug 1813 - Discharged on 15 Apr 1815 - Muster - Number: 1 - Entry Date: 23 Aug 1813 - Muster ended on 6 Apr 1814

Barney, Lewis - Clerk - Muster - Number: 12 - Entry Date: 1 Sep 1813 - Discharged on 15 Dec 1814 - Payroll 1 - Number: 12 - Entry Date: 1 Sep 1813 - Discharged on 15 Dec 1814 - Payroll 2 - Number: 12 - Entry Date: 1 Sep 1813

Barney, William B. - Sailing Master (Major) - Payroll 2 - Number: 636 - Entry Date: 17 Apr 1814 – Resigned on 14 Aug 1814 - BLW 41277-40-50 & BLW 56686-120-55 - Pension: WO-271, WC-177 - Also served as a major in Colonel Biays' Regiment, Maryland Militia - U.S. Frigate United States - Number: 636 - Entry Date: 17 Apr 1814 - Resigned on 14 Aug 1814

Barrett, Thomas - Seaman - Payroll 2 - Number: 697 - Entry Date: 27 May 1814 - Discharged on 1 Apr 1815

Barry, John J. - Master's Mate - Payroll 2 - Number: 809 - Entry Date: 9 Jul 1814 - Discharged on 2 Jan 1815 - BLW 3091-160-55 - Pension: SO-25667, SC-20227

Barry, Joseph L. (Berry) - Midshipman - Payroll 1 - Number: 301 - Entry Date: 7 Mar 1814 - Payroll ended on 6 Apr 1814 - Payroll 2 - Number: 301 - Entry Date: 7 Mar 1814 - Discharged on 1 Apr 1815

Bartheson, William - Seaman - Payroll 2 - Number: 439 - Entry Date: 4 Apr 1814 - Discharged on 1 Apr 1815

Bartley, Henry - Cook - Payroll 1 - Number: 99 - Entry Date: 28 Sep 1813 - Payroll ended on 6 Apr 1814 - Payroll 2 - Number: 99 - Entry Date: 28 Sep 1813 - Discharged on 28 Sep 1814

Bassett, H. W. - Midshipman - Muster - Number: 24 - Entry Date: 20 Oct 1813 - Discharged on 2 Mar 1814 - Payroll 1 - Number: 24 - Entry Date: 20 Oct 1813 - Discharged on 2 Mar 1814 - Payroll 2 - Number: 24 - Entry Date: 20 Oct 1813

Bastian, Adam - Ordinary Seaman - U.S. Sloop-of-War Ontario - Number: 125 - Entry Date: 20 Feb 1814 - Discharged on 14 Apr 1814 to the flotilla (ran) - Muster - Number: 957 - Entry Date: 17 Feb 1814 - Discharged on 24 Aug 1814 to U.S. Sloop-of-War Ontario - Payroll 2 - Number: 957 - Entry Date: 17 Feb 1814 - Ran

Bastian, James - Volunteer Seaman - Prisoner of War at Halifax, prisoner number 7316, captured on 24 Aug 1814 near Washington, D.C. by British forces; received at Halifax on 30 Sep 1814 on HMS Surprize; discharged on 5 Mar 1815 and sent to Salem, Massachusetts on Cartel Lingan

Batis, John (1) - Seaman - Payroll 1 - Number: 61 - Entry Date: 12 Oct 1813 - Payroll ended on 6 Apr 1814 - Payroll 1a - Number: 61 - Entry Date: 12 Oct 1813 - Payroll 2 - Number: 61 - Entry Date: 12 Oct 1813 - Discharged on 13 Oct 1814

Batis, John (2) - Seaman - Payroll 1 - Number: 353 - Entry Date: 5 Apr 1814 - Payroll ended on 6 Apr 1814 - Payroll 2 - Number: 353 - Entry Date: 5 Apr 1814 - Discharged on 1 Apr 1815

Batist, John (Baptist) - Boy - U.S. Gunboat 138 - Number: 67 - Paid on 6 Apr 1814 - Payroll 2 - Number: 865 - Entry Date: 10 Sep 1813 - Ran on 18 Feb 1815 - Wounded at Bladensburg - U.S. Frigate United States - Number: 865 - Entry Date: 7 Apr 1814 - Ran on 18 Feb 1815 from US Gunboat 138- Seaman - Washington Naval Hospital - Number: 11 - Wounded at Bladensburg, neck wound, admitted on 24 Aug 1814, deserted on 28 Sep 1814

Battle, Timothy - Marine Private - Washington Naval Hospital - Number: 24 - Wounded at Bladensburg, head wound, admitted on 26 Aug 1814, deserted on 26 Oct 1814 - Enlisted on 11 Dec 1810 at Charleston SC Navy Yard

Baxter, Alexander - Seaman - U.S. Sloop-of-War Ontario - Number: 25 - Entry Date: 14 Jan 1814 - Discharged on 13 Apr 1814 to the flotilla - Transfers - Number: 16 - Entry Date: 14 Apr 1814 - Discharged on 6 Dec 1814 - Payroll 2 - Number: 632 - Entry Date: 12 Nov 1813 - Discharged on 6 Dec 1814 to U.S. Sloop-of-War Ontario - U.S. Frigate United States - Number: 632 - Entry Date: 17 Apr 1814 - Discharged on 6 Dec 1814 to U.S. Sloop-of-War Ontario - U.S. Sloop-of-War Ontario - Number: 632 - Entry Date: 7 Dec 1814 - Discharged on 5 Mar 1815 from the flotilla

Baxter, John - Seaman - Payroll 2 - Number: 954 - Entry Date: 28 Jan 1814 - Discharged on 1 Apr 1815 - U.S. Sloop-of-War Ontario - Number: 104 - Entry Date: 1 Feb 1814 - Discharged on 14 Apr 1814 to the flotilla (prisoner) - Prisoner of War at Dartmoor, prisoner number 5502, captured on 22 Aug 1814 from the U.S. Flotilla Service, Gunboat Number 2 on the Chesapeake Bay by British forces; sent to Halifax on H.M. Transport Loire; received at Dartmoor on 17 Dec 1814; released on 29 Jun 1815 - Born: Philadelphia - Age: 40 - Muster - Number: 954 - Entry Date: 28 Jan 1814 - Discharged on 1 Apr 1815

Baxter, Thomas - Boy - U.S. Frigate United States - Number: 575 - Entry Date: 12 Feb 1814 - Discharged on 26 Oct 1814 to U.S. Battery Scorpion - U.S. Sloop Scorpion - Number: 2 - Entry Date: 26 Oct 1812 - Payroll ended on 11 Feb 1814 - Payroll 2 - Number: 575 - Entry Date: 26 Oct 1812 - Discharged on 26 Oct 1814

Bay, John - Volunteer Seaman - Washington Naval Hospital - Number: 7 - Wounded at Bladensburg, head wound, admitted 24 Aug 1814, deserted on 24 Aug 1814

Bayer, Ferdinand - Landsman - Payroll 2 - Number: 707 - Entry Date: 5 Jun 1814 - Ran on 19 Feb 1815

Beach, William - Seaman - Payroll 1 - Number: 213 - Entry Date: 22 Jan 1814 - Payroll ended on 6 Apr 1814 - Seaman - Payroll 2 - Number: 213 - Entry Date: 22 Jan 1814 - Discharged on 2 Jan 1815

Beandesive, Lewis - Master's Mate - Muster - Number: 18 - Entry Date: 28 Sep 1813 - Discharged on 15 Dec 1814 - Payroll 1 - Number: 18 - Entry Date: 27 Sep 1813 - Payroll ended on 6 Apr 1814 - Payroll 2 - Number: 18 - Entry Date: 27 Sep 1813 - Discharged on 15 Dec 1814

Beaty, Johsua - Seaman - Muster - Number: 747 - Entry Date: 19 May 1814 - Discharged on 2 Jan 1815 - Payroll 2 - Number: 747 - Entry Date: 19 May 1814 - Discharged on 2 Jan 1815 - Payroll 2 - Number: 977 - Entry Date: 8 Apr 1814 - Discharged on 18 May 1814

Beggs, Beverly - Sailing Master - Payroll 1 - Number: 291 - Entry Date: 1 Mar 1814 - Payroll ended on 6 Apr 1814 - Payroll 2 - Number: 291 - Entry Date: 1 Mar 1814 - Discharged on 1 Feb 1815

Bell, David - Ordinary Seaman - Payroll 2 - Number: 959 - Entry Date: 25 Aug 1814 - Discharged on 1 Apr 1815 – Race: Negro - Muster - Number: 959 - Entry Date: 25 Aug 1814 - Discharged on 1 Apr 1815

Bell, Thomas - Landsman - Payroll 2 - Number: 578 - Entry Date: 4 May 1814 - Ran on 20 Oct 1814

Bellowry, Matthias - Cook - Payroll 1 - Number: 146 - Entry Date: 8 Nov 1813 - Discharged on 28 Nov 1813 - Payroll 2 - Number: 146 - Entry Date: 8 Nov 1813 - Ran on 28 Nov 1813

Belt, Joseph - Ordinary Seaman - Payroll 2 - Number: 886 - Entry Date: 25 Aug 1814 - Discharged on 1 Apr 1815

Bennett, William - Ordinary Seaman - Payroll 2 - Number: 701 - Entry Date: 31 May 1814 - Discharged on 1 Apr 1815

Benold, Matthias - Seaman - Payroll 1 - Number: 359 - Entry Date: 3 Jan 1814 - Payroll ended on 6 Apr 1814 - Payroll 2 - Number: 359 - Entry Date: 3 Jan 1814 - Discharged on 3 Jan 1815

Benson, William B. - Master's Mate - Muster - Number: 20 - Entry Date: 28 Sep 1813 - Muster ended on 6 Apr

1814 - Payroll 1 - Number: 20 - Entry Date: 28 Sep 1813 - Payroll ended on 6 Apr 1814 - Payroll 2 - Number: 20 - Entry Date: 28 Sep 1813 - Discharged on 18 Dec 1814

Besse, Claudius (also Claude) - Sailing Master - Muster - Number: 9 - Entry Date: 10 Sep 1813 - Muster ended on 6 Apr 1814 - Payroll 1 - Number: 9 - Entry Date: 10 Sep 1813 - Payroll ended on 6 Apr 1814 - Payroll 2 - Number: 9 - Entry Date: 10 Sep 1813 - Discharged on 15 Apr 1815 - Warranted as a sailing master on 16 Sep 1813

Besse, John - Master's Mate - Muster - Number: 21 - Entry Date: 28 Sep 1813 - Discharged on 15 Dec 1814 - BLW 5162-160-55 - Pension: WO-15703, WC-9771 - Payroll 1 - Number: 21 - Entry Date: 28 Sep 1813 - Payroll ended on 6 Apr 1814 - Payroll 2 - Number: 21 - Entry Date: 28 Sep 1813 - Discharged on 15 Dec 1814

Besse, Simmons - Midshipman - Payroll 1 - Number: 25 - Entry Date: 28 Sep 1813 - Payroll ended on 6 Apr 1814 - Payroll 2 - Number: 25 - Entry Date: 28 Sep 1813 - Discharged on 18 Nov 1814 - Muster - Number: 25 - Entry Date: 28 Sep 1813 - Discharged on 16 Dec 1814

Betsworth, Peter C. - Seaman - Payroll 1 - Number: 71 - Entry Date: 14 Nov 1813 - Discharged on 19 Mar 1814 - Payroll 1a - Number: 71 - Entry Date: 14 Nov 1813 - Ran on 19 May 1814 - Payroll 2 - Number: 71 - Entry Date: 14 Nov 1813 - Ran on 19 Mar 1814

Billings, John - Seaman - Payroll 2 - Number: 781 - Entry Date: 12 Jul 1814 - Discharged on 1 Apr 1815

Bing, George - Seaman - Payroll 2 - Number: 759 - Entry Date: 18 Apr 1814 - Ran on 25 Jan 1815

Birch, David - Seaman - Payroll 1 - Number: 273 - Date: 11 Mar 1814 - Payroll ended on 6 Apr 1814 - Payroll 2 - Number: 273 - Entry Date: 11 Mar 1814 - Discharged on 1 Apr 1815 - Prisoner of War at Halifax, prisoner number 7317, captured on 24 Aug 1814 near Washington, D.C. by British forces; received at Halifax on 30 Sep 1814 on HMS Surprize; discharged on 5 Mar 1815 and sent to Salem, Massachusetts on Cartel Lingan

Bird, William - Landsman - Payroll 2 - Number: 803 - Entry Date: 15 Jul 1814 - Discharged on 1 Apr 1815

Bisbee, John - Armorer - U.S. Sloop-of-War Ontario - Number: 133 - Entry Date: 9 Mar 1814 - Discharged on 14 Apr 1814 to the flotilla (died) - Payroll 2 - Number: 390 - Entry Date: 7 Mar 1814 - Died on 7 Sep 1814

Blackburne, William - Ordinary Seaman - Payroll 1 - Number: 109 - Entry Date: 11 Nov 1813 - Payroll ended on 6 Apr 1814 - Payroll 2 - Number: 109 - Entry Date: 11 Nov 1813 - Discharged on 12 Nov 1814

Blades, William Cooper - Seaman - Payroll 2 - Number: 406 - Entry Date: 6 Mar 1814 - Discharged on 6 Mar 1815 - BLW 11696-165-55

Blakeman, Peter - Seaman - Payroll 2 - Number: 910 - Entry Date: 25 Aug 1814 - Ran on 4 Mar 1815

Boater, Alexander - Volunteer Seaman - Washington Naval Hospital - Number: 46 - Wounded at Bladensburg; admitted on 24 Aug 1814, discharged on 28 Sep 1814

Bobbit, Samuel - Seaman - Payroll 1 - Number: 216 - Entry Date: 26 Jan 1814 - Payroll ended on 6 Apr 1814 - Payroll 2 - Number: 216 - Entry Date: 26 Jan 1814 - Discharged on 26 Jan 1815

Boice, Cornelius (or Boyce) - Seaman - U.S. Sloop-of-War Ontario - Number: 113 - Entry Date: 8 Feb 1814 - Discharged on 13 Apr 1814 to the flotilla - Payroll 2 - Number: 514 - Entry Date: 4 Feb 1814 - Discharged on 6 Dec 1814 to U.S. Sloop-of-War Ontario - Transfers - Number: 7 - Entry Date: 14 Apr 1814 - Discharged on 6 Dec 1814 - U.S. Sloop-of-War Ontario - Number: 230 - Entry Date: 7 Dec 1814 - Discharged on 5 Mar 1815 from the flotilla - U.S. Frigate United States - Number: 514 - Entry Date: 7 Apr 1814 - Discharged on 6 Dec 1814 to U.S. Sloop-of-War Ontario

Boice, Sutton - Landsman - Payroll 2 - Number: 817 - Entry Date: 17 Jul 1814 - Discharged on 1 Apr 1815

Bomberger, George - Boy - U.S. Frigate United States - Number: 484 - Entry Date: 12 Feb 1814 - Discharged on 1 Oct 1814 to U.S. Battery Scorpion - U.S. Sloop Scorpion - Number: 6 - Entry Date: 28 Sep 1812 - Payroll ended on 11 Feb 1814 - Payroll 2 - Number: 484 - Entry Date: 28 Sep 1812 - Discharged on 1 Oct 1814

Bory, John - Boy - Payroll 2 - Number: 386 - Entry Date: 13 Apr 1814 - Ran on 6 Sep 1814

Bowan, Henry - Ordinary Seaman - Payroll 2 - Number: 531 - Entry Date: 9 May 1814 - Ran on 6 Jan 1815

Bowden, James - Ordinary Seaman - Payroll 2 - Number: 375 - Entry Date: 31 Mar 1814 - Discharged on 1 Apr 1815

Bowen, John - Master's Mate - Payroll 1 - Number: 296 - Entry Date: 10 Mar 1814 - Payroll ended on 6 Apr 1814 - Payroll 2 - Number: 296 - Entry Date: 10 Mar 1814 - Discharged on 1 Apr 1815

Bower, Jacob - Landsman - Payroll 1 - Number: 181 - Entry Date: 18 Dec 1813 - Discharged on 28 Feb 1814 - Payroll 2 - Number: 181 - Entry Date: 18 Dec 1813 - Discharged on 28 Feb 1814

Bowie, James - Seaman - Payroll 2 - Number: 922 - Entry Date: 13 Aug 1814 - Ran of 19 Oct 1814

Bowmaker, William - Seaman - Payroll 1 - Number: 77 - Entry Date: 1 Nov 1813 - Payroll ended on 6 Apr 1814 - Payroll 1a - Number: 77 - Entry Date: 1 Nov 1813 - Payroll 2 - Number: 77 - Entry Date: 1 Nov 1813 - Discharged on 7 Nov 1814

Bowman, Edward - Seaman - Payroll 2 - Number: 764 - Entry Date: 13 Mar 1814 - Discharged on 1 Apr 1815

Boyd, John - Ordinary Seaman - Payroll 1 - Number: 106 - Entry Date: 12 Oct 1813 - Payroll ended on 6 Apr 1814 - Payroll 2 - Number: 106 - Entry Date: 12 Oct 1813 - Discharged on 12 Oct 1814

Braden, Elisha - Cook - Payroll 1 - Number: 100 - Entry Date: 15 Sep 1813 - Payroll ended on 6 Apr 1814 - Payroll 2 - Number: 100 - Entry Date: 15 Sep 1813 - Discharged on 23 Sep 1814

Brady, Edward - Seaman - Payroll 2 - Number: 638 - Entry Date: 15 Mar 1814 - Discharged on 1 Apr 1815

Brant, John - Seaman - U.S. Sloop-of-War Ontario - Number: 94 - Entry Date: 26 Jan 1814 - Discharged on 13 Apr 1814 to the flotilla (ran) - Payroll 2 - Number: 934 - Entry Date: 22 Jan 1814 - Ran on 25 Aug 1814 - Muster - Number: 934 - Entry Date: 22 Jan 1814 - Ran on 25 Apr 1814 from Potomac

Breese, John M. - Sailing Master - Muster - Number: 7 - Entry Date: 12 Oct 1813 - Muster ended on 6 Apr 1814 - Payroll 1 - Number: 7 - Entry Date: 12 Oct 1813 - Payroll ended on 6 Apr 1814 - Payroll 2 - Number: 7 - Entry Date: 12 Oct 1813 - Discharged on 15 Apr 1815

Breese, Joseph - Seaman - U.S. Sloop-of-War Ontario - Number: 93 - Entry Date: 26 Jan 1814 - Discharged on 13 Apr 1814 to the flotilla - Transfers - Number: 13 - Entry Date: 14 Apr 1814 - Discharged on 6 Dec 1814 - Payroll 2 - Number: 486 - Entry Date: 22 Jan 1814 - Discharged on 6 Dec 1814 to U.S. Sloop-of-War Ontario - U.S. Frigate United States - Number: 486 - Entry Date: 7 Apr 1814 - Discharged on 6 Dec 1814 to U.S. Sloop-of-War Ontario - U.S. Sloop-of-War Ontario - Number: 219 - Entry Date: 7 Dec 1814 - Discharged on 5 Mar 1815 from the flotilla

Briscoe, George - Ordinary Seaman - Payroll 1 - Number: 326 - Entry Date: 24 Mar 1814 - Payroll ended on 6 Apr 1814 - Payroll 2 - Number: 326 - Entry Date: 24 Mar 1814 - Discharged on 24 Mar 1815

Briso, Alexander - Sailing Master - Payroll 2 - Number: 626 - Entry Date: 1 Mar 1814 - Discharged on 15 Apr 1815

Bromwell, Robert (1) - Boatswain - Payroll 2 - Number: 996 - Entry Date: 2 May 1814 - Discharged on 1 Apr 1815 - Muster - Number: 996 - Entry Date: 20 May 1814 - Discharged on 1 Apr 1815

Bromwell, Robert (2) - Seaman - Payroll 2 - Number: 735 - Entry Date: 23 Apr 1814 - Discharged on 19 May 1814

Brown, Benjamin G. (alias Brooks, Benjamin) - Ordinary Seaman - Payroll 2 - Number: 264 - Entry Date: 19 Feb 1814 - Died on 2 Jun 1814 - Ordinary Seaman - Payroll 1 - Number: 437 - Payroll ended on 6 Apr 1814 - Payroll 2 - Number: 264 - Entry Date: 8 Mar 1814 - Killed on 2 Jun 1814

Brown, Daniel - Seaman - U.S. Sloop Scorpion - Number: 4 - Entry Date: 10 Feb 1812 - Payroll ended on 11 Feb 1814 - Payroll 2 - Number: 425 - Entry Date: 9 Feb 1814 - Ran on 5 Jan 1815

Brown, Edward P. - Seaman - Payroll 2 - Number: 909 - Entry Date: 2 Feb 1814 - Discharged on 6 Dec 1814 to U.S. Sloop-of-War Ontario - U.S. Sloop-of-War Ontario - Number: 227 - Entry Date: 7 Dec 1814 - Discharged on 5 Mar 1815 from the flotilla - Pension: Navy IF-142 - Transfers - Number: 22 - Entry Date: 14 Apr 1814 - Discharged on 6 Dec 1814 - U.S. Frigate United States - Number: 909 - Entry Date: 14 Apr 1814 - Discharged on 6 Dec 1814 to U.S. Sloop-of-War Ontario - U.S. Sloop-of-War Ontario - Number: 108 - Entry Date: 8 Feb 1814 - Discharged on 14 Apr 1814 to the flotilla

Brown, Francis - Midshipman - Payroll 2 - Number: 633 - Entry Date: 19 May 1814 - Discharged on 7 Jan 1815

Brown, James (1) - Seaman - Payroll 2 - Number: 427 - Entry Date: 23 Apr 1814 - Ran (no date)

Brown, James (2) - Ordinary Seaman - U.S. Frigate United States - Number: 905 - Entry Date: 7 Apr 1814 - Discharged on 6 Dec 1814 to U.S. Sloop-of-War Ontario - Transfers - Number: 21 - Entry Date: 15 Apr 1814 - Discharged on 6 Dec 1814 - Payroll 2 - Number: 905 - Entry Date: 31 Jan 1814 - Discharged on 6 Dec 1814 to U.S. Sloop-of-War Ontario

Brown, James (3) - Seaman - U.S. Frigate Adams Payroll - Number: 78 - Entry Date: 18 Jan 1813 - Discharged on 10 Nov 1813 to U.S. Galley Shark - U.S. Sloop-of-War Ontario - Number: 106 - Entry Date: 6 Feb 1814 - Discharged on 14 Apr 1814 to the flotilla - U.S. Frigate United States - Number: 908 - Entry Date: 7 Apr 1814 - Discharged on 10 Feb 1815 to U.S. Battery Scorpion - U.S. Sloop-of-War Ontario - Number: 225 - Entry Date: 7 Dec 1814 - Discharged on 5 Mar 1815 from the flotilla - U.S. Flotilla Service - Number: 908 - BLW 24841-160-55 - U.S. Sloop Scorpion - Number: 908 - Entry Date: 10 Feb 1813 - Payroll ended on 11 Feb 1814 - Payroll 2 - Number: 908 - Entry Date: 10 Feb 1813 - Discharged on 10 Feb 1815

Brown, John - Ordinary Seaman - U.S. Sloop-of-War Ontario - Number: 119 - Entry Date: 13 Feb 1814 - Discharged on 13 Apr 1814 to the flotilla - U.S. Frigate United States - Number: 655 - Entry Date: 7 Apr 1814 - Ran on 24 Aug 1814 from Bladensburg - Seaman - Payroll 2 - Number: 655 - Entry Date: 14 Apr 1814 - Ran on 26 Aug 1814

Brown, Sylvester - Gunner - Payroll 2 - Number: 685 - Entry Date: 20 Apr 1814 - Discharged on 1 Apr 1815 - BLW 5160-177-55 - U.S. Frigate United States - Number: 685 - Entry Date: 27 Apr 1814 - Discharged on 1 Apr 1815 - Lazaretto (Baltimore)

Brown, Thomas (1) - Seaman - U.S. Frigate United States - Number: 481 - Entry Date: 7 Apr 1814 - Discharged on 6 Dec 1814 to U.S. Sloop-of-War Ontario - U.S. Sloop-of-War Ontario - Number: 28 - Entry Date: 14 Jan 1814 - Discharged on 13 Apr 1814 to the flotilla - Transfers - Number: 54 - Entry Date: 14 Apr 1814 - Discharged on 6 Dec 1814 - Payroll 2 - Number: 481 - Entry Date: 15 Nov 1813 - Discharged on 6 Dec 1814 to U.S. Sloop-of-War Ontario

Brown, Thomas (2) - Seaman - U.S. Sloop-of-War Ontario - Number: 90 - Entry Date: 18 Jan 1814 - Discharged on 14 Apr 1814 to the flotilla - U.S. Sloop-of-War Ontario - Number: 191 - Entry Date: 7 Dec 1814 - Discharged on 5 Mar 1815 from the flotilla - Payroll 2 - Number: 898 - Entry Date: 22 Jan 1814 - Died on 15 Apr 1814

Brown, William (1) - Seaman - Payroll 1 - Number: 714 - Entry Date: 26 Mar 1814 - Payroll ended on 6 Apr 1814 - Payroll 2 - Number: 714 - Entry Date: 26 Mar 1814 - Discharged on 7 Jun 1814

Brown, William (2) - Seaman - Payroll 2 - Number: 752 - Entry Date: 6 Jun 1814 - Ran on 14 Dec 1814

Brown, William (3) - Seaman - U.S. Sloop-of-War Ontario - Number: 139 - Entry Date: 16 Mar 1814 - Discharged on 14 Apr 1814 to the flotilla - Muster - Number: 937 - Entry Date: 15 Mar 1814 - Ran on 24 Aug 1814 - Payroll 2 - Number: 937 - Entry Date: 15 Mar 1814 - Ran on 24 Aug 1814

Brown, William (4) - Gunner - Payroll 2 - Number: 329 - Entry Date: 18 Jun 1814 - Discharged on 1 Apr 1815

Bruff, William T. - Boy - Payroll 1 - Number: 136 - Entry Date: 13 Oct 1813 - Discharged on 15 Nov 1813 - Payroll 2 - Number: 136 - Entry Date: 13 Oct 1813 - Discharged on 15 Nov 1813

Bryson, James - Seaman - U.S. Frigate Adams Muster - Number: 319 - Entry Date: 3 Apr 1813 - Discharged on 10 Nov 1813 to U.S. Gunboat 137 - U.S. Frigate United States - Number: 509 - Entry Date: 7 Apr 1814 - Discharged on 23 Nov 1814 to U.S. Battery Scorpion - U.S. Sloop Scorpion - Number: 15 - Entry Date: 23 Nov 1812 - Payroll ended on 11 Feb 1814 - Payroll 2 - Number: 509 - Entry Date: 23 Nov 1812 - Discharged on 12 Feb 1814

Buckley, John H. - Seaman - U.S. Sloop-of-War Ontario - Number: 101 - Entry Date: 30 Jan 1814 - Discharged on 13 Apr 1814 to the flotilla - U.S. Frigate United States - Number: 882 - Entry Date: 7 Apr 1814 - Ran on 14 Nov 1814 to U.S. Sloop-of-War Ontario - U.S. Sloop-of-War Ontario - Number: 222 - Entry Date: 7 Dec 1814 - Discharged on 5 Mar 1815 from the flotilla - Payroll 2 - Number: 882 - Entry Date: 25 Jan 1814 - Ran on 14 Nov 1814

Buckley, Thomas - Midshipman - Payroll 1 - Number: 351 - Entry Date: 2 Apr 1814 - Payroll ended on 6 Apr 1814 - Payroll 2 - Number: 351 - Entry Date: 2 Apr 1814 - Discharged on 22 Oct 1814

Buddy, Peter - Steward - Payroll 1 - Number: 347 - Entry Date: 6 Apr 1814 - Payroll ended on 6 Apr 1814 - Payroll 2 - Number: 347 - Entry Date: 6 Apr 1814 - Discharged on 24 Dec 1814

Bulgdin, James - Ordinary Seaman - U.S. Sloop-of-War Ontario - Number: 154 - Entry Date: 16 Mar 1814 - Discharged on 5 Apr 1814 to the flotilla - U.S. Frigate United States - Number: 804 - Entry Date: 7 Apr 1814 - Discharged on 6 Oct 1814 to U.S. Sloop-of-War Ontario - Payroll 2 - Number: 804 - Entry Date: 15 Mar 1814 - Discharged on 6 Oct 1814

Bullen, Henry - Steward - Payroll 2 - Number: 527 - Entry Date: 26 Mar 1814 - Discharged on 20 Oct 1814

Bundy, Jacob S. - Gunner - Muster - Number: 41 - Entry Date: 16 Sep 1813 - Muster ended on 6 Apr 1814 - Payroll 1 - Number: 41 - Entry Date: 16 Oct 1813 - Payroll ended on 6 Apr 1814 - Payroll 1a - Number: 41 - Entry Date: 16 Sep 1813 - Payroll 2 - Number: 41 - Entry Date: 16 Oct 1813 - Discharged on 30 Sep 1814

Burgess, John - Ordinary Seaman - U.S. Sloop Scorpion - Number: 11 - Entry Date: 22 Jan 1813 - Payroll ended on 11 Feb 1814 - U.S. Frigate Adams Muster - Number: 189 - Entry Date: 15 Mar 1813 - Discharged on 10 Nov 1813 to U.S. Galley Shark - Payroll 2 - Number: 421 - Entry Date: 22 Jan 1813 - Discharged on 27 Jan 1815

Burke, Thomas - Quarter Gunner - U.S. Sloop-of-War Ontario - Number: 52 - Entry Date: 14 Jan 1814 - Discharged on 14 Apr 1814 to the flotilla - Transfers - Number: 42 - Entry Date: 15 Apr 1814 - Discharged on 6 Dec 1814 - Payroll 2 - Number: 640 - Entry Date: 7 Dec 1813 - Discharged on 6 Dec 1814 to U.S. Sloop-of-War Ontario - U.S. Sloop-of-War Ontario - Number: 201 - Entry Date: 7 Dec 1814 - Discharged on 19 Mar 1815 from the flotilla

Burnes, John - Seaman - Payroll 1 - Number: 175 - Entry Date: 9 Dec 1813 - Payroll ended on 6 Apr 1814 - Payroll 2 - Number: 175 - Entry Date: 9 Dec 1813 - Discharged on 9 Dec 1814

Burnes, William - Seaman - Payroll 1 - Number: 183 - Entry Date: 8 Dec 1813 - Payroll ended on 6 Apr 1814 - Payroll 2 - Number: 183 - Entry Date: 8 Dec 1813 - Discharged on 8 Dec 1814

Burnham, John B. - Gunner - Payroll 2 - Number: 896 - Entry Date: 14 Jul 1814 - Discharged on 1 Apr 1815 - U.S. Frigate United States - Number: 896 - Entry Date: 18 Apr 1814 - Discharged on 1 Apr 1815 to Patuxent

Burrows, Edward - Boatswain - Muster - Number: 36 - Entry Date: 24 Sep 1813 - Discharged on 16 Oct 1814 - Payroll 1 - Number: 36 - Entry Date: 24 Sep 1813 - Payroll ended on 6 Apr 1814 - Payroll 2 - Number: 36 - Entry Date: 24 Sep 1813 - Discharged on 10 Oct 1814

Busher, Thomas - Ordinary Seaman - U.S. Sloop-of-War Ontario - Number: 65 - Entry Date: 14 Jan 1814 - Discharged on 14 Apr 1814 to the flotilla - Muster - Number: 933 - Entry Date: 15 Apr 1815 - Ran on 17 Apr 1814 - Muster - Number: 976 - Entry Date: 15 Apr 1815 - Ran on 17 Apr 1814 - Payroll 2 - Number: 976 - Entry Date: 15 Apr 1815 - Ran on 17 Apr 1814- Payroll 2 - Number: 933 - Entry Date: 15 Apr 1815 - Ran on 17 Apr 1814

Butler, Charles - Seaman - Payroll 2 - Number: 590 - Entry Date: 7 May 1814 - Discharged on 1 Apr 1815

Butler, Henry - Landsman - Muster - Number: 1002 - Entry Date: 7 Apr 1814 - Discharged on 1 Apr 1815 - Seaman - Payroll 2 - Number: 1002 - Entry Date: 7 Apr 1814 - Discharged on 1 Apr 1815

Butler, Matthias - Cook - Payroll 1 - Number: 95 - Entry Date: 15 Sep 1813 Payroll ended on 6 Apr 1814 - Payroll 2 - Number: 95 - Entry Date: 15 Sep 1813 - Discharged on 21 Sep 1814

Butler, Peter - Seaman - Payroll 2 - Number: 875 - Entry Date: 19 Aug 1814 - Ran on 16 Mar 1815

Byers, Joseph M. - Midshipman - Muster - Number: 981 - Entry Date: 12 Dec 1814 - Discharged on 1 Apr 1815 - Payroll 2 - Number: 981 - Entry Date: 12 Dec 1814 - Discharged on 1 Apr 1815

Byers, William - Sailing Master - Payroll 2 - Number: 448 - Entry Date: 1 Feb 1814 - Discharged on 15 Apr 1815

Cadle, Archibald - Seaman - Payroll 2 - Number: 694 - Entry Date: 19 May 1814 - Discharged on 1 Apr 1815

Cain, George - Ordinary Seaman - U.S. Sloop-of-War Ontario - Number: 129 - Entry Date: 26 Feb 1814 - Discharged on 14 Apr 1814 to the flotilla (ran) - Payroll 2 - Number: 941 - Entry Date: 14 Apr 1814 - Ran on 24 Aug 1814 - Muster - Number: 941 - Entry Date: 23 Feb 1814 - Ran on 24 Aug 1814

Caldwell, John - Armorer - Payroll 1 - Number: 147 - Entry Date: 17 Nov 1813 - Payroll ended on 6 Apr 1814 -

Payroll 2 - Number: 147 - Entry Date: 17 Nov 1813 - Discharged on 17 Nov 1814

Calwell, James - Ordinary Seaman - Payroll 1 - Number: 211 - Entry Date: 22 Jan 1814 - Payroll ended on 6 Apr 1814 - Payroll 2 - Number: 211 - Entry Date: 22 Jan 1814 - Discharged on 28 Jan 1815

Card, Nathaniel - Seaman - Payroll 1 - Number: 343 - Entry Date: 5 Apr 1814 - Payroll ended on 6 Apr 1814 - Payroll 2 - Number: 343 - Entry Date: 5 Apr 1814 - Discharged on 1 Apr 1815

Carmichael, Levin - Seaman - Payroll 1 - Number: 322 - Entry Date: 23 Mar 1814 - Payroll ended on 6 Apr 1814 - Payroll 2 - Number: 322 - Entry Date: 23 Mar 1814 - Discharged on 1 Apr 1815

Carr, John - Landsman - Payroll 2 - Number: 403 - Entry Date: 25 Mar 1814 - Payroll 2 - Number: 382 - Entry Date: 25 Mar 1814 - Discharged on 1 Apr 1815

Carr, John B. - Boy - U.S. Frigate United States - Number: 571 - Entry Date: 12 Feb 1814 - Discharged on 2 Jan 1815 to U.S. Battery Scorpion - U.S. Sloop Scorpion - Number: 7 - Entry Date: 2 Jan 1813 - Payroll ended on 11 Feb 1814 - Payroll 2 - Number: 571 - Entry Date: 2 Jan 1813 - Discharged on 2 Jan 1815 - BLW 6052-160-55

Carrew, James - Sailing Master - Payroll 1 - Number: 85 - Entry Date: 27 Oct 1813 - Payroll ended on 6 Apr 1814 - Payroll 2 - Number: 85 - Entry Date: 27 Oct 1813 - Discharged on 27 Oct 1814

Carrigen, Neil - Marine Private - U.S. Marine Corps - Taken at Bladensburg on 24 Aug 1814 - Halifax Prisoner number: 7314 - Date received: 30 Sep 1814 from what ship: HMS Surprize - Discharged on 5 Mar 1815 and sent to Salem, Massachusetts on Cartel Lingan

Carroll, John H. - Midshipman - U.S. Frigate United States - Number: 891 - Entry Date: 31 Apr 1814 - Discharged on 1 Mar 1815 to Patuxent - Payroll 2 - Number: 891 - Entry Date: 31 Jul 1814 - Discharged on 1 Mar 1815

Carter, John - Seaman - Payroll 1 - Number: 339 - Entry Date: 29 Mar 1814 - Payroll ended on 6 Apr 1814 - Payroll 2 - Number: 339 - Entry Date: 29 Mar 1814 - Ran on 30 Jun 1814

Carter, William - Master's Mate - U.S. Gunboat 138 - Number: 852 - Paid on 6 Apr 1814 - Payroll 2 - Number: 852 - Payroll 2 - Number: 852 - Entry Date: 10 Sep 1813 - Discharged on 11 Nov 1814 - Pension: Navy IF-287

Caso, George - Seaman - Payroll 1 - Number: 272 - Entry Date: 12 Mar 1814 - Payroll ended on 6 Apr 1814

Cassidy, Daniel - Cook - Payroll 1 - Number: 96 - Entry Date: 16 Sep 1813 - Payroll ended on 6 Apr 1814 - Payroll 2 - Number: 96 - Entry Date: 16 Sep 1813 - Discharged on 21 Sep 1814

Chambers, David - Gunner - Payroll 1 - Number: 42 - Entry Date: 28 Oct 1813 - Payroll ended on 6 Apr 1814 - Payroll 1a - Number: 42 - Entry Date: 28 Sep 1813 - Payroll 2 - Number: 42 - Entry Date: 28 Oct 1813 - Discharged on 11 May 1814 - Muster - Number: 42 - Entry Date: 28 Sep 1813 - Discharged on 11 May 1814

Chapman, Nathan - Cook - Muster - Number: 995 - Entry Date: 6 Jul 1814 - Discharged on 1 Apr 1815 - Payroll 2 - Number: 995 - Entry Date: 6 Jul 1814 - Discharged on 1 Apr 1815

Chapman, Nathaniel - Payroll 2 - Number: 436 - Entry Date: 10 Apr 1814 - Discharged on 5 Jul 1814

Chase, Joseph - Ordinary Seaman - U.S. Sloop Scorpion - Number: 13 - Entry Date: 12 Jan 1813 - Payroll ended on 11 Feb 1814 - BLW 15218-160-55 - Payroll 2 - Number: 430 - Entry Date: 12 Jan 1813 - Discharged on 16 Feb 1815

Chete, Crawford - Seaman - Payroll 2 - Number: 674 - Entry Date: 6 May 1814 - Discharged on 1 Apr 1815

Chilcut, Joshua - Ordinary Seaman - Payroll 1 - Number: 285 - Entry Date: 15 Mar 1814 - Payroll ended on 6 Apr 1814 - Payroll 2 - Number: 285 - Entry Date: 15 Mar 1814 - Discharged on 1 Apr 1815

Christall, Peter - Seaman - Payroll 2 - Number: 725 - Entry Date: 13 Apr 1814 - Ran on 17 Apr 1814

Christie, Daniel - Marine Private - U.S. Marine Corps – Halifax Prison - Prisoner number: 7320 – Taken at Bladensburg on 24 Aug 1814 - Date received: 30 Sep 1814 from what ship: HMS Surprize - Discharged on 5 Mar 1815 and sent to Salem, Massachusetts on Cartel Lingan

Christie, George - Master's Mate - Payroll 2 - Number: 738 - Entry Date: 28 Apr 1814 - Discharged on 14 Aug 1814

Christy, John - Seaman - Payroll 1 - Number: 83 - Entry Date: 21 Oct 1813 - Payroll ended on 6 Apr 1814 - Payroll

2 - Number: 83 - Entry Date: 21 Oct 1813 - Discharged on 21 May 1814

Clark, Francis - Ordinary Seaman - Payroll 1 - Number: 241 - Entry Date: 2 Mar 1814 - Payroll ended on 6 Apr 1814 - Payroll 2 - Number: 241 - Entry Date: 2 Mar 1814 - Discharged on 1 Apr 1815

Clife, James W. - Steward - Payroll 2 - Number: 422 - Entry Date: 4 Apr 1814 - Discharged on 1 Apr 1815

Clifford, William - Seaman - U.S. Frigate Adams Payroll - Number: 242 - Entry Date: 17 Mar 1813 - Discharged on 10 Nov 1813 to U.S. Schooner Asp - U.S. Frigate United States - Number: 812 - Entry Date: 21 Apr 1814 - Discharged on (Not known) to U.S. Schooner Asp - U.S. Sloop Asp - Number: 5 - Entry Date: 11 Nov 1813 - Discharged on 20 Apr 1814 - Payroll 2 - Number: 812 - Entry Date: 12 Feb 1813 - Discharged on Unknown

Cloud, Daniel - Landsman - Payroll 1 - Number: 411 - Entry Date: 10 Feb 1814 - Payroll ended on 6 Apr 1814 - Payroll 2 - Number: 411 - Entry Date: 10 Feb 1814 - Discharged on 10 Feb 1815

Cloues, Philip - Ordinary Seaman - Payroll 2 - Number: 840 - Entry Date: 3 Aug 1814 - Ran on 2 Dec 1814

Cobb, William B. - Landsman - Payroll 1 - Number: 159 - Entry Date: 10 Dec 1813 - Payroll ended on 6 Apr 1814 - BLW 39153-160-55 - Pension: SO-25678, SC-13509 - Payroll 2 - Number: 159 - Entry Date: 10 Dec 1813 - Discharged on 10 Dec 1814

Cobbit, Matthew - Seaman - Payroll 1 - Number: 86 - Entry Date: 29 Oct 1813 - Payroll ended on 6 Apr 1814 - Payroll 2 - Number: 86 - Entry Date: 29 Oct 1813 - Discharged on 29 Oct 1814

Cochran, John T. - Master's Mate - Payroll 1 - Number: 191 - Entry Date: 3 Jan 1814 - Payroll ended on 6 Apr 1814 - Payroll 2 - Number: 191 - Entry Date: 3 Jan 1814 - Discharged on 3 Jan 1815

Cochran, Thomas (1) - Midshipman - Payroll 1 - Number: 214 - Entry Date: 22 Jan 1814 - Payroll ended on 6 Apr 1814 - Payroll 2 - Number: 214 - Entry Date: 22 Jan 1814 - Discharged on 22 Jan 1815

Cochran, Thomas (2) - Master's Mate - Muster - Number: 983 - Entry Date: 23 Jan 1815 - Discharged on 1 Apr 1815 - Payroll 2 - Number: 983 - Entry Date: 23 Jan 1815 - Discharged on 1 Apr 1815

Cockey, Thomas - Seaman - Payroll 2 - Number: 378 - Entry Date: 3 Apr 1814 - Discharged on 1 Apr 1815

Collins, John - Landsman - Payroll 1 - Number: 184 - Entry Date: 20 Dec 1813 - Discharged 10 Dec 1814 - Payroll 2 - Number: 184 - Entry Date: 20 Dec 1813 - Ran on 11 Dec 1813

Collins, Philip - Ordinary Seaman - Payroll 2 - Number: 684 - Entry Date: 31 May 1814 - Ran on 26 Jan 1815

Conner, Timothy - Seaman - Payroll 2 - Number: 740 - Entry Date: 17 May 1814 - Discharged on 28 May 1814

Conner, William - Seaman - Payroll 1 - Number: 236 - Entry Date: 19 Feb 1814 - Payroll ended on 6 Apr 1814 - Payroll 2 - Number: 236 - Entry Date: 19 Feb 1814 - Discharged on 19 Feb 1815

Conway, John - Ordinary Seaman - Payroll 1 - Number: 327 - Entry Date: 24 Mar 1814 - Payroll ended on 6 Apr 1814 - Payroll 2 - Number: 327 - Entry Date: 24 Mar 1814 - Discharged on 2 Mar 1815

Conway, John O. - Seaman - Payroll 1 - Number: 311 - Entry Date: 17 Mar 1814 - Payroll ended on 6 Apr 1814 - Payroll 2 - Number: 311 - Entry Date: 17 Mar 1814 - Ran on 11 Apr 1814

Cook, James - Seaman - U.S. Sloop-of-War Ontario - Number: 103 - Entry Date: 31 Jan 1814 - Discharged on 14 Apr 1814 to the flotilla - Transfers - Number: 27 - Entry Date: 15 Apr 1814 - Discharged on 6 Dec 1814 - U.S. Frigate United States - Number: 888 - Entry Date: 7 Apr 1814 - Discharged on 6 Dec 1814 to U.S. Sloop-of-War Ontario - Transfers - Number: 27 - Entry Date: 15 Apr 1814 - Discharged on 6 Dec 1814 - Payroll 2 - Number: 888 - Entry Date: 15 Apr 1814 - Discharged on 6 Dec 1814 to U.S. Sloop-of-War Ontario

Cook, John - Boy - Payroll 1 - Number: 356 - Entry Date: 6 Apr 1814 - Payroll ended on 6 Apr 1814 - Payroll 2 - Number: 356 - Entry Date: 6 Apr 1814 - Discharged on 31 Mar 1815

Cooper, Benjamin - Seaman - Payroll 2 - Number: 388 - Entry Date: 2 Apr 1814 - Discharged on 1 Apr 1815 - BLW 84492-161-55

Cooper, Edward - Ordinary Seaman - Payroll 2 - Number: 719 - Entry Date: 10 Jun 1814 - Discharged on 1 Apr 1815

Cooper, John - Ordinary Seaman - Payroll 2 - Number: 593 - Entry Date: 14 May 1814 - Discharged on 1 Apr 1815

Cooper, John W. - Seaman - Payroll 2 - Number: 445 - Entry Date: 14 Mar 1814 - Discharged on 14 Mar 1815

Cooper, Thomas - Master's Mate - U.S. Frigate United States - Number: 913 - Discharged on 14 Jan 1815 - Lazaretto (Baltimore) - Payroll 2 - Number: 913 - Entry Date: 12 Jul 1814 - Discharged on 14 Jul 1815

Cope, George - Seaman - Payroll 2 - Number: 558 - Entry Date: 3 Feb 1813 - Discharged on 3 Feb 1815 - Payroll 2 - Number: 624 - U.S. Frigate United States - Number: 558 - Entry Date: 7 Apr 1814 - Discharged on 3 Feb 1815 to Potomac Flotilla

Corrain, James - Seaman - Payroll 2 - Number: 782 - Entry Date: 19 Jul 1814 - Discharged on 1 Apr 1815

Corrie, George - Ordinary Seaman - U.S. Frigate United States - Number: 525 - Entry Date: 7 Apr 1814 - Discharged on 6 Dec 1814 to U.S. Sloop-of-War Ontario - Transfers - Number: 40 - Entry Date: 6 Apr 1814 - Discharged on 6 Dec 1814 - Seaman - Payroll 2 - Number: 525 - Entry Date: 5 Mar 1814 - Discharged on 6 Dec 1814

Coulson, David - Ordinary Seaman - Payroll 2 - Number: 678 - Entry Date: 27 May 1814 - Discharged on 1 Apr 1815

Couran, William - Boy - U.S. Frigate Adams Payroll - Number: 255 - Entry Date: 17 Mar 1813 - Discharged on 10 Nov 1813 to U.S. Schooner Asp - U.S. Frigate United States - Number: 560 - Entry Date: 7 Apr 1814 - Discharged on 19 Feb 1815 to U.S. Galley Shark - U.S. Schooner Shark - Number: 21 - Entry Date: 11 Nov 1813 - Discharged on 29 Mar 1814 - Payroll 2 - Number: 560 - Entry Date: 19 Feb 1813 - Discharged on 19 Feb 1815 - Payroll 2 - Number: 522 - - Entry Date: 19 Feb 1813 - Discharged on 19 Feb 1815

Cox, William - Ordinary Seaman - Payroll 2 - Number: 788 - Entry Date: 8 Jun 1814 - Ran on 16 Nov 1814

Coy, Frederick - Seaman - Payroll 1 - Number: 350 - Entry Date: 2 Apr 1814 - Payroll ended on 6 Apr 1814 - Payroll 2 - Number: 350 - Entry Date: 2 Apr 1814 - Discharged on 1 Apr 1815

Craig, William - Ordinary Seaman - Payroll 2 - Number: 733 - Entry Date: 10 Jun 1814 - Ran on 14 Oct 1814 - U.S. Frigate United States - Number: 733 - Entry Date: 10 Apr 1814 - Ran on 14 Oct 1814 at Lazaretto (Baltimore)

Crawford, John - Landsman - Payroll 1 - Number: 122 - Entry Date: 29 Sep 1813 - Payroll ended on 6 Apr 1814 - Payroll 2 - Number: 122 - Entry Date: 29 Sep 1813 - Discharged on 7 Apr 1814

Croacher, Daniel - Seaman - Payroll 1 - Number: 225 - Entry Date: 5 Feb 1814 - Payroll ended on 6 Apr 1814 - Payroll 2 - Number: 225 - Entry Date: 5 Feb 1814 - Discharged on 1 Feb 1815 - Payroll 2 - Number: 997 - Entry Date: 8 Mar 1814 - Discharged on 1 Apr 1815 - Muster - Number: 997 - Entry Date: 9 Mar 1815 - Discharged on 1 Apr 1815

Croft, Lewis R. (Craft) - Quarter Gunner - U.S. Sloop Scorpion - Number: 17 - Entry Date: 9 Jan 1813 - Payroll ended on 11 Feb 1814 - U.S. Frigate United States - Number: 569 - Entry Date: 12 Feb 1814 - Discharged on 1 Apr 1815 to U.S. Battery Scorpion - Payroll 2 - Number: 569 - Entry Date: 9 Jan 1813 - Discharged on 1 Apr 1815 - Prisoner of War at Halifax, number 7327, captured on 22 Aug 1814 during the Battle of Bladensburg, discharged on 18 Nov 1814 and sent to England on HMS Loire - Prisoner of War at Halifax, prisoner number 7327, captured on 22 Aug 1814 near Washington, D.C. by British forces; received at Halifax on 30 Sep 1814 on HMS Surprize; discharged on 18 Nov 1814 and sent to England on HMS Loire - Prisoner of War at Dartmoor, prisoner number 5503, captured on 22 Aug 1814 from the U.S. Flotilla Service, Gunboat Number 2 on the Chesapeake Bay by British forces; sent to Halifax on H.M. Transport Loire; received at Dartmoor on 17 Dec 1814; released on 29 Jun 1815 - Born: Marblehead - Age: 34

Crooker, Joseph - Boatswain - Muster - Number: 35 - Entry Date: 6 Oct 1813 - Discharged on 13 Oct 1814 - Payroll 1 - Number: 35 - Entry Date: 6 Oct 1813 - Payroll ended on 6 Apr 1814 - Payroll 2 - Number: 35 - Entry Date: 6 Oct 1813 - Discharged on 13 Oct 1814

Crow, John - Ordinary Seaman - Payroll 1 - Number: 117 - Entry Date: 23 Oct 1813 - Payroll ended on 6 Apr 1814 - Payroll 2 - Number: 117 - Entry Date: 23 Oct 1813 - Discharged on 25 Oct 1814

Cuff, Jacob - Ordinary Seaman - Payroll 1 - Number: 263 - Payroll ended on 6 Apr 1814 - Payroll 2 - Number: 263 - Entry Date: 25 Feb 1814 - Discharged on 24 Feb 1815

Cunningham, Thomas - Seaman - Payroll 1 - Number: 154 - Entry Date: 17 Nov 1813 - Discharged on 12 Mar 1814 - Payroll 2 - Number: 154 - Entry Date: 17 Nov 1813 - Ran on 12 Mar 1814

Currie, George W. - Ordinary Seaman - U.S. Sloop-of-War Ontario - Number: 156 - Entry Date: 16 Mar 1814 - Discharged on 5 Apr 1814 to the flotilla - U.S. Sloop-of-War Ontario - Number: 240 - Entry Date: 7 Dec 1814 - Discharged on 5 Mar 1815 from the flotilla

Curry, Benjamin L. - Seaman - Payroll 1 - Number: 323 - Entry Date: 23 Mar 1814 - Payroll ended on 6 Apr 1814 - Payroll 2 - Number: 323 - Entry Date: 23 Mar 1814 - Discharged on 1 Apr 1815

Dailey, James - Landsman - Payroll 2 - Number: 771 - Entry Date: 26 Jun 1814 - Discharged on 1 Apr 1815

Daily, Daniel - Seaman - Payroll 2 - Number: 715 - Entry Date: 6 Jun 1814 - Discharged on 1 Apr 1815

Daniels, Charlie - Seaman - U.S. Sloop-of-War Ontario - Number: 60 - Entry Date: 14 Jan 1814 - Discharged on 14 Apr 1814 to the flotilla

Daniels, James - Boy - Payroll 2 - Number: 504 - Entry Date: 26 Dec 1812 - Discharged on 30 Mar 1814 - U.S. Frigate Adams Muster - Number: 110 - Entry Date: 18 Jan 1813 - Discharged on 10 Nov 1813 to U.S. Schooner Asp - U.S. Schooner Shark - Number: 14 - Entry Date: 11 Nov 1813 - Discharged on 29 Mar 1814 - U.S. Frigate United States - Number: 504 - Entry Date: 7 Apr 1814 - Discharged on 17 Feb 1815 to U.S. Galley Shark

Daniels, Joab - Ordinary Seaman - U.S. Frigate United States - Number: 918 - Entry Date: 7 Apr 1814 - Ran on 2 Dec 1814 from U.S. Sloop-of-War Ontario - U.S. Sloop-of-War Ontario - Number: 121 - Entry Date: 13 Feb 1814 - Discharged on 14 Apr 1814 to the flotilla (ran) - Payroll 2 - Number: 918 - Entry Date: 12 Feb 1814 - Ran on 2 Dec 1814

Danvers, William - Seaman - Payroll 2 - Number: 765 - Entry Date: 15 Mar 1814 - Ran on 18 Jan 1815

Daudney, Hiram - Ordinary Seaman - U.S. Sloop-of-War Ontario - Number: 153 - Entry Date: 16 Mar 1814 - Discharged on 5 Apr 1814 to the flotilla (killed) - U.S. Frigate United States - Number: 489 - Entry Date: 7 Apr 1814 - Killed on 24 Aug 1814 at Bladensburg - Payroll 2 - Number: 489 - Entry Date: 15 Mar 1814 - Killed on 24 Aug 1814 at Bladensburg

David, Charles - Seaman - Payroll 1 - Number: 88 - Entry Date: 1 Dec 1813 - Payroll ended on 6 Apr 1814 - Wounded at Bladensburg - Payroll 2 - Number: 88 - Entry Date: 1 Dec 1813 - Discharged on 1 Nov 1814 - Washington Naval Hospital - Number: 6 - Fever, admitted on 24 Aug 1814 and discharged on 4 Sep 1814

Davidson, William - Landsman - Payroll 1 - Number: 312 - Entry Date: 19 Mar 1814 - Payroll ended on 6 Apr 1814 - Payroll 2 - Number: 312 - Entry Date: 19 Mar 1814 - Discharged on 19 Mar 1815

Davis, C. - Master's Mate - Payroll 1 - Number: 345 - Entry Date: 6 Apr 1814 - Payroll ended on 6 Apr 1814 - Payroll 2 - Number: 345 - Entry Date: 6 Apr 1814 - Ran on 3 May 1814

Davis, John - Sailing Master - Payroll 1 - Number: 290 - Entry Date: 1 Mar 1814 Payroll ended on 6 Apr 1814 - Payroll 2 - Number: 290 - Entry Date: 1 Mar 1814 - Discharged on 1 Feb 1815

Davis, Samuel - Ordinary Seaman - Payroll 2 - Number: 467 - Entry Date: 8 Mar 1813 - Ran on 28 Nov 1814

Davis, Samuel - Ordinary Seaman - U.S. Gunboat 137 - Number: 12 - Entry Date: 8 Mar 1813 - Payroll ended on 4 Mar 1814 - U.S. Frigate Adams Payroll - Number: 383 - Entry Date: 6 Apr 1813 - Discharged on 10 Nov 1813 to U.S. Galley Shark - U.S. Frigate Adams Muster - Number: 383 - Entry Date: 6 Apr 1813 - Discharged on 10 Nov 1813 to U.S. Galley Shark

Davis, Thomas - Seaman - Muster - Number: 942 - Entry Date: 1 Jan 1814 - Discharged on 18 Aug 1814 to U.S. Sloop-of-War Ontario - Transfers - Number: 55 - Entry Date: 15 Apr 1814 - Discharged on 6 Dec 1814 - U.S. Sloop-of-War Ontario - Number: 75 - Entry Date: 14 Jan 1814 - Discharged on 13 Apr 1814 to the flotilla - Payroll 2 - Number: 942 - Entry Date: 1 Jan 1814 - Discharged on 6 Dec 1814 to U.S. Sloop-of-War Ontario

Davison, Henry - Seaman - Payroll 2 - Number: 801 - Entry Date: 25 Jul 1814 - Ran on 19 Jan 1815

Davison, John - Seaman - Muster - Number: 953 - Entry Date: 22 Jan 1814 - Ran on 24 Aug 1814 - U.S. Sloop-of-War Ontario - Number: 92 - Entry Date: 26 Jan 1814 - Discharged on 14 Apr 1814 to the flotilla (ran) - Payroll 2 - Number: 953 - Entry Date: 22 Jan 1814 - Ran on 24 Aug 1814

Davison, Lancelot - Seaman - Payroll 1 - Number: 201 - Entry Date: 8 Jan 1814 - Payroll ended on 6 Apr 1814 - Payroll 2 - Number: 201 - Entry Date: 8 Jan 1814 - Discharged on 5 Feb 1815

Dawson, Edward - Seaman - Payroll 2 - Number: 542 - Entry Date: 26 Mar 1814 - Discharged on 2 Dec 1814

Dawson, Nicholas - Seaman - Payroll 1 - Number: 258 - Payroll ended on 6 Apr 1814 - Payroll 2 - Number: 258 - Entry Date: 19 Feb 1814 - Discharged on 19 Feb 1815

Dawson, Woolman - Seaman - Payroll 2 - Number: 365 - Entry Date: 30 Mar 1814 - Discharged on 1 Apr 1815

Dean, Melville - Steward - Payroll 2 - Number: 424 - - Entry Date: Mar 1814 - Discharged on 1 Apr 1815

Dean, William - Steward - Payroll 2 - Number: 423 - Entry Date: 30 Mar 1814 - Discharged on 31 Dec 1814

Dearing, Noah - Ordinary Seaman - U.S. Sloop Scorpion - Number: 8 - Entry Date: 1 Feb 1813 - Payroll ended on 11 Feb 1814 - U.S. Frigate Adams Payroll - Number: 290 - Entry Date: 23 Mar 1813 - Discharged on 10 Nov 1813 to U.S. Galley Shark - U.S. Frigate Adams Muster - Number: 290 - Entry Date: 23 Mar 1813 - Discharged on 10 Nov 1813 to U.S. Galley Shark - Payroll 2 - Number: 429 - Entry Date: 1 Feb 1813 - Discharged on 1 Feb 1815

Dennett, George (or Dennitt) - Ordinary Seaman - U.S. Frigate Adams Muster - Number: 275 - Entry Date: 22 Mar 1813 - Discharged on 10 Nov 1813 to U.S. Schooner Scorpion- Ordinary Seaman - U.S. Schooner Shark - Number: 16 - Entry Date: 11 Nov 1813 - Discharged on 29 Mar 1814 - U.S. Frigate United States - Number: 508 - Entry Date: 7 Apr 1814 - Discharged on 26 Jan 1815 to U.S. Galley Shark - Payroll 2 - Number: 508 - Entry Date: 26 Jan 1813 - Discharged on 2 Jan 1815

Dennight, Willson - Boy - U.S. Sloop-of-War Ontario - Number: 81 - Entry Date: 14 Jan 1814 - Discharged on 14 Apr 1814 to the flotilla - Transfers - Number: 26 - Entry Date: 15 Apr 1814 - Discharged on 6 Dec 1814 - Muster - Number: 928 - Entry Date: 6 Jun 1814 - Discharged on 6 Dec 1814 - Wounded at Bladensburg - U.S. Sloop-of-War Ontario - Number: 212 - Entry Date: 7 Dec 1814 - Discharged on 5 Mar 1815 from the flotilla - Payroll 2 - Number: 928 - Entry Date: 6 Jan 1814 - Discharged on 6 Dec 1814 to U.S. Sloop-of-War Ontario - Seaman - Washington Naval Hospital - Number: 34 - Wounded at Bladensburg, admitted on 3 Sep 1814, discharged on 10 Oct 1814

Denny, John - Seaman - U.S. Frigate United States - Number: 923 - Entry Date: 7 Apr 1814 - Discharged on 6 Dec 1814 to U.S. Sloop-of-War Ontario - U.S. Sloop-of-War Ontario - Number: 59 - Entry Date: 14 Jan 1814 - Discharged on 14 Apr 1814 to the flotilla - Transfers - Number: 45 - Entry Date: 15 Apr 1814 - Discharged on 6 Dec 1814 - Wounded at Bladensburg - U.S. Sloop-of-War Ontario - Number: 204 - Entry Date: 7 Dec 1814 - Discharged on 3 Mar 1815 from the flotilla (crippled) - Payroll 2 - Number: 923 - Entry Date: 15 Apr 1814 - Discharged on 6 Dec 1814 to U.S. Sloop-of-War Ontario - Washington Naval Hospital - Number: 37 - Wounded at Bladensburg, admitted on 3 Sep 1814, discharged on 4 Jan 1815 - Pension: Naval IF-325 (USS Ontario)

Dentworth, Ceasar - Ordinary Seaman - U.S. Gunboat 138 – Number 36 - Paid on 6 Apr 1814

Deshield, Adam - Gunner - Payroll 2 - Number: 846 - Entry Date: 6 Aug 1814 - Discharged on 1 Apr 1815

Deteer, Abraham - Landsman - Payroll 2 - Number: 858 - Entry Date: 15 Aug 1814 - Ran on 13 Feb 1815

Devetre, Joseph - Seaman - Payroll 2 - Number: 625 - Entry Date: 16 Apr 1814 - Discharged on 1 Apr 1815

Dick, David - Seaman - Payroll 1 - Number: 54 - Entry Date: 27 Sep 1813 - Payroll ended on 6 Apr 1814 - Payroll 1a - Number: 54 - Entry Date: 27 Sep 1813 - Payroll 2 - Number: 54 - Entry Date: 27 Sep 1813 - Discharged on 27 Sep 1814

Dickerson, James - Seaman - Payroll 1 - Number: 58 - Entry Date: 30 Sep 1813 - Discharged on 20 Feb 1814 - Payroll 1a - Number: 58 - Entry Date: 30 Sep 1813 - Discharged on 20 Feb 1814 - Payroll 2 - Number: 58 - Entry Date: 30 Sep 1813

Dicks, Isaac - Seaman - Payroll 1 - Number: 65 - Entry Date: 18 Oct 1813 - Payroll ended on 6 Apr 1814 - Payroll 1a - Number: 65 - Entry Date: 18 Oct 1813 - Payroll 2 - Number: 65 - Entry Date: 18 Oct 1813 - Discharged on 18 Oct 1814

Didolph, Owen - Gunner - U.S. Frigate United States - Number: 866 - Entry Date: 7 Apr 1814 - Discharged on 1 Apr 1815 to US Gunboat 138 - Payroll 2 - Number: 866 - Entry Date: 18 Mar 1814 - Discharged on 1 Apr 1815

Dill, Eli - Boatswain - Payroll 1 - Number: 34 - Entry Date: 3 Oct 1813 - Payroll ended on 6 Apr 1814 - Payroll 2 - Number: 34 - Entry Date: 3 Oct 1813 - Discharged on 5 Jan 1815 - Muster - Number: 34 - Entry Date: 20 Sep 1813 - Muster ended on 6 Apr 1814

Dixon, James - Steward - Muster - Number: 989 - Entry Date: 16 Apr 1814 - Discharged on 1 Apr 1815 - Payroll 2 - Number: 989 - Entry Date: 16 Apr 1814 - Discharged on 1 Apr 1815

Dixon, Richard (also Dickson) - Seaman - U.S. Sloop-of-War Ontario - Number: 100 - Entry Date: 30 Jan 1814 - Discharged on 14 Apr 1814 to the flotilla (ran) - Seaman - Payroll 2 - Number: 681 - Entry Date: 24 Jan 1814 - Ran on 4 Jul 1814

Dixon, Thomas - Ordinary Seaman - U.S. Schooner Shark - Number: 8 - Entry Date: 21 May 1813 - Discharged on 29 Mar 1814 - Payroll 2 - Number: 483 - Entry Date: 21 May 1812 - Discharged on 23 May 1814

Dodson, William - Sailing Master - Payroll 2 - Number: 603 - Entry Date: 1 Mar 1814 -: Discharged on 15 Apr 1815

Dolliver, Benjamin - Ordinary Seaman - U.S. Frigate Adams Payroll - Number: 244 - Entry Date: 17 Mar 1813 - Discharged on 10 Nov 1813 to U.S. Schooner Scorpion - U.S. Frigate United States - Number: 520 - Entry Date: 7 Apr 1814 - Discharged on 24 Jan 1815 to U.S. Galley Shark - U.S. Schooner Shark - Number: 20 - Entry Date: 11 Nov 1813 - Discharged on 29 Mar 1814 - Payroll 2 - Number: 520 - Entry Date: 25 Jan 1813 - Discharged on 24 Jan 1815

Donaldson, John - Boy - Payroll 2 - Number: 530 - Entry Date: 10 May 1814 - Discharged on 1 Apr 1815 - BLW 8039-160-55

Doniven, James - Ordinary Seaman - Payroll 2 - Number: 731 - Entry Date: 8 Jun 1814 - Ran on 10 Jul 1814

Donohue, Timothy - Seaman - U.S. Sloop-of-War Ontario - Number: 114 - Entry Date: 8 Feb 1814 - Discharged on 14 Apr 1814 to the flotilla (ran) - Muster - Number: 932 - Entry Date: 4 Feb 1814 - Ran on 17 Apr 1814 - Payroll 2 - Number: 932 - Entry Date: 4 Feb 1814 - Ran on 17 Apr 1814

Doogood, Abraham - Volunteer Seaman - Prisoner of War at Halifax, prisoner number 7329, captured on 22 Aug 1814 near Washington, D.C. by British forces; received at Halifax on 30 Sep 1814 on HMS Surprize; discharged on 18 Nov 1814 and sent to England on HMS Loire - Prisoner of War at Dartmoor, prisoner number 5505, captured on 22 Aug 1814 from the U.S. Flotilla Service, Gunboat Number 2 on the Chesapeake Bay by British forces; sent to Halifax on H.M. Transport Loire; received at Dartmoor on 17 Dec 1814; released on 29 Jun 1815 - Born: Waterford - Age: 60

Dorgan, Andrew - Sailing Master - Muster - Number: 10 - Entry Date: 11 Sep 1813 - Discharged on 4 Oct 1813 - Warranted as a sailing master on 8 Jul 1812; resigned on 15 Apr 1813 - Payroll 1 - Number: 10 - Entry Date: 22 Sep 1813 - Discharged on 11 Oct 1813 - Reinstated as a sailing master on 11 Sep 1813; discharged on 5 Oct 1813 - Payroll 2 - Number: 10 - Entry Date: 22 Sep 1813

Dorman, Thomas - Ordinary Seaman - Payroll 2 - Number: 586 - Entry Date: 7 May 1814 - Discharged on 1 Apr 1815

Dormett, Joseph N. - Seaman - U.S. Frigate United States - Number: 708 - Entry Date: 21 Apr 1814 - Discharged on 12 Feb 1815 to U.S. Schooner Asp - U.S. Sloop Asp - Number: 3 - Entry Date: 11 Nov 1813 - Discharged on 20 Apr 1814 - Payroll 2 - Number: 708 - Entry Date: 12 Feb 1813 - Discharged on 12 Feb 1815

Dougherty, Hugh - Seaman - U.S. Frigate United States - Number: 879 - Entry Date: 14 Apr 1814 - Discharged on 6 Dec 1814 to U.S. Sloop-of-War Ontario - U.S. Sloop-of-War Ontario - Number: 38 - Entry Date: 14 Jan 1814 - Discharged on 13 Apr 1814 to the flotilla - Transfers - Number: 2 - Entry Date: 14 Apr 1814 - Discharged on 6 Dec 1814 - Payroll 2 - Number: 879 - Entry Date: 23 Nov 1813 - Discharged on 6 Dec 1814 to U.S. Sloop-of-War Ontario - U.S. Sloop-of-War Ontario - Number: 196 - Entry Date: 7 Dec 1814 - Discharged on 5 Mar 1815 from the flotilla

Doyle, Patrick - Ordinary Seaman - Payroll 2 - Number: 756 - Entry Date: 14 Jun 1814 - Died on 28 Oct 1814

Drew, Enoch - Ordinary Seaman - U.S. Frigate Adams Payroll - Number: 325 - Entry Date: 3 Apr 1813 - Discharged on 10 Nov 1813 to U.S. Galley Shark - U.S. Frigate Adams Muster - Number: 325 - Entry Date: 3 Apr 1813 - Discharged on 10 Nov 1813 to U.S. Galley Shark - U.S. Frigate United States - Number: 713 - Entry Date: 21 Apr 1814 - Discharged on 3 Feb 1815 to U.S. Schooner Asp - U.S. Sloop Asp - Number: 8 - Entry

Date: 3 Feb 1814 - Discharged on 20 Apr 1814 - Payroll 2 - Number: 713 - Entry Date: 3 Feb 1813 - Ran on 3 Feb 1815

Duck, Thomas - Ordinary Seaman - Payroll 1 - Number: 275 - Entry Date: 8 Mar 1814 - Payroll ended on 6 Apr 1814 - Payroll 2 - Number: 275 - Entry Date: 8 Mar 1814 - Discharged on 8 Mar 1815

Dugan, James - Master's Mate - Payroll 2 - Number: 670 - Entry Date: 27 May 1814 - Discharged on 3 Nov 1814

Dukehart, Thomas F. - Master's Mate - Muster - Number: 30 - Entry Date: 1 Nov 1813 - Discharged on 11 Dec 1814 - Payroll 1 - Number: 30 - Entry Date: 1 Nov 1813 - Payroll ended on 6 Apr 1814 - Payroll 2 - Number: 30 - Entry Date: 1 Nov 1813 - Discharged on 11 Dec 1814 - BLW 14298-160-55

Dunan, Aymond - Midshipman - Payroll 1 - Number: 305 - Entry Date: 23 Mar 1814 - Payroll ended on 6 Apr 1814 - Payroll 2 - Number: 305 - Entry Date: 23 Mar 1814 - Discharged on 24 Aug 1814

Dunegan, Benjamin - Ordinary Seaman - Payroll 2 - Number: 806 - Entry Date: 14 Jun 1814 - Discharged on 1 Apr 1815

Dunlap, Samuel - Steward - Payroll 1 - Number: 198 - Entry Date: 5 Jan 1814 - Payroll ended on 6 Apr 1814 - Payroll 2 - Number: 198 - Entry Date: 5 Jan 1814 - Discharged on 1 Dec 1814

Dunn, Richard - Ordinary Seaman - U.S. Frigate Adams Payroll - Number: 130 - Entry Date: 6 Feb 1813 - Ran on 24 May 1814 from U.S. Gunboat 71 - U.S. Frigate United States - Number: 492 - Entry Date: 12 Feb 1814 - Ran on 19 Jan 1815 to U.S. Battery Scorpion - U.S. Frigate Adams Muster - Number: 482 - Entry Date: 20 Aug 1813 - Discharged on 10 Nov 1813 to U.S. Schooner Scorpion - U.S. Sloop Scorpion - Number: 14 - Entry Date: 20 Aug 1812 - Payroll ended on 11 Feb 1814 - Payroll 2 - Number: 492 - Entry Date: 20 Aug 1812 - Ran on 2 Jan 1815

Dunn, Walter - Ordinary Seaman - Payroll 2 - Number: 839 - Entry Date: 8 Aug 1814 - Discharged on 1 Apr 1815

Dunwoody, John - Seaman - U.S. Sloop-of-War Ontario - Number: 96 - Entry Date: 29 Jan 1814 - Discharged on 14 Apr 1814 to the flotilla (killed) - Muster - Number: 927 - Entry Date: 24 Jan 1814 - Killed on 24 Aug 1814 at Bladensburg - Payroll 2 - Number: 927 - Entry Date: 15 Apr 1814 - Killed on 24 Aug 1814 at Bladensburg

Dutill, Peter - Ordinary Seaman - U.S. Sloop-of-War Ontario - Number: 84 - Entry Date: 18 Jan 1814 - Discharged on 14 Apr 1814 to the flotilla - Transfers - Number: 537 - 36 - Entry Date: 15 Apr 1814 - Discharged on 6 Dec 1814 - U.S. Sloop-of-War Ontario - Number: 214 - Entry Date: 7 Dec 1814 - Discharged on 5 Mar 1815 from the flotilla - U.S. Frigate United States - Number: 537 - Entry Date: 7 Apr 1814 - Discharged on 6 Dec 1814 to U.S. Sloop-of-War Ontario - Payroll 2 - Number: 537 - Entry Date: 7 Jan 1814 - Discharged on 6 Dec 1814 to U.S. Sloop-of-War Ontario

Duvall, Edmund T. - Midshipman - Payroll 1 - Number: 286 - Entry Date: 5 Mar 1814 - Payroll ended on 6 Apr 1814 - Payroll 2 - Number: 286 - Entry Date: 5 Mar 1814 - Discharged on 1 Apr 1815 - BLW 58138-160-55 - Pension: SO-2629, SC-5769 - Also served in Captain James Wimp's Company, Ohio Militia, between Jun 1812 and 20 Dec 1812; sailor was in the Battle of Bladensburg

Duvall, George W. - Master's Mate - Payroll 1 - Number: 247 - Entry Date: 25 Feb 1814 - Payroll ended on 6 Apr 1814 - BLW 7122-160-55 - Payroll 2 - Number: 247 - Entry Date: 25 Feb 1814 - Discharged on 5 Jan 1815

Earnest, Frederick Airns - Seaman - U.S. Frigate United States - Number: 814 - Entry Date: 12 Feb 1814 - Discharged on 1 Mar 1815 to U.S. Battery Scorpion - U.S. Frigate United States - Number: 814 - Battery Scorpion - Pension: Navy IF-494 - U.S. Sloop Scorpion - Number: 5 - Entry Date: 18 Sep 1812 - Payroll ended on 11 Feb 1814 - Payroll 2 - Number: 517 - Entry Date: 18 Sep 1812 - Payroll 2 - Number: 814 - Entry Date: 18 Sep 1813 - Discharged on 1 Mar 1815 - Washington Naval Hospital - Number: 41 - Wounded at Bladensburg, admitted on 9 Sep 1814, discharged on 10 Oct 1814 - Pension: Navy IF-494

Eaton, John - Ordinary Seaman - Payroll 1 - Number: 171 - Entry Date: 7 Dec 1813 - Payroll ended on 6 Apr 1814 - Payroll 2 - Number: 171 - Entry Date: 7 Dec 1813 - Discharged on 7 Dec 1814

Eccleston, Archibald - Landsman - Payroll 2 - Number: 391 - Entry Date: 1 Jan 1814 - Discharged on 1 Jan 1815 - BLW 49102-160-55

Edwards, Joseph - Landsman - Payroll 2 - Number: 579 - Entry Date: 4 May 1814 - Ran on 4 Nov 1814 - Discharged on 4 Nov 1814 - BLW 5177-160-55 - Pension: WO-13311- WC-14589

Edwards, Paul - Gunner - Payroll 2 - Number: 724 - Entry Date: 8 Apr 1814 - Discharged on 1 Apr 1815 - Prisoner of War at Halifax, prisoner number 7328, captured on 22 Aug 1814 near Washington, D.C. by British forces; received at Halifax on 30 Sep 1814 on HMS Surprize; discharged on 18 Nov 1814 and sent to England on HMS Loire - Prisoner of War at Dartmoor, prisoner number 5504, captured on 22 Aug 1814 from the U.S. Flotilla Service, Gunboat Number 2 on the Chesapeake Bay by British forces; sent to Halifax on H.M. Transport Loire; received at Dartmoor on 17 Dec 1814; released on 29 Jun 1815 - Born: Harlem - Age: 63

Elderkin, Stephen - Ordinary Seaman - U.S. Frigate Adams Payroll - Number: 31 - Entry Date: 29 Dec 1812 - Discharged on 10 Nov 1813 to U.S. Galley Shark - U.S. Sloop-of-War Ontario - Number: 127 - Entry Date: 23 Feb 1814 - Discharged on 13 Apr 1814 to the flotilla - U.S. Frigate United States - Number: 635 - Entry Date: 7 Apr 1814 - Discharged on 3 Jan 1815 to U.S. Sloop-of-War Ontario

Elliott, James - Master's Mate - Muster - Number: 19 - Entry Date: 28 Sep 1813 Muster ended on 6 Apr 1814 - Payroll 1 - Number: 19 - Entry Date: 28 Sep 1813 - Payroll ended on 6 Apr 1814 - Payroll 2 - Number: 19 - Entry Date: 28 Sep 1813 - Discharged on 26 Apr 1814

Elliott, Robert - Seaman - Payroll 1 - Number: 257 - Payroll ended on 6 Apr 1814 - Payroll 2 - Number: 257 - Entry Date: 12 Feb 1814 - Discharged on 1 Apr 1815 - Prisoner of War at Halifax, prisoner number 7324, captured on 22 Aug 1814 near Washington, D.C. by British forces; received at Halifax on 30 Sep 1814 on HMS Surprize; discharged on 5 Mar 1815 and sent to Salem, Massachusetts on Cartel Lingan

Ellis, Elihu - Ordinary Seaman - Payroll 2 - Number: 494 - Entry Date: 3 Apr 1814 - Discharged on 1 Apr 1815

Ellis, James - Ordinary Seaman - U.S. Frigate United States - Number: 726 - Entry Date: 17 Apr 1814 - Ran on 24 Aug 1814 - Muster - Number: 925 - Entry Date: 14 Apr 1814 - Discharged on 1 Apr 1815 - Payroll 2 - Number: 726 - Entry Date: 14 Apr 1814 - Ran on 24 Aug 1814 - Payroll 2 - Number: 925 - Entry Date: 14 Apr 1814 - Discharged on 1 Apr 1815

Ellison, David - Seaman - Payroll 1 - Number: 153 - Entry Date: 27 Nov 1813 - Discharged on 12 Mar 1814 - Payroll 2 - Number: 153 - Entry Date: 27 Nov 1813 - Ran on 12 Mar 1814

Elliston, James - Ordinary Seaman - Payroll 1 - Number: 240 - Entry Date: 26 Feb 1814 - Payroll ended on 6 Apr 1814 - Payroll 2 - Number: 240 - Entry Date: 26 Feb 1814 - Discharged on 26 Feb 1815

Elliston, Thomas S. - Seaman - Payroll 2 - Number: 691 - Entry Date: 7 May 1814 - Ran on 31 Aug 1814

Elwell, Asa - Ordinary Seaman - U.S. Sloop-of-War Ontario - Number: 149 - Entry Date: 16 Mar 1814 - Discharged on 5 Apr 1814 to the flotilla - Transfers - Number: 43 - Entry Date: 6 Apr 1814 - Discharged on 6 Dec 1814 - U.S. Frigate United States - Number: 654 - Entry Date: 7 Apr 1814 - Discharged on 6 Dec 1814 to U.S. Sloop-of-War Ontario - U.S. Sloop-of-War Ontario - Number: 237 - Entry Date: 7 Dec 1814 - Discharged on 5 Mar 1815 from the flotilla - Payroll 2 - Number: 654 - Entry Date: 6 Apr 1814 - Discharged on 6 Dec 1814

Emory, Daniel (Emery) - Seaman - U.S. Frigate Adams Muster - Number: 375 - Entry Date: 6 Apr 1813 - Discharged on 10 Nov 1813 to U.S. Galley Shark - U.S. Schooner Shark - Number: 25 - Entry Date: 11 Nov 1813 - Discharged on 29 Mar 1814 - U.S. Frigate United States - Number: 557 - Entry Date: 7 Apr 1814 - Discharged on 3 Mar 1815 to U.S. Galley Shark - Payroll 2 - Number: 557 - Entry Date: 3 Mar 1813 - Discharged on 3 Mar 1815

English, David - Seaman - Payroll 2 - Number: 821 - Entry Date: 5 Jul 1814 - Discharged on 1 Apr 1815

Ennis, Henry - Boy - U.S. Frigate United States - Number: 501 - Entry Date: 7 Apr 1814 - Ran on 26 Feb 1815 from U.S. Gunboat 138 - U.S. Gunboat 138 - Number: 57 - Paid on 6 Apr 1814 - Payroll 2 - Number: 501 - Entry Date: 10 Sep 1813 - Ran on 26 Feb 1815

Ennolds, John - Landsman - Payroll 1 - Number: 124 - Entry Date: 30 Sep 1813 - Payroll ended on 6 Apr 1814 - Payroll 2 - Number: 124 - Entry Date: 30 Sep 1813 - Discharged on 18 Oct 1814

Ervin, George - Seaman - Payroll 2 - Number: 696 - Entry Date: 26 May 1814 - Ran on 9 Jul 1814

Evans, Ebenezer - Boy - U.S. Frigate Adams Muster - Number: 58 - Entry Date: 1 Jan 1813 - Discharged on 10 Nov 1813 to U.S. Gunboat 137 - U.S. Frigate United States - Number: 528 - Entry Date: 7 Apr 1814 - Discharged on 1 Apr 1815 - Lost his right arm on 26 June at St. Leonard's Creek - U.S. Sloop-of-War Ontario - Number: 128 - Entry Date: 23 Feb 1814 - Discharged on 13 Apr 1814 to the flotilla - Payroll 2 - Number: 528 - Entry Date: 19

Feb 1814 - Discharged on 1 Apr 1815

Evans, John P. - Seaman - Payroll 1 - Number: 197 - Entry Date: 5 Jan 1814 - Payroll ended on 6 Apr 1814 - Payroll 2 - Number: 197 - Entry Date: 5 Jan 1814 - Discharged on 5 Jan 1815

Everett, John - Seaman - Payroll 1 - Number: 56 - Entry Date: 30 Sep 1813 - Payroll ended on 6 Apr 1814 - Payroll 1a - Number: 56 - Entry Date: 30 Sep 1813 - Discharged on 30 Sep 1814 - Payroll 2 - Number: 56 - Entry Date: 30 Sep 1813 -: Discharged on 30 Sep 1814

Farmer, Ceasar - Seaman - U.S. Sloop-of-War Ontario - Number: 32 - Entry Date: 14 Jan 1814 - Discharged on 14 Apr 1814 to the flotilla - U.S. Frigate United States - Number: 878 - Entry Date: 14 Apr 1814 - Discharged on 6 Dec 1814 to U.S. Sloop-of-War Ontario - Transfers - Number: 23 - Entry Date: 15 Apr 1814 - Discharged on 6 Dec 1814 - U.S. Sloop-of-War Ontario - Number: 194 - Entry Date: 7 Dec 1814 - Discharged on 5 Mar 1815 from the flotilla - Payroll 2 - Number: 878 - Entry Date: 16 Nov 1813 - Discharged on 6 Dec 1814 to U.S. Sloop-of-War Ontario

Farr, William - Ordinary Seaman - Payroll 2 - Number: 720 - Entry Date: 8 Jun 1814 - Ran on 14 Jan 1814

Fearson, Benjamin F. - Midshipman - Muster - Number: 27 - Entry Date: 28 Sep 1813 - Muster ended on 6 Apr 1814 - Payroll 1 - Number: 27 - Entry Date: 27 Oct 1813 - Payroll ended on 6 Apr 1814 - Payroll 2 - Number: 27 - Entry Date: 27 Oct 1813 - Discharged on 5 Nov 1814

Fearson, John - Midshipman - Payroll 2 - Number: 773 - Entry Date: 22 Jul 1814 - Discharged on 2 Jan 1815

Fedrolph, Frederick B. - Seaman - Muster - Number: 963 - Entry Date: 29 Apr 1814 - Discharged on 1 Apr 1815 - Payroll 2 - Number: 963 - Entry Date: 29 Apr 1814 - Discharged on 1 Apr 1815

Fee, John - Boy - Payroll 1 - Number: 131 - Entry Date: 20 Sep 1813 - Discharged on 25 Feb 1814 - Payroll 2 - Number: 131 - Entry Date: 20 Sep 1813 - Ran on 25 Feb 1814

Fields, George - Ordinary Seaman - Payroll 2 - Number: 718 - Entry Date: 6 Jun 1814 - Discharged on 9 Mar 1815

Fisher, Henry - Seaman - Payroll 2 - Number: 822 - Entry Date: 27 Jul 1814 - Discharged on 1 Apr 1815

Flannel, William - Ordinary Seaman - Payroll 2 - Number: 818 - Entry Date: 17 Jul 1814 - Ran on 24 Aug 1814

Fleming William - Boy - Payroll 1 - Number: 265 - Payroll ended on 6 Apr 1814 - Payroll 2 - Number: 265 - Entry Date: 14 Feb 1814 - Discharged on 1 Apr 1815

Fleming, Charles - Carpenter - U.S. Frigate United States - Number: 598 - Entry Date: 7 Apr 1814 - Discharged on 9 Sep 1814 to U.S. Battery Scorpion - U.S. Sloop Scorpion - Number: 7 - Entry Date: 5 Sep 1812 - Payroll ended on 11 Feb 1814 - Payroll 2 - Number: 598 - Entry Date: 5 Sep 1812 - Discharged on 9 Sep 1814

Fleming, Michael - Seaman - Payroll 1 - Number: 69 - Entry Date: 9 Nov 1813 - Payroll ended on 6 Apr 1814 - Payroll 1a - Number: 69 - Entry Date: 4 Nov 1813 - Payroll 2 - Number: 69 - Entry Date: 9 Nov 1813 - Discharged on 9 Nov 1814 - Washington Naval Hospital - Number: 16 - Wounded at Bladensburg, admitted on 24 Aug 1814, deserted on 28 Sep 1814

Fleming, William - Ordinary Seaman - Payroll 2 - Number: 780 - Entry Date: 15 Jul 1814 - Discharged on 1 Apr 1815 - Wounded at Bladensburg

Fletcher, Henry - Seaman - Payroll 2 - Number: 836 - Entry Date: 12 Aug 1814 - Ran on 22 Feb 1815

Foble, John - Landsman - Payroll 2 - Number: 829 - Entry Date: 30 Jul 1814 - Ran on 24 Aug 1814

Foman, Thomas - Ordinary Seaman - U.S. Schooner Shark - Number: 10 - Entry Date: 22 Sep 1813 - Discharged on 29 Mar 1814 - U.S. Frigate United States - Number: 459 - Entry Date: 7 Apr 1814 - Discharged on 26 Sep 1814 to U.S. Galley Shark - Payroll 2 - Number: 459 - Entry Date: 7 Apr 1814 - Discharged on 26 Sep 1814

Foster, Greenbury - Ordinary Seaman - Payroll 2 - Number: 407 - Entry Date: 2 Apr 1814 - Discharged on 1 Apr 1815

Foster, James - Quarter Gunner - U.S. Sloop-of-War Ontario - Number: 148 - Entry Date: 16 Mar 1814 - Discharged on 5 Apr 1814 to the flotilla (ran) - U.S. Frigate United States - Number: 555 - Entry Date: 7 Apr 1814 - Ran on 24 Aug 1814 from U.S. Sloop-of-War Ontario - Payroll 2 - Number: 555 - Entry Date: 15 Mar 1814

Foster, Nathan - Boatswain - Payroll 1 - Number: 32 - Entry Date: 27 Sep 1813 - Payroll ended on 6 Apr 1814 - Payroll 2 - Number: 32 - Entry Date: 27 Sep 1813 - Discharged on 28 Oct 1814 - Muster - Number: 32 - Entry Date: 27 Sep 1813 - Discharged on 24 Oct 1814

Foster, Thomas - Master's Mate - Payroll 1 - Number: 295 - Entry Date: 10 Mar 1814 - Payroll ended on 6 Apr 1814 - Payroll 2 - Number: 295 - Entry Date: 10 Mar 1814 - Discharged on 2 Dec 1814

Foster, William - Ordinary Seaman - Payroll 1 - Number: 173 - Entry Date: 8 Dec 1813 - Payroll ended on 6 Apr 1814 - BLW 3909-160-55 or BLW 65138-160-55 - Payroll 2 - Number: 173 - Entry Date: 8 Dec 1813 - Discharged on 7 Dec 1814

Founder, Joseph - Ordinary Seaman - Payroll 1 - Number: 342 - Entry Date: 4 Apr 1814 - Payroll ended on 6 Apr 1814 - Payroll 2 - Number: 342 - Entry Date: 4 Apr 1814 - Ran on 24 Aug 1814

Fowler, John - Seaman - Payroll 1 - Number: 333 - Entry Date: 8 Mar 1814 - Payroll ended on 6 Apr 1814 - Payroll 2 - Number: 333 - Entry Date: 8 Mar 1814 - Ran on 8 Dec 1814

Fox, Henry - Ordinary Seaman - Payroll 1 - Number: 161 - Entry Date: 19 Nov 1813 - Payroll ended on 6 Apr 1814 - Payroll 2 - Number: 161 - Entry Date: 19 Nov 1813 - Discharged on 1 Nov 1814

Frame, Edward - Marine Private - U.S. Marine Corps - Enlisted 13 Jun 1809 at Baltimore Navy Yard Sep 1813 - Pension: Navy IF-583

Francis, John (1) - Boy - U.S. Frigate Adams Muster - Number: 120 - Entry Date: 5 Feb 1813 - Discharged on 10 Nov 1813 to U.S. Schooner Asp - U.S. Frigate United States - Number: 458 - Entry Date: 7 Apr 1814 - Discharged on 1 Feb 1815 to Potomac Flotilla - Payroll 2 - Number: 458 - Entry Date: 11 Jun 1813 - Discharged on 1 Feb 1815

Francis, John (2) - Seaman - Payroll 2 - Number: 693 - Entry Date: 19 May 1814 - Discharged on 1 Apr 1815

Francisco, Joseph - Ordinary Seaman - U.S. Frigate United States - Number: 639 - Entry Date: 13 Apr 1814 - Discharged on 6 Dec 1814 to U.S. Sloop-of-War Ontario - Transfers - Number: 48 - Entry Date: 14 Apr 1814 - Discharged on 6 Dec 1814 - Seaman - U.S. Sloop-of-War Ontario - Number: 217 - Entry Date: 7 Dec 1814 - Discharged on 5 Mar 1815 from the flotilla - Payroll 2 - Number: 639 - Entry Date: 27 Jan 1814 - Discharged on 9 Feb 1816

Frazier, James - Midshipman - Payroll 2 - Number: 393 - Entry Date: 1 Mar 1814 - Discharged on 16 Dec 1814 - BLW 10040-160-55 - Pension: Navy WF-394, WO-40717, WC-31406 - Also served in Captain Thomas Woodford's Company, Maryland Militia between 1 Mar and 16 Dec 1814

Frazier, John (1) - Seaman - Payroll 2 - Number: 649 - Entry Date: 11 Apr 1813 - Discharged on 11 Apr 1814 - BLW 3027-160-55

Frazier, John (2) - Boatswain - Payroll 2 - Number: 518 - Entry Date: 12 Apr 1814 - Discharged on 11 Jan 1815

Frazier, John (3) - Master's Mate - Payroll 2 - Number: 743 - Entry Date: 17 Dec 1813 - Died on 17 Jul 1814

Frazier, John (4) - Marine Private - Washington Naval Hospital - Number: 14 - Wounded at Bladensburg, admitted on 24 Aug 1814, discharged on 26 Sep 1814

Frazier, Ross - Master's Mate - Payroll 2 - Number: 392 - Entry Date: 12 Feb 1814 - Discharged on 16 Dec 1814

Frazier, Solomon - Lieutenant - Payroll 2 - Number: 602 - Entry Date: 1 Feb 1814 - Discharged on 1 Apr 1815 - U.S. Frigate United States - Number: 602 - Discharged on 1 Apr 1815

Freeze, Frederick - Seaman - Payroll 2 - Number: 699 - Entry Date: 31 May 1814 - Ran on 9 Jul 1814

Frew, John - Steward - Payroll 1 - Number: 91 - Entry Date: 5 Oct 1813 - Payroll ended on 6 Apr 1814 - Payroll 2 - Number: 91 - Entry Date: 5 Oct 1813 - Discharged on 5 Oct 1814

Fuller, Daniel - Ordinary Seaman - Payroll 1 - Number: 102 - Entry Date: 15 Oct 1813 - Payroll ended on 6 Apr 1814 - Payroll 2 - Number: 102 - Entry Date: 15 Oct 1813 - Discharged on 16 Sep 1814

Fuller, Zachariah - Seaman - Muster - Number: 951 - Entry Date: 31 Dec 1813 - Died on 22 Aug 1814 - U.S. Sloop-of-War Ontario - Number: 73 - Entry Date: 14 Jan 1814 - Discharged on 13 Apr 1814 to the flotilla (died) -

Payroll 2 - Number: 951 - Entry Date: 31 Dec 1813 - Died on 22 May 1814

Fullerton, Charles - Gunner - Payroll 2 - Number: 841 - Entry Date: 13 Jul 1814 - Discharged on 1 Apr 1815

Fulson, Stephen - Ordinary Seaman - Muster - Number: 975 - Entry Date: 18 Jul 1814 - Discharged on 1 Apr 1815 - Payroll 2 - Number: 975 Entry Date: 18 Jul 1814 - Discharged on 1 Apr 1815

Gade, Henry - Ordinary Seaman - Payroll 2 - Number: 438 - Entry Date: 4 Apr 1814 - Discharged on 1 Apr 1815

Galatin, Daniel - Master's Mate - Payroll 1 - Number: 292 - Entry Date: 3 Mar 1814 - Payroll ended on 6 Apr 1814 - Payroll 2 - Number: 292 - Entry Date: 3 Mar 1814 - Discharged on 6 Mar 1815

Gale, Joshua - Seaman - Payroll 1 - Number: 321 - Entry Date: 23 Mar 1814 - Payroll ended on 6 Apr 1814 - Payroll 2 - Number: 321 - Entry Date: 23 Mar 1814 - Discharged on 1 Apr 1815

Gallagher, George - Boy - Payroll 1 - Number: 132 - Entry Date: 20 Sep 1813 - Payroll ended on 6 Apr 1814 - Payroll 2 - Number: 132 - Entry Date: 20 Sep 1813 - Discharged on 1 Mar 1815 - Wounded at Bladensburg - Pension: Navy IF-611 1/2 - Washington Naval Hospital - Number: 43 - Wounded at Montgomery Court House, admitted on 17 Sep 1814, discharged on 8 Dec 1814 - Pension: Navy IF-611 1/2

Gannon, James - Seaman - Payroll 1 - Number: 306 - Entry Date: 4 Mar 1814 - Payroll ended on 6 Apr 1814 - Payroll 2 - Number: 306 - Entry Date: 4 Mar 1814 - Discharged on 1 Apr 1815

Gannon, William - Landsman - Payroll 2 - Number: 901 - Discharged on Unknown

Gardiner, Conyman - Landsman - Payroll 2 - Number: 870 - Entry Date: 19 Aug 1814 - Discharged on 1 Apr 1815

Gardiner, Isaac - Ordinary Seaman - Payroll 2 - Number: 452 - Entry Date: 18 Aug 1814 - Discharged on 1 Apr 1815

Garend, Osbern - Seaman - Payroll 2 - Number: 695 - Entry Date: 25 May 1814 - Discharged on 1 Apr 1815

Garnsay, Isaac - Ordinary Seaman - Payroll 1 - Number: 332 - Entry Date: 28 Mar 1814 - Payroll ended on 6 Apr 1814 - Payroll 2 - Number: 332 - Entry Date: 28 Mar 1814 - Discharged on 1 Apr 1815

Garrish, John - Seaman - Payroll 1 - Number: 160 - Entry Date: 16 Dec 1813 - Payroll ended on 6 Apr 1814 - Payroll 2 - Number: 160 - Entry Date: 16 Dec 1813 - Died on 13 Oct 1814

Geoghegan, John - Sailing Master - U.S. Gunboat 138 - Number: 3 - Paid on 6 Apr 1814 - Payroll 2 - Number: 850 - Entry Date: 10 Sep 1813 - Discharged on 1 Apr 1815 - BLW 43702-160-55

Gibbons, John - Seaman - Payroll 1 - Number: 330 - Entry Date: 26 Mar 1814 - Payroll ended on 6 Apr 1814 - Payroll 2 - Number: 330 - Entry Date: 26 Mar 1814 - Died on 7 Jan 1815

Gibbons, Thomas - Landsman - Payroll 2 - Number: 798 - Entry Date: 29 Apr 1814 - Discharged on 24 Jul 1814

Gibbs, Richard - Seaman - Payroll 1 - Number: 193 - Entry Date: 3 Jan 1814 - Payroll ended on 6 Apr 1814 - Payroll 2 - Number: 193 - Entry Date: 3 Jan 1814 - Discharged on 3 Jan 1815

Gibson, John (1) - Volunteer Seaman - Prisoner of War at Halifax, prisoner number 7331, captured on 22 Aug 1814 near Washington, D.C. by British forces; received at Halifax on 30 Sep 1814 on HMS Surprize; discharged on 5 Mar 1815 and sent to Salem, Massachusetts on Cartel Lingan

Gibson, John (2) - Marine Private - Washington Naval Hospital - Number: 10 - Wounded at Bladensburg, admitted on 24 Aug 1814, discharged on 19 Oct 1814 - Pension: Navy IF-624 - POW: Enlisted 10 Jul 1811 at US Frigate Guerriere

Giddleman, John - Ordinary Seaman - Payroll 2 - Number: 832 - Entry Date: 7 Aug 1814 - Discharged on 1 Apr 1815

Gilbert, Thomas P. - Seaman - Payroll 1 - Number: 68 - Entry Date: 4 Nov 1813 - Payroll ended on 6 Apr 1814 - Payroll 1a - Number: 68 - Entry Date: 4 Nov 1813 - Payroll 2 - Number: 68 - Entry Date: 4 Nov 1813 - Died on 10 Jun 1814

Gilham, Thomas - Ordinary Seaman - Payroll 1 - Number: 315 - Entry Date: 20 Mar 1814 - Payroll ended on 6 Apr 1814 - Payroll 2 - Number: 315 - Entry Date: 20 Mar 1814 - Discharged on 1 Apr 1815

Gilpatrick, Jotham - Seaman - U.S. Sloop Scorpion - Number: 12 - Entry Date: 1 Mar 1813 - Payroll ended on 11 Feb 1814 - U.S. Frigate Adams Muster - Number: 393 - Entry Date: 13 Apr 1813 - Discharged on 10 Nov 1813 to U.S. Schooner Scorpion - U.S. Frigate United States - Number: 544 - Entry Date: 12 Feb 1814 - Discharged on 1 Mar 1815 to U.S. Battery Scorpion - Payroll 2 - Number: 544 - Entry Date: 1 Mar 1813 - Discharged on 1 Mar 1815

Gladden, Simeon (or Glasden) - Ordinary Seaman - U.S. Frigate Adams Payroll - Number: 139 - Entry Date: 6 Feb 1813 - Discharged on 10 Nov 1813 to U.S. Schooner Asp- Ordinary Seaman - U.S. Frigate United States - Number: 499 - Entry Date: 7 Apr 1814 - Discharged on 9 Jan 1815 to U.S. Battery Scorpion- Ordinary Seaman - U.S. Sloop Scorpion - Number: 20 - Entry Date: 9 Jan 1813 - Payroll ended on 11 Feb 1814 - Ordinary Seaman - Payroll 2 - Number: 499 - Entry Date: 9 Jan 1813 - Discharged on 9 Jan 1815

Glenn, James - Seaman - U.S. Schooner Shark - Number: 12 - Entry Date: 11 Nov 1813 - Discharged on 29 Mar 1814 - U.S. Frigate United States - Number: 564 - Entry Date: 7 Apr 1814 - Discharged on 18 Dec 1814 to U.S. Galley Shark - Payroll 2 - Number: 564 - Entry Date: 18 Dec 1812 - Discharged on 18 Dec 1814

Glenn, Thomas - Gunner - Payroll 2 - Number: 730 - Entry Date: 15 Apr 1814 - Discharged on 1 Apr 1815 - BLW 41863-160-55 - Pension: WO-13335, WC-7901

Godfrey, Joseph - Seaman - U.S. Sloop-of-War Ontario - Number: 117 - Entry Date: 10 Feb 1814 - Discharged on 13 Apr 1814 to the flotilla (ran) - Muster - Number: 955 - Entry Date: 7 Feb 1814 - Ran on 24 Aug 1814 - Payroll 2 - Number: 955 - Entry Date: 7 Feb 1814 - Ran on 24 Aug 1814

Goodman, John (or Godman) - Landsman - Payroll 1 - Number: 340 - Entry Date: 31 Mar 1814 - Payroll ended on 6 Apr 1814 - Payroll 2 - Number: 340 - Entry Date: 31 Mar 1814 - Discharged on 1 Apr 1815 - BLW 34037-160-55

Goodridge, Benjamin - Ordinary Seaman - U.S. Frigate Adams Payroll - Number: 273 - Entry Date: 21 Mar 1813 - Discharged on 10 Nov 1813 to U.S. Gunboat 137 - U.S. Gunboat 137 - Number: 19 - Entry Date: 15 Feb 1813 - Payroll ended on 4 Mar 1814 - U.S. Frigate United States - Number: 468 - Entry Date: 7 Apr 1814 - Discharged on 15 Feb 1815 to U.S. Gunboat 137 - Payroll 2 - Number: 468 - Entry Date: 15 Feb 1813 - Discharged on 15 Feb 1815

Gordon, Benjamin - Boatswain - Payroll 2 - Number: 40 - Entry Date: 28 Sep 1813 - Discharged on 12 Oct 1814 - Payroll 1 - Number: 40 - Entry Date: 28 Sep 1813 - Payroll ended on 6 Apr 1814 - Payroll 1a - Number: 40 - Entry Date: 28 Sep 1813 - Muster - Number: 40 - Entry Date: 27 Sep 1813 - Discharged on 12 Oct 1814

Gordon, James - Boy - Payroll 1 - Number: 137 - Entry Date: 27 Oct 1813 - Payroll ended on 6 Apr 1814 - BLW 49101-160-55 - Payroll 2 - Number: 137 - Entry Date: 27 Oct 1813 - Discharged on 27 Oct 1814

Gordon, John - Seaman - Payroll 1 - Number: 84 - Entry Date: 27 Oct 1813 - Payroll ended on 6 Apr 1814 - Payroll 2 - Number: 84 - Entry Date: 27 Oct 1813 - Discharged on 27 Oct 1814

Gordon, Peter - Quartermaster - U.S. Sloop-of-War Ontario - Number: 64 - Entry Date: 14 Jan 1814 - Discharged on 14 Apr 1814 to the flotilla (ran) - U.S. Frigate United States - Number: 585 - Entry Date: 7 Apr 1814 to U.S. Sloop-of-War Ontario - Payroll 2 - Number: 585 - Entry Date: 23 Dec 1813 - Ran on 19 Dec 1814 - BLW 76085-160-55

Gordon, Thomas - Ordinary Seaman - Payroll 1 - Number: 118 - Entry Date: 27 Oct 1813 - Payroll ended on 6 Apr 1814 - Payroll 2 - Number: 118 - Entry Date: 27 Oct 1813 - Discharged on 27 Oct 1814

Gore, William - Landsman - Payroll 1 - Number: 143 - Entry Date: 6 Oct 1813 - Payroll ended on 6 Apr 1814 - BLW 3506-160-55 - Payroll 2 - Number: 143 - Entry Date: 6 Oct 1813 - Discharged on 6 Oct 1814

Gorsuch, Garrard - Master's Mate - Payroll 1 - Number: 15 - Entry Date: 25 Sep 1813 - Discharged on 9 Mar 1814 - Payroll 2 - Number: 15 - Entry Date: 25 Sep 1813 - Muster - Number: 15 - Entry Date: 25 Sep 1813 - Discharged on 9 Mar 1814

Gossage, Francis - Seaman - Payroll 2 - Number: 644 - Entry Date: 24 Mar 1814 - Discharged on 26 Mar 1815

Gowen, Charles - Ordinary Seaman - U.S. Gunboat 137 - Number: 13 - Entry Date: 14 Jan 1812 - Payroll ended on 4 Mar 1814 - U.S. Frigate Adams Payroll - Number: 158 - Entry Date: 22 Feb 1813 - Discharged on 10 Nov 1813 to U.S. Schooner Asp - Payroll 2 - Number: 443 - Entry Date: 13 Jan 1813 - Discharged on 13 Jan 1815

Grace, John - Ordinary Seaman - U.S. Sloop-of-War Ontario - Number: 50 - Entry Date: 14 Jan 1814 - Discharged on 14 Apr 1814 to the flotilla - Transfers - Number: 37 - Entry Date: 15 Apr 1814 - Discharged on 6 Dec 1814 - U.S. Sloop-of-War Ontario - Number: 200 - Entry Date: 7 Dec 1814 - Discharged on 19 Mar 1815 from the flotilla - U.S. Frigate United States - Number: 659 - Entry Date: 7 Apr 1814 - Discharged on 6 Dec 1814 to U.S. Sloop-of-War Ontario - Payroll 2 - Number: 659 - Entry Date: 1 Dec 1813 - Discharged on 6 Dec 1814 to U.S. Sloop-of-War Ontario

Graham, Thomas - Ordinary Seaman - Payroll 1 - Number: 328 - Entry Date: 25 Mar 1814 - Payroll ended on 6 Apr 1814 - Payroll 2 - Number: 328 - Entry Date: 25 Mar 1814 - Discharged on 1 Apr 1815

Grandison, Jeremiah (1) - Ordinary Seaman - Payroll 1 - Number: 992 - Entry Date: 15 Mar 1814 - Payroll ended on 6 Apr 1814 - Payroll 2 - Number: 992 - Entry Date: 15 Mar 1814 - Discharged on 2 Sep 1814

Grandison, Jeremiah (2)- Cook - Payroll 2 - Number: 309 - Entry Date: 13 Sep 1814 - Discharged on 15 Mar 1815 - Muster - Number: 309 - Entry Date: 13 Sep 1814 - Discharged on 15 Mar 1815

Grant, William (1) - Seaman - U.S. Frigate Adams Muster - Number: 380 - Entry Date: 6 Apr 1813 - Discharged on 10 Nov 1813 to U.S. Schooner Scorpion - U.S. Schooner Shark - Number: 4 - Entry Date: 11 Nov 1813 - Discharged on 29 Mar 1814 - U.S. Frigate United States - Number: 552 - Entry Date: 7 Apr 1814 - Discharged on 4 Feb 1815 to U.S. Galley Shark - Payroll 2 - Number: 552 - Entry Date: 4 Feb 1813 - Discharged on 4 Feb 1815

Grant, William (2) - Seaman - Payroll 2 - Number: 769 - Entry Date: 17 May 1814 - Ran on 5 Aug 1814

Graves, Jonathan - Marine Corporal - Washington Naval Hospital - Number: 26 - Wounded at Bladensburg, admitted on 27 Aug 1814, discharged on 7 Oct 1814 - Enlisted 5 Aug 1809 at Point Petre, Georgia

Gray, Henry - Seaman - U.S. Sloop-of-War Ontario - Number: 42 - Entry Date: 14 Jan 1814 - Discharged on 13 Apr 1814 to the flotilla (ran) - Payroll 2 - Number: 451 - Entry Date: 25 Nov 1813 - Ran on 24 Aug 1814

Gray, John - Ordinary Seaman - U.S. Frigate Adams Muster - Number: 278 - Entry Date: 22 Mar 1813 - Discharged on 10 Nov 1813 to U.S. Schooner Asp - U.S. Sloop Asp - Number: 6 - Entry Date: 11 Nov 1813 - Discharged on 20 Apr 1814 - U.S. Frigate United States - Number: 711 - Entry Date: 21 Apr 1814 - Discharged on 28 Jan 1815 to U.S. Schooner Asp - Payroll 2 - Number: 711 - Entry Date: 21 Jan 1813 - Discharged on 28 Jan 1815

Grayson, Alfred - Marine Brevet Captain - U.S. Marine Corps - Quartermaster; commissioned as a 2nd lieutenant on 26 Jul 1810, promoted to 1st lieutenant on 14 Apr 1812, breveted captain on 18 Jun 1814, died on 28 Jun 1823

Green, Charles - Seaman - Payroll 1 - Number: 352 - Entry Date: 2 Apr 1814 - Payroll ended on 6 Apr 1814 - Payroll 2 - Number: 352 - Entry Date: 2 Apr 1814 - Discharged on 1 Apr 1815

Green, John - Seaman - Payroll 1 - Number: 267 - Entry Date: 2 Jan 1814 - Payroll ended on 6 Apr 1814 - Payroll 2 - Number: 267 - Entry Date: 2 Jan 1814 - Discharged on 25 Jan 1815 - U.S. Frigate Adams Muster - Number: 167 - Entry Date: 22 Feb 1813 - Discharged on 14 Jul 1813 - Taken from U.S. Schooner Asp at Kinsale by the British on 20 Jul 1813 - Prisoner of War at Bermuda, number 1143, taken on 20 Jul 1813, discharged on 13 Aug 1813 and released to U.S. ship Rolla

Green, Robert - Seaman - Muster - Number: 52 - Entry Date: 14 Sep 1813 - Died on 16 Aug 1814 - Payroll 1 - Number: 52 - Entry Date: 18 Sep 1813 - Payroll ended on 6 Apr 1814 - Payroll 1a - Number: 52 - Entry Date: 18 Sep 1813 - Died on 16 Aug 1814 at Baltimore - Payroll 2 - Number: 52 - Entry Date: 18 Sep 1813 - Died on 16 Aug 1814

Gregory, William - Marine Private - Washington Naval Hospital - Number: 33 - Wounded at Bladensburg, admitted on 3 Sep 1814, discharged on 17 Oct 1814 - Pension: Navy IF-673 (U.S. Frigate Adams) - Enlisted on 25 Sep 1812 in U.S. Frigate Adams

Griffin, Richard - Clerk - Payroll 2 - Number: 401 - Entry Date: 21 Mar 1814 - Discharged on 1 Apr 1815

Griffitt, Peter - Ordinary Seaman - Payroll 2 - Number: 723 - Entry Date: 7 Apr 1814 - Ran on 24 Aug 1814

Groot, John D. - Seaman - U.S. Sloop Scorpion - Number: 2 - Entry Date: 2 Feb 1813 - Payroll ended on 11 Feb 1814 - U.S. Frigate Adams Payroll - Number: 203 - Entry Date: 15 Mar 1813 - Discharged on 10 Nov 1813 to U.S. Gunboat 137 - U.S. Frigate Adams Muster - Number: 203 - Entry Date: 15 Mar 1813 - Discharged on 10 Nov 1813 to U.S. Gunboat 137 - U.S. Frigate United States - Number: 536 - Entry Date: 7 Apr 1814 - Ran on 6

Dec 1814 form U.S. Battery Scorpion - Payroll 2 - Number: 536 - Entry Date: 2 Feb 1813 - Ran on 6 Dec 1814

Gustiff, Ralph - Ordinary Seaman - Payroll 1 - Number: 260 - Entry Date: 19 Feb 1814 - Payroll ended on 6 Apr 1814 - Payroll 2 - Number: 260 - Entry Date: 19 Feb 1814 - Discharged on 19 Feb 1815

Guthridge, William - Gunner - Muster - Number: 45 - Entry Date: 12 Oct 1813 - Discharged on 12 Oct 1814 - Payroll 1 - Number: 45 - Entry Date: 12 Oct 1813 - Payroll ended on 6 Apr 1814 - Payroll 1a - Number: 45 - Entry Date: 12 Oct 1813 - Payroll 2 - Number: 45 - Entry Date: 12 Oct 1813 - Discharged on 2 Oct 1814

Hague, Forbes - Seaman - Payroll 2 - Number: 651 - Entry Date: 3 Mar 1814 - Ran on 28 Dec 1814

Halfpenny, Robert - Ordinary Seaman - Payroll 2 - Number: 869 - Entry Date: 18 Aug 1814 - Ran on 24 Feb 1815

Hall, Francis - Ordinary Seaman - Payroll 2 - Number: 279 - Entry Date: 11 Mar 1814 - Payroll 1 - Number: 435 - Entry Date: 11 Mar 1814 - Payroll ended on 6 Apr 1814 - Payroll 2 - Number: 435 - Entry Date: 11 Mar 1814 - Discharged on 12 Mar 1814

Hall, James - Master's Mate - Payroll 1 - Number: 22 - Entry Date: 28 Sep 1813 - Payroll ended on 6 Apr 1814 - Payroll 2 - Number: 22 - Entry Date: 28 Sep 1813 - Discharged on 6 Dec 1814 - Muster - Number: 22 - Entry Date: 28 Sep 1813 - Discharged on 16 Dec 1814

Hall, John - Seaman - Payroll 1 - Number: 75 - Entry Date: 18 Oct 1813 - Discharged on 16 Jan 1814 - Payroll 1a - Number: 75 - Entry Date: 18 Oct 1813 - Discharge on 16 Jan 1814 - Payroll 2 - Number: 75 - Entry Date: 18 Oct 1813

Halsey, George - Ordinary Seaman - Payroll 2 - Number: 770 - Entry Date: 7 Jun 1814 - Discharged on 1 Apr 1815

Hambleton, Asa - Ordinary Seaman - Payroll 2 - Number: 385 - Entry Date: 7 Apr 1814 - Discharged on 5 Mar 1815

Hamilton, John - Landsman - Payroll 2 - Number: 604 - Entry Date: 17 May 1814 - Ran on 24 Dec 1814 - BLW 3153-160-55

Hamilton, Robert M. - Sailing Master - U.S. Frigate United States - Number: 912 - Resigned on 21 Nov 1814, transferred to Commodore Barney - Payroll 2 - Number: 912 - Entry Date: 3 May 1814 - Resigned on 21 Nov 1814 - Warranted as a sailing master on 1 Mar 1814

Hamilton, Thomas - Surgeon - Payroll 1 - Number: 14 - Entry Date: 22 Dec 1813 - Payroll ended on 6 Apr 1814 - Pension: Navy WF-456 - Payroll 2 - Number: 14 - Entry Date: 22 Dec 1813 - Discharged on 7 Apr 1815 - Muster - Number: 14 - Entry Date: 22 Dec 1813 - Muster ended on 6 Apr 1814

Hammon, Reuben - Seaman - U.S. Frigate Adams Muster - Number: 220 - Entry Date: 16 Mar 1813 - Discharged on 10 Nov 1813 to U.S. Schooner Asp - U.S. Sloop Asp - Number: 7 - Entry Date: 11 Nov 1813 - Discharged on 20 Apr 1814 - U.S. Frigate United States - Number: 709 - Entry Date: 21 Apr 1814 - Ran on 1 Dec 1814 from U.S. Schooner Asp - Payroll 2 - Number: 709 - Entry Date: 2 Feb 1813 - Ran on 1 Dec 1814

Hand, John - Master's Mate - Payroll 2 - Number: 792 - Entry Date: 24 May 1814 - Discharged on 23 Dec 1814

Hanson, Charles - Ordinary Seaman - Payroll 2 - Number: 757 - Entry Date: 15 Apr 1814 - Ran on 23 Feb 1815

Hardacre, Moses - Volunteer Seaman - Prisoner of War at Halifax, prisoner number 7330, captured on 22 Aug 1814 near Washington, D.C. by British forces; received at Halifax on 30 Sep 1814 on HMS Surprize; discharged on 5 Mar 1815 and sent to Salem, Massachusetts on Cartel Lingan

Hardestry, Joseph H. - Payroll 2 - Number: 383 – Discharged: date unknown

Hardesty, Charles R. - Midshipman - Payroll 1 - Number: 302 - Entry Date: 11 Mar 1814 - Payroll ended on 6 Apr 1814 - Payroll 2 - Number: 302 - Entry Date: 11 Mar 1814 - Discharged on 1 Apr 1815 - BLW 3034-160-55

Hardy, Joseph - Ordinary Seaman - Payroll 1 - Number: 103 - Entry Date: 18 Oct 1813 - Payroll ended on 6 Apr 1814 - Payroll 2 - Number: 103 - Entry Date: 18 Oct 1813 - Discharged on 28 Sep 1814

Hardy, Samuel T. - Boy - Payroll 1 - Number: 133 - Entry Date: 25 Sep 1813 - Discharged on 4 Dec 1813 - Payroll 2 - Number: 133 - Entry Date: 25 Sep 1813 - Discharged on Oct 1813

Harkens, John - Boy - U.S. Sloop-of-War Ontario - Number: 29 - Entry Date: 14 Jan 1814 - Discharged on 13 Apr 1814 to the flotilla - Payroll 2 - Number: 412 - Entry Date: 16 Nov 1813 - Ran on 28 Oct 1814

Harman, Gabriel - Ordinary Seaman - Payroll 2 - Number: 610 - Entry Date: 2 May 1814 - Discharged on 1 Apr 1815

Harper, Henry - Seaman - Payroll 1 - Number: 251 - Payroll ended on 6 Apr 1814 - Payroll 2 - Number: 251 - Entry Date: 22 Feb 1814 - Died on 12 Nov 1814

Harper, Robert - Gunner's Mate - U.S. Sloop-of-War Ontario - Number: 16 - Entry Date: 14 Jan 1814 - Discharged on 13 Apr 1814 to the flotilla - U.S. Frigate United States - Number: 876 - Entry Date: 14 Apr 1814 - Discharged on 23 Aug 1814 to U.S. Sloop-of-War Ontario - Payroll 2 - Number: 876 - Entry Date: 28 Oct 1813 - Discharged on 23 Apr 1814

Harrington, Robert - Seaman - Payroll 1 - Number: 64 - Entry Date: 15 Oct 1813 - Payroll ended on 6 Apr 1814 - Payroll 1a - Number: 64 - Entry Date: 16 Oct 1813 - Discharged on 16 Oct 1814 - Payroll 2 - Number: 64 - Entry Date: 15 Oct 1813 - Discharged on 16 Oct 1814

Harrington, William - Seaman - U.S. Frigate United States - Number: 646 - Ran on 24 Aug 1814 - Payroll 2 - Number: 646 - Entry Date: 15 May 1814 - Ran on 24 May 1814

Harris, Ebenezer - Ordinary Seaman - U.S. Frigate Adams Payroll - Number: 165 - Entry Date: 22 Feb 1813 - Discharged on 10 Nov 1813 to U.S. Galley Shark - U.S. Schooner Shark - Number: 9 - Entry Date: 11 Nov 1813 - Discharged on 29 Mar 1814 - U.S. Frigate United States - Number: 524 - Entry Date: 7 Apr 1814 - Ran on 13 Nov 1814 from U.S. Galley Shark - Payroll 2 - Number: 553 - Entry Date: 21 Jan 1813 - Discharged on 13 Nov 1814 - Payroll 2 - Number: 524 - Entry Date: 21 Jan 1813 - Ran on 13 Nov 1813

Harris, John - Steward - Payroll 1 - Number: 94 - Entry Date: 7 Oct 1813 - Discharged on 9 Feb 1814 - Payroll 2 - Number: 94 - Entry Date: 7 Oct 1813 - Ran on 9 Feb 1814

Harris, Thomas - Ordinary Seaman - Payroll 2 - Number: 736 - Entry Date: 26 Apr 1814 - Discharged on 1 Apr 1815 - BLW 3888-160-55

Harris, William - Landsman - U.S. Frigate United States - Number: 772 - Entry Date: 10 Apr 1814 - Ran on 30 Sep 1814 at Fort McHenry - Payroll 2 - Number: 772 - Entry Date: 9 Jul 1814 - Ran on 30 Sep 1814

Harrison, James - Ordinary Seaman - Payroll 2 - Number: 368 - Entry Date: 16 Mar 1814 - Discharged on 1 Apr 1815

Harrison, William - Quarter Gunner - U.S. Frigate United States - Number: 461 - Entry Date: 11 Apr 1814 - Discharged on 28 Sep 1814 to U.S. Gunboat 137 - Quarter Gunner - U.S. Gunboat 137 - Number: 7 - Entry Date: 17 Sep 1812 - Payroll ended on 4 Mar 1814 - Payroll 2 - Number: 461 - Entry Date: 17 Sep 1812 - Discharged on 29 Sep 1814

Hart, James - Landsman - Payroll 1 - Number: 320 - Entry Date: 23 Mar 1814 - Payroll ended on 6 Apr 1814 - Payroll 2 - Number: 320 - Entry Date: 23 Mar 1814 - Discharged on 1 Apr 1815

Hartman, John - Seaman - Payroll 1 - Number: 152 - Entry Date: 17 Nov 1813 - Discharged on 11 Dec 1813 - Payroll 2 - Number: 152 - Entry Date: 17 Nov 1813 - Ran on 11 Dec 1813

Harvey, James (1) - Seaman - U.S. Sloop-of-War Ontario - Number: 95 - Entry Date: 29 Jan 1814 - Discharged on 14 Apr 1814 to the flotilla (ran) - Payroll 2 - Number: 935 - Entry Date: 24 Jan 1814 - Ran on 21 Apr 1814 - Muster - Number: 935 - Entry Date: 24 Jun 1814 - Ran on 21 Apr 1814

Harvey, James (2) - Seaman - Payroll 1 - Number: 82 - Entry Date: 6 Oct 1813 - Payroll ended on 6 Apr 1814 - Payroll 2 - Number: 82 - Entry Date: 6 Oct 1813 - Discharged on 7 Oct 1814

Harvey, Nathaniel - Seaman - Payroll 2 - Number: 737 - Entry Date: 27 Apr 1814 - Discharged on 8 Mar 1815

Harvey, Thomas H. - Gunner - Payroll 2 - Number: 581 - Entry Date: 6 Apr 1814 - Discharged on 11 Jan 1815 - Payroll 2 - Number: 973 - Entry Date: 6 Apr 1814 - Discharged on 14 May 1814 - Muster - Number: 581 - Entry Date: 15 May 1814 - Discharged on 1 Jan 1815

Hawkins, Samuel - Landsman - Payroll 1 - Number: 123 - Entry Date: 30 Sep 1813 - Payroll ended on 6 Apr 1814 - Payroll 2 - Number: 123 - Entry Date: 30 Sep 1813 - Discharged on 30 Sep 1814

Hay, Stacy - Landsman - Payroll 2 - Number: 606 - Entry Date: 23 Apr 1814 - Ran on 28 Oct 1814

Hayley, Joseph (or Hailey) - Ordinary Seaman - U.S. Frigate Adams Muster - Number: 382 - Entry Date: 6 Apr 1813 - Discharged on 10 Nov 1813 to U.S. Galley Shark - U.S. Schooner Shark - Number: 23 - Entry Date: 11 Nov 1813 - Discharged on 29 Mar 1814 - U.S. Frigate United States - Number: 521 - Entry Date: 7 Apr 1814 - Discharged on 6 Feb 1815 from U.S. Galley Shark - Payroll 2 - Number: 521 - Entry Date: 6 Feb 1813 - Discharged on 6 Feb 1815

Haynie, Samuel - Master's Mate - Payroll 2 - Number: 739 - Entry Date: 6 May 1814 - Ran on 3 Jan 1815 - Payroll 2 - Number: 911 - Entry Date: 4 May 1814

Hayward, John - Ordinary Seaman - Payroll 1 - Number: 208 - Entry Date: 17 Jan 1814 - Payroll ended on 6 Apr 1814 - Pension: Navy WF-477 - Payroll 2 - Number: 208 - Entry Date: 17 Jan 1814 - Discharged on 7 Feb 1815

Heinzman, John - Ordinary Seaman - Payroll 2 - Number: 727 - Entry Date: 14 Apr 1814 - Discharged on 1 Apr 1815

Henry, Joseph - Ordinary Seaman - U.S. Sloop-of-War Ontario - Number: 82 - Entry Date: 14 Jan 1814 - Discharged on 13 Apr 1814 to the flotilla - Transfers - Number: 14 - Entry Date: 14 Apr 1814 - Discharged on 6 Dec 1814 - U.S. Sloop-of-War Ontario - Number: 213 - Entry Date: 7 Dec 1814 - Discharged on 5 Mar 1815 from the flotilla - U.S. Frigate United States - Number: 890 - Entry Date: 7 Apr 1814 - Discharged on 6 Dec 1814 to U.S. Sloop-of-War Ontario - Payroll 2 - Number: 890 - Entry Date: 6 Jun 1814 - Discharged on 6 Dec 1814 to U.S. Sloop-of-War Ontario

Herring, Thomas - Seaman - Payroll 1 - Number: 283 - Entry Date: 9 Mar 1814 - Payroll ended on 6 Apr 1814 - Payroll 2 - Number: 283 - Entry Date: 9 Mar 1814 - Discharged on 1 Apr 1815 - Prisoner of War at Halifax, prisoner number 7291, captured on 22 Aug 1814 near Washington, D.C. by British forces; received at Halifax on 30 Sep 1814 on HMS Surprize; discharged on 5 Mar 1815 and sent to Salem, Massachusetts on Cartel Lingan

Herron, William - Seaman - Payroll 2 - Number: 802 - Entry Date: 11 Jul 1814 - Discharged on 1 Apr 1815

Hill, Richard - Seaman - Payroll 1 - Number: 212 - Entry Date: 22 Jan 1814 - Payroll ended on 6 Apr 1814 - Payroll 2 - Number: 212 - Entry Date: 22 Jan 1814 - Discharged on 30 Jan 1815 - Wounded at Bladensburg - Washington Naval Hospital - Number: 15 - Wounded at Bladensburg, admitted on 24 Aug 1814, discharged on 30 Oct 1814 - BLW 32293-160-55 - Pension: Navy IF-747

Hill, Thomas (1) - Seaman - U.S. Frigate Adams Payroll - Number: 118 - Entry Date: 5 Feb 1813 - Discharged on 10 Nov 1813 to U.S. Galley Shark - U.S. Frigate United States - Number: 495 - Entry Date: 7 Apr 1814 - Ran on 24 Aug 1814 from U.S. Battery Scorpion - Payroll 2 - Number: 495 - Entry Date: 18 Jan 1812 - Ran on 26 Aug 1814

Hill, Thomas (2) - Seaman - U.S. Sloop-of-War Ontario - Number: 137 - Entry Date: 13 Mar 1814 - Discharged on 13 Apr 1814 to the flotilla - U.S. Sloop Scorpion - Number: 19 - Entry Date: 18 Jan 1813 - Payroll ended on 11 Feb 1814 - Payroll 2 - Number: 940 - Entry Date: 14 Apr 1814 - Ran on 24 Aug 1814 - Muster - Number: 940 - Entry Date: 13 Mar 1814 - Ran on 24 Aug 1814

Hilliday, (William) - Marine Sergeant - U.S. Marine Corps – At Bladensburg

Hindman, John H. - Seaman - Payroll 1 - Number: 140 - Entry Date: 29 Oct 1813 - Payroll ended on 6 Apr 1814- Seaman - Payroll 2 - Number: 140 - Entry Date: 29 Oct 1813 - Discharged on 29 Oct 1814

Hodges, Benjamin - Boy - U.S. Frigate Adams Payroll - Number: 54 - Entry Date: 1 Jan 1813 - Discharged on 10 Nov 1813 to U.S. Schooner Asp - U.S. Schooner Shark - Number: 3 - Entry Date: 11 Nov 1813 - Discharged on 29 Mar 1814 - U.S. Frigate United States - Number: 554 - Entry Date: 7 Apr 1814 - Payroll 2 - Number: 457 - Entry Date: 17 Nov 1812 - Payroll 2 - Number: 554 - Entry Date: 30 Mar 1814 - Ran on 24 Aug 1814

Holbrook, Asa - Ordinary Seaman - U.S. Frigate Adams Muster - Number: 164 - Entry Date: 22 Feb 1813 - Discharged on 10 Nov 1813 to U.S. Galley Shark - U.S. Schooner Shark - Number: 15 - Entry Date: 11 Nov 1813 - Discharged on 29 Mar 1814 - Muster - Number: 943 - Entry Date: 20 Jan 1814 – Payroll 2 - Number: 943 - Entry Date: 20 Jan 1814 – Discharged: never appeared

Holbrook, Lemuel - Ordinary Seaman - U.S. Gunboat 137 - Number: 4 - Entry Date: 19 Jan 1813 - Payroll ended on 4 Mar 1814 - U.S. Frigate Adams Muster - Number: 169 - Entry Date: 22 Feb 1813 - Discharged on 10 Nov 1813 to U.S. Galley Shark - U.S. Frigate United States - Number: 523 - Entry Date: 7 Apr 1814 - Ran on 19 Jan 1815 from U.S. Gunboat 137 - Payroll 2 - Number: 523 - Entry Date: 19 Jan 1813 - Discharged on 19 Jan 1815

Holden, Peter G. - Seaman - Payroll 2 - Number: 596 - Entry Date: 9 May 1814 - Ran on 30 Sep 1814

Holland, Samuel - Ordinary Seaman - U.S. Sloop-of-War Ontario - Number: 110 - Entry Date: 8 Feb 1814 - Discharged on 14 Apr 1814 to the flotilla - U.S. Frigate United States - Number: 572 - Entry Date: 7 Apr 1814 - Discharged on 5 Dec 1814 to U.S. Sloop-of-War Ontario - Transfers - Number: 41 - Entry Date: 15 Apr 1814 - Discharged on 6 Dec 1814 - U.S. Sloop-of-War Ontario - Number: 228 - Entry Date: 7 Dec 1814 - Discharged on 5 Mar 1815 from the flotilla - Payroll 2 - Number: 572 - Discharged on 6 Dec 1814 to U.S. Sloop-of-War Ontario

Holliday, Philip - Boy - U.S. Sloop-of-War Ontario - Number: 62 - Entry Date: 14 Jan 1814 - Discharged on 13 Apr 1814 to the flotilla - Transfers - Number: 15 - Entry Date: 14 Apr 1814 - Discharged on 6 Dec 1814 - U.S. Frigate United States - Number: 906 - Entry Date: 7 Apr 1814 - Discharged on 6 Dec 1814 to U.S. Sloop-of-War Ontario - U.S. Sloop-of-War Ontario - Number: 205 - Entry Date: 7 Dec 1814 - Discharged on 14 Jan 1815 from the flotilla - Payroll 2 - Number: 906 - Entry Date: 23 Dec 1813 - Discharged on 6 Dec 1814 to U.S. Sloop-of-War Ontario

Holmes, Emanuel - Seaman - Payroll 2 - Number: 657 - Entry Date: 14 Apr 1814 - Discharged on 1 Apr 1815 - Payroll 2 - Number: 904 - Entry Date: 14 Apr 1814 - Discharged on 1 Apr 1815

Holt, Enoch - Seaman - Payroll 2 - Number: 434 - Entry Date: 8 Mar 1814 - Discharged on 8 Mar 1815

Honlton, George - Seaman - Payroll 2 - Number: 800 - Entry Date: 27 Jul 1814 - Ran on 30 Nov 1814

Hook, William (1) - Gunner - Payroll 1 - Number: 200 - Entry Date: 8 Jan 1814 - Payroll ended on 6 Apr 1814 - Payroll 2 - Number: 200 - Entry Date: 8 Jan 1814 - Discharged on 8 Jan 1815

Hook, William (2) - Boatswain - Payroll 2 - Number: 982 - Entry Date: 12 Jan 1815 - Discharged on 1 Apr 1815 - Muster - Number: 982 - Entry Date: 12 Jan 1815 - Discharged on 1 Apr 1815

Hooker, James - Ordinary Seaman - Payroll 1 - Number: 310 - Entry Date: 17 Mar 1814 - Payroll ended on 6 Apr 1814 - Payroll 2 - Number: 310 - Entry Date: 17 Mar 1814 - Discharged on 28 May 1814

Hooper, James - Seaman - U.S. Sloop-of-War Ontario - Number: 120 - Entry Date: 13 Feb 1814 - Discharged on 14 Apr 1814 to the flotilla (died) - Muster - Number: 930 - Entry Date: 10 Feb 1814 - Died from wounds on 1 Sep 1814, wounded at Bladensburg - Payroll 2 - Number: 930 - Entry Date: 14 Apr 1814 - Died from wounds on 1 Sep 1814, wounded at Bladensburg - BLW 69644-160-55

Horn, Henry M. (1) - Steward - Muster - Number: 337 - Entry Date: 10 Jul 1814 - Discharged on 1 Apr 1815 - Payroll 2 - Number: 337 - Entry Date: 10 Jul 1814: Discharged on 1 Apr 1815

Horn, Henry M. (2) - Seaman - Payroll 1 - Number: 1000 - Entry Date: 29 Mar 1814 - Payroll ended on 6 Apr 1814 - Payroll 2 - Number: 1000 - Entry Date: 29 Mar 1814 - Discharged on 9 Jul 1814

Howard, Henry - Boatswain - Muster - Number: 39 - Entry Date: 16 Oct 1813 - Muster ended on 6 Apr 1814 - Payroll 1 - Number: 39 - Entry Date: 16 Oct 1813 - Payroll ended on 6 Apr 1814 - Payroll 2 - Number: 39 - Entry Date: 16 Oct 1813 - Discharged on 16 Oct 1814

Howard, John - Boatswain - Muster - Number: 37 - Entry Date: 12 Oct 1813 - Discharged on 12 Oct 1814 - Payroll 1 - Number: 37 - Entry Date: 12 Oct 1813 - Payroll ended on 6 Apr 1814 - Payroll 2 - Number: 37 - Entry Date: 12 Oct 1813 - Discharged on 12 Oct 1814

Howland, George - Ordinary Seaman - Payroll 1 - Number: 170 - Entry Date: 7 Dec 1813 - Payroll ended on 6 Apr 1814 - Payroll 2 - Number: 170 - Entry Date: 7 Dec 1813 - Discharged on 7 Dec 1814

Hubbard, James - Master's Mate - Payroll 2 - Number: 627 - Entry Date: 10 Mar 1814 - Discharged on 1 Apr 1815

Hubbard, John - Seaman - Payroll 2 - Number: 472 - Entry Date: 12 Feb 1814 - Discharged on 12 Feb 1815

Hubbard, Thomas - Landsman - Payroll 2 - Number: 396 - Entry Date: 28 Mar 1814 - Died on 26 Jun 1814 - Pension: Navy WF-1239

Huberre, Joseph - Marine Private - Washington Naval Hospital - Number: 29 - Wounded at Bladensburg, admitted on 28 Aug 1814, discharged on 7 Oct 1814

Huffington, Jesse - Sailing Master - Muster - Number: 4 - Entry Date: 21 Sep 1813 - Muster ended on 6 Apr 1814 -

Payroll 1 - Number: 4 - Entry Date: 21 Sep 1813 - Payroll ended on 6 Apr 1814 - Payroll 2 - Number: 4 - Entry Date: 21 Sep 1813 - Discharged on 20 Dec 1814

Hugg, Henry - Ordinary Seaman - Payroll 1 - Number: 187 - Entry Date: 3 Jan 1814 - Discharged on 2 Feb 1814 - Payroll 2 - Number: 187 - Entry Date: 3 Jan 1814 - Discharged on 2 Feb 1814

Hunt, Nathaniel - Seaman - Payroll 2 - Number: 594 - Entry Date: 23 Apr 1814 - Ran on 7 Jan 1815

Hutchings, Theodore - Ordinary Seaman - U.S. Frigate United States - Number: 561 - Entry Date: 7 Apr 1814 - Discharged on 3 Feb 1815 to U.S. Galley Shark - U.S. Schooner Shark - Number: 5 - Entry Date: 29 Dec 1813 - Discharged on 29 Mar 1814 - Payroll 2 - Number: 561 - Entry Date: 3 Feb 1813 - Discharged on 3 Feb 1815

Huza, Robert - Seaman - Payroll 1 - Number: 252 - Payroll ended on 6 Apr 1814 - Payroll 2 - Number: 252 - Entry Date: 23 Feb 1814 - Discharged on 23 Feb 1815

Hyatt, George F. - Midshipman - Payroll 2 - Number: 969 - Entry Date: 22 Nov 1814 - Discharged on 1 Apr 1815 - Muster - Number: 969 - Entry Date: 28 Nov 1814 - Discharged on 1 Apr 1815 - BLW 12804-160-55

Hymer, Jacob - Landsman - Payroll 2 - Number: 795 - Entry Date: 23 Jul 1814 - Discharged on 1 Apr 1815

Ignacious, John - Seaman - Payroll 1 - Number: 87 - Entry Date: 30 Oct 1813 - Payroll ended on 6 Apr 1814 - Payroll 2 - Number: 87 - Entry Date: 30 Oct 1813 - Discharged on 30 Oct 1814

Inez, Peter - Ordinary Seaman - Payroll 1 - Number: 185 - Entry Date: 30 Dec 1813 - Discharged on 27 Feb 1814 - Payroll 2 - Number: 185 - Entry Date: 30 Dec 1813 - Ran on 28 Feb 1814

Inez, Samuel - Ordinary Seaman - Payroll 2 - Number: 192 - Entry Date: 3 Jan 1814 - Discharged on 3 Jan 1815 - Payroll 1 - Number: 192 - Entry Date: 3 Jan 1814 - Payroll ended on 6 Apr 1814

Inlose, John - Ordinary Seaman - Payroll 2 - Number: 199 - Entry Date: 6 Jan 1814 - Payroll 1 - Number: 199 - Entry Date: 6 Jan 1814 - Discharged on 20 Jul 1814

Ireson, Samuel - Seaman - U.S. Frigate Adams Muster - Number: 331 - Entry Date: 4 Apr 1813 - Discharged on 10 Nov 1813 to U.S. Schooner Asp - U.S. Schooner Shark - Number: 22 - Entry Date: 11 Nov 1813 - Discharged on 29 Mar 1814 - U.S. Frigate United States - Number: 505 - Entry Date: 7 Apr 1814 - Discharged on 21 Jan 1815 to U.S. Galley Shark - Payroll 2 - Number: 505 - Entry Date: 21 Jan 1813 - Discharged on 21 Jan 1815

Isley, Matthias - Master's Mate - Muster - Number: 17 - Entry Date: 27 Sep 1813 - Discharged on 17 Jun 1814 - Payroll 1 - Number: 17 - Entry Date: 27 Sep 1813 - Payroll ended on 6 Apr 1814 - Payroll 2 - Number: 17 - Entry Date: 27 Sep 1813 - Discharged on 17 Jun 1814

Jackson, Elisha - Seaman - Payroll 1 - Number: 167 - Entry Date: 7 Dec 1813 - Payroll ended on 6 Apr 1814 - Payroll 2 - Number: 167 - Entry Date: 7 Dec 1813 - Discharged on 7 Dec 1814

Jackson, Solomon - Landsman - Payroll 2 - Number: 400 - Entry Date: 1 Apr 1814 - Discharged on 1 Apr 1815

Jacobs, John (1) - Seaman - Payroll 2 - Number: 473 - Entry Date: 1 Apr 1814 - Ran on 5 Jan 1815

Jacobs, John (2) - Seaman - U.S. Frigate United States - Number: 919 - Discharged on 6 Feb 1815 to U.S. Gunboat 137 - U.S. Gunboat 137 - Number: 2 - Entry Date: 6 Feb 1813 - Payroll ended on 4 Mar 1814 - U.S. Frigate Adams Muster - Number: 376 - Entry Date: 6 Apr 1813 - Discharged on 10 Nov 1813 to U.S. Galley Shark - U.S. Frigate Adams Payroll - Number: 376 - Entry Date: 6 Apr 1813 - Discharged on 10 Nov 1813 to U.S. Galley Shark - Payroll 2 - Number: 919 - Entry Date: 6 Feb 1814 - Discharged on 6 Feb 1815

James, Leonard - Ordinary Seaman - U.S. Frigate United States - Number: 894 - Entry Date: 26 Apr 1814 - Discharged on 1 Apr 1815 to Patuxent - Payroll 2 - Number: 894 - Entry Date: 20 Jul 1814 - Discharged on 1 Apr 1815

James, Garrison - Seaman - Payroll 2 - Number: 658 - Entry Date: 14 Mar 1814 - Discharged on 1 Apr 1815

Jamison, Thomas - Seaman - Payroll 2 - Number: 374 - Entry Date: 31 Mar 1814 - Died on 13 May 1814

Jarboe, Joseph - Master's Mate - Muster - Number: 827 - Entry Date: 6 Aug 1814 - Discharged on 16 Dec 1814 - Midshipman - Payroll 2 - Number: 827 - Entry Date: 6 Aug 1814 - Discharged on 15 Dec 1814 - Seaman - Payroll 2 - Number: 972 - Entry Date: 30 Jul 1814 - Discharged on 5 Aug 1814

Jefferson, John - Ordinary Seaman - Payroll 2 - Number: 373 - Entry Date: 19 Mar 1814 - Discharged on 1 Apr 1815

Jenkins, Henry - Midshipman - Payroll 2 - Number: 372 - Entry Date: 1 Apr 1814 - Discharged on 1 Apr 1815 - Payroll 2 - Number: 398 - BLW 1470-160-55 - Pension: Navy WF-530

Jenkins, James - Seaman - Payroll 2 - Number: 409 - Entry Date: 26 Mar 1814 - Discharged on 1 Apr 1815 - BLW 10051-160-55 - Payroll 2 - Number: 551

Jenkins, John - Ordinary Seaman - Payroll 1 - Number: 115 - Entry Date: 2 Oct 1813 - Payroll ended on 6 Apr 1814 - Payroll 2 - Number: 115 - Entry Date: 2 Oct 1813 - Discharged on 2 Oct 1814

Jenkins, Purnel - Payroll 2 - Number: 402 - Discharged on Unknown

Jenkins, Richard - Cook - U.S. Frigate United States - Number: 500 - Entry Date: 7 Apr 1814 - Discharged on 26 Sep 1814 to U.S. Battery Scorpion - U.S. Sloop Scorpion - Number: 1 - Entry Date: 17 Sep 1812 - Payroll ended on 11 Feb 1814 - Payroll 2 - Number: 500 - Entry Date: 17 Sep 1812 - Discharged on 26 Sep 1814

Jenkins, Thomas - Ordinary Seaman - U.S. Frigate Adams Payroll - Number: 378 - Entry Date: 6 Apr 1813 - Discharged on 10 Nov 1813 to U.S. Galley Shark - U.S. Frigate Adams Muster - Number: 378 - Entry Date: 6 Apr 1813 - Discharged on 10 Nov 1813 to U.S. Galley Shark - Steward - Payroll 2 - Number: 619 - Entry Date: 30 Mar 1814 - Discharged on 29 Dec 1814

Jenny, Joseph - Midshipman - Payroll 1 - Number: 249 - Entry Date: 28 Feb 1814 - Payroll ended on 6 Apr 1814 - Payroll 2 - Number: 249 - Entry Date: 28 Feb 1814 - Discharged on 15 Dec 1814

Johnson, Edward - Ordinary Seaman - Payroll 2 - Number: 755 - Entry Date: 8 Jun 1814 - Payroll 2 - Number: 793 - Entry Date: 14 Jun 1814 - Discharged on 1 Apr 1815

Johnson, Henry - Ordinary Seaman - Payroll 1 - Number: 166 - Entry Date: 7 Dec 1813 - Payroll ended on 6 Apr 1814 - Payroll 1a - Number: 67 - Entry Date: 23 Oct 1813 - Died on 15 Dec 1813 - Payroll 2 - Number: 166 - Entry Date: 7 Dec 1813 - Discharged on 7 Dec 1814

Johnson, James - Seaman - Payroll 1 - Number: 67 - Entry Date: 23 Oct 1813 - Discharged on 5 Dec 1813 - Payroll 2 - Number: 67 - Entry Date: 23 Oct 1813 - Died on 15 Dec 1813

Johnson, Kelly - Seaman - Payroll 2 - Number: 477 - Entry Date: 5 May 1814 - Ran on 16 Oct 1814

Johnson, Peter - Seaman - U.S. Frigate United States - Number: 512 - - Entry Date: 7 Apr 1814 - Discharged on 6 Dec 1814 to U.S. Sloop-of-War Ontario - Transfers - Number: 33 - Entry Date: 18 Apr 1814 - Discharged on 6 Dec 1814 - BLW 32330-160-55 - U.S. Sloop-of-War Ontario - Number: 99 - Entry Date: 30 Jan 1814 - Discharged on 17 Apr 1814 to the flotilla - Payroll 2 - Number: 512 - Entry Date: 28 Jan 1814 - Discharged on 6 Dec 1814 to U.S. Sloop-of-War Ontario

Johnson, Richard - Muster - Number: 926 - Discharged on Unknown - Payroll 2 - Number: 926 - Discharged on Unknown

Jones, Benjamin - Seaman - Payroll 2 - Number: 794 - Entry Date: 30 Jul 1814 - Discharged on 1 Apr 1815

Jones, Charles - Seaman - Payroll 1 - Number: 218 - Entry Date: 26 Jan 1814 - Payroll ended on 6 Apr 1814 - Payroll 2 - Number: 218 - Entry Date: 26 Jan 1814 - Discharged on 26 Jan 1815

Jones, Harry - Boy - Payroll 1 - Number: 134 - Entry Date: 29 Sep 1813 - Payroll ended on 6 Apr 1814 - Wounded at Bladensburg - Race: Black - Payroll 2 - Number: 134 - Entry Date: 29 Sep 1813 - Discharged on 2 Nov 1814 - Wounded at Bladensburg - Race: Black - Washington Naval Hospital - Number: 35 - Wounded at Bladensburg, admitted on 3 Sep 1814; discharged on 30 Oct 1814 - Race: Black

Jones, Henry - Ordinary Seaman - Payroll 1 - Number: 223 - Entry Date: 1 Feb 1814 - Payroll ended on 6 Apr 1814 - Payroll 2 - Number: 223 - Entry Date: 1 Feb 1814 - Discharged on 1 Feb 1815

Jones, James - Boatswain - Muster - Number: 31 - Entry Date: 18 Sep 1813 - Discharged on 26 Sep 1814 - Payroll 1 - Number: 31 - Entry Date: 18 Sep 1813 - Payroll ended on 6 Apr 1814 - Payroll 2 - Number: 31 - Entry Date: 18 Sep 1813 - Discharged on 26 Sep 1814 - BLW 18480-160-55

Jones, Jonas - Seaman - Payroll 2 - Number: 872 - Entry Date: 17 Aug 1814 - Discharged on 5 May 1815

Jones, Perry - Boy - Payroll 2 - Number: 763 - Entry Date: 4 Mar 1814 - Discharged on 1 Apr 1815

Jones, Thomas - Seaman - U.S. Sloop-of-War Ontario - Number: 105 - Entry Date: 6 Feb 1814 - Discharged on 13 Apr 1814 to the flotilla - Transfers - Number: 3 - Entry Date: 14 Apr 1814 - Discharged on 6 Dec 1814 - U.S. Frigate United States - Number: 607 - Entry Date: 7 Apr 1814 - Discharged on 6 Dec 1814 to U.S. Sloop-of-War Ontario - Payroll 2 - Number: 607 - Entry Date: 14 Apr 1814 - Discharged on 6 Dec 1814 to U.S. Sloop-of-War Ontario - U.S. Sloop-of-War Ontario - Number: 224 - Entry Date: 7 Dec 1814 - Discharged on 5 Mar 1815 from the flotilla

Jones, William - Boy - Payroll 2 - Number: 490 - Entry Date: 9 Apr 1814 - Discharged on 1 Apr 1815 - BLW 149-160-55

Jones, William R. - Steward - Muster - Number: 768 - Entry Date: 13 May 1814 - Discharged on 1 Apr 1815 - Payroll 2 - Number: 768 - Entry Date: 13 May 1814 - Discharged on 1 Apr 1815 - Pension: SO-7870, SC-4633 - Ordinary Seaman - Payroll 2 - Number: 1001 - Entry Date: 5 May 1814 - Discharged on 12 Mar 1814

Jory, John - Ordinary Seaman - Payroll 2 - Number: 864 - Entry Date: 15 Aug 1814 - Discharged on 1 Apr 1815 - BLW 13059-160-55 - Pension: WO-3259, WC-5621

Joshua, James - Seaman - Payroll 2 - Number: 431 - Entry Date: 26 Mar 1814 - Ran on 24 Aug 1814

Jutt, Samuel L. - Master's Mate - Payroll 2 - Number: 671 - Entry Date: 28 Jun 1814 - Discharged on 12 Jan 1815

Kashaden, Robert - Master's Mate - Payroll 1 - Number: 232 - Entry Date: 15 Feb 1814 - Payroll ended on 6 Apr 1814 - Payroll 2 - Number: 232 - Entry Date: 15 Feb 1814 - Discharged on 10 Aug 1814

Kelly, James - Ordinary Seaman - Payroll 2 - Number: 868 - Entry Date: 16 Aug 1814 - Discharged on 1 Apr 1815

Kelly, Thomas - Steward - Payroll 2 - Number: 745 - Entry Date: 7 Apr 1814 - Never appeared

Kelly, Zacharias - Gunner - Payroll 2 - Number: 618 - Entry Date: 25 Mar 1814 - Discharged on 1 Apr 1815

Kendricks, William - Seaman - Payroll 1 - Number: 168 - Entry Date: 7 Dec 1813 - Payroll ended on 6 Apr 1814 - Payroll 2 - Number: 168 - Entry Date: 7 Dec 1813 - Discharged on 7 Dec 1814 - Wounded at Bladensburg - Washington Naval Hospital - Number: 13 - Wounded at Bladensburg, admitted on 24 Aug 1814, discharged on 28 Sep 1814

Kennard, Nathaniel - Seaman - Payroll 2 - Number: 766 - Entry Date: 16 Mar 1814 - Ran on 22 Sep 1814

Kennedy, John - Landsman - Payroll 2 - Number: 705 - Entry Date: 2 Jun 1814 - Ran on 18 Jun 1814

Kenny, Richard - Steward - Payroll 2 - Number: 491 - Entry Date: 3 Apr 1814 - Discharged on 1 Apr 1815

Keptner, John - Ordinary Seaman - Payroll 1 - Number: 341 - Entry Date: 4 Apr 1814 - Payroll ended on 6 Apr 1814 - Payroll 2 - Number: 341 - Entry Date: 4 Apr 1814 - Discharged on 1 Apr 1815

Kerry, Thomas (1) - Seaman - U.S. Frigate United States - Number: 762 - Payroll 2 - Number: 449 - Entry Date: 26 Mar 1814 - Payroll 2 - Number: 762 - Entry Date: 26 Mar 1814 - Discharged on 1 Apr 1815

Keys, Thomas (2) - Seaman - Payroll 1 - Number: 250 - Payroll ended on 6 Apr 1814 - Payroll 2 - Number: 250 - Entry Date: 17 Feb 1814 - Discharged on 17 Feb 1815

Kiddall, John - Sailing Master - Payroll 1 - Number: 8 - Entry Date: 16 Oct 1813 - Payroll ended on 6 Apr 1814 - Payroll 2 - Number: 8 - Entry Date: 16 Oct 1813 - Discharged on 1 Apr 1815 - Warranted as a sailing master on 6 Oct 1813 - Muster - Number: 8 - Entry Date: 16 Oct 1813 - Muster ended on 6 Apr 1814

Kimbol, Rowland - Seaman - Payroll 2 - Number: 605 - Entry Date: 16 Apr 1814 - Ran on 23 Jan 1815

Kinn, John - Seaman - Payroll 1 - Number: 74 - Entry Date: 14 Oct 1813 - Payroll ended on 6 Apr 1814 - Payroll 1a - Number: 74 - Entry Date: 14 Oct 1813 - Payroll 2 - Number: 74 - Entry Date: 14 Oct 1813 - Discharged on 1 Nov 1814

Kinsey, George - Seaman - Payroll 2 - Number: 433 - Entry Date: 12 Mar 1814 - Discharged on 9 Mar 1815

Kirby, James (2) - Ordinary Seaman - Payroll 2 - Number: 920 - Entry Date: 28 Nov 1814 - Discharged on 1 Apr 1815

Koon, Peter - Seaman - Payroll 2 - Number: 758 - Entry Date: 16 Apr 1814 - Discharged on 1 Apr 1815

Krebs, Jacob - Ordinary Seaman - Payroll 2 - Number: 790 - Entry Date: 23 Jul 1814 - Ran on 17 Feb 1815

Krull, Henderick - Seaman - Payroll 1 - Number: 145 - Entry Date: 30 Oct 1813 - Payroll ended on 6 Apr 1814 - Payroll 2 - Number: 145 - Entry Date: 30 Oct 1813 - Discharged on 30 Oct 1814

Labee, Constant - Seaman - U.S. Frigate United States - Number: 611 - Entry Date: 17 Apr 1814 - Killed on 24 Aug 1814 at Bladensburg - Payroll 2 - Number: 611 - Entry Date: 16 May 1814 - Died on 24 Aug 1814

Lambert, Joshua - Seaman - U.S. Frigate United States - Number: 474 - Entry Date: 7 Apr 1814 - Died on 18 Oct 1814, sick on U.S. Gunboat 137 - U.S. Schooner Shark - Number: 2 - Entry Date: 11 Nov 1813 - Discharged on 29 Mar 1814 - Payroll 2 - Number: 474 - Entry Date: 30 Mar 1814 - Died on 18 Oct 1814

Lang, Thomas - Quartermaster - U.S. Sloop-of-War Ontario - Number: 115 - Entry Date: 8 Feb 1814 - Discharged on 14 Apr 1814 to the flotilla (ran) - Payroll 2 - Number: 936 - Entry Date: 5 Feb 1814 - Ran on 24 Aug 1814 - Muster - Number: 936 - Entry Date: 5 Feb 1814 - Ran on 24 Aug 1814

Lashford, Thomas - Ordinary Seaman - Payroll 1 - Number: 148 - Entry Date: 23 Nov 1813 - Payroll ended on 6 Apr 1814 - Payroll 2 - Number: 148 - Entry Date: 23 Nov 1813 - Discharged on 23 Nov 1814

Launey, John - Ordinary Seaman - U.S. Gunboat 137 - Number: 18 - Entry Date: 26 Jan 1813 - Payroll ended on 4 Mar 1814 - U.S. Frigate United States - Number: 857 - Entry Date: 11 Apr 1814 - Ran on 26 Apr 1814 from U.S. Gunboat 137 - Payroll 2 - Number: 857 - Entry Date: 26 Jan 1813 - Ran on 26 Apr 1814

Lawder, George (1) - Seaman - Payroll 1 - Number: 233 - Entry Date: 15 Feb 1814 - Payroll ended on 6 Apr 1814 - BLW 3912-160-55 - Pension: Navy IF-903 - Payroll 2 - Number: 233 - Entry Date: 15 Feb 1814 - Discharged on 1 Aug 1814 - BLW 3912-160-55 - Pension: Navy IF-903 - Washington Naval Hospital - Number: 49 - Severely wounded at Bladensburg, admitted on 7 Oct 1814, discharged on 1 Apr 1815

Lawder, George (2) - Marine Private - U.S. Marine Corps - Pension: Navy IF-1271

Lawrence, William - Seaman - Payroll 2 - Number: 688 - Entry Date: 7 May 1814 - Discharged on 1 Apr 1815

Lawson, William - Seaman - Payroll 2 - Number: 830 - Entry Date: 8 Aug 1814 - Discharged on 1 Apr 1815

Lednum, Jesse - Ordinary Seaman - Payroll 2 - Number: 799 - Entry Date: 25 Jul 1814 - Ran on 25 Jan 1815

Lee, Washington - Steward - Payroll 2 - Number: 534 - Entry Date: 23 Apr 1814 - Died on 8 Nov 1814

Lemouse, Francis - Seaman - U.S. Frigate Adams Payroll - Number: 102 - Entry Date: 17 Jan 1813 - Discharged on 10 Nov 1813 to U.S. Schooner Scorpion - U.S. Sloop Scorpion - Number: 9 - Entry Date: 31 Dec 1812 - Payroll ended on 11 Feb 1814 - U.S. Frigate United States - Number: 543 - Entry Date: 12 Feb 1814 - Discharged on 31 Dec 1814 to U.S. Battery Scorpion - Payroll 2 - Number: 543 - Entry Date: 3 Dec 1812 - Discharged on 31 Dec 1814

Levering, William - Ordinary Seaman - U.S. Frigate United States - Number: 595 - Entry Date: 7 Apr 1814 - Discharged on 6 Dec 1814 to U.S. Sloop-of-War Ontario - Transfers - Number: 19 - Entry Date: 15 Apr 1814 - Discharged on 6 Dec 1814 - Payroll 2 - Number: 595 - Entry Date: 9 Dec 1813 - Discharged on 6 Dec 1814 to U.S. Sloop-of-War Ontario

Leverton, Greenbury - Ordinary Seaman - Payroll 2 - Number: 861 - Entry Date: 11 Aug 1814 - Discharged on 1 Apr 1815

Lewis, Thomas - Ordinary Seaman - Payroll 2 - Number: 641 - Entry Date: 14 Apr 1814 - Discharged on 1 Apr 1815

Lezar, Lawrence - Seaman - Payroll 1 - Number: 79 - Entry Date: 4 Nov 1813 - Discharged on 10 Dec 1813 - Payroll 2 - Number: 79 - Entry Date: 4 Nov 1813 - Discharged on 10 Dec 1813

Linderman, Frederick - Seaman - Payroll 1 - Number: 235 - Entry Date: 17 Feb 1814 - Payroll ended on 6 Apr 1814 - Payroll 2 - Number: 235 - Entry Date: 17 Feb 1814

Linthrum, Thomas - Master's Mate - Payroll 2 - Number: 744 - Entry Date: 28 Mar 1814 - Discharged on 17 Dec 1815

Littlefield, Joseph - Seaman - U.S. Frigate United States - Number: 466 - Entry Date: 11 Apr 1814 - Discharged on 3 Feb 1815 to U.S. Gunboat 137 - U.S. Gunboat 137 - Number: 11 - Entry Date: 3 Feb 1813 - Payroll ended on 4 Mar 1814 - Payroll 2 - Number: 466 - Entry Date: 3 Feb 1813 - Discharged on 3 Feb 1815

Lloyd, James - Seaman - Payroll 2 - Number: 419 - Entry Date: 28 Apr 1814 - Discharged on 1 Apr 1815

Locherman, Josiah - Midshipman - Payroll 2 - Number: 541 - Entry Date: 10 Mar 1814 - Discharged on 1 Apr 1815

London, Robert - Seaman - Payroll 2 - Number: 652 - Entry Date: 21 Mar 1814 - Ran on 24 Aug 1814

Lont, Sylvester A. - Seaman - Payroll 2 - Number: 748 - Entry Date: 22 Apr 1814 - Ran on 1 Apr 1815

Lorano, James - Seaman - Payroll 1 - Number: 243 - Entry Date: 22 Feb 1814 - Payroll ended on 6 Apr 1814 - Payroll 2 - Number: 243 - Entry Date: 22 Feb 1814 - Discharged on 22 Feb 1815

Lord, John - Boatswain - U.S. Frigate United States - Number: 550 - Entry Date: 15 Apr 1814 - Discharged on 6 Dec 1814 to U.S. Sloop-of-War Ontario - U.S. Sloop-of-War Ontario - Number: 37 - Entry Date: 14 Jan 1814 - Discharged on 14 Apr 1814 to the flotilla - Transfers - Number: 28 - Entry Date: 15 Apr 1814 - Discharged on 6 Dec 1814 - BLW 28856-152-55 - U.S. Sloop-of-War Ontario - Number: 195 - Entry Date: 7 Dec 1814 - Discharged on 5 Mar 1815 from the flotilla - Payroll 2 - Number: 550 - Entry Date: 23 Mar 1813 - Discharged on 6 Dec 1814 to U.S. Sloop-of-War Ontario

Loring, Eliphalet - Quartermaster - U.S. Sloop-of-War Ontario - Number: 145 - Entry Date: 16 Mar 1814 - Discharged on 13 Apr 1814 to the flotilla - U.S. Frigate United States - Number: 482 - Entry Date: 7 Apr 1814 - Discharged on 6 Dec 1814 to U.S. Sloop-of-War Ontario - Transfers - Number: 53 - Entry Date: 14 Apr 1814 - Discharged on 6 Dec 1814 - U.S. Sloop-of-War Ontario - Number: 233 - Entry Date: 7 Dec 1814 - Discharged on 5 Mar 1815 from the flotilla - Payroll 2 - Number: 482 - Entry Date: 15 Mar 1814 - Discharged on 6 Dec 1814 to U.S. Sloop-of-War Ontario

Loughborough, Foster (Greenbury) - Volunteer Seaman - Washington Naval Hospital - Number: 17 - Wounded at Bladensburg, admitted on 24 Aug 1814, discharged on 28 Aug 1815

Louis, Lloyd - Landsman - Payroll 1 - Number: 358 - Entry Date: 2 Dec 1813 - Payroll ended on 6 Apr 1814 - Payroll 2 - Number: 358 - Entry Date: 2 Dec 1813 - Discharged on 1 Apr 1815

Lovedory, John - Steward - Payroll 2 - Number: 511 - Entry Date: 2 Mar 1814 - Discharged on 10 Nov 1814

Loverling, William - Ordinary Seaman - U.S. Sloop-of-War Ontario - Number: 53 - Entry Date: 14 Jan 1814 - Discharged on 14 Apr 1814 to the flotilla - U.S. Sloop-of-War Ontario - Number: 202 - Entry Date: 7 Dec 1814 - Discharged on 19 Mar 1815 from the flotilla

Lowry, Benjamin - Seaman - Payroll 2 - Number: 366 - Entry Date: 11 Apr 1814 - Discharged on 1 Apr 1815

Lowry, John - Ordinary Seaman - Payroll 1 - Number: 113 - Entry Date: 2 Nov 1813 - Payroll ended on 6 Apr 1814 - Payroll 2 - Number: 113 - Entry Date: 2 Nov 1813 - Discharged on 2 Nov 1814

Lowry, William - Landsman - Payroll 1 - Number: 128 - Entry Date: 2 Nov 1813 - Payroll ended on 6 Apr 1814 - Payroll 2 - Number: 128 - Entry Date: 2 Nov 1813 - Discharged on 2 Nov 1814

Lucas, Benjamin - Seaman - Payroll 2 - Number: 845 - Entry Date: 4 Aug 1814 - Ran on 31 Aug 1814 - Payroll 2 - Number: 859 - Entry Date: 3 Aug 1814

Lucas, George - Seaman - Muster - Number: 50 - Entry Date: 14 Sep 1813 - Discharged on 14 Sep 1814 - Payroll 1 - Number: 50 - Entry Date: 14 Sep 1813 - Payroll ended on 6 Apr 1814 - Payroll 1a - Number: 50 - Entry Date: 14 Sep 1813 - Payroll 2 - Number: 50 - Entry Date: 14 Sep 1813 - Discharged on 14 Sep 1814

Lucas, Peter - Ordinary Seaman - Payroll 2 - Number: 884 - Entry Date: 1 Aug 1814 - Ran on 25 Nov 1814 - BLW 3089-160-55

Luke, Norris - Gunner - Muster - Number: 46 - Entry Date: 16 Oct 1813 - Discharged on 16 Oct 1814 - Payroll 1 - Number: 46 - Entry Date: 16 Oct 1813 - Payroll ended on 6 Apr 1814 - Payroll 1a - Number: 46 - Entry Date: 14 Oct 1813 - Payroll 2 - Number: 46 - Entry Date: 16 Oct 1813 - Discharged on 16 Oct 1814

Lundgram, Andrew - Seaman - Payroll 1 - Number: 244 - Entry Date: 25 Feb 1814 - Payroll ended on 6 Apr 1814 - Payroll 2 - Number: 244 - Entry Date: 25 Feb 1814 - Discharged on 25 Feb 1815

Lynch, Timothy - Seaman - Payroll 2 - Number: 786 - Entry Date: 21 Jul 1814 - Ran on 2 Nov 1814

MacKay, William - Seaman - Payroll 1 - Number: 344 - Entry Date: 5 Apr 1814 - Payroll ended on 6 Apr 1814 - Payroll 2 - Number: 344 - Entry Date: 5 Apr 1814 - Discharged on 1 Apr 1815

Mann, John - Ordinary Seaman - Payroll 2 - Number: 965 - Entry Date: 3 Aug 1814 - Discharged on 1 Apr 1815 - Muster - Number: 965 - Entry Date: 3 Aug 1814 - Discharged on 1 Apr 1815

Maria, John (1) - Ordinary Seaman - U.S. Sloop Scorpion - Number: 6 - Entry Date: 11 Jan 1813 - Payroll ended on 11 Feb 1814 - U.S. Frigate United States - Number: 813 - Entry Date: 12 Feb 1814 - Killed on 24 Aug 1814 at Bladensburg - Seaman - Payroll 2 - Number: 813 - Payroll 2 - Number: 485 - Entry Date: 11 Jan 1813 - Killed on 24 Aug 1814 at Bladensburg

Marie, John (2) - Ordinary Seaman - U.S. Frigate Adams Muster - Number: 121 - Entry Date: 5 Feb 1813 - Discharged on 10 Nov 1813 to U.S. Gunboat 137 - Seaman - Payroll 1 - Number: 354 - Entry Date: 5 Apr 1814 - Payroll ended on 6 Apr 1814 - Payroll 2 - Number: 354 - Entry Date: 5 Apr 1814 - Discharged on 1 Apr 1815

Mars, John - Ordinary Seaman - Payroll 2 - Number: 842 - Entry Date: 3 Aug 1814 - Ran on 24 Aug 1814

Marshall, John - Master's Mate - Payroll 2 - Number: 783 - Entry Date: 11 Jul 1814 - Discharged on 16 Dec 1814 - BLW 13057-160-55

Marshall, Philip - Steward - Payroll 2 - Number: 617 - Entry Date: 4 Mar 1814 - Discharged on 4 Mar 1815 - BLW 2194-160-55

Martin, ----- - Sea Captain - Washington Naval Hospital - Number: 32 - Wounded at Bladensburg, admitted on 30 Aug 1814, discharged on 26 Sep 1814

Martin, Caleb - Landsman - Payroll 1 - Number: 125 - Entry Date: 20 Nov 1813 - Payroll ended on 6 Apr 1814 - BLW 78158-160-55 - Payroll 2 - Number: 125 - Entry Date: 20 Nov 1813 - Discharged on 26 Nov 1814

Martin, Isaac - Landsman - Payroll 1 - Number: 129 - Entry Date: 1 Oct 1813 - Payroll ended on 6 Apr 1814 - Payroll 2 - Number: 129 - Entry Date: 1 Oct 1813 - Discharged on 24 Jun 1814 - Cook - Muster - Number: 999 - Entry Date: 25 Jun 1814 - Discharged on 1 Oct 1814 - Payroll 2 - Number: 999 - Entry Date: 25 Jun 1814 - Discharged on 1 Oct 1814

Martin, James H. (1) - Sailing Master - Muster - Number: 246 - Entry Date: 5 Jul 1814 - Discharged on 15 Apr 1815 - Wounded at Bladensburg - Payroll 2 - Number: 246 - Entry Date: 6 Jul 1814 - Discharged on 1 Apr 1815 - Wounded at Bladensburg - Washington Naval Hospital - Number: 25 - Wounded at Bladensburg, admitted on 26 Aug 1814, discharged on 4 Jan 1815 - Pension: Navy IF-972

Martin, James H. (2) - Master's Mate - Payroll 1 - Number: 988 - Entry Date: 1 Mar 1814 - Payroll ended on 6 Apr 1814 - Wounded at Bladensburg - Payroll 2 - Number: 988 - Entry Date: 1 Mar 1814 - Discharged on 4 Jul 1814 - Wounded at Bladensburg - Pension: Navy IF-972

Martin, John - Seaman - U.S. Sloop-of-War Ontario - Number: 79 - Entry Date: 14 Jan 1814 - Discharged on 14 Apr 1814 to the flotilla (ran) - U.S. Frigate United States - Number: 539 - Entry Date: 7 Apr 1814 - Ran on 24 Aug 1814 from U.S. Sloop-of-War Ontario - Payroll 2 - Number: 539 - Entry Date: 5 Jan 1814 - Ran on 24 May 1814 - BLW 55512-160-55

Martin, Peter (1) - Gunner - Payroll 2 - Number: 825 - Entry Date: 14 Jul 1814 - Ran on 24 Aug 1814

Martin, Peter (2) - Seaman - Muster - Number: 874 - Entry Date: 19 Aug 1814 - Discharged on 1 Apr 1815 - Payroll 2 - Number: 874 - Entry Date: 19 Aug 1814 - Discharged on 1 Apr 1815- Seaman - Payroll 2 - Number: 964 - Entry Date: 19 Aug 1814

Martin, Robert F. - Ordinary Seaman - Payroll 2 - Number: 417 - Entry Date: 13 Mar 1814 - Discharged on 1 Apr 1815

Martin, William (1) - Ordinary Seaman - Payroll 2 - Number: 645 - Entry Date: 10 Apr 1814 - Discharged on 1 Apr 1815

Martin, William (2) - Sailing Master - Payroll 1 - Number: 205 - Entry Date: 13 Jan 1814 - Payroll ended on 6 Apr 1814 - Payroll 2 - Number: 205 - Entry Date: 13 Jan 1814 - Discharged on 15 Apr 1815 - Warranted as a sailing master on 12 Jan 1814

Martin, William (3) - Boatswain - Muster - Number: 844 - Entry Date: 21 Aug 1814 - Discharged on 1 Apr 1815 - Payroll 2 - Number: 844 - Entry Date: 21 Aug 1814 - Discharged on 1 Apr 1815 - Payroll 2 - Number: 931 - Entry Date: 4 Aug 1814 - Discharged on 20 Aug 1814

Maryjohn, Loronz - Seaman - Payroll 1 - Number: 274 - Entry Date: 14 Mar 1814 - Payroll ended on 6 Apr 1814 - Payroll 2 - Number: 274 - Entry Date: 14 Mar 1814 - Discharged on 1 Apr 1815

Mason, Andrew - Seaman - U.S. Frigate United States - Number: 547 - Entry Date: 5 Apr 1814 - Ran on 25 Jan 1815 from U.S. Sloop-of-War Ontario - Payroll 2 - Number: 547 - Entry Date: 4 Mar 1814 - Ran on 25 Jan 1815

Massington, Charles - Ordinary Seaman - Payroll 1 - Number: 111 - Entry Date: 10 Oct 1813 - Payroll ended on 6 Apr 1814 - Payroll 2 - Number: 111 - Entry Date: 10 Oct 1813 - Died on 13 Sep 1814 at Fort McHenry, MD

Masson, William - Gunner - BLW 108846-160-55

Matthews, Andrew - Ordinary Seaman - U.S. Frigate Adams Payroll - Number: 196 - Entry Date: 15 Mar 1813 - Discharged on 10 Nov 1813 to U.S. Schooner Asp - U.S. Frigate United States - Number: 510 - Entry Date: 7 Apr 1814 - Ran on 3 Dec 1814 to U.S. Battery Scorpion - U.S. Sloop Scorpion - Number: 21 - Entry Date: 22 Jan 1813 - Payroll ended on 11 Feb 1814 - Payroll 2 - Number: 510 - Entry Date: 22 Jan 1813 - Ran on 23 Dec 1814 - BLW 42262-160-55

Mattis, Michael - Seaman - U.S. Sloop-of-War Ontario - Number: 138 - Entry Date: 16 Mar 1814 - Discharged on 13 Apr 1814 to the flotilla - U.S. Frigate United States - Number: 907 - Entry Date: 7 Apr 1814 - Discharged on 28 Feb 1815 to U.S. Sloop-of-War Ontario - Transfers - Number: 56 - Entry Date: 14 Apr 1814 - Discharged on 6 Dec 1814 - Payroll 2 - Number: 907 - Entry Date: 15 Mar 1814 - Discharged on 28 Feb 1815 to U.S. Sloop-of-War Ontario

McAllen, Dennis - Seaman - U.S. Sloop-of-War Ontario - Number: 157 - Entry Date: 16 Mar 1814 - Discharged on 5 Apr 1814 to the flotilla - U.S. Frigate United States - Number: 885 - Entry Date: 7 Apr 1814 - Died on 11 Oct 1814 on U.S. Sloop-of-War Ontario - Payroll 2 - Number: 885 - Entry Date: 15 Mar 1814 - Died on 11 Oct 1814

McAllister, John - Landsman - Payroll 1 - Number: 316 - Entry Date: 21 Mar 1814 - Payroll ended on 6 Apr 1814

McBain, Daniel - Ordinary Seaman - Payroll 2 - Number: 677 - Entry Date: 23 May 1814 - Ran on 1 Aug 1814

McCallister, Charles - Boy - Payroll 1 - Number: 317 - Entry Date: 21 Mar 1814 - Payroll ended on 6 Apr 1814 - Payroll 2 - Number: 317 - Entry Date: 21 Mar 1814 - Discharged on 28 Feb 1814

McCallister, John - Landsman - Payroll 2 - Number: 316 - Entry Date: 21 Mar 1814 - Discharged on 28 Feb 1815

McCarty, John - Ordinary Seaman - Payroll 1 - Number: 144 - Entry Date: 6 Oct 1813 - Discharged on 20 Oct 1813 - Payroll 2 - Number: 144 - Entry Date: 6 Oct 1813 - Ran on 21 Oct 1813

McClanahan, William - Landsman - Payroll 1 - Number: 215 - Entry Date: 25 Jan 1814 - Payroll ended on 6 Apr 1814 - Payroll 2 - Number: 215 - Entry Date: 25 Jan 1814 - Discharged on 25 Jan 1815

McClellan, Bennet - Seaman - Payroll 1 - Number: 174 - Entry Date: 9 Dec 1813 - Payroll ended on 6 Apr 1814 - Payroll 2 - Number: 174 - Entry Date: 9 Dec 1813 - Discharged on 9 Dec 1814

McClellan, Robert - Volunteer Seaman - Washington Naval Hospital - Number: 42 - Wounded at Upper Marlboro, admitted on 12 Sep 1814, discharged on 30 Oct 1814

McClelland, John - Steward - Payroll 1 - Number: 334 - Entry Date: 17 Mar 1814 - Payroll ended on 6 Apr 1814 - Payroll 2 - Number: 334 - Entry Date: 17 Mar 1814 - Died on 26 Jul 1814

McClemmy, Ezekiel - Landsman - Payroll 1 - Number: 121 - Entry Date: 29 Sep 1813 - Payroll ended on 6 Apr 1814 - Payroll 2 - Number: 121 - Entry Date: 29 Sep 1813 - Discharged on 28 Sep 1814

McConnell, John - Ordinary Seaman - U.S. Sloop-of-War Ontario - Number: 27 - Entry Date: 14 Jan 1814 - Discharged on 13 Apr 1814 to the flotilla - Transfers - Number: 9 - Entry Date: 14 Apr 1814 - Discharged on 6 Dec 1814 - U.S. Sloop-of-War Ontario - Number: 190 - Entry Date: 7 Dec 1814 - Discharged on 5 Mar 1815 from the flotilla - Payroll 2 - Number: 415 - Entry Date: 15 Nov 1813 - Discharged on 6 Dec 1814 to U.S. Sloop-of-War Ontario

McCormick, Benson L. - Landsman - Payroll 1 - Number: 126 - Entry Date: 6 Oct 1813 - Payroll ended on 6 Apr 1814 - Payroll 2 - Number: 126 - Entry Date: 6 Oct 1813 - Discharged on 7 Oct 1814

McDonald, John - Seaman - U.S. Frigate Adams Payroll - Number: 145 - Entry Date: 6 Feb 1813 - Discharged on 10 Nov 1813 to U.S. Galley Shark - U.S. Frigate Adams Muster - Number: 145 - Entry Date: 6 Feb 1813 - Discharged on 10 Nov 1813 to U.S. Galley Shark - U.S. Sloop Asp - Number: 1 - Entry Date: 11 Nov 1813 - Discharged on 20 Apr 1814

McDonald, Patrick - Steward - Payroll 2 - Number: 479 - Entry Date: 25 Mar 1814 - Discharged on 24 Nov 1814

McDonough, Andrew - Seaman - Payroll 2 - Number: 405 - Entry Date: 28 Apr 1814 - Discharged on 1 Apr 1815

McDonough, John (1) - Boatswain - Payroll 2 - Number: 710 - Entry Date: 13 Jan 1813 - Discharged on 24 Jan 1815 - Muster - Number: 710 - Entry Date: 18 May 1814 - Discharged on 24 Jan 1815

McDonough, John (2) - Seaman - U.S. Frigate United States - Number: 710 - Entry Date: 21 Apr 1814 - Discharged on 17 May 1814 to U.S. Schooner Asp - Payroll 2 - Number: 984 - Entry Date: 13 Jan 1813 - Discharged on 17 May 1814

McMahon, Charles - Ordinary Seaman - Payroll 2 - Number: 615 - Entry Date: 14 Apr 1814 - Discharged on 1 Apr 1815

McNichols, Thomas - Ordinary Seaman - Payroll 2 - Number: 863 - Entry Date: 15 Aug 1814 - Discharged on 1 Apr 1815 - BLW 76328-160-55

McRiff, George - Seaman - Payroll 1 - Number: 142 - Entry Date: 18 Oct 1813 - Discharged on 28 Oct 1813 - Payroll 2 - Number: 142 - Entry Date: 18 Oct 1813 - Discharged on 28 Oct 1813

Medcalf, George - Seaman - Payroll 1 - Number: 355 - Entry Date: 5 Apr 1814 - Payroll ended on 6 Apr 1814 - Payroll 2 - Number: 355 - Entry Date: 5 Apr 1814 - Discharged on 31 Mar 1815

Meine, Benjamin - Ordinary Seaman - Payroll 2 - Number: 791 - Entry Date: 11 Jul 1814 - Ran on 17 Feb 1815

Melville, William - Ordinary Seaman - U.S. Frigate Adams Payroll - Number: 134 - Entry Date: 6 Feb 1813 - Discharged on 10 Nov 1813 to U.S. Galley Shark - U.S. Gunboat 137 - Number: 17 - Entry Date: 21 May 1813 - Payroll ended on 4 Mar 1814 - Payroll 2 - Number: 470 - Entry Date: 21 May 1812 - Ran on 24 Aug 1814

Merchant, Richard - Ordinary Seaman - Payroll 1 - Number: 110 - Entry Date: 19 Nov 1813 - Payroll ended on 6 Apr 1814 - Payroll 2 - Number: 110 - Entry Date: 19 Nov 1813 - Discharged on 19 Nov 1814

Middleton, Moses - Master's Mate - Payroll 1 - Number: 16 - Entry Date: 25 Sep 1813 - Payroll ended on 6 Apr 1814 - Payroll 2 - Number: 16 - Entry Date: 25 Sep 1813 - Discharged on 1 Apr 1815 - Muster - Number: 16 - Entry Date: 25 Sep 1813 - Discharged on Muster ended on 6 Apr 1814

Milam, Barney - Seaman - Payroll 2 - Number: 689 - Entry Date: 7 May 1814 - Ran on 10 Oct 1814

Miller, George (1) - Ordinary Seaman - Payroll 1 - Number: 112 - Entry Date: 13 Oct 1813 - Payroll ended on 6 Apr 1814 - Payroll 2 - Number: 112 - Entry Date: 13 Oct 1813 - Discharged on 13 Oct 1814

Miller, George (2) - Seaman - U.S. Sloop-of-War Ontario - Number: 142 - Entry Date: 18 Mar 1814 - Discharged on 14 Apr 1814 to the flotilla (ran) - Payroll 2 - Number: 938 - Entry Date: 15 Mar 1814 - Ran on 24 Aug 1814 - Muster - Number: 938 - Entry Date: 15 Mar 1814 - Ran on 24 Aug 1814

Miller, John - Seaman - Payroll 1 - Number: 158 - Entry Date: 6 Dec 1813 - Payroll ended on 6 Apr 1814 - Payroll 2 - Number: 158 - Entry Date: 6 Dec 1813 - Discharged on 3 Sep 1814

Miller, Joseph - Seaman - Payroll 1 - Number: 80 - Entry Date: 10 Nov 1813 - Payroll ended on 6 Apr 1814 - Payroll 2 - Number: 80 - Entry Date: 10 Nov 1813 - Discharged on 10 Oct 1814

Miller, Michael - Seaman - Payroll 1 - Number: 78 - Entry Date: 3 Nov 1813 - Payroll ended on 6 Apr 1814 - Payroll 1a - Number: 78 - Entry Date: 3 Nov 1813 - Payroll 2 - Number: 78 - Entry Date: 3 Nov 1813 - Discharged on 3 Nov 1814

Miller, Samuel - Marine Captain - Washington Naval Hospital - Number: 31 - Wounded at Bladensburg, admitted on 28 Aug 1814, discharged - Pension: Navy IF-1066 - Commissioned as a second lieutenant on 1 June 1808, promoted to first lieutenant on 7 March 1809, promoted to captain on 18 June 1814 promoted to major on 1 July 1834, promoted to lieutenant colonel on 6 October 1841, breveted major on 24 August 1814, breveted lieutenant colonel on 3 March 1827, died on 9 December 1855

Miller, William - Ordinary Seaman - Payroll 1 - Number: 172 - Entry Date: 7 Dec 1813 - Payroll ended on 6 Apr 1814 - Payroll 2 - Number: 172 - Entry Date: 7 Dec 1813 - Discharged on 7 Dec 1814

Millfield, William - Seaman - Payroll 1 - Number: 207 - Entry Date: 13 Jan 1814 - Payroll ended on 6 Apr 1814 - Payroll 2 - Number: 207 - Entry Date: 13 Jan 1814 - Discharged on 13 Jan 1815

Mills, Armory - Landsman - U.S. Frigate United States - Number: 456 - Entry Date: 7 Apr 1814 - Discharged on 6 Dec 1814 to U.S. Sloop-of-War Ontario - U.S. Sloop-of-War Ontario - Number: 144 - Entry Date: 16 Mar 1814 - Discharged on 13 Apr 1814 to the flotilla - Transfers - Number: 50 - Entry Date: 14 Apr 1814 - Discharged on 6 Dec 1814 - U.S. Sloop-of-War Ontario - Number: 232 - Entry Date: 7 Dec 1814 - Discharged on 5 Mar 1815 from the flotilla - Payroll 2 - Number: 456 - Entry Date: 14 Apr 1814 - Discharged on 6 Dec 1814 to U.S. Sloop-of-War Ontario

Minzies, James - Boatswain's Mate - U.S. Sloop Scorpion - Number: 1 - Entry Date: 18 Dec 1812 - Payroll ended on 11 Feb 1814 - U.S. Frigate United States - Number: 601 - Entry Date: 12 Feb 1814 - Discharged on 31 Dec 1814 to U.S. Battery Scorpion - Boatswain - Payroll 2 - Number: 601 - Entry Date: 18 Dec 1812 - Discharged on 31 Dec 1814 - BLW 10165-160-55

Mitchell, Francis - Seaman - Payroll 1 - Number: 63 - Entry Date: 15 Oct 1813 - Payroll ended on 6 Apr 1814 - Payroll 1a - Number: 63 - Entry Date: 15 Oct 1813 - Payroll 2 - Number: 63 - Entry Date: 15 Oct 1813 - Discharged on 15 Oct 1814

Mitchell, James - Ordinary Seaman - Payroll 2 - Number: 835 - Entry Date: 11 Aug 1814 - Ran on 12 Dec 1814

Mitchell, Reuben - Gunner - U.S. Frigate United States - Number: 673 - Entry Date: 7 Apr 1814 - Prisoner of War at Dartmoor, number 5500, captured on 22 Aug 1814 in Chesapeake Bay on U.S. Gunboat No. 2; died on 11 May 1815 from variola (small pox) - Born: Maryland - Age: 29 - Prisoner of War at Halifax, prisoner number 7326, captured on 22 Aug 1814 near Washington, D.C. by British forces; received at Halifax on 30 Sep 1814 on HMS Surprize; discharged on 18 Nov 1814 and sent to England on HMS Loire - Prisoner of War at Dartmoor, prisoner number 5500, captured on 22 Aug 1814 from the U.S. Flotilla Service, Gunboat Number 2 on the Chesapeake Bay by British forces; sent to Halifax on H.M. Transport Loire; received at Dartmoor on 17 Dec 1814; died on 11 May 1815 from variola (small pox) - Born: Maryland - Age: 29 - Payroll 2 - Number: 673 - Entry Date: 5 Apr 1814 - Died on 12 Jan 1815

Mohool, Thomas - Gunner - Muster - Number: 48 - Entry Date: 27 Dec 1814 - Discharged on 1 Apr 1815 - Payroll 2 - Number: 48 - Entry Date: 27 Dec 1814 - Discharged on 1 Apr 1815 - Payroll 1 - Number: 998 - Entry Date: 12 Nov 1813 - Payroll ended on 6 Apr 1814 - Payroll 1a - Number: 998 - Entry Date: 12 Nov 1813 - Payroll 2 - Number: 998 - Entry Date: 12 Nov 1813 - Discharged on 14 Nov 1814 - Muster - Number: 998 - Entry Date: 12 Nov 1813 - Discharged on 14 Nov 1814

Montell, John - Seaman - Payroll 2 - Number: 779 - Entry Date: 2 Apr 1814 - Discharged on 1 Apr 1815

Montgomery, Hugh - Boy - Payroll 1 - Number: 324 - Entry Date: 24 Mar 1814 - Payroll ended on 6 Apr 1814 - Payroll 2 - Number: 324 - Entry Date: 24 Mar 1814 - Discharged on 1 Apr 1815 - BLW 34875-160-55

Montgomery, Richard - Master's Mate - U.S. Frigate United States - Number: 574 - Entry Date: 14 Apr 1814 - Discharged on 6 Jun 1814 to U.S. Sloop-of-War Ontario - Ordinary Seaman - Payroll 2 - Number: 574 - Entry Date: 28 Apr 1813 - Discharged on 6 Jun 1814

Mooney, George - Master's Mate - U.S. Gunboat 138 - Number: 53 - Paid on 6 Apr 1814 - Payroll 2 - Number: 851 - Entry Date: 10 Sep 1813 - Died on 2 May 1814

Moore, Edward - Seaman - U.S. Frigate Adams Payroll - Number: 379 - Entry Date: 6 Apr 1813 - Discharged on 10 Nov 1813 to U.S. Schooner Asp - U.S. Frigate United States - Number: 562 - Entry Date: 5 Mar 1814 - Discharged on 23 Aug 1814 to U.S. Gunboat 137 - U.S. Gunboat 137 - Number: 6 - Entry Date: 3 Feb 1813 - Payroll ended on 4 Mar 1814 - Payroll 2 - Number: 562 - Entry Date: 3 Feb 1813 - Discharged on 23 Aug 1814 – Prisoner of War at Halifax, prisoner number 7322, captured on 22 Aug 1814 near Washington, D.C. by British forces; received at Halifax on 30 Sep 1814 on HMS Surprize; discharged on 5 Mar 1815 and sent to Salem,

Massachusetts on Cartel Lingan

Moore, Sharp D. - Midshipman - U.S. Frigate United States - Number: 889 - Entry Date: 7 Aug 1814 - Discharged on 23 Dec 1814 to U.S. Sloop-of-War Ontario - Payroll 2 - Number: 889 - Entry Date: 18 Jul 1814 - Discharged on 23 Dec 1814

Moore, Thomas - Sailing Master - Payroll 2 - Number: 647 - Entry Date: 6 Mar 1814 - Discharged on 2 Aug 1814 - BLW 24810-160-55

Moore, William - Ordinary Seaman - U.S. Sloop-of-War Ontario - Number: 77 - Entry Date: 14 Jan 1814 - Discharged on 17 Apr 1814 to the flotilla (ran) - Payroll 2 - Number: 950 - Entry Date: 3 Jan 1814 - Ran on 24 Aug 1814 - Muster - Number: 950 - Entry Date: 3 Jan 1814 - Ran on 24 Aug 1814

Morris, Fisher - Landsman - Payroll 1 - Number: 163 - Entry Date: 19 Nov 1813 - Payroll ended on 6 Apr 1814 - Payroll 2 - Number: 163 - Entry Date: 19 Nov 1813 - Discharged on 26 Nov 1814

Morris, John - Seaman - Payroll 2 - Number: 895 - Entry Date: 15 Apr 1814 - Ran on 28 Aug 1814

Morris, Joseph - Seaman - Payroll 1 - Number: 62 - Entry Date: 12 Oct 1813 - Payroll ended on 6 Apr 1814 - Payroll 1a - Number: 62 - Entry Date: 12 Oct 1813 - Payroll 2 - Number: 62 - Entry Date: 12 Oct 1813 - Discharged on 12 Oct 1814

Morrison, George - Seaman - Payroll 1 - Number: 180 - Entry Date: 10 Dec 1813 - Payroll ended on 6 Apr 1814 - Payroll 2 - Number: 180 - Entry Date: 10 Dec 1813 - Discharged on 19 Dec 1814

Mortimer, John - Seaman - U.S. Frigate United States - Number: 661 - Entry Date: 7 Apr 1814 - Discharged on 6 Dec 1814 to U.S. Sloop-of-War Ontario - Transfers – Number 18 - Entry Date: 14 Apr 1814 - Discharged on 6 Dec 1814 - U.S. Sloop-of-War Ontario - Number: 146 - Entry Date: 16 Mar 1814 - Discharged on 13 Apr 1814 to the flotilla - U.S. Sloop-of-War Ontario - Number: 234 - Entry Date: 7 Dec 1814 - Discharged on 5 Mar 1815 from the flotilla - Payroll 2 - Number: 661 - Entry Date: 15 Mar 1814 - Discharged on 6 Dec 1814 to U.S. Sloop-of-War Ontario

Mortimore, Lester - Seaman - Payroll 2 - Number: 698 - Entry Date: 31 May 1814 - Discharged on 1 Apr 1815

Much, James - Seaman - Payroll 2 - Number: 883 - Entry Date: 20 Aug 1814 - Discharged on 1 Apr 1815

Mullen, James - Volunteer Seaman - Washington Naval Hospital - Number: 44 - Wounded at Montgomery Court House, admitted on 17 Sep 1814, discharged on 8 Dec 1814

Mullinix, James - Ordinary Seaman - Muster - Number: 952 - Entry Date: 5 Jan 1815 - Discharged on 6 Dec 1814 to U.S. Sloop-of-War Ontario - Transfers - Number: 47 - Entry Date: 15 Apr 1814 - Discharged on 6 Dec 1814 - U.S. Sloop-of-War Ontario - Number: 80 - Entry Date: 14 Jan 1814 - Discharged on 14 Apr 1814 to the flotilla - U.S. Sloop-of-War Ontario – Number 211 - Entry Date: 7 Dec 1814 - Discharged on 5 Mar 1815 from the flotilla - Payroll 2 - Number: 952 - Entry Date: 5 Dec 1814 - Discharged on 6 Dec 1814 to U.S. Sloop-of-War Ontario

Munday, William (Monday) - Seaman - U.S. Frigate United States - Number: 502 - Entry Date: 7 Apr 1814 - Discharged on 1 Apr 1815 - Lost both arms and an eye at St. Leonard's Creek - Payroll 2 - Number: 502 - Entry Date: 28 Mar 1814 - Discharged on 1 Apr 1815- Seaman - Washington Naval Hospital - Number: 21 - Lost both arms and an eye at St. Leonard's Creek, admitted on 24 Aug 1814, discharged on 10 Oct 1814 - Pension: Navy IF 1107

Murphy, Thomas - Ordinary Seaman - Payroll 1 - Number: 169 - Entry Date: 7 Dec 1813 - Payroll ended on 6 Apr 1814 - Payroll 2 - Number: 169 - Entry Date: 7 Dec 1813 - Discharged on 7 Dec 1814

Murray, James - Seaman - Payroll 1 - Number: 229 - Entry Date: 9 Feb 1814 - Payroll ended on 6 Apr 1814 - Payroll 2 - Number: 229 - Entry Date: 9 Feb 1814 - Discharged on 9 Feb 1815

Nabbs, William - Landsman - Payroll 1 - Number: 319 - Entry Date: 22 Mar 1814 - Payroll ended on 6 Apr 1814 - Payroll 2 - Number: 319 - Entry Date: 22 Mar 1814 - Died on 26 Jun 1814

Nalum, Ennolds - Ordinary Seaman - Payroll 1 - Number: 262 - Payroll ended on 6 Apr 1814 - Payroll 2 - Number: 262 - Entry Date: 19 Feb 1814 - Discharged on 19 Feb 1815

Nashville, Thomas - Payroll 2 - Number: 453 - Discharged date not known

Neal, Charles - Seaman - Payroll 1 - Number: 255 - Payroll ended on 6 Apr 1814 - Payroll 2 - Number: 255 - Entry Date: 6 Feb 1814 - Discharged on 7 Mar 1815

Neal, John - Ordinary Seaman - U.S. Frigate United States - Number: 881 - Entry Date: 26 Apr 1814 - Ran on 20 Nov 1814 at Annapolis (Patuxent) - Payroll 2 - Number: 881 - Entry Date: 26 Jul 1814 - Ran on 20 Nov 1814

Neel, Samuel - Seaman - Payroll 2 - Number: 506 - Entry Date: 6 Mar 1814 - Discharged on 6 Mar 1815

Negley, Michael - Seaman - Payroll 2 - Number: 582 - Entry Date: 14 Apr 1814 - Discharged on 6 Dec 1814 to U.S. Sloop-of-War Ontario - U.S. Frigate United States - Number: 582 - Entry Date: 13 Apr 1814 - Discharged on 6 Dec 1814 to U.S. Sloop-of-War Ontario - Transfers - Number: 49 - Entry Date: 14 Apr 1814 - Discharged on 6 Dec 1814 - U.S. Sloop-of-War Ontario - Number: 226 - Entry Date: 7 Dec 1814 - Discharged on 5 Mar 1815 from the flotilla - U.S. Sloop-of-War Ontario - Number: 107 - Entry Date: 8 Feb 1814 - Discharged on 13 Apr 1814 to the flotilla

Neil, Thomas - Ordinary Seaman - Payroll 1 - Number: 105 - Entry Date: 25 Oct 1813 - Payroll ended on 6 Apr 1814 - Payroll 2 - Number: 105 - Entry Date: 25 Oct 1813 - Discharged on 7 Oct 1814

Newbold, Pursel (Newbolt) - Ordinary Seaman - Muster - Number: 956 - Entry Date: 17 Feb 1814 - Ran on 24 Aug 1814 - U.S. Sloop-of-War Ontario - Number: 956 - Entry Date: 20 Feb 1814 - Discharged on 14 Apr 1814 to the flotilla (prisoner) - Prisoner of War at Halifax, prisoner number 7312, captured on 24 Aug 1814 near Washington, D.C. by British forces; received at Halifax on 30 Sep 1814 on HMS Surprize; discharged on 5 Mar 1815 and sent to Salem, Massachusetts on Cartel Lingan- Ordinary Seaman - Payroll 2 - Number: 956 - Entry Date: 17 Feb 1814 - Discharged on 24 Aug 1814

Newton, Samuel (or Vinton) - Seaman - Payroll 1 - Number: 464 - Payroll ended on 6 Apr 1814 - Payroll 2 - Number: 464 - Entry Date: 6 Feb 1814 - Died on 4 Jan 1815

Nicholas, John - Seaman - Payroll 1 - Number: 196 - Entry Date: 5 Jan 1814 - Payroll ended on 6 Apr 1814 - Payroll 2 - Number: 196 - Entry Date: 5 Jan 1814 - Discharged on 5 Jan 1815

Nichols, John (1) - Ordinary Seaman - Payroll 2 - Number: 946 - Entry Date: 23 Dec 1813 - Discharged on 6 Dec 1814 to U.S. Sloop-of-War Ontario - Transfers - Number: 32 - Entry Date: 18 Apr 1814 - Discharged on 6 Dec 1814 - U.S. Sloop-of-War Ontario - Number: 206 - Entry Date: 7 Dec 1814 - Discharged on 5 Mar 1815 from the flotilla - U.S. Sloop-of-War Ontario - Number: 66 - Entry Date: 14 Jan 1814 - Discharged on 17 Apr 1814 to the flotilla - Muster - Number: 946 - Entry Date: 23 Dec 1813 - Discharged on 6 Dec 1814 to U.S. Sloop-of-War Ontario

Nichols, John (2) - Seaman - Payroll 2 - Number: 797 - Entry Date: 1 Aug 1814 - Ran on 6 Dec 1814

Nicholson, Benjamin - Cook - Wounded at St. Leonard's Creek and at Bladensburg - Pension: Navy IF-707

Nicholson, Isaac - Cook - Payroll 1 - Number: 139 - Entry Date: 28 Sep 1813 - Payroll ended on 6 Apr 1814 - Pension: Navy IF-1131 - Payroll 2 - Number: 139 - Entry Date: 28 Sep 1813 - Discharged on 28 Sep 1814

Nicholson, James - Sailing Master - Payroll 1 - Number: 3 - Entry Date: 6 Sep 1813 - Payroll ended on 6 Apr 1814 - Payroll 2 - Number: 3 - Entry Date: 6 Sep 1813 - Discharged on 15 Apr 1815 - Warranted as a sailing master on 31 Aug 1813 - Muster - Number: 3 - Entry Date: 6 Sep 1813 - Discharged on Muster ended on 6 Apr 1814

Nicholson, Jesse - Seaman - U.S. Sloop-of-War Ontario - Number: 86 - Entry Date: 18 Jan 1814 - Discharged on 13 Apr 1814 to the flotilla - Transfers - Number: 8 - Entry Date: 14 Apr 1814 - Discharged on 6 Dec 1814 - U.S. Frigate United States - Number: 916 - Entry Date: 7 Apr 1814 - Discharged on 6 Dec 1814 to U.S. Sloop-of-War Ontario - U.S. Sloop-of-War Ontario - Number: 216 - Entry Date: 7 Dec 1814 - Discharged on 5 Mar 1815 from the flotilla - Payroll 2 - Number: 916 - Entry Date: 7 Jun 1814 - Discharged on 6 Dec 1814 to U.S. Sloop-of-War Ontario

Nisbet, George - Seaman - U.S. Gunboat 137 - Number: 8 - Entry Date: 28 Jul 1813 - Payroll ended on 4 Mar 1814 - Payroll 2 - Number: 440 - Entry Date: 28 Jul 1812 - Discharged on 17 Aug 1814

Nixon, John - Seaman - Payroll 2 - Number: 687 - Entry Date: 7 May 1814 - Died on 7 Oct 1814

Noble, John - Boy - Payroll 2 - Number: 706 - Entry Date: 1 Jun 1814 - Ran on 10 Dec 1814

Norman, William - Seaman - U.S. Sloop-of-War Ontario - Number: 155 - Entry Date: 16 Mar 1814 - Discharged on 5 Apr 1814 to the flotilla - Transfers - Number: 51 - Entry Date: 6 Apr 1814 - Discharged on 6 Dec 1814 - U.S. Frigate United States - Number: 563 - Entry Date: 7 Apr 1814 - Discharged on 6 Dec 1814 to U.S. Sloop-of-War Ontario - U.S. Sloop-of-War Ontario - Number: 239 - Entry Date: 7 Dec 1814 - Discharged on 5 Mar 1815 from the flotilla - Payroll 2 - Number: 563 - Entry Date: 15 May 1813 - Discharged on 6 Dec 1814 to U.S. Sloop-of-War Ontario

Nouvell, Peter - Seaman - Payroll 2 - Number: 774 - Entry Date: 15 Jun 1814 - Discharged on 1 Apr 1815

Oldham, Thomas (1) - Seaman - U.S. Frigate Adams Muster - Number: 133 - Entry Date: 6 Feb 1813 - Discharged on 10 Nov 1813 to U.S. Schooner Asp - U.S. Sloop Asp - Number: 4 - Entry Date: 11 Nov 1813 - Discharged on 20 Apr 1814 - U.S. Frigate United States - Number: 721 - Entry Date: 11 Apr 1814 - Discharged on 12 Jul 1814 to U.S. Schooner Asp - Seaman - Payroll 2 - Number: 721 - Entry Date: 4 Jul 1812 - Discharged on 12 Jul 1814

Oldham, Thomas (2) - Seaman - U.S. Frigate United States - Number: 824 - Entry Date: 2 Aug 1814 - Ran on 24 Aug 1814 - Payroll 2 - Number: 824 - Entry Date: 29 Jul 1814 - Ran on 24 Aug 1814

Oliver, Edward - Seaman - Payroll 1 - Number: 70 - Entry Date: 11 Nov 1813 - Discharged on 7 Dec 1813 - Payroll 1a - Number: 70 - Entry Date: 11 Nov 1813 - Discharged on 7 Dec 1813 - Payroll 2 - Number: 70 - Entry Date: 11 Nov 1813

Onion, Stephen B. - Master's Mate - Payroll 1 - Number: 231 - Entry Date: 12 Feb 1814 - Payroll ended on 6 Apr 1814 - Payroll 2 - Number: 231 - Entry Date: 12 Feb 1814 - Discharged on 21 May 1814

Oram, John (1) - Master's Mate - Muster - Number: 303 - Entry Date: 6 Jun 1814 - Discharged on 1 Apr 1815 - BLW 29797-160-55 - Pension: WO-374, WC-855 - Payroll 2 - Number: 303 - Entry Date: 6 Jun 1814 - Discharged on 1 Apr 1815

Oram, John (2) - Midshipman - Payroll 1 - Number: 994 - Entry Date: 16 Mar 1814 - Payroll ended on 6 Apr 1814 - Payroll 2 - Number: 994 - Entry Date: 16 Mar 1814 - Discharged on 5 Mar 1814

Organ, Henry - Ordinary Seaman - Payroll 1 - Number: 114 - Entry Date: 12 Nov 1813 - Payroll ended on 6 Apr 1814 - Payroll 2 - Number: 114 - Entry Date: 12 Nov 1813 - Discharged on 12 Nov 1814

Ormsby, Robert - Purser - Muster - Number: 11 - Payroll 1 - Number: 11 - Discharged on 6 Apr 1815 - Warranted as a purser on 25 Apr 1812; furloughed in 1816 - Purser - Payroll 2 - Number: 11

Orr, John - Ordinary Seaman - U.S. Sloop-of-War Ontario - Number: 158 - Entry Date: 16 Mar 1814 - Discharged on 5 Apr 1814 to the flotilla - Transfers - Number: 44 - Entry Date: 6 Apr 1814 - Discharged on 6 Dec 1814 - U.S. Sloop-of-War Ontario - Number: 241 - Entry Date: 7 Dec 1814 - Discharged on 5 Mar 1815 from the flotilla - U.S. Frigate United States - Number: 487 - Entry Date: 7 Apr 1814 - Discharged on 6 Dec 1814 to U.S. Sloop-of-War Ontario - Payroll 2 - Number: 487 - Entry Date: 15 Mar 1814 - Discharged on 6 Dec 1814 to U.S. Sloop-of-War Ontario

Osborne, Elisha - Marine Private - Washington Naval Hospital - Number: 36 - Wounded at Bladensburg, admitted on 3 Sep 1814, discharged on 31 Dec 1814 - Pension: Navy IF-1154

Osgood, Abram - Landsman - Payroll 1 - Number: 120 - Entry Date: 29 Sep 1813 - Payroll ended on 6 Apr 1814 - Payroll 2 - Number: 120 - Entry Date: 29 Sep 1813 - Discharged on 1 Apr 1815

Overholtz, Samuel - Ordinary Seaman - Payroll 2 - Number: 750 - Entry Date: 13 Apr 1814 - Discharged on 1 Apr 1815

Owens, Peter - Seaman - Payroll 1 - Number: 325 - Entry Date: 24 Mar 1814 - Payroll ended on 6 Apr 1814 - Payroll 2 - Number: 325 - Entry Date: 24 Mar 1814 - Ran on 28 Dec 1814

Page, Robert - Ordinary Seaman - U.S. Frigate Adams Muster - Number: 283 - Entry Date: 23 Mar 1813 - Discharged on 10 Nov 1813 to U.S. Schooner Asp - BLW 5121-160-55 - U.S. Schooner Shark - Number: 17 - Entry Date: 11 Nov 1813 - Discharged on 29 Mar 1814 - U.S. Frigate United States - Number: 507 - Entry Date: 7 Apr 1814 - Discharged on 3 Feb 1815 to U.S. Galley Shark - Payroll 2 - Number: 507 - Entry Date: 3 Feb 1813 - Discharged on 3 Feb 1815 - BLW 5121-160-55

Palmer, Henry - Landsman - Payroll 2 - Number: 775 - Entry Date: 11 Jul 1814 - Ran on 11 Nov 1814

Palmer, Tristram S. - Ordinary Seaman - Payroll 1 - Number: 206 - Entry Date: 13 Jan 1814 - Payroll ended on 6 Apr 1814 - Payroll 2 - Number: 206 - Entry Date: 13 Jan 1814 - Discharged on 13 Jan 1815

Parish, Nicholas - Ordinary Seaman - Payroll 2 - Number: 408 - Entry Date: 6 Apr 1814 - Discharged on 1 Apr 1815 - Payroll 2 - Number: 450

Parker, Peter - Seaman - Payroll 2 - Number: 834 - Entry Date: 9 Aug 1814 - Ran on 30 Nov 1814

Parker, Samuel (alias Henry Parker) - Seaman - U.S. Frigate United States - Number: 899 - Entry Date: 19 Aug 1814 - Discharged on 6 Dec 1814 to U.S. Sloop-of-War Ontario, taken in Patuxent (Prisoner) - Seaman - Transfers - Number: 52 - Discharged on 6 Dec 1814 - Boy - U.S. Sloop-of-War Ontario - Number: 236 - Entry Date: 7 Dec 1814 - Discharged on 5 Mar 1815 from the flotilla (prisoner) - Seaman - Payroll 2 - Number: 899 - Discharged on 6 Dec 1814 to U.S. Sloop-of-War Ontario

Pasco, John - Seaman - Payroll 1 - Number: 335 - Entry Date: 28 Mar 1814 - Payroll ended on 6 Apr 1814 - Payroll 2 - Number: 335 - Entry Date: 28 Mar 1814 - Discharged on 1 Apr 1815

Patterson, Cato - Cook - Payroll 1 - Number: 101 - Entry Date: 20 Oct 1813 - Payroll ended on 6 Apr 1814 - Ordinary Seaman - Payroll 2 - Number: 833 - Entry Date: 8 Aug 1814 - Ran on 24 Mar 1815 - Pension: Navy IF-1164

Patterson, Cato - Cook - Payroll 2 - Number: 101 - Entry Date: 20 Oct 1813 - Discharged on 10 Oct 1814

Patterson, Harm - Seaman - Payroll 1 - Number: 349 - Entry Date: 2 Apr 1814 - Payroll ended on 6 Apr 1814 - Payroll 2 - Number: 349 - Entry Date: 2 Apr 1814 - Discharged on 1 Apr 1815

Paulding, George - Ordinary Seaman - Payroll 2 - Number: 831 - Entry Date: 10 Aug 1814 - Ran on 22 Oct 1814

Peabeck, Richard - Ordinary Seaman - Payroll 2 - Number: 728 - Entry Date: 14 Apr 1814 - Discharged on 1 Apr 1815

Peace, John W. - Sailing Master - Payroll 2 - Number: 893 - Entry Date: 20 Nov 1814 - Discharged on 1 Apr 1815

Peach, William - Ordinary Seaman - U.S. Sloop-of-War Ontario - Number: 57 - Entry Date: 14 Jan 1814 - Discharged on 14 Apr 1814 to the flotilla

Peak, John (1) - Volunteer Pilot - Washington Naval Hospital - Number: 20 - Wounded at Bladensburg, admitted on 24 Aug 1814, discharged on 28 Aug 1814

Peak, John (2) - Master's Mate - Payroll 2 - Number: 404 - Entry Date: 26 Aug 1812 - Discharged on 9 Sep 1814 - BLW 1606-160-55

Peak, Samuel - Master's Mate - Muster - Number: 945 - Entry Date: 13 Jul 1814 - Discharged on 23 Dec 1814 - Payroll 2 - Number: 945 - Entry Date: 13 Jul 1814 - Discharged on 23 Dec 1814

Peck, John - Landsman - Payroll 2 - Number: 648 - Entry Date: 24 Mar 1814 - Discharged on 1 Apr 1815

Peck, Joseph - Ordinary Seaman - Payroll 2 - Number: 960 - Entry Date: 25 Jun 1814 - Discharged on 1 Apr 1815 - Muster - Number: 960 - Entry Date: 25 Aug 1814 - Discharged on 1 Apr 1815

Pembroke, James - Cook - Payroll 2 - Number: 686 - Entry Date: 23 May 1814 - Died on 29 May 1814

Pendegast, Robert - Ordinary Seaman - Payroll 1 - Number: 224 - Entry Date: 1 Feb 1814 - Payroll ended on 6 Apr 1814 - Payroll 2 - Number: 224 - Entry Date: 1 Feb 1814 - Died

Penn, John - Ordinary Seaman - Payroll 2 - Number: 630 - Entry Date: 19 May 1814 - Ran on 26 Oct 1814

Penn, William - Seaman - Payroll 2 - Number: 816 - Entry Date: 2 Sep 1814 - Ran on 19 Feb 1814

Pents, James - Ordinary Seaman - Payroll 1 - Number: 281 - Entry Date: 8 Mar 1814 - Payroll ended on 6 Apr 1814 - Payroll 2 - Number: 281 - Entry Date: 8 Mar 1814 - Discharged on 8 Mar 1815

Perkins, Benjamin - Midshipman - Payroll 1 - Number: 304 - Entry Date: 22 Mar 1814 - Payroll ended on 6 Apr 1814 - Payroll 2 - Number: 304 - Entry Date: 22 Mar 1814 - Discharged on 22 Mar 1815

Perry, Hugh - Ordinary Seaman - Muster - Number: 967 - Entry Date: 1 Feb 1814 - Discharged on 1 Apr 1815h - Landsman - Payroll 2 - Number: 967 - Entry Date: 1 Feb 1814 - Discharged on 1 Apr 1815

Peterkin, William - Sailing Master - Payroll 1 - Number: 288 - Entry Date: 1 Mar 1814 - Payroll ended on 6 Apr 1814 - Payroll 2 - Number: 288 - Entry Date: 1 Mar 1814 - Discharged on 6 Jul 1814 - Warranted as a sailing master on 1 Mar 1814; resigned on 2 Jul 1814

Peters, John (1) - Quartermaster - U.S. Sloop-of-War Ontario - Number: 85 - Entry Date: 18 Jan 1814 - Discharged on 14 Apr 1814 to the flotilla - Transfers - Number: 30 - Entry Date: 15 Apr 1814 - Discharged on 6 Dec 1814 - U.S. Sloop-of-War Ontario - Number: 215 - Entry Date: 7 Dec 1814 - Discharged on 5 Mar 1815 from the flotilla - U.S. Frigate United States - Number: 535 - Entry Date: 7 Apr 1814 - Discharged on 6 Dec 1814 to U.S. Sloop-of-War Ontario - Payroll 2 - Number: 535 - Entry Date: 7 Jan 1814 - Discharged on 6 Dec 1814 to U.S. Sloop-of-War Ontario

Peters, John (2) - Seaman - U.S. Frigate United States - Number: 587 - Entry Date: 7 Apr 1814 - Discharged on 19 Sep 1814 to U.S. Gunboat 138 - U.S. Gunboat 138 - Number: 42 - Paid on 6 Apr 1814 - Payroll 2 - Number: 587 - Entry Date: 4 Jan 1814 - Discharged on 1 Sep 1814

Peters, John (3) - Ordinary Seaman - Payroll 2 - Number: 612 - Entry Date: 16 May 1814 - Discharged on 1 Apr 1815

Peters, Samuel - Ordinary Seaman - Payroll 1 - Number: 234 - Entry Date: 17 Feb 1814 - Payroll ended on 6 Apr 1814 - Payroll 2 - Number: 234 - Entry Date: 17 Feb 1814 - Discharged on 17 Feb 1815

Peterson, Daniel - Ordinary Seaman - Payroll 1 - Number: 149 - Entry Date: 22 Nov 1813 - Payroll ended on 6 Apr 1814 - Payroll 2 - Number: 149 - Entry Date: 22 Nov 1813 - Discharged on 22 Nov 1814

Peterson, Joseph - Ordinary Seaman - U.S. Sloop-of-War Ontario - Number: 123 - Entry Date: 13 Feb 1814 - Discharged on 14 Apr 1814 to the flotilla - Transfers - Number: 1 - Entry Date: 15 Apr 1814 - Discharged on 12 Dec 1814 - U.S. Frigate United States - Number: 634 - Entry Date: 7 Apr 1814 - Discharged on 12 Dec 1814 to U.S. Sloop-of-War Ontario - U.S. Sloop-of-War Ontario - Number: 243 - Entry Date: 7 Dec 1814 - Discharged on 5 Mar 1815 from the flotilla - Payroll 2 - Number: 634 - Entry Date: 12 Feb 1814 - Discharged on 12 Dec 1814 to U.S. Sloop-of-War Ontario

Peterson, Samuel - Seaman - Payroll 2 - Number: 716 - Entry Date: 6 Jun 1814 - Discharged on 1 Apr 1815

Phelan, John V. - Seaman - Payroll 1 - Number: 59 - Entry Date: 30 Sep 1813 - Discharged on 30 Dec 1813 - Payroll 1a - Number: 59 - Entry Date: 30 Sep 1813 - Discharged on 30 Dec 1813 - Payroll 2 - Number: 59 - Entry Date: 30 Sep 1813

Phillips, Jacob - Ordinary Seaman - U.S. Sloop-of-War Ontario - Number: 143 - Entry Date: 18 Mar 1814 - Discharged on 13 Apr 1814 to the flotilla (ran) - U.S. Frigate United States - Number: 892 - Entry Date: 7 Apr 1814 - Ran on 31 Oct 1814 to U.S. Sloop-of-War Ontario - Payroll 2 - Number: 892 - Entry Date: 1 Apr 1814 - Ran on 31 Oct 1814

Phillips, Jeremiah - Landsman - Payroll 2 - Number: 389 - Entry Date: 14 Apr 1814 - Discharged on 1 Apr 1815

Phillips, Noah - Ordinary Seaman - Payroll 1 - Number: 336 - Entry Date: 29 Mar 1814 - Payroll ended on 6 Apr 1814 - Payroll 2 - Number: 336 - Entry Date: 29 Mar 1814 - Ran on 24 Aug 1814

Pierce, Thomas - Ordinary Seaman - Payroll 1 - Number: 164 - Entry Date: 19 Nov 1813 - Payroll ended on 6 Apr 1814 - Payroll 2 - Number: 164 - Entry Date: 19 Nov 1813 - Discharged on 19 Nov 1814

Piles, John - Ordinary Seaman - Payroll 1 - Number: 104 - Entry Date: 25 Oct 1813 - Payroll ended on 6 Apr 1814 - Payroll 2 - Number: 104 - Entry Date: 25 Oct 1813 - Discharged on 26 Sep 1814

Pincel, Stephen W. - Master's Mate - Payroll 2 - Number: 369 - Entry Date: 21 Mar 1814 - Discharged on 1 Apr 1815

Pintz, Joseph - Seaman - Payroll 2 - Number: 749 - Entry Date: 22 Apr 1814 - Discharged on 30 Apr 1814

Plaster, Stephen - Seaman - Payroll 1 - Number: 150 - Entry Date: 22 Nov 1813 - Payroll ended on 6 Apr 1814 - Payroll 2 - Number: 150 - Entry Date: 22 Nov 1813 - Discharged on 22 Nov 1814 - BLW 21757-160-55

Pluck, Michael - Seaman - Payroll 1 - Number: 53 - Entry Date: 27 Sep 1813 - Payroll ended on 6 Apr 1814 - Payroll 1a - Number: 53 - Entry Date: 27 Sep 1813 - Payroll 2 - Number: 53 - Entry Date: 27 Sep 1813 - Discharged on 27 Sep 1814

Plumb, Peter - Seaman - Payroll 2 - Number: 360 - Entry Date: 3 Apr 1814 - Discharged on 1 Apr 1815 - BLW 15308-163-55

Plummer, James - Ordinary Seaman - Payroll 2 - Number: 361 - Entry Date: 3 Apr 1814 - Discharged on 1 Apr 1815 - Pension: SO-9303, SC-6080

Polk, William W. - Sailing Master - Payroll 2 - Number: 970 - Entry Date: 24 Jul 1814 - Discharged on 2 Dec 1814 - Warranted as a sailing master on 18 Jul 1814; resigned on 27 Jul 1825 - BLW 51229-160-55 - Muster - Number: 970 - Entry Date: 24 Jul 1814 - Discharged on 2 Dec 1814

Porter, Philemon - Seaman - Payroll 2 - Number: 362 - Entry Date: 3 Apr 1814 - Discharged on 1 Apr 1815

Porter, Robert L. - Gunner - Payroll 1 - Number: 266 - Payroll ended on 6 Apr 1814 - Payroll 2 - Number: 266 - Entry Date: 1 Mar 1814 - Discharged on 27 Jan 1815 - BLW 5115-160-55

Porter, William - Seaman - Payroll 2 - Number: 488 - Entry Date: 19 Apr 1814 - Discharged on 1 Apr 1815

Potales, Anthony - Steward - Payroll 1 - Number: 90 - Entry Date: 12 Oct 1813 - Payroll ended on 6 Apr 1814 - Payroll 2 - Number: 90 - Entry Date: 12 Oct 1813 - Discharged on 12 Oct 1814

Poulson, John - Seaman - U.S. Sloop-of-War Ontario - Number: 97 - Entry Date: 29 Jan 1814 - Discharged on 13 Apr 1814 to the flotilla - U.S. Frigate United States - Number: 914 - Entry Date: 7 Apr 1814 - Ran on 14 Nov 1814 to U.S. Sloop-of-War Ontario - U.S. Sloop-of-War Ontario - Number: 220 - Entry Date: 7 Dec 1814 - Discharged on 5 Mar 1815 from the flotilla - Payroll 2 - Number: 914 - Entry Date: 24 Jan 1814 - Ran on 14 Nov 1814

Powers, John - Seaman - Payroll 2 - Number: 704 - Entry Date: 2 Jun 1814 - Ran on 24 Dec 1814

Pradier, Martin - Seaman - Payroll 2 - Number: 532 - Entry Date: 9 May 1814 - Ran on 29 Nov 1814

Pritchard, Richard (1) - Seaman - Payroll 1 - Number: 226 - Entry Date: 2 Feb 1814 - Payroll ended on 6 Apr 1814 - Payroll 2 - Number: 226 - Entry Date: 2 Feb 1814 - Discharged on 7 May 1814

Pritchard, Richard (2) - Boatswain - Muster - Number: 986 - Entry Date: 8 May 1814 - Discharged on 2 Feb 1815 - Boatswain - Payroll 2 - Number: 986 - Entry Date: 8 May 1814 - Discharged on 2 Feb 1815

Pritchard, Thomas - Ordinary Seaman - U.S. Frigate Adams Payroll - Number: 33 - Entry Date: 29 Dec 1812 - Discharged on 10 Nov 1813 to U.S. Galley Shark - U.S. Sloop Scorpion - Number: 10 - Entry Date: 7 Dec 1812 - Payroll ended on 11 Feb 1814 - U.S. Frigate Adams Muster - Number: 33 - Entry Date: 29 Dec 1812 - Discharged on 10 Nov 1813 to U.S. Galley Shark - Payroll 2 - Number: 428 - Entry Date: 7 Dec 1812 - Discharged on 7 Dec 1814

Pulley, Edward - Ordinary Seaman - Payroll 1 - Number: 238 - Entry Date: 26 Feb 1814 - Payroll ended on 6 Apr 1814 - Payroll 2 - Number: 238 - Entry Date: 26 Feb 1814 - Discharged on 26 Feb 1815

Quigins, David - Ordinary Seaman - Payroll 2 - Number: 944 - Entry Date: 12 Jul 1814 - Discharged on 1 Apr 1815 - Muster - Number: 944 - Entry Date: 12 Jul 1814 - Discharged on 1 Apr 1815

Quinn, Edward - Seaman - Payroll 1 - Number: 194 - Entry Date: 3 Jan 1814 - Discharged on 16 Feb 1814 - Payroll 2 - Number: 194 - Entry Date: 3 Jan 1814 - Discharged on 16 Feb 1814

Ratcliff, Richard - Ordinary Seaman - Payroll 1 - Number: 195 - Entry Date: 3 Jan 1814 - Discharged on 27 Feb 1814 - Payroll 2 - Number: 195 - Entry Date: 3 Jan 1814 - Ran on 27 Feb 1814

Ratcliff, William - Boy - U.S. Frigate United States - Number: 570 - Entry Date: 20 Apr 1814 - Died on 12 Nov 1814 to U.S. Galley Shark - U.S. Schooner Shark - Number: 1 - Entry Date: 1 Jan 1813 - Discharged on 11 Feb 1814 - Payroll 2 - Number: 570 - Entry Date: 1 Jan 1813 - Died

Rattle, Robert - Ordinary Seaman - Payroll 2 - Number: 856 - Entry Date: 16 Aug 1814 - Ran on 26 Sep 1814

Ravenburgh, Lewis - Boatswain - U.S. Gunboat 138 - Number: 66 - Paid on 6 Apr 1814

Ray, David - Ordinary Seaman - U.S. Sloop-of-War Ontario - Number: 69 - Entry Date: 14 Jan 1814 - Discharged on 17 Apr 1814 to the flotilla (ran) - U.S. Frigate United States - Number: 663 - Entry Date: 7 Apr 1814 - Ran on 24 Aug 1814 - Payroll 2 - Number: 663 - Entry Date: 18 Apr 1814 - Ran on 24 Aug 1814

Ray, Robert - Steward - Payroll 2 - Number: 621 - Entry Date: 14 Apr 1814 - Discharged on 1 Apr 1815

Read, Nathaniel - Ordinary Seaman - U.S. Frigate Adams Payroll - Number: 197 - Entry Date: 15 Mar 1813 - Discharged on 10 Nov 1813 to U.S. Galley Shark - U.S. Sloop Scorpion - Number: 16 - Entry Date: 25 Jan 1813 - Payroll ended on 11 Feb 1814 - Payroll 2 - Number: 426 - Entry Date: 25 Jan 1813 - Discharged on 24 Jan 1815

Reading, William - Boatswain - Payroll 1 - Number: 33 - Entry Date: 3 Oct 1813 - Payroll ended on 6 Apr 1814 - Payroll 2 - Number: 33 - Entry Date: 3 Oct 1813 - Discharged on 30 Sep 1814 - Muster - Number: 33 - Entry Date: 30 Sep 1813 - Discharged on 20 Sep 1814

Reynolds, John - Ordinary Seaman - Payroll 2 - Number: 785 - Entry Date: 29 Jul 1814 - Ran on 3 Feb 1815

Ricard, Richard - Sailing Master - Payroll 2 - Number: 902 - Entry Date: 1 Aug 1814 - Discharged on 15 Apr 1815

Rice, Urban - Ordinary Seaman - U.S. Frigate Adams Payroll - Number: 161 - Entry Date: 22 Feb 1813 - Discharged on 10 Nov 1813 to U.S. Galley Shark - U.S. Gunboat 137 - Number: 3 - Entry Date: 19 Jan 1813 - Payroll ended on 4 Mar 1814 - Steward - Payroll 2 - Number: 985 - Entry Date: 1 Mar 1813 - Discharged on 27 Mar 1814 - Muster – Number 442 - Entry Date: 28 Mar 1814 - Discharged on 15 Feb 1815 - Payroll 2 - Number: 442 - Entry Date: 28 Mar 1814 - Discharged on 15 Feb 1815

Richardson, Benjamin - Marine First Lieutenant - U.S. Marine Corps – Commissioned as second lieutenant on 5 June 1813, promoted to first lieutenant on 18 June 1814, resigned on 1 October 1824.

Richardson, George - Seaman - U.S. Sloop-of-War Ontario - Number: 45 - Entry Date: 14 Jan 1814 - Discharged on 17 Apr 1814 to the flotilla - Transfers - Number: 46 - Entry Date: 18 Apr 1814 - Discharged on 6 Dec 1814 - U.S. Sloop-of-War Ontario - Number: 198 - Entry Date: 7 Dec 1814 - Discharged on 5 Mar 1815 from the flotilla - Payroll 2 - Number: 880 - Entry Date: 27 Nov 1813 - Discharged on 6 Dec 1814 to U.S. Sloop-of-War Ontario

Richardson, Richard - Seaman - U.S. Sloop-of-War Ontario - Number: 147 - Entry Date: 16 Mar 1814 - Discharged on 13 Apr 1814 to the flotilla - U.S. Sloop-of-War Ontario - Number: 235 - Entry Date: 7 Dec 1814 - Discharged on 5 Mar 1815 from the flotilla

Richerson, George - Seaman - U.S. Frigate United States - Number: 880 - Entry Date: 18 Apr 1814 - Discharged on 6 Dec 1814 to U.S. Sloop-of-War Ontario - Transfers - Number: 17 - Entry Date: 14 Apr 1814 - Discharged on 6 Dec 1814 - U.S. Frigate United States - Number: 465 - Entry Date: 7 Apr 1814 - Discharged on 6 Dec 1814 to U.S. Sloop-of-War Ontario - Payroll 2 - Number: 465 - Entry Date: 14 Apr 1814 - Discharged on 6 Dec 1814 to U.S. Sloop-of-War Ontario

Risk, John - Ordinary Seaman - Payroll 1 - Number: 318 - Entry Date: 22 Mar 1814 - Payroll ended on 6 Apr 1814 - Payroll 2 - Number: 318 - Entry Date: 22 Mar 1814 - Discharged on 24 Aug 1814

Roach, James - Seaman - U.S. Schooner Shark - Number: 19 - Entry Date: 11 Nov 1813 - Discharged on 29 Mar 1814 - U.S. Frigate Adams Payroll - Number: 125 - Entry Date: 5 Feb 1813 - Discharged on 10 Nov 1813 to U.S. Schooner Scorpion - U.S. Frigate United States - Number: 565 - Entry Date: 7 Apr 1814 - Discharged on 17 Aug 1814 to U.S. Galley Shark - Payroll 2 - Number: 565 - Entry Date: 14 Jul 1812 - Discharged on 17 Jan 1814

Roach, John - Seaman - Payroll 2 - Number: 642 - Entry Date: 18 May 1814 - Ran on 24 Aug 1814

Roads, Samuel (or Rhoads) - Seaman - U.S. Frigate United States - Number: 761 - Entry Date: 20 Apr 1814 - Ran on 21 Oct 1814 - U.S. Frigate United States - Number: 692 - Payroll 2 - Number: 761 - Entry Date: 17 May 1814 - Payroll 2 - Number: 692 - Entry Date: 17 May 1814 - Ran on 21 Oct 1814

Roberson, David - Landsman - Payroll 2 - Number: 742 - Entry Date: 19 May 1814 - Discharged on 1 Apr 1815

Roberts, Asa - Seaman - U.S. Frigate Adams Muster - Number: 254 - Entry Date: 17 Mar 1813 - Discharged on 10 Nov 1813 to U.S. Galley Shark - U.S. Sloop Scorpion - Number: 3 - Entry Date: 24 Feb 1813 - Payroll ended on 11 Feb 1814 - U.S. Frigate United States - Payroll 2 - Number: 597 - Entry Date: 24 Feb 1813 - Discharged on 24 Feb 1815

Roberts, Asabel - Boy - U.S. Frigate United States - Number: 877 - Entry Date: 14 Apr 1814 - Ran on 24 Aug 1814 to U.S. Sloop-of-War Ontario - U.S. Sloop-of-War Ontario - Number: 26 - Entry Date: 14 Jan 1814 - Discharged on 13 Apr 1814 to the flotilla (ran) - Payroll 2 - Number: 877 - Entry Date: 13 Nov 1813 - Ran on 24 Aug 1814

Roberts, Thomas - Seaman - Payroll 2 - Number: 377 - Entry Date: 10 Apr 1814 - Discharged on 1 Apr 1815

Robinson, Dorsey - Ordinary Seaman - Payroll 1 - Number: 155 - Entry Date: 27 Nov 1813 - Payroll ended on 6 Apr 1814 - Payroll 2 - Number: 155 - Entry Date: 27 Nov 1813 - Died on 2 Oct 1814

Robinson, John - Seaman - Payroll 2 - Number: 635 - Entry Date: 19 Feb 1814 - Discharged on 3 Jan 1815

Roderick, Peter - Boatswain - Muster - Number: 38 - Entry Date: 16 Oct 1813 - Discharged on 16 Oct 1814 - Payroll 1 - Number: 38 - Entry Date: 16 Oct 1813 - Payroll ended on 6 Apr 1814 - Payroll 2 - Number: 38 - Entry Date: 16 Oct 1813 - Discharged on 16 Oct 1814

Rodman, Solomon - Sailing Master - Muster - Number: 287 - Entry Date: 22 Jan 1814 - Discharged on 15 Apr 1815 - BLW 20774-160-55 - Payroll 2 - Number: 287 - Entry Date: 22 Jun 1814 - Master's Mate - Payroll 1 - 991 - Entry Date: 10 Mar 1814 - Payroll ended on 6 Apr 1814 - Payroll 2 - 991 - Entry Date: 10 Mar 1814 - Discharged on 21 Jun 1814

Rook, Hicks - Boy - Payroll 1 - Number: 314 - Entry Date: 19 Mar 1814 - Payroll ended on 6 Apr 1814 - Payroll 2 - Number: 314 - Entry Date: 19 Mar 1814 - Discharged on 19 Mar 1815

Rook, Hollinsworth - Seaman - Payroll 1 - Number: 204 - Entry Date: 12 Jan 1814 - Payroll ended on 6 Apr 1814 - Payroll 2 - Number: 204 - Entry Date: 12 Jan 1814 - Discharged on 16 Oct 1814

Rook, Joshua - Seaman - Payroll 1 - Number: 190 - Entry Date: 3 Jan 1814 - Payroll ended on 6 Apr 1814 - Payroll 2 - Number: 190 - Entry Date: 3 Jan 1814 - Discharged on 3 Jan 1815

Rosenburgh, Lewis - Boatswain - Payroll 2 - Number: 1003 - Entry Date: 7 Apr 1814 - Never appeared

Ross, William - Ordinary Seaman - Payroll 2 - Number: 381 - Entry Date: 16 Mar 1814 - Ran on 20 Jan 1815

Rossin, John - Master's Mate - Payroll 1 - Number: 23 - Entry Date: 18 Sep 1813 - Payroll ended on 6 Apr 1814 - Payroll 2 - Number: 23 - Entry Date: 18 Sep 1813 - Discharged on 6 Dec 1814 - Muster - Number: 23 - Entry Date: 18 Sep 1813 - Discharged on 16 Dec 1814

Roud, William (or Peach) - Ordinary Seaman - Payroll 2 - Number: 513 - Entry Date: 21 Dec 1812 - Died on 29 Sep 1814

Roulson, Gabriel - Ordinary Seaman - U.S. Frigate United States - Number: 660 - Entry Date: 15 Apr 1814 - Ran on 31 Oct 1814 - Taken on July 20th or 26th (Prisoner) - Payroll 2 - Number: 660 - Entry Date: 24 Nov 1813 - Ran on 31 Oct 1814

Rowlins, James - Ordinary Seaman - Payroll 1 - Number: 116 - Entry Date: 25 Oct 1813 - Payroll ended on 6 Apr 1814 - Payroll 2 - Number: 116 - Entry Date: 25 Oct 1813 - Discharged on 17 Oct 1814

Rusk, John - Ordinary Seaman - Payroll 2 - Number: 676 - Entry Date: 24 Mar 1814 - Discharged on 1 Apr 1815

Russell, Francis - Ordinary Seaman - U.S. Schooner Shark - Number: 13 - Entry Date: 1 Jan 1814 - Discharged on 29 Mar 1814 - U.S. Frigate United States - Number: 463 - Entry Date: 7 Apr 1814 - Discharged on 1 Apr 1815 to U.S. Gunboat 137 - Seaman - Payroll 2 - Number: 463 - Entry Date: 1 Jan 1814 - Discharged on 1 Apr 1815

Rutter, Edward - Midshipman - Muster - Number: 980 - Entry Date: 9 Jan 1815 - Discharged on 1 Apr 1815 - Payroll 2 - Number: 980 - Entry Date: 9 Jan 1815 - Discharged on 1 Apr 1815

Rutter, John - Midshipman - Payroll 2 - Number: 979 - Entry Date: 9 Jan 1815 - Discharged on 1 Apr 1815 - Muster - Number: 979 - Entry Date: 9 Jan 1815 - Discharged on 1 Apr 1815

Rutter, Josiah - Sailing Master - Payroll 1 - Number: 289 - Entry Date: 1 Mar 1814 - Payroll ended on 6 Apr 1814 - BLW 886-160-55 - Payroll 2 - Number: 289 - Entry Date: 1 Mar 1814 - Discharged on 15 Apr 1815 - Warranted as a sailing master on 1 Mar 1814

Rutter, Solomon (1) - Lieutenant - Muster - Number: 2 - Entry Date: 20 Sep 1813 - Muster ended on 6 Apr 1814 - Payroll 1 - Number: 2 - Entry Date: 20 Sep 1813 - Payroll ended on 6 Apr 1814 - Payroll 2 - Number: 2 - Entry Date: 20 Sep 1813 - Discharged on 1 Apr 1815

Rutter, Solomon (2) - Midshipman - Muster - Number: 26 - Entry Date: 28 Sep 1813 - Discharged on 5 Mar 1814 - Warranted as a midshipman on 26 Feb 1814; resigned on 1 Feb 1822 - Payroll 1 - Number: 26 - Entry Date: 28

Sep 1813 - Discharged on 5 Mar 1814 - Payroll 2 - Number: 26 - Entry Date: 28 Sep 1813 - Discharged on 5 Mar 1814

Rutter, Valentine - Master's Mate - Payroll 1 - Number: 29 - Entry Date: 29 Sep 1813 - Discharged on 9 Feb 1814 - Payroll 2 - Number: 29 - Entry Date: 29 Sep 1813 - Muster - Number: 29 - Entry Date: 29 Sep 1813 - Discharged on 9 Feb 1814

Sampson, Joseph - Seaman - U.S. Frigate United States - Number: 476 - Entry Date: 5 Mar 1814 - Discharged on 30 Jan 1815 to U.S. Gunboat 137

Sanders, Daniel - Landsman - Payroll 2 - Number: 545 - Entry Date: 11 Mar 1814 - Discharged on 1 Apr 1815

Sanford, John - Seaman - Payroll 1 - Number: 203 - Entry Date: 11 Jan 1814 - Discharged on 22 Jan 1814 - Payroll 2 - Number: 203 - Entry Date: 11 Jan 1814 - Ran of 22 Jan 1814

Santo, Emanuel - Seaman - Payroll 1 - Number: 72 - Entry Date: 5 Oct 1813 - Payroll ended on 6 Apr 1814 - Payroll 1a - Number: 72 - Entry Date: 5 Oct 1813 - Payroll 2 - Number: 72 - Entry Date: 5 Oct 1813 - Discharged on 14 Nov 1814

Saucer, Benjamin - Ordinary Seaman - Payroll 2 - Number: 777 - Entry Date: 12 Jul 1814 - Ran on 3 Dec 1814

Saucer, John - Ordinary Seaman - Muster - Number: 961 - Entry Date: 25 Aug 1814 - Discharged on 1 Apr 1815 - Payroll 2 - Number: 961 - Entry Date: 25 Jun 1814 - Discharged on 1 Apr 1815

Saul, Emanuel - Volunteer Seaman - Washington Naval Hospital - Number: 12 - Wounded at Bladensburg, admitted on 24 Aug 1814, discharged on 29 Sep 1814

Sawyer, Robert - Ordinary Seaman - Payroll 1 - Number: 107 - Entry Date: 15 Oct 1813 - Payroll ended on 6 Apr 1814 - Payroll 2 - Number: 107 - Entry Date: 15 Oct 1813 - Discharged on 27 Aug 1814

Scarlett, James - Seaman - Payroll 1 - Number: 55 - Entry Date: 30 Sep 1813 - Payroll ended on 6 Apr 1814 - Payroll 1a - Number: 55 - Entry Date: 30 Sep 1813 - Discharged on 30 Sep 1814 - Payroll 2 - Number: 55 - Entry Date: 30 Sep 1813 - Discharged on 30 Sep 1814

Schweickardt, George - Steward - U.S. Frigate United States - Number: 588 – Transferred on 23 Aug 1814 to U.S. Gunboat 138 - Ordinary Seaman - U.S. Gunboat 138 - Number: 7 - Paid on 6 Apr 1814 - Steward - Payroll 2 - Number: 588 - Entry Date: 10 Sep 1813 - Discharged on 23 Aug 1814

Scott, John - Seaman - Payroll 1 - Number: 268 - Entry Date: 7 Mar 1814 - Payroll ended on 6 Apr 1814 - Payroll 2 - Number: 268 - Entry Date: 7 Mar 1814 - Discharged on 7 Mar 1815

Seabolt, Adam - Seaman - Payroll 2 - Number: 722 - Entry Date: 5 Apr 1814 - Discharged on 1 Apr 1815

Sedley, Edward - Ordinary Seaman - U.S. Frigate United States - Number: 665 - Entry Date: 11 Apr 1814 - Ran on 24 Aug 1814 to U.S. Gunboat 137 - U.S. Gunboat 137 - Number: 14 - Entry Date: 18 May 1813 - Payroll ended on 4 Mar 1814 - Payroll 2 - Number: 665 - Entry Date: 5 Mar 1814 - Discharged on 24 Aug 1814 - Prisoner of War at Halifax, prisoner number 7323, captured on 22 Aug 1814 near Washington, D.C. by British forces; received at Halifax on 30 Sep 1814 on HMS Surprize; discharged on 5 Mar 1815 and sent to Salem, Massachusetts on Cartel Lingan

Sellers, James - Sailing Master - Payroll 1 - Number: 221 - Entry Date: 27 Jan 1814 - Payroll ended on 6 Apr 1814 - Payroll 2 - Number: 221 - Entry Date: 27 Jan 1814 - Discharged on 15 Apr 1815 - Warranted as a sailing master on 27 Jan 1814

Sevier, Alexander G. - Marine Captain - U.S. Marine Corps - Paymaster; commissioned as a 2nd lieutenant on 27 Apr 1810, promoted to 1st lieutenant on 17 Apr 1812; promoted to captain on 18 Jun 1814; brevet major in 1814; resigned on 3 April 1816; wounded at Bladensburg - Pension: Navy IF-1066

Seward, Daniel - Ordinary Seaman - Payroll 2 - Number: 444 - Entry Date: 2 Jan 1813 - Discharged on 6 Jan 1815

Shammeau, Samuel - Seaman - Payroll 2 - Number: 515 - Entry Date: 2 Mar 1814 - Discharged on 1 Apr 1815

Shaw, Ichabod - Cook - U.S. Frigate United States - Number: 567 - Entry Date: 7 Apr 1814 - Discharged on 30 Jan 1815 to U.S. Galley Shark - U.S. Schooner Shark - Number: 24 - Entry Date: 13 Jan 1814 - Discharged on 29 Mar 1814 - Payroll 2 - Number: 567 - Entry Date: 13 Jan 1813 - Discharged on 30 Jan 1815

Shellingham, Christopher - Ordinary Seaman - Payroll 2 - Number: 820 - Entry Date: 21 Jul 1814 - Discharged on 1 Apr 1815

Shepherd, James - Ordinary Seaman - U.S. Sloop-of-War Ontario - Number: 48 - Entry Date: 14 Jan 1814 - Discharged on 14 Apr 1814 to the flotilla - U.S. Sloop-of-War Ontario - Number: 151 - Entry Date: 16 Mar 1814 - Discharged on 5 Apr 1814 to the flotilla - U.S. Frigate United States - Number: 556 - Entry Date: 7 Apr 1814 - Discharged on 1 Apr 1815 to U.S. Sloop-of-War Ontario - Payroll 2 - Number: 556 - Entry Date: 15 Mar 1814 - Discharged on 1 Apr 1815

Shepherd, John - Ordinary Seaman - Muster - Number: 949 - Entry Date: 29 Nov 1813 - Ran on 24 Aug 1814 - BLW 5114-160-55 - Payroll 2 - Number: 949 - Entry Date: 29 Nov 1813 - Ran on 24 Aug 1814

Sherwood, Hugh - Master's Mate - Payroll 2 - Number: 741 - Entry Date: 19 May 1814 - Discharged on 1 Apr 1815 - BLW 2195-160-55 - Pension: WO-1614, WC-461

Shillingsbury, Isaac (or Schillingburgh) - Seaman - Payroll 1 - Number: 338 - Entry Date: 28 Mar 1814 - Payroll ended on 6 Apr 1814 - BLW 451-160-55- Seaman - Payroll 2 - Number: 338 - Entry Date: 28 Mar 1814 - Discharged on 1 Apr 1815

Shortill, Robert - Steward - Payroll 1 - Number: 93 - Entry Date: 9 Oct 1813 - Discharged on 26 Jan 1814 - Payroll 2 - Number: 93 - Entry Date: 9 Oct 1813

Simmons, James R. - Ordinary Seaman - Payroll 2 - Number: 668 - Entry Date: 26 May 1814 - Discharged on 2 Nov 1814

Simpson, John - Ordinary Seaman - U.S. Frigate Adams Payroll - Number: 105 - Entry Date: 17 Jan 1813 - Discharged on 10 Nov 1813 to U.S. Galley Shark - U.S. Frigate United States - Number: 566 - Entry Date: 12 Feb 1814 - Discharged on 22 Dec 1814 to U.S. Battery Scorpion - U.S. Sloop Scorpion - Number: 4 - Entry Date: 22 Dec 1812 - Payroll ended on 11 Feb 1814 - Payroll 2 - Number: 566 - Entry Date: 22 Dec 1812 - Discharged on 22 Dec 1814 - BLW 3404-160-55

Simpson, Joseph - Seaman - U.S. Gunboat 137 - Number: 1 - Entry Date: 26 Jan 1813 - Payroll ended on 4 Mar 1814 - U.S. Frigate Adams Payroll - Number: 221 - Entry Date: 16 Mar 1813 - Discharged on 10 Nov 1813 to U.S. Schooner Scorpion - Payroll 2 - Number: 476 - Entry Date: 26 Jan 1813 - Discharged on 30 Jan 1815

Sinclair, Haddaway - Seaman - Payroll 2 - Number: 384 - Entry Date: 26 Mar 1814 - Discharged on 1 Apr 1815

Sippit, Charles - Seaman - Payroll 1 - Number: 66 - Entry Date: 18 Oct 1813 - Payroll ended on 6 Apr 1814 - Payroll 1a - Number: 66 - Entry Date: 18 Oct 1813 - Discharged on 18 Oct 1814 - BLW 33345-160-55 - Payroll 2 - Number: 66 - Entry Date: 18 Oct 1813 - Discharged on 18 Oct 1814

Skinner, John S. - Purser - Payroll 2 - Number: 990 - Entry Date: 16 Apr 1814 - Muster - Number: 990 - Entry Date: 16 Apr 1814 - Warranted as a purser on 24 Mar 1814; resigned in 1815

Slater, James - Ordinary Seaman - Payroll 2 - Number: 843 - Entry Date: 2 Aug 1814 - Ran on 29 Nov 1814

Sloane, Samuel - Ordinary Seaman - Payroll 2 - Number: 679 - Entry Date: 28 Apr 1814 - Discharged on 14 Jan 1814

Small, John - Ordinary Seaman - Payroll 1 - Number: 270 - Entry Date: 7 Feb 1814 - Payroll ended on 6 Apr 1814 - Payroll 2 - Number: 270 - Entry Date: 7 Feb 1814 - Discharged on 1 Apr 1815

Smith, Charles (1) - Seaman - U.S. Frigate United States - Number: 493 - Entry Date: 7 Apr 1814 - Ran on 15 Nov 1814 to U.S. Sloop-of-War Ontario - Payroll 2 - Number: 493 - Entry Date: 22 Dec 1813 - Ran on 15 Nov 1814

Smith, Charles (2) - Landsman - Payroll 2 - Number: 577 - Entry Date: 4 May 1814 - Ran on 12 Nov 1814 - BLW 24636-160-55

Smith, George - Boy - Payroll 1 - Number: 217 - Entry Date: 26 Jan 1814 - Payroll ended on 6 Apr 1814 - Payroll 2 - Number: 217 - Entry Date: 26 Jan 1814 - Discharged on 26 Jan 1815

Smith, James - Seaman - Payroll 1 - Number: 348 - Entry Date: 2 Apr 1814 - Payroll ended on 6 Apr 1814 - Payroll 2 - Number: 348 - Entry Date: 2 Apr 1814 - Discharged on 1 Apr 1815 - BLW 15346-160-55 - Pension: SO-225, SC-428, WO-16511, WC-10902

Smith, John (1) - Seaman - Payroll 1 - Number: 242 - Entry Date: 24 Feb 1814 - Payroll ended on 6 Apr 1814 - Payroll 2 - Number: 242 - Entry Date: 24 Feb 1814 - Discharged on 25 Feb 1815

Smith, John (2) - Seaman - U.S. Frigate United States - Number: 549 - Entry Date: 7 Apr 1814 - Discharged on 20 Jan 1815 to U.S. Battery Scorpion - U.S. Sloop Scorpion - Number: 18 - Entry Date: 20 Jan 1813 - Payroll ended on 11 Feb 1814 - Payroll 2 - Number: 549 - Entry Date: 20 Jan 1813 - Discharged on 20 Jan 1815

Smith, John (3) - Seaman - U.S. Frigate United States - Number: 584 - Entry Date: 7 Apr 1814 - Ran on 21 Oct 1814 to U.S. Sloop-of-War Ontario - U.S. Sloop-of-War Ontario - Number: 116 - Entry Date: 8 Feb 1814 - Discharged on 13 Apr 1814 to the flotilla (ran) - Payroll 2 - Number: 584 - Entry Date: 14 Apr 1814 - Ran on 24 Oct 1814

Smith, John (4) - Seaman - U.S. Flotilla Service - BLW 57235-160-55 - Pension: SO-1643, SC-13989, WO-33044, WC-25030 - U.S. Frigate Adams Payroll - Number: 210 - Entry Date: 16 Mar 1813 - Discharged on 10 Nov 1813 to U.S. Gunboat 137

Smith, Joseph - Marine Private - Washington Naval Hospital - Number: 8 - Wounded at Bladensburg, admitted on 24 Aug 1814, discharged on 31 Dec 1814 - Pension: Navy IF-1398

Smith, Levin - Ordinary Seaman - Payroll 1 - Number: 276 - Entry Date: 7 Mar 1814 - Payroll ended on 6 Apr 1814 - Payroll 2 - Number: 276 - Entry Date: 7 Mar 1814 - Discharged on 7 Mar 1815 - BLW 61250-160-55

Smith, Thomas J. - Landsman - Payroll 2 - Number: 613 - Entry Date: 18 Apr 1814 - Discharged on 1 Apr 1815

Smith, William (1) - Seaman - Payroll 1 - Number: 60 - Entry Date: 30 Sep 1813 - Discharged on 29 Jan 1814 - Payroll 1a - Number: 60 - Entry Date: 30 Sep 1813 - Ran on 29 Jan 1814 - Payroll 2 - Number: 60 - Entry Date: 30 Sep 1813 - Ran on 29 Jan 1814

Smith, William (2) - Seaman - Payroll 1 - Number: 81 - Entry Date: 16 Nov 1813 - Discharged on 20 Feb 1814 - Payroll 2 - Number: 81 - Entry Date: 16 Nov 1813 - Discharged on 20 Feb 1814

Smith, William (3) - Landsman - Payroll 2 - Number: 614 - Entry Date: 23 Apr 1814 - Ran on 30 Nov 1814

Smith, William (4) - Seaman - U.S. Gunboat 138 - Number: 50 - Paid on 6 Apr 1814 - No such man

Smoot, John H. - Master's Mate - Payroll 2 - Number: 370 - Entry Date: 22 Feb 1814 - Discharged on 1 Apr 1815

Snoday, Thomas - Boy - U.S. Sloop-of-War Ontario - Number: 70 - Entry Date: 14 Jan 1814 - Discharged on 17 Apr 1814 to the flotilla - U.S. Frigate United States - Number: 666 - Entry Date: 7 Apr 1814 - Discharged on 6 Dec 1814 to U.S. Sloop-of-War Ontario - Transfers - Number: 34 - Entry Date: 18 Apr 1814 - Discharged on 6 Dec 1814 - U.S. Sloop-of-War Ontario - Number: 207 - Entry Date: 7 Dec 1814 - Discharged on 5 Mar 1815 from the flotilla - Payroll 2 - Number: 666 - Entry Date: 28 Dec 1813 - Discharged on 6 Dec 1814 to U.S. Sloop-of-War Ontario

Sodderstack, Frederick - Ordinary Seaman - U.S. Sloop-of-War Ontario - Number: 150 - Entry Date: 16 Mar 1814 - Discharged on 13 Apr 1814 to the flotilla - Ordinary Seaman - Transfers - Number: 10 - Entry Date: 14 Apr 1814 - Discharged on 6 Dec 1814 - Ordinary Seaman - U.S. Sloop-of-War Ontario - Number: 231 - Entry Date: 7 Dec 1814 - Discharged on 5 Mar 1815 from the flotilla - Ordinary Seaman - Payroll 2 - Number: 413 - Entry Date: 15 Mar 1814 - Discharged on 6 Dec 1814 to U.S. Sloop-of-War Ontario

Soller, James - Seaman - Payroll 2 - Number: 592 - Entry Date: 25 Mar 1814 - Ran on 25 Nov 1814

Sollers, Seabert - Ordinary Seaman - Payroll 2 - Number: 837 - Entry Date: 6 Aug 1814 - Ran on 13 Nov 1814

Somersfield, William - Ordinary Seaman - Payroll 2 - Number: 838 - Entry Date: 3 Aug 1814 - Discharged on 1 Apr 1815

Southerton, Samuel - Landsman - Payroll 2 - Number: 395 - Entry Date: 28 Mar 1814 - Discharged on 1 Apr 1815

Sparrow, Stephen - Ordinary Seaman - U.S. Sloop Asp - Number: 9 - Entry Date: 3 Feb 1814 - Discharged on 20 Apr 1814 - U.S. Frigate Adams Muster - Number: 372 - Entry Date: 6 Apr 1813 - Discharged on 10 Nov 1813 to U.S. Gunboat 137 - U.S. Frigate United States - Number: 683 - Entry Date: 21 Apr 1814 - Discharged on 3 Mar 1815 to U.S. Schooner Asp - Payroll 2 - Number: 683 - Entry Date: 3 Mar 1813 - Discharged on 3 Mar 1815

Spencer, James - Seaman - Payroll 1 - Number: 156 - Entry Date: 1 Dec 1813 - Payroll ended on 6 Apr 1814 -

Payroll 2 - Number: 156 - Entry Date: 1 Dec 1813 - Discharged on 1 Dec 1814

Stafford, John - Seaman - Payroll 1 - Number: 189 - Entry Date: 3 Jan 1814 - Payroll ended on 6 Apr 1814 - Payroll 2 - Number: 189 - Entry Date: 3 Jan 1814 - Discharged on 3 Jan 1815

Stallings, Levi - Ordinary Seaman - Payroll 1 - Number: 210 - Entry Date: 21 Jan 1814 - Payroll ended on 6 Apr 1814 - Payroll 2 - Number: 210 - Entry Date: 21 Jan 1814 - Discharged on 24 Jan 1815

Stanton, William - Seaman - U.S. Sloop-of-War Ontario - Number: 47 - Entry Date: 14 Jan 1814 - Discharged on 17 Apr 1814 to the flotilla - U.S. Frigate United States - Number: 475 - - Entry Date: 7 Apr 1814 - Discharged on 6 Dec 1814 to U.S. Sloop-of-War Ontario - Transfers - Number: 31 - Entry Date: 18 Apr 1814 - Discharged on 6 Dec 1814 - U.S. Sloop-of-War Ontario - Number: 199 - Entry Date: 7 Dec 1814 - Discharged on 19 Mar 1815 from the flotilla - Payroll 2 - Number: 475 - Entry Date: 27 Nov 1813 - Discharged on 6 Dec 1814 to U.S. Sloop-of-War Ontario

Steiger, John - Landsman - Payroll 2 - Number: 399 - Entry Date: 20 Apr 1814 - Discharged on 1 Apr 1815

Stephenson, Robert - Ordinary Seaman - U.S. Frigate United States - Number: 496 - Entry Date: 7 Apr 1814 - Discharged on 6 Dec 1814 to U.S. Sloop-of-War Ontario - U.S. Sloop-of-War Ontario - Number: 41 - Entry Date: 14 Jan 1814 - Discharged on 13 Apr 1814 to the flotilla - Transfers - Number: 5 - Entry Date: 14 Apr 1814 - Discharged on 6 Dec 1814 - U.S. Sloop-of-War Ontario - Number: 197 - Entry Date: 7 Dec 1814 - Discharged on 5 Mar 1815 from the flotilla - Ordinary Seaman - Payroll 2 - Number: 496 - Entry Date: 23 Nov 1814 - Discharged on 6 Dec 1814 to U.S. Sloop-of-War Ontario

Sterling, Zachariah - Ordinary Seaman - Payroll 2 - Number: 754 - Entry Date: 9 Jun 1814 - Discharged on 1 Apr 1815

Stevens, John - Cook - Payroll 2 - Number: 680 - Entry Date: 16 Mar 1814 - Discharged on 1 Apr 1815

Stevens, Timothy - Seaman - U.S. Frigate Adams Payroll - Number: 138 - Entry Date: 6 Feb 1813 - Discharged on 10 Nov 1813 to U.S. Schooner Scorpion - U.S. Frigate United States - Number: 622 - Entry Date: 12 Feb 1814 - Discharged on 21 Jul 1814 to U.S. Battery Scorpion - U.S. Sloop Scorpion - Number: 5 - Entry Date: 10 Jun 1812 - Payroll ended on 11 Feb 1814 - Payroll 2 - Number: 622 - Entry Date: 10 Jun 1812 - Discharged on 21 Jul 1814

Steward, Arthur - Seaman - Payroll 2 - Number: 568 - Entry Date: 9 May 1814 - Ran on 30 Sep 1814

Steward, John J. - Steward - Payroll 2 - Number: 609 - Entry Date: 10 Mar 1814 - Discharged on 28 Dec 1814

Stewart, Joseph - Gunner - Muster - Number: 47 - Entry Date: 30 Oct 1813 - Discharged on 30 Oct 1814 - BLW 27824-160-55 - Payroll 1 - Number: 47 - Entry Date: 30 Oct 1813 - Payroll ended on 6 Apr 1814 - Payroll 1a - Number: 47 - Entry Date: 30 Oct 1813 - Payroll 2 - Number: 47 - Entry Date: 30 Oct 1813 - Discharged on 30 Oct 1814

Still, William (1) - Quartermaster - U.S. Frigate Adams Payroll - Number: 45 - Entry Date: 29 Dec 1812 - Discharged on 10 Nov 1813 to U.S. Galley Shark

Still, William (2) - Master's Mate - Payroll 1 - Number: 298 - Entry Date: 12 Mar 1814 - Payroll ended on 6 Apr 1814 - Payroll 2 - Number: 298 - Entry Date: 12 Mar 1814 - Discharged on 12 May 1812

Stines, John (alias Stains) - Boatswain - Muster - Number: 978 - Entry Date: 27 Dec 1814 - Discharged on 1 Apr 1815 - BLW 53801-160-55 - Payroll 2 - Number: 978 - Entry Date: 27 Dec 1814 - Discharged on 1 Apr 1815

Stines, William - Seaman - Payroll 2 - Number: 873 - Entry Date: 16 Aug 1814 - Discharged on 1 Apr 1815

Stockard, Mathias - Boy - U.S. Sloop-of-War Ontario - Number: 54 - Entry Date: 14 Jan 1814 - Discharged on 14 Apr 1814 to the flotilla - Transfers - Number: 20 - Entry Date: 14 Apr 1814 - Discharged on 6 Dec 1814 - U.S. Frigate United States - Number: 643 - Entry Date: 7 Apr 1814 - Discharged on 6 Dec 1814 to U.S. Sloop-of-War Ontario - U.S. Sloop-of-War Ontario - Number: 203 - Entry Date: 7 Dec 1814 - Discharged on 19 Mar 1815 from the flotilla - Payroll 2 - Number: 643 - Entry Date: 10 Dec 1812 - Discharged on 6 Dec 1814 to U.S. Sloop-of-War Ontario

Stoker, Tristan - Ordinary Seaman - Payroll 2 - Number: 573 - Entry Date: 25 Mar 1814 - Discharged on 1 Apr 1815

Stokes, Andrew - Seaman - Payroll 2 - Number: 631 - Entry Date: 6 Mar 1814 - Discharged on 6 Mar 1815

Stokes, Ezekiel - Seaman - Payroll 1 - Number: 282 - Entry Date: 15 Mar 1814 - Payroll ended on 6 Apr 1814 - Payroll 2 - Number: 282 - Entry Date: 15 Mar 1814 - Discharged on 15 Mar 1814

Stokes, John - Seaman - Payroll 1 - Number: 151 - Entry Date: 17 Nov 1813 - Discharged on 27 Dec 1813 - Payroll 2 - Number: 151 - Entry Date: 17 Nov 1813 - Discharged on 24 Aug 1814 - Ran and returned on 1 Jan 1814

Stone, Wesley - Ordinary Seaman - Payroll 1 - Number: 176 - Entry Date: 9 Dec 1813 - Payroll ended on 6 Apr 1814 - Payroll 2 - Number: 176 - Entry Date: 9 Dec 1813 - Ran on 7 Jan 1814

Stover, Daniel H. - Steward - Payroll 2 - Number: 968 - Entry Date: 21 Nov 1814 - Discharged on 1 Apr 1815 - Midshipman - Muster - Number: 968 - Entry Date: 21 Nov 1814 - Discharged on 1 Apr 1815

Streamel, Christian - Landsman - Payroll 1 - Number: 446 - Entry Date: 27 Jan 1814 - Payroll ended on 6 Apr 1814 - Payroll 2 - Number: 446 - Entry Date: 27 Jan 1814 - Discharged on 28 Jan 1815 - Payroll 2 - Number: 220 - Entry Date: 27 Jan 1814 - Discharged on 28 Jan 1815

Street, William - Midshipman - Muster - Number: 28 - Entry Date: 9 Nov 1813 - Discharged on Muster ended on 6 Apr 1814 - Payroll 1 - Number: 28 - Entry Date: 9 Nov 1813 - Payroll ended on 6 Apr 1814 - Payroll 2 - Number: 28 - Entry Date: 9 Nov 1813 - Discharged on 1 Apr 1815

Stretch, William - Ordinary Seaman - Payroll 1 - Number: 178 - Entry Date: 9 Dec 1813 - Discharged on 27 Jan 1814 - Payroll 2 - Number: 178 - Entry Date: 9 Dec 1813 - Ran on 7 Jan 1814

Stuard, Siosos - U.S. Frigate United States - Number: 662 - Lazaretto (Baltimore) - Payroll 2 - Number: 662 - Discharged on Unknown

Sturges, William (1) - Seaman - U.S. Gunboat 138 - Number: 44 - Paid on 6 Apr 1814 - Payroll 1 - Number: 854 - Entry Date: 16 Nov 1813 - Payroll ended on 6 Apr 1814 - Payroll 2 - Number: 854 - Entry Date: 16 Nov 1813

Sturges, William (2) - Gunner - Payroll 2 - Number: 138 - Entry Date: 13 Sep 1813 - Discharged on 26 Sep 1814

Suter, Richard S. - Midshipman - Payroll 2 - Number: 929 - Entry Date: 6 Jul 1814 - Ran on 15 Dec 1814 - Muster - Number: 929 - Entry Date: 6 May 1814 - Ran on 15 Dec 1814 - Pension: Navy IF-1480

Sutton, William - Seaman - Payroll 1 - Number: 269 - Entry Date: 10 Mar 1814 - Discharged on 21 Mar 1814 - Payroll 2 - Number: 269 - Entry Date: 10 Mar 1814 - Ran of 22 Mar 1814

Swards, Daniel - Ordinary Seaman - U.S. Gunboat 137 - Number: 5 - Entry Date: 21 Jan 1813 - Payroll ended on 4 Mar 1814

Taff, Emanuel - Seaman - U.S. Sloop-of-War Ontario - Number: 98 - Entry Date: 29 Jan 1814 - Discharged on 13 Apr 1814 to the flotilla (ran) - U.S. Frigate United States - Number: 924 - Entry Date: 7 Apr 1814 - Ran on 26 Aug 1814 from Bladensburg - Payroll 2 - Number: 924 - Entry Date: 24 Jan 1814 - Discharged on 26 Aug 1814 - On U.S. Sloop-of-War Ontario

Talveris, Joseph - Seaman - Payroll 2 - Number: 76 - Entry Date: 20 Oct 1813 - Ran on 6 Nov 1813 - Payroll 1a - Number: 76 - Entry Date: 20 Oct 1813 - Ran on 9 Nov 1813 - Payroll 1 - Number: 76 - Entry Date: 20 Oct 1813 - Discharged on 1 Nov 1813

Tarbox, Haven - Seaman - U.S. Frigate Adams Muster - Number: 277 - Entry Date: 22 Mar 1813 - Discharged on 10 Nov 1813 to U.S. Gunboat 137 - U.S. Schooner Shark - Number: 6 - Entry Date: 11 Nov 1813 - Discharged on 29 Mar 1814 - U.S. Frigate United States - Number: 447 - Entry Date: 7 Apr 1814 - Discharged on 5 Feb 1815 to U.S. Galley Shark - Payroll 2 - Number: 447 - Entry Date: 5 Feb 1813 - Discharged on 5 Feb 1815

Tate, Thomas - Seaman - Payroll 2 - Number: 700 - Entry Date: 31 May 1814 - Discharged on 1 Apr 1815 - BLW 39924-160-55

Taylor Jr., James - Master's Mate - Payroll 1 - Number: 294 - Entry Date: 10 Mar 1814 - Payroll ended on 6 Apr 1814 - Payroll 2 - Number: 294 - Entry Date: 10 Mar 1814 - Discharged on 10 Aug 1814

Taylor, Henry - Boatswain - Payroll 1 - Number: 346 - Entry Date: 6 Apr 1814 - Payroll ended on 6 Apr 1814 - Payroll 2 - Number: 346 - Entry Date: 6 Apr 1814 - Discharged on 1 Apr 1815

Taylor, James (1) - Landsman - Payroll 2 - Number: 826 - Entry Date: 14 Jul 1814 - Discharged on 1 Apr 1815

Taylor, James (2) - Master's Mate - Payroll 1 - Number: 248 - Entry Date: 2 Mar 1814 - Payroll ended on 6 Apr 1814 - BLW 24644-160-55 - Payroll 2 - Number: 248 - Entry Date: 2 Mar 1814 - Discharged on 2 May 1814

Taylor, John - Seaman - Payroll 2 - Number: 650 - Entry Date: 12 May 1814 - Discharged on 1 Apr 1815

Taylor, Matthew - Steward - Payroll 1 - Number: 89 - Entry Date: 14 Sep 1813 - Payroll ended on 6 Apr 1814 - Payroll 2 - Number: 89 - Entry Date: 14 Sep 1813 - Discharged on 21 May 1814

Taylor, Purnel - Cook - Payroll 2 - Number: 379 - Entry Date: 2 Mar 1814 - Discharged on 1 Apr 1815

Taylor, Robert - Seaman - Muster - Number: 958 - Entry Date: 20 Aug 1814 - Discharged on 1 Apr 1815 - Payroll 2 - Number: 958 - Entry Date: 20 Aug 1814 - Discharged on 1 Apr 1815

Taylor, William - Ordinary Seaman - Payroll 1 - Number: 278 - Entry Date: 10 Mar 1814 - Payroll ended on 6 Apr 1814 - Payroll 2 - Number: 278 - Entry Date: 10 Mar 1814 - Discharged on 20 Jun 1814

Teshey, John - Seaman - Payroll 2 - Number: 73 - Entry Date: 13 Oct 1813 - Discharged on 13 Oct 1814 - Payroll 1a - Number: 73 - Entry Date: 13 Oct 1813 - Payroll 1 - Number: 73 - Entry Date: 13 Oct 1813 - Payroll ended on 6 Apr 1814

Thomas, Henry - Sailing Master - Payroll 2 - Number: 637 - Entry Date: 25 Jan 1814 - Discharged on 1 Feb 1815

Thomas, John - Gunner - Payroll 2 - Number: 746 - Entry Date: 13 Apr 1814 - Never appeared

Thomas, Joseph - Landsman - Payroll 1 - Number: 357 - Entry Date: 15 Nov 1813 - Payroll ended on 6 Apr 1814 - Payroll 2 - Number: 357 - Entry Date: 15 Nov 1813 - Never appeared

Thomas, Richard - Landsman - Payroll 2 - Number: 397 - Entry Date: 28 Mar 1814 - Discharged on 1 Apr 1815 - BLW 576-160-55

Thompkins, William - Ordinary Seaman - Payroll 1 - Number: 331 - Entry Date: 2 Apr 1814 - Payroll ended on 6 Apr 1814 - Payroll 2 - Number: 331 - Entry Date: 2 Apr 1814 - Discharged on 1 Apr 1815

Thompson, Alexander - Seaman - U.S. Sloop-of-War Ontario - Number: 31 - Entry Date: 14 Jan 1814 - Discharged on 13 Apr 1814 to the flotilla - Transfers - Number: 11 - Entry Date: 14 Apr 1814 - Discharged on 6 Dec 1814 - U.S. Sloop-of-War Ontario - Number: 193 - Entry Date: 7 Dec 1814 - Discharged on 5 Mar 1815 from the flotilla - Payroll 2 - Number: 416 - Entry Date: 16 Nov 1813 - Discharged on 6 Dec 1814 to U.S. Sloop-of-War Ontario

Thompson, Anthony C. - Surgeon's Mate - Payroll 2 - Number: 855 - Entry Date: 17 Jul 1814 - Discharged on 7 Sep 1814 - BLW 67782-160-55

Thompson, Barrett - Seaman - Payroll 2 - Number: 702 - Entry Date: 31 May 1814 - Ran on 12 Jan 1815

Thompson, Elisha - Ordinary Seaman - Payroll 1 - Number: 239 - Entry Date: 25 Feb 1814 - Payroll ended on 6 Apr 1814 - Payroll 2 - Number: 239 - Entry Date: 25 Feb 1814 - Ran on 9 Jul 1814

Thompson, James - Master's Mate - Payroll 1 - Number: 300 - Entry Date: 15 Mar 1814 - Payroll ended on 6 Apr 1814 - Payroll 2 - Number: 300 - Entry Date: 15 Mar 1814 - Discharged on 2 Jul 1814

Thompson, John (1) - Ordinary Seaman - U.S. Sloop-of-War Ontario - Number: 152 - Entry Date: 16 Mar 1814 - Discharged on 5 Apr 1814 to the flotilla - Transfers - Number: 39 - Entry Date: 6 Apr 1814 - Discharged on 6 Dec 1814 - U.S. Sloop-of-War Ontario - Number: 238 - Entry Date: 7 Dec 1814 - Discharged on 5 Mar 1815 from the flotilla - Payroll 2 - Number: 414 - Entry Date: 15 Mar 1814 - Discharged on 6 Dec 1814 to U.S. Sloop-of-War Ontario

Thompson, John (2) - Master's Mate - Payroll 2 - Number: 616 - Entry Date: 12 Mar 1814 - Discharged on 1 Apr 1815

Thrackera, George - Ordinary Seaman - U.S. Frigate United States - Number: 480 - - Entry Date: 7 Apr 1814 - Discharged on 1 Apr 1815 to U.S. Sloop-of-War Ontario - U.S. Sloop-of-War Ontario - Number: 480 - Entry Date: 14 Jan 1814 - Discharged on 13 Apr 1814 to the flotilla (prisoner) - Payroll 2 - Number: 480 - Entry Date: 27 Dec 1813 - Discharged on 24 Aug 1814 - Prisoner of War at Halifax, prisoner number 7321, captured on 24

Aug 1814 near Washington, D.C. by British forces; received at Halifax on 30 Sep 1814 on HMS Surprize; discharged on 5 Mar 1815 and sent to Salem, Massachusetts on Cartel Lingan

Tobin, Francis L. - Boy - Payroll 1 - Number: 135 - Entry Date: 15 Sep 1813 - Discharged on 15 Nov 1813 - Payroll 2 - Number: 135 - Entry Date: 15 Sep 1813 - Discharged on 15 Nov 1813

Tobin, John - Steward - Payroll 1 - Number: 92 - Entry Date: 15 Sep 1813 - Payroll ended on 6 Apr 1814 - Payroll 2 - Number: 92 - Entry Date: 15 Sep 1813 - Discharged on 24 May 1814

Tonlson, John - Seaman - Payroll 2 - Number: 420 - Entry Date: 2 May 1814 - Discharged on 1 Apr 1815

Tooly, Thomas - Seaman - U.S. Sloop-of-War Ontario - Number: 102 - Entry Date: 31 Jan 1814 - Discharged on 14 Apr 1814 to the flotilla - Transfers - Number: 29 - Entry Date: 15 Apr 1814 - Discharged on 6 Dec 1814 - U.S. Frigate United States - Number: 903 - Entry Date: 7 Apr 1814 - Discharged on 6 Dec 1814 to U.S. Sloop-of-War Ontario - U.S. Sloop-of-War Ontario - Number: 223 - Entry Date: 7 Dec 1814 - Discharged on 5 Mar 1815 from the flotilla - Payroll 2 - Number: 903 - Entry Date: 27 Jan 1814 - Discharged on 6 Dec 1814 to U.S. Sloop-of-War Ontario

Townsend, David - Ordinary Seaman - Payroll 2 - Number: 669 - Entry Date: Mar 1814 - Died on 1 Jul 1814

Townsend, Nathan - Master's Mate - Muster - Number: 364 - Entry Date: 24 May 1814 - Discharged on 1 Apr 1815 - Payroll 2 - 364 - Entry Date: 24 Aug 1814 - Discharged on 1 Apr 1815 - Payroll 2 - Number: 939 - Entry Date: 5 Feb 1814 - Discharged on 23 May 1814

Townsley, John - Seaman - Payroll 2 - Number: 849 - Entry Date: 20 Jul 1814 - Ran on 29 Nov 1814

Tracy, Alexander - Seaman - Payroll 2 - Number: 787 - Entry Date: 30 Jul 1814 - Discharged on 16 Mar 1815

Trenton, Anthony - Seaman - Payroll 2 - Number: 811 - Entry Date: 11 Jul 1814 - Discharged on 1 Apr 1815

Trust, James - Landsman - Payroll 2 - Number: 776 - Entry Date: 15 Jul 1814 - Discharged on 1 Apr 1815

Tucker, James - Seaman - U.S. Frigate Adams Muster - Number: 183 - Entry Date: 23 Feb 1813 - Discharged on 10 Nov 1813 to U.S. Gunboat 137 - U.S. Frigate United States - Number: 559 - Entry Date: 7 Apr 1814 - Discharged on 1 Apr 1815 to U.S. Galley Shark - U.S. Schooner Shark - Number: 18 - Entry Date: 11 Nov 1813 - Discharged on 29 Mar 1814 - Payroll 2 - Number: 559 - Entry Date: 17 Sep 1812 - Discharged on 1 Apr 1815 - Prisoner of War at Halifax, prisoner number 7325, captured on 22 Aug 1814 near Washington, D.C. by British forces; received at Halifax on 30 Sep 1814 on HMS Surprize; discharged on 18 Nov 1814 and sent to England on HMS Loire - Prisoner of War at Dartmoor, prisoner number 5501, captured on 22 Aug 1814 from the U.S. Flotilla Service, Gunboat Number 2 on the Chesapeake Bay by British forces; sent to Halifax on H.M. Transport Loire; received at Dartmoor on 17 Dec 1814; released on 29 Jun 1815 - Born: New Jersey - Age: 42

Tucker, John - Seaman - U.S. Sloop-of-War Ontario - Number: 30 - Entry Date: 14 Jan 1814 - Discharged on 13 Apr 1814 to the flotilla - Number: 4 - Entry Date: 14 Apr 1814 - Discharged on 6 Dec 1814 - U.S. Frigate United States - Number: 623 - Entry Date: 7 Apr 1814 - Discharged on 6 Dec 1814 to U.S. Sloop-of-War Ontario - U.S. Sloop-of-War Ontario - Number: 192 - Entry Date: 7 Dec 1814 - Discharged on 5 Mar 1815 from the flotilla - Payroll 2 - Number: 623 - Entry Date: 16 Nov 1813 - Discharged on 6 Dec 1814 to U.S. Sloop-of-War Ontario

Turner, Alexander - Seaman - Payroll 2 - Number: 363 - Entry Date: 11 Apr 1814 - Discharged on 1 Apr 1815

Turner, Jacob (1) - Seaman - Payroll 1 - Number: 202 - Entry Date: 9 Jan 1814 - Payroll ended on 6 Apr 1814 - Payroll 2 - Number: 202 - Entry Date: 9 Jan 1814 - Discharged on 9 Jan 1815

Turner, Jacob (2) - Gunner - Muster - Number: 993 - Entry Date: 12 Jan 1815 - Discharged on 1 Apr 1815 - Payroll 2 - Number: 993 - Entry Date: 12 Jan 1814 - Discharged on 1 Apr 1815

Turner, John - Seaman - Payroll 2 - Number: 478 - Entry Date: 6 Apr 1814 - Ran on 26 Dec 1814

Turner, Richard - Seaman - Payroll 2 - Number: 367 - Entry Date: 3 Apr 1814 - Discharged on 1 Apr 1815 - Payroll 2 - Number: 380 - Entry Date: 3 Mar 1814

Uhl, Andrew - Seaman - Payroll 2 - Number: 591 - Entry Date: 7 Apr 1814 - Ran on 24 May 1814 - BLW 45152-160-55

Underwood, John - Ordinary Seaman - U.S. Frigate Adams Payroll - Number: 282 - Entry Date: 22 Mar 1813 -

Discharged on 10 Nov 1813 to U.S. Galley Shark - Ordinary Seaman - U.S. Gunboat 137 - Number: 16 - Entry Date: 26 Jan 1813 - Payroll ended on 4 Mar 1814 - Wounded at Bladensburg - U.S. Frigate United States - Number: 462 - Entry Date: 7 Apr 1814 - Discharged on 24 Jan 1815 to U.S. Gunboat 137 - Payroll 2 - Number: 462 - Entry Date: 26 Jan 1813 - Discharged on 24 Jan 1815 - Washington Naval Hospital - Number: 18 - Contusion, admitted on 24 Aug 1814, discharged on 5 Sep 1814 - BLW 103447-160-55

Valiant, Thomas - Ordinary Seaman - U.S. Frigate United States - Number: 503 - Entry Date: 7 Apr 1814 - Discharged on 11 Oct 1814 to U.S. Gunboat 138 - U.S. Gunboat 138 - Number: 64 - Paid on 6 Apr 1814 - Payroll 2 - Number: 503 - Entry Date: 11 Oct 1813 - Discharged on 11 Oct 1814

Van Blake, Isaac - Gunner - Payroll 1 - Number: 43 - Entry Date: 28 Oct 1813 - Payroll ended on 6 Apr 1814 - Payroll 1a - Number: 43 - Entry Date: 28 Sep 1813 - Killed on 24 Aug 1814 at Bladensburg - Payroll 2 - Number: 43 - Entry Date: 28 Oct 1813 - Killed on 24 Aug 1814 at Bladensburg - Muster - Number: 43 - Entry Date: 28 Sep 1813 - Killed on 24 Aug 1814 at Bladensburg

Vaughn, William - Master's Mate - U.S. Frigate United States - Number: 526 - Entry Date: 7 Apr 1814 - Discharged on 8 Feb 1815 to U.S. Battery Scorpion - Midshipman - Payroll 2 - Number: 526 - Entry Date: 30 Mar 1814 - Discharged on 8 Feb 1815

Venoms, Gabriel - Boy - Payroll 1 - Number: 284 - Entry Date: 9 Mar 1814 - Payroll ended on 6 Apr 1814 - Payroll 2 - Number: 284 - Entry Date: 9 Mar 1814 - Discharged on 9 Mar 1815

Verby, James - Seaman - Payroll 2 - Number: 387 - Entry Date: 26 Mar 1814 - Discharged on 1 Apr 1815

Vermillion, James - Ordinary Seaman - U.S. Schooner Shark - Number: 11 - Entry Date: 31 Jan 1814 - Discharged on 29 Mar 1814 - Payroll 2 - Number: 441 - Entry Date: 7 Feb 1813 - Discharged on 13 Feb 1814

Vickers, John - Ordinary Seaman - Payroll 1 - Number: 261 - Payroll ended on 6 Apr 1814 - Payroll 2 - Number: 261 - Entry Date: 19 Feb 1814 - Discharged on 20 Feb 1815

Vickers, William O. - Ordinary Seaman - Payroll 1 - Number: 108 - Entry Date: 30 Oct 1813 - Payroll ended on 6 Apr 1814 - Payroll 2 - Number: 108 - Entry Date: 30 Oct 1813 - Discharged on 11 Nov 1814

Vinton, Samuel - Seaman - Payroll 2 - Number: 254 - Entry Date: 6 Mar 1814 - Died on 4 Jan 1815

Waddell, John - Seaman - Payroll 1 - Number: 245 - Entry Date: 24 Feb 1814 - Payroll ended on 6 Apr 1814 - Payroll 2 - Number: 245 - Entry Date: 24 Feb 1814 - Died on 2 Apr 1814

Waddell, William - Boy - Payroll 1 - Number: 307 - Entry Date: 5 Mar 1814 - Payroll ended on 6 Apr 1814 - Payroll 2 - Number: 307 - Entry Date: 5 Mar 1814 - Discharged on 5 Mar 1814

Walker, Alexis - Ordinary Seaman - Payroll 2 - Number: 867 - Discharged on 1 Apr 1815

Walker, John - Cook - Payroll 1 - Number: 98 - Entry Date: 25 Sep 1813 - Payroll ended on 6 Apr 1814 - Payroll 2 - Number: 98 - Entry Date: 25 Sep 1813 - Discharged on 26 Sep 1814

Walker, Robert - Master's Mate - Payroll 2 - Number: 789 - Entry Date: 15 Jul 1814 - Ran on 30 Dec 1814

Wall, Samuel - Boatswain - Payroll 2 - Number: 672 - Entry Date: 14 May 1814 - Ran on 7 Jan 1814

Walleader, Daniel - Seaman - Payroll 2 - Number: 796 - Entry Date: 16 Jul 1814 - Discharged on 1 Apr 1815

Walters, Jacob - Seaman - Payroll 2 - Number: 418 - Entry Date: 28 Apr 1814 - Ran on 18 Oct 1814

Ward, James - Ordinary Seaman - U.S. Frigate Adams Muster - Number: 49 - Entry Date: 29 Dec 1812 - Discharged on 10 Nov 1813 to U.S. Galley Shark - U.S. Frigate Adams Payroll - Number: 49 - Entry Date: 1 Jan 1813 - Discharged on 10 Nov 1813 to U.S. Galley Shark - U.S. Frigate United States - Number: 628 - Entry Date: 7 Apr 1814 - Ran on 21 Nov 1814 to U.S. Sloop-of-War Ontario - U.S. Sloop-of-War Ontario - Number: 126 - Entry Date: 23 Feb 1814 - Discharged on 13 Apr 1814 to the flotilla (ran) - Payroll 2 - Number: 628 - Entry Date: 14 Apr 1814 - Ran on 21 Nov 1814

Ware, Joseph - Ordinary Seaman - Payroll 1 - Number: 179 - Entry Date: 9 Dec 1813 - Payroll ended on 6 Apr 1814 - Payroll 2 - Number: 179 - Entry Date: 9 Dec 1813 - Discharged on 9 Dec 1814

Warner, John - Sailing Master - Muster - Number: 6 - Entry Date: 22 Sep 1813 - Killed on 24 Aug 1814 at

Bladensburg - Warranted as a sailing master on 15 Sep 1813 - Pension: Navy WF-1244 - Payroll 1 - Number: 6 - Entry Date: 22 Sep 1813 - Payroll ended on 6 Apr 1814 - Payroll 2 - Number: 6 - Entry Date: 22 Sep 1813 - Killed on 24 Aug 1814 at Bladensburg

Warren, William - Seaman - Payroll 1 - Number: 222 - Entry Date: 29 Jan 1814 - Payroll ended on 6 Apr 1814 - Payroll 2 - Number: 222 - Entry Date: 29 Jan 1814 - Discharged on 30 Jan 1815

Watson, William - Seaman - Payroll 1 - Number: 177 - Entry Date: 9 Dec 1813 - Payroll ended on 6 Apr 1814 - Payroll 2 - Number: 177 - Entry Date: 9 Dec 1813 - Discharged on 7 Dec 1814

Watts, Joseph - Ordinary Seaman - Payroll 1 - Number: 277 - Entry Date: 7 Mar 1814 - Payroll ended on 6 Apr 1814 - Payroll 2 - Number: 277 - Entry Date: 7 Mar 1814 - Discharged on 9 Mar 1814

Way, John - Ordinary Seaman - Payroll 2 - Number: 667 - Entry Date: 16 Sep 1813 - Ran 17 Dec 1814

Webb, Henry - Ordinary Seaman - Payroll 1 - Number: 280 - Entry Date: 9 Mar 1814 - Payroll ended on 6 Apr 1814 - Payroll 2 - Number: 280 - Entry Date: 9 Mar 1814 - Discharged on 5 Jun 1814

Webber, George - Seaman - Payroll 2 - Number: 313 - Entry Date: 18 Mar 1814 - Payroll 1 - Number: 454 - Entry Date: 18 Mar 1814 - Payroll ended on 6 Apr 1814 - Payroll 2 - Number: 454 - Entry Date: 18 Mar 1814 - Discharged on 1 Apr 1815

Webber, James - Ordinary Seaman - U.S. Gunboat 137 - Number: 10 - Entry Date: 9 Feb 1813 - Payroll ended on 4 Mar 1814 - U.S. Frigate Adams Muster - Number: 299 - Entry Date: 24 Mar 1813 - Discharged on 10 Nov 1813 to U.S. Galley Shark - U.S. Frigate United States - Number: 656 - Entry Date: 5 Mar 1814 - Discharged on 7 Feb 1815 to U.S. Gunboat 137 - Payroll 2 - Number: 656 - Entry Date: 9 Feb 1813 - Discharged on 7 Feb 1815

Webber, John A. - Master's Mate - Payroll 1 - Number: 299 - Entry Date: 1 Mar 1814 - Payroll ended on 6 Apr 1814 - Payroll 2 - Number: 299 - Entry Date: 1 Mar 1814 - Discharged on 15 Apr 1815

Webster, Isaac - Landsman - Payroll 1 - Number: 182 - Entry Date: 16 Dec 1813 - Discharged on 29 Jan 1814 - Payroll 2 - Number: 182 - Entry Date: 16 Dec 1813 - Discharged on 29 Jan 1814

Weeds, Ebenestus - Seaman - U.S. Gunboat 138 - Number: 47 - Paid on 6 Apr 1814 - Payroll 2 - Number: 853 - Entry Date: 10 Sep 1813 - Discharged on 27 Sep 1814

Weeks, John - Landsman - Payroll 2 - Number: 871 - Entry Date: 12 Aug 1814 - Discharged on 1 Apr 1815

Weigthman, William - Ordinary Seaman - Payroll 2 - Number: 767 - Entry Date: 3 May 1814

Wentworth, Ceasar - Cook - U.S. Frigate United States - Number: 589 - Discharged on 23 Feb 1815 to U.S. Gunboat 138 - Payroll 2 - Number: 589 - Entry Date: 10 Sep 1813 - Discharged on 23 Feb 1815

Wheeler, James - Midshipman - Payroll 2 - Number: 620 - Entry Date: 10 Mar 1814

Wheeler, John - Master's Mate - Payroll 2 - Number: 371 - Entry Date: 28 Mar 1814 - Discharged on 1 Apr 1815

White, Joseph - Ordinary Seaman - Payroll 2 - Number: 848 - Entry Date: 5 Aug 1814 - Ran on 22 Feb 1815

White, Michael - Seaman - U.S. Sloop-of-War Ontario - Number: 91 - Entry Date: 26 Jan 1814 - Discharged on 14 Apr 1814 to the flotilla - U.S. Frigate United States - Number: 498 - Entry Date: 7 Apr 1814 - Discharged on 6 Dec 1814 to U.S. Sloop-of-War Ontario - Transfers - Number: 35 - Entry Date: 15 Apr 1814 - Discharged on 6 Dec 1814 - U.S. Sloop-of-War Ontario - Number: 218 - Entry Date: 7 Dec 1814 - Discharged on 5 Mar 1815 from the flotilla - Payroll 2 - Number: 498 - Entry Date: 22 Jan 1814 - Discharged on 6 Dec 1814 to U.S. Sloop-of-War Ontario

White, Stephen - Master's Mate - U.S. Frigate United States - Number: 808 - Entry Date: 10 Apr 1814 - Discharged on 1 Apr 1815 - Lazaretto (Baltimore) - Midshipman - Payroll 2 - Number: 808 - Entry Date: 9 Jul 1814 - Discharged on 1 Apr 1815

Whitemore, John - Seaman - Payroll 1 - Number: 228 - Entry Date: 8 Feb 1814 - Payroll ended on 6 Apr 1814 - Payroll 2 - Number: 228 - Entry Date: 8 Feb 1814 - Discharged on 12 Feb 1815

Whittington, Samuel B. - Master's Mate - Payroll 2 - Number: 917 - Entry Date: 15 Sep 1814 - Discharged on 25 Dec 1814

Wier, Alexander - Seaman - Muster - Number: 51 - Entry Date: 14 Sep 1813 - Discharged on 14 Sep 1814 - Payroll 1 - Number: 51 - Entry Date: 14 Sep 1813 - Payroll ended on 6 Apr 1814 - Payroll 1a - Number: 51 - Payroll 2 - Number: 51 - Entry Date: 14 Sep 1813 - Discharged on 14 Sep 1814

Wightmore, John - Ordinary Seaman - Payroll 2 - Number: 580 - Entry Date: 25 Apr 1814 - Discharged on 7 Jan 1815

Wilkins, David - Ordinary Seaman - U.S. Frigate Adams Payroll - 336 - Entry Date: 4 Apr 1813 - Discharged on 10 Nov 1813 to U.S. Gunboat 137 - U.S. Frigate United States - Number: 469 - Entry Date: 7 Apr 1814 - Discharged on 21 Jan 1815 to U.S. Gunboat 137 - U.S. Gunboat 137 - Number: 15 - Entry Date: 21 Jan 1813 - Payroll ended on 4 Mar 1814 - Payroll 2 - Number: 469 - Entry Date: 21 Jan 1813 - Discharged on 24 Jan 1815

Wilkinson, Joseph - Ordinary Seaman - Payroll 2 - Number: 810 - Entry Date: 11 Jul 1814 - Discharged on 1 Apr 1815 - BLW 41977-149-55 - Pension: WO-17075, WC-14201

Willet, George - Seaman - Payroll 1 - Number: 219 - Entry Date: 26 Jan 1814 - Payroll ended on 6 Apr 1814 - Payroll 2 - Number: 219 - Entry Date: 26 Jan 1814 - Discharged on 30 Jan 1815

Williams, George - Seaman - Payroll 1 - Number: 57 - Entry Date: 30 Sep 1813 - Payroll ended on 6 Apr 1814 - Payroll 1a - Number: 57 - Entry Date: 30 Sep 1813 - Discharged on 5 Oct 1814 - Payroll 2 - Number: 57 - Entry Date: 30 Sep 1813 - Discharged on 5 Oct 1814

Williams, John (1) - Landsman - Payroll 2 - Number: 394 - Entry Date: 28 Mar 1814 - Discharged on 1 Apr 1815

Williams, John (2) - Ordinary Seaman - U.S. Frigate Adams Payroll - Number: 178 - Entry Date: 22 Feb 1813 - Discharged on 10 Nov 1813 to U.S. Schooner Asp - U.S. Sloop Asp - Number: 10 - Entry Date: 3 Feb 1814 - Discharged on 20 Apr 1814 - U.S. Frigate United States - Number: 729 - Entry Date: 21 Apr 1814 - Ran on 11 Sep 1814 to U.S. Schooner Asp - U.S. Frigate Adams Muster - Number: 729 - Entry Date: 22 Feb 1813 - Discharged on 10 Nov 1813 to U.S. Schooner Asp - Payroll 2 - Number: 729 - Entry Date: 23 Dec 1812 - Ran on 11 Sep 1814

Williams, Robert - Ordinary Seaman - Payroll 1 - Number: 165 - Entry Date: 19 Nov 1813 - Payroll ended on 6 Apr 1814 - Payroll 2 - Number: 165 - Entry Date: 19 Nov 1813 - Discharged on 19 Nov 1814

Williams, William - Seaman - Payroll 2 - Number: 860 - Entry Date: 12 Aug 1814 - Ran on 24 Feb 1815

Williamson, Frederick - Ordinary Seaman - Payroll 2 - Number: 664 - Entry Date: 23 Apr 1814 - Discharged on 1 Apr 1815 - Wounded at Bladensburg - Pension: Navy IF-1651 - Seaman - Washington Naval Hospital - Number: 9 - Wounded at Bladensburg, admitted on 24 Aug 1814, discharged on 10 Oct 1814

Willslager, Daniel - Landsman - Payroll 2 - Number: 778 - Entry Date: 23 Jul 1814 - Discharged on 1 Apr 1815

Wilson, David - Boy - U.S. Sloop-of-War Ontario - Number: 209 - Entry Date: 7 Dec 1814 - Discharged on 5 Mar 1815 from the flotilla U.S. Sloop-of-War Ontario - Number: 72 - Entry Date: 14 Jan 1814 - Discharged on 13 Apr 1814 to the flotilla - Transfers - Number: 12 - Entry Date: 14 Apr 1814 - Discharged on 6 Dec 1814 - U.S. Frigate United States - Number: 629 - Entry Date: 7 Apr 1814 - Discharged on 6 Dec 1814 to U.S. Sloop-of-War Ontario - Payroll 2 - Number: 629 - Entry Date: 30 Dec 1813 - Discharged on 6 Dec 1814 to U.S. Sloop-of-War Ontario

Wilson, George - Seaman - Payroll 2 - Number: 540 - Entry Date: 25 Apr 1814 - Discharged on 1 Apr 1815 - Prisoner - BLW 50335-160-55 - Prisoner of War at Halifax, prisoner number 7319, captured on 24 Aug 1814 near Washington, D.C. by British forces; received at Halifax on 30 Sep 1814 on HMS Surprize; discharged on 5 Mar 1815 and sent to Salem, Massachusetts on Cartel Lingan

Wilson, Jacob - Boy - Payroll 1 - Number: 130 - Entry Date: 20 Sep 1813 - Discharged on 30 Oct 1813 - Payroll 2 - Number: 130 - Entry Date: 20 Sep 1813 - Discharged on 31 Oct 1813

Wilson, James (1) - Seaman - Payroll 1 - Number: 259 - Payroll ended on 6 Apr 1814 - Payroll 2 - Number: 259 - Entry Date: 2 Mar 1814 - Discharged on 2 Mar 1815

Wilson, James (2) - Master's Mate - U.S. Frigate United States - Number: 815 - Entry Date: 20 Feb 1814 - Discharged on 17 Nov 1814 to Commodore Barney - Payroll 2 - Number: 815 - Entry Date: 16 Jul 1814 - Discharged on 17 Nov 1814

Wilson, John (1) - Seaman - Payroll 2 - Number: 410 - Landsman - Payroll 2 - Number: 455 - Entry Date: 12 Mar 1814 - Discharged on 15 Mar 1815

Wilson, John (2) - Ordinary Seaman - Payroll 2 - Number: 760 - Entry Date: 23 Apr 1814 - Ran on 24 Aug 1814

Wilson, Joseph - Seaman - Payroll 2 - Number: 717 - Entry Date: 4 Jun 1814 - Discharged on 1 Apr 1815

Wilson, Joseph I. - Seaman - Payroll 2 - Number: 529 - Entry Date: 6 Apr 1814 - Ran on 1 Oct 1814

Wilson, William - Ordinary Seaman - Payroll 1 - Number: 162 - Entry Date: 19 Nov 1813 - Payroll ended on 6 Apr 1814 - Payroll 2 - Number: 162 - Entry Date: 19 Nov 1813 - Discharged on 19 Nov 1814 - BLW 98118-150-55

Winder, John T. - Muster - Number: 947 – Discharged: never appeared- Payroll 2 - Number: 947 – Discharged: never appeared

Wingate, Levin - Boatswain - Payroll 2 - Number: 751 - Entry Date: 8 Jun 1814 - Discharged on 26 Dec 1814 - Payroll 2 - Number: 805 - Entry Date: 11 Jun 1814

Wingate, Samuel (1) - Steward - Payroll 2 - Number: 533 - Entry Date: 15 Aug 1814 - Discharged on 28 Oct 1814

Wingate, Samuel (2) - Carpenter - Payroll 2 - Number: 962 - Entry Date: 29 Oct 1814 - Discharged on 1 Apr 1815 - Muster - Number: 962 - Entry Date: 29 Oct 1813 - Discharged on 1 Apr 1815

Winingder, Stephen - Gunner - Payroll 2 - Number: 653 - Entry Date: 20 Apr 1814 - Discharged on 2 Dec 1814 - Barge No. 6 - BLW 23461-160-55

Winters, James - Seaman - Payroll 2 - Number: 823 - Entry Date: 28 Jul 1814 - Discharged on 1 Apr 1815

Wiseman, Joseph - Midshipman - Muster - Number: 971 - Entry Date: 2 Dec 1814 - Discharged on 1 Apr 1815 - Payroll 2 - Number: 971 - Entry Date: 2 Jun 1814 - Discharged on 1 Apr 1815

Witham, James - Seaman - U.S. Frigate Adams Muster - Number: 367 - Entry Date: 5 Apr 1813 - Discharged on 10 Nov 1813 to U.S. Schooner Asp - U.S. Schooner Shark - Number: 26 - Entry Date: 5 Feb 1814 - Discharged on 29 Mar 1814 - U.S. Frigate United States - Number: 519 - Entry Date: 7 Apr 1814 - Ran on 24 Dec 1814 to U.S. Galley Shark - Payroll 2 - Number: 519 - Entry Date: 5 Feb 1813 - Ran on 24 Dec 1814

Wood, George - Seaman - Payroll 2 - Number: 682 - Entry Date: 22 May 1814 - Discharged on 21 Oct 1814

Woodford, Thomas (1) - Seaman - U.S. Frigate Adams Payroll - Number: 92 - Entry Date: 17 Jan 1813 - Discharged on 10 Nov 1813 to U.S. Schooner Asp - U.S. Frigate United States - Number: 712 - Entry Date: 21 Apr 1814 - Discharged on 16 May 1814 to U.S. Schooner Asp - U.S. Sloop Asp - Number: 2 - Entry Date: 11 Nov 1813 - Discharged on 20 Apr 1814 - Payroll 2 – Number 974 - Entry Date: 21 Dec 1812 - Discharged on 16 May 1814

Woodford, Thomas (1) - Gunner - Muster - Number: 712 - Entry Date: 17 May 1814 - Discharged on Dec 1814 - Payroll 2 - Number: 712 - Entry Date: 17 May 1814 - Discharged on 2 Dec 1814

Woods Jr., John - Master's Mate - Payroll 2 - Number: 887 - Entry Date: 14 Jun 1814 - Discharged on 10 Aug 1814

Woodward, William - Ordinary Seaman - U.S. Gunboat 138 - Number: 35 - Paid on 6 Apr 1814 - U.S. Frigate United States - Number: 548 - Entry Date: 7 Apr 1814 - Ran on 24 Aug 1814 from Gunboat 138 - Payroll 2 - Number: 548 - Entry Date: 10 Sep 1813 - Ran on 24 Aug 1814

Woolford, William - Seaman - Payroll 2 - Number: 734 - Entry Date: 22 Apr 1814 - Discharged on 1 Apr 1815 - Pension: Navy IF-1696

Worthington, Henry - Sailing Master - Payroll 1 - Number: 5 - Entry Date: 18 Sep 1813 - Payroll ended on 6 Apr 1814 - Muster - Number: 5 - Entry Date: 12 Sep 1813 - Discharged on Muster ended on 6 Apr 1814 - Payroll 2 - Number: 5 - Entry Date: 18 Sep 1813 - Discharged on 15 Apr 1815 - Warranted as a sailing master on 15 Sep 1813

Wright, George - Boy - U.S. Gunboat 138 - Number: 58 - Paid on 6 Apr 1814 - U.S. Frigate United States - Number: 497 - Entry Date: 7 Apr 1814 - Ran on 24 Aug 1814 to U.S. Sloop-of-War Ontario - Payroll 2 - Number: 497 - Entry Date: 10 Sep 1813 - Ran on 24 Aug 1814

Wright, James - Sailing Master - Payroll 2 - Number: 703 - Entry Date: 16 Feb 1814 - Discharged on 1 Feb 1815 - Warranted as a sailing master on 18 Feb 1814

Wright, Lloyd - Landsman - Payroll 2 - Number: 576 - Entry Date: 5 May 1814 - Discharged on 1 Apr 1815 - BLW 1409-160-55

Young, Henry - Ordinary Seaman - Payroll 2 - Number: 675 - Entry Date: 27 May 1814 - Ran on 2 Dec 1814

Young, William (1) - Landsman - Payroll 1 - Number: 127 - Entry Date: 8 Oct 1813 - Payroll ended on 6 Apr 1814 - Payroll 2 - Number: 127 - Entry Date: 8 Oct 1813 - Discharged on 7 Oct 1814 - BLW 61539-160-55 - Pension: WO-34206, WC-31742

Young, William (2) - Seaman - U.S. Sloop-of-War Ontario - Number: 111 - Entry Date: 8 Feb 1814 - Discharged on 14 Apr 1814 to the flotilla - Transfers - Number: 24 - Entry Date: 15 Apr 1814 - Discharged on 6 Dec 1814 - U.S. Frigate United States - Number: 599 - Entry Date: 7 Apr 1814 - Discharged on 6 Dec 1814 to U.S. Sloop-of-War Ontario - U.S. Sloop-of-War Ontario - Number: 229 - Entry Date: 7 Dec 1814 - Discharged on 5 Mar 1815 from the flotilla - Payroll 2 - Number: 599 - Entry Date: 3 Feb 1813 - Discharged on 6 Dec 1814 to U.S. Sloop-of-War Ontario

Young, William J. - Master's Mate - Payroll 2 - Number: 732 - Entry Date: 24 May 1815 - Discharged on 31 Dec 1814 - BLW 41548-160-55

New York Flotilla Squadron Roster

Abbott, Stephen - Master's Mate - Payroll 2 - Number: 2169 - Entry Date: 2 Nov 1815 - Discharged to the U.S. Storeship Tom Bowline

Adams, Thomas - Seaman - Payroll 1 - Number: 56 - Entry Date: 3 Oct 1813 - Gunboat No. 6 - Statement - Number: 56 - Entry Date: 3 Oct 1813 - Gunboat No. 6

Alert, Richard - Seaman - Payroll 2 - Number: 218 - Entry Date: 9 Feb 1814 - Discharged to the U.S. Frigate John Adams

Allen, Tirah - Ordinary Seaman - Payroll 2 - Number: 1013 - Entry Date: 18 May 1814

Allwell, Edward - Seaman - Payroll 2 - Number: 1802 - Entry Date: 1 Jan 1815

Ames, John - Ordinary Seaman - Payroll 2 - Number: 969 - Entry Date: 30 Nov 1813

Anderson, John (1) - Seaman - Payroll 1 - Number: 23 - Entry Date: 3 Oct 1813 - Gunboat No. 6 - Statement - Number: 22 - Entry Date: 3 Oct 1813 - Gunboat No. 6 - Discharged on 28 Jul 1814

Anderson, John (2) - Quarter Gunner - Payroll 1 - Number: 84 - Entry Date: 3 Oct 1813 - Gunboat No. 8 - Discharged on 22 Mar 1814 at New York - Statement - Number: 87 - Entry Date: 3 Oct 1813 - Gunboat No. 8

Andreas, Robert - Seaman - Payroll 2 - Number: 907 - Entry Date: 27 Nov 1813 - Ran

Anthony, Robert - Boy - Payroll 1 - Number: 9 - Entry Date: 3 Oct 1813 - Gunboat No. 6 - Statement - Number: 8 - Entry Date: 3 Oct 1813 - Gunboat No. 6

Antonio, Charles - Ordinary Seaman - Payroll 2 - Number: 991 - Entry Date: 1 Dec 1813 - Ran

Antony, Peter - Seaman - Statement - Number: 802 - Entry Date: 27 Sep 1813 - Gunboat No. 109 - Discharged on 12 Jul 1814

Antrim, Purnel G. - Seaman - Payroll 2 - Number: 207 - Entry Date: 9 Feb 1814 - Gunboat No. A - Statement - Number: 176 - Entry Date: 26 Jan 1814 - Gunboat No. A - Discharged on 28 Jan 1814 - Discharged to the U.S. Frigate John Adams

Archer, James - Boy - Payroll 2 - Number: 956 - Entry Date: 5 Oct 1813 - Ran

Armstrong, George - Carpenter - Payroll 2 - Number: 180 - Entry Date: 9 Feb 1814 - Discharged to the U.S. Frigate John Adams

Armstrong, John - Ordinary Seaman - Payroll 2 - Number: 1816 - Entry Date: 1 Apr 1815 - Discharged

Ash, Charles - Seaman - Payroll 1 - Number: 22 - Entry Date: 3 Oct 1813 - Gunboat No. 6 - Statement - Number: 21 - Entry Date: 3 Oct 1813 - Gunboat No. 6 - Discharged on 14 Jul 1814

Atwood, Morris A. - Ordinary Seaman - Payroll 2 - Number: 1795 - Entry Date: 1 Apr 1815 - Discharged

Augustus, Abraham - Ordinary Seaman - Payroll 2 - Number: 1813 - Entry Date: 1 Apr 1815 - Discharged

Babbit, Corner - Seaman - Payroll 2 - Number: 996 - Entry Date: 6 Nov 1813 - Gunboat No. 112 Statement - Number: 862 - Entry Date: 27 Sep 1813 - Gunboat No. 112 - Ran on 6 Nov 1813 at New York

Bacon, Benjamin - Seaman - Payroll 1 - Number: 124 - Entry Date: 3 Oct 1813 - Gunboat No. 29 - Statement - Number: 128 - Entry Date: 3 Oct 1813 - Gunboat No. 29 - Discharged on 11 Sep 1814

Bailey, Robert - Seaman - Statement - Number: 200 - Entry Date: 3 Oct 1813 - Gunboat No. B

Baldwin, James M. - Master's Mate - Payroll 1 - Number: 155 - Entry Date: 26 Sep 1813 - Gunboat No. 30 - Discharged on 28 Mar 1814 at New York - Master's Mate - Statement - Number: 157 - Entry Date: 27 Sep 1813 - Gunboat No. 30

Balls, William - Quarter Gunner - Payroll 1 - Number: 29 - Entry Date: 3 Oct 1813 - Gunboat No. 6 - Statement - Number: 29 - Entry Date: 3 Oct 1813 - Gunboat No. 6 - Discharged on 19 Sep 1814 - BLW 3510-160-50

Baptist, John - Seaman - Statement - Number: 915 - Entry Date: 27 Sep 1813 - Gunboat No. 114 - Discharged on 13 Jun 1814

Barker, George - Ordinary Seaman - Payroll 2 - Number: 972 - Entry Date: 14 Nov 1813 - Gunboat No. 103 - Statement - Number: 672 - Entry Date: 27 Sep 1813 - Gunboat No. 103 - Ran on 14 Nov 1813 at New York

Barnwall, William - Surgeon's Mate - Payroll 2 - Number: 2170 - Entry Date: 31 Oct 1815 - Discharged to the U.S. Ship-of-the-Line Franklin

Barnwell, William - Seaman - Payroll 2 - Number: 215 - Entry Date: 9 Feb 1814 - Gunboat No. 114 - Statement - Number: 912 - Entry Date: 27 Sep 1813 - Gunboat No. 114 - Discharged on 9 Feb 1814 - Discharged to the U.S. Frigate John Adams

Barry, John - Seaman - Payroll 2 - Number: 212 - Entry Date: 9 Feb 1814 - Discharged to the U.S. Frigate John Adams

Bartley, James - Ordinary Seaman - Payroll 2 - Number: 1789 - Entry Date: 11 Jan 1815 - Ran

Baston, Samuel - Landsman - Payroll 2 - Number: 891 - Entry Date: 4 Oct 1813 - Ran

Batties, John - Seaman - Payroll 2 - Number: 836 - Entry Date: 5 Dec 1813 - Discharged to the U.S. Frigate President

Beall, John - Boatswain's Mate - Payroll 2 - Number: 193 - Entry Date: 9 Feb 1814 - Gunboat No. 109 - Statement - Number: 786 - Entry Date: 27 Sep 1813 - Gunboat No. 109 - Discharged on 9 Feb 1814 - Discharged to the U.S. Frigate John Adams

Beeman, Elam - Seaman - Statement - Number: 883 - Entry Date: 27 Sep 1813 - Gunboat No. 113 - Discharged on 9 Jul 1814

Beish, George - Seaman - Payroll 2 - Number: 2063 - Entry Date: 28 Sep 1815 - Ran

Bellise, John - Seaman - Payroll 2 - Number: 1792 - Entry Date: 1 Apr 1815 - Discharged

Beman, William - Ordinary Seaman - Statement - Entry Date: 21 Jul 1814 - Gunboat No. 30 - Discharged to the U.S. Frigate President

Benedict, George - Ordinary Seaman - Payroll 2 - Number: 1061 - Entry Date: 24 Nov 1813 - Ran

Benjamin, David - Seaman - Payroll 2 - Number: 750 - Entry Date: 4 Mar 1814 - Discharged to the U.S. Sloop-of-War Peacock

Benjamin, John - Landsman - Payroll 2 - Number: 1691 - Entry Date: 1 Apr 1814 - Discharged

Berrian, William (1) - Ordinary Seaman - Payroll 2 - Number: 791 - Entry Date: 14 Jul 1814 - Discharged to the U.S. Frigate President

Berrian, William (2) - Ordinary Seaman - Payroll 2 - Number: 1859 - Entry Date: 16 Dec 1814 - Ran

Berry, William - Landsman - Statement - Number: 1108 - Entry Date: 2 Mar 1814 - Gunboat No. 37- Seaman - Payroll 2 - Number: 1695 - Entry Date: 17 Jun 1814 - Gunboat No. 37 - New York Naval Yard Muster 1 Aug 1815 - Number: 1072 - Entry Date: 2 Mar 1814 - Gunboat No. 37 - Discharged on 17 Jun 1814

Bettise, John - Seaman - Payroll 2 - Number: 1794 - Entry Date: 1 Apr 1815 - Discharged

Betts, William - Master's Mate - Payroll 1 - Number: 131 - Entry Date: 3 Oct 1813 - Gunboat No. 29 - Statement - Number: 135 - Entry Date: 3 Oct 1813 - Gunboat No. 29

Bickford, James - Ordinary Seaman - Payroll 2 - Number: 1057 - Entry Date: 15 Apr 1814 - Ran

Biddley, William - Landsman - Payroll 2 - Number: 1741 - Entry Date: 30 Oct 1814 - Ran

Bills, James - Master's Mate - Payroll 2 - Number: 835 - Entry Date: 5 Dec 1813 - Discharged to the U.S. Frigate President

Blake, James (1) - Boy - Payroll 2 - Number: 948 - Entry Date: 19 Nov 1813 - Ran on 19 Nov 1813 at New York

Blake, James (2) - Seaman - New York Naval Yard Muster 1 Aug 1815 - Number: 1411 - Entry Date: 8 Jun 1814 -

Gunboat No. 50 - Discharged on 8 Feb 1815 - BLW 5843-160-55 - Payroll 2 - Number: 1780 - Entry Date: 8 Feb 1815 - Gunboat No. 50

Bleumer, Michael - Boy - Statement - Number: 342 - Entry Date: 4 Oct 1813 - Gunboat No. 40 - Discharged on 31 May 1814

Bliss, William - Seaman - Payroll 2 - Number: 1967 - Entry Date: 31 Jul 1815 - Ran

Blosson, George - Ordinary Seaman - Payroll 2 - Number: 177 - Entry Date: 9 Feb 1814 - Discharged to the U.S. Frigate John Adams

Bodge, John - Boy - Payroll 2 - Number: 1985 - Entry Date: 21 Jul 1815 - Discharged to the U.S. Brig Boxer

Bogett, John - Landsman - New York Naval Yard Muster 1 Aug 1815 - Number: 1369 - Entry Date: 30 May 1814 - Gunboat No. 43 - Discharged on 1 Apr 1815 - Landsman - Payroll 2 - Number: 1759 - Entry Date: 1 Apr 1815 - Gunboat No. 43

Bonds, Isaac - Ordinary Seaman - Statement - Number: 171 - Entry Date: 3 Oct 1813 - Gunboat No. A

Boston, Samuel - Landsman - Payroll 1 - Number: 128 - Entry Date: 3 Oct 1813 - Gunboat No. 29 - Ran on 4 Oct 1813 at New York - Statement - Number: 132 - Entry Date: 3 Oct 1813 - Gunboat No. 29

Bowen, William - Seaman - Statement - Number: 328 - Entry Date: 3 Oct 1813 - Gunboat No. 40 - Discharged on 9 Nov 1813

Bowie, Henry - Sailing Master - Payroll 2 - Number: 833 - Entry Date: 5 Dec 1813

Bowman, John - Boy - Statement - Number: 327 - Entry Date: 3 Oct 1813 - Gunboat No. 40

Boyd, Robertson - Ordinary Seaman - Payroll 1 - Number: 150 - Entry Date: 26 Sep 1813 - Gunboat No. 30 - Statement - Number: 152 - Entry Date: 27 Sep 1813 - Gunboat No. 30 - Discharged on 12 Jul 1814

Bradberry, James - Seaman - Payroll 1 - Number: 51 - Entry Date: 3 Oct 1813 - Gunboat No. 6 - Statement - Number: 51 - Entry Date: 3 Oct 1813 - Gunboat No. 6 - Discharged on 24 Feb 1814 at New York

Bradford, Jacob - Ordinary Seaman - Payroll 2 - Number: 1720 - Entry Date: 1 Apr 1815 - Ran

Bradwell, Benjamin - Ordinary Seaman - Payroll 2 - Number: 1676 - Entry Date: 22 Mar 1815 - Discharged

Branham, Stephen - Seaman - Payroll 2 - Number: 1008 - Entry Date: 5 Apr 1814 - Ran

Breid, John - Ordinary Seaman - Statement - Number: 216 - Entry Date: 3 Oct 1813 - Gunboat No. B - Discharged on 26 Feb 1814

Brewer, Joshua - Landsman - Payroll 2 - Number: 1693 - Entry Date: 6 Sep 1814 - Ran

Briggs, David - Landsman - Payroll 2 - Number: 1694 - Entry Date: 15 Oct 1814 - Ran

Briggs, Jeremiah - Master's Mate - Statement - Number: 185 - Entry Date: 3 Oct 1813 - Gunboat No. A - BLW 6466-160-55

Briggs, Samuel R. - Sailing Master - Statement - Number: 309 - Entry Date: 3 Oct 1813 - Gunboat No. 40

Broadlin, William - Seaman - Statement - Number: 686 - Entry Date: 27 Sep 1813 - Gunboat No. 103 - Discharged on 13 Jun 1814

Brooks, John - Ordinary Seaman - Payroll 2 - Number: 1075 - Entry Date: 20 Jun 1814 - Sent to Lake Ontario

Broun, Jacob - Seaman - Payroll 2 - Number: 1852 - Entry Date: 1 Apr 1815 - Discharged to the U.S. Sloop-of-War Peacock

Brown, Benjamin - Seaman - Payroll 1 - Number: 58 - Entry Date: 4 Nov 1813 - Gunboat No. 6 - Discharged on 9 Feb 1814 - Discharged to the U.S. Frigate John Adams - Statement - Number: 58 - Entry Date: 3 Nov 1813 - Gunboat No. 6 - Seaman - Statement - Number: 1180 - Entry Date: 29 Mar 1814 - Gunboat No. 6

Brown, Charles - Landsman - Payroll 1 - Number: 87 - Entry Date: 3 Oct 1813 - Gunboat No. 8 - Statement - Number: 90 - Entry Date: 3 Oct 1813 - Gunboat No. 8

Brown, Daniel - Seaman - Payroll 2 - Number: 194 - Entry Date: 9 Feb 1814 - Gunboat No. 109 - Discharged to the U.S. Frigate John Adams - Statement - Number: 796 - Entry Date: 27 Sep 1813 - Gunboat No. 109

Brown, George - Boy - Payroll 2 - Number: 2579 - Entry Date: 7 Jun 1817 - Discharged to Enterprize

Brown, Henry - Seaman - Payroll 2 - Number: 1861 - Entry Date: 25 Feb 1815 - Gunboat No. 103 - Statement - Number: 673 - Entry Date: 27 Sep 1813 - Gunboat No. 103 - Discharged on 29 Nov 1813 - Statement - Number: 1446 - Entry Date: 29 Jul 1814 - Gunboat No. 103

Brown, James (1) - Cook - Payroll 2 - Number: 1961 - Entry Date: 23 Jul 1815 - Discharged

Brown, John (2) - Seaman - Payroll 1 - Number: 116 - Entry Date: 3 Oct 1813 - Gunboat No. 29 - Discharged on 16 Oct 1813 at New York - New York - Payroll 2 - Number: 1867 - Entry Date: 27 Apr 1815 - Gunboat No. 29 - Statement - Number: 120 - Entry Date: 3 Oct 1813 - Gunboat No. 29

Brown, Joseph - Seaman - Payroll 2 - Number: 1881 - Entry Date: 9 Dec 1814 - Ran

Brown, Patrick - Seaman - Payroll 2 - Number: 1809 - Entry Date: 29 Jul 1814 - Discharged

Brown, Peter (1) - Seaman - Payroll 1 - Number: 98 - Entry Date: 3 Oct 1813 - Gunboat No. 8 - Discharged on 25 Feb 1814 at New York - Statement - Number: 101 - Entry Date: 3 Oct 1813 - Gunboat No. 8 - Statement - Number: 1231 - Entry Date: 17 Mar 1814 - Gunboat No. 8

Brown, Peter (2) - Seaman - Statement - Number: 892 - Entry Date: 27 Sep 1813 - Gunboat No. 113 - Discharged on 13 Jun 1814

Brown, Thomas (1) - Boatswain's Mate - Payroll 2 - Number: 800 - Entry Date: 14 Jul 1814 - Gunboat No. B - Statement - Number: 214 - Entry Date: 3 Oct 1813 - Gunboat No. B - Statement - Number: 1048 - Entry Date: 15 Feb 1814 - Gunboat No. B - Discharged on 14 Jul 1814 - Discharged to the U.S. Frigate President

Brown, Thomas (2) - Landsman - Payroll 2 - Number: 1733 - Entry Date: 1 Apr 1815 - Discharged

Brown, William (1) - Seaman - Payroll 2 - Number: 994 - Entry Date: 2 Nov 1813 - Gunboat No. 112 - Statement - Number: 845 - Entry Date: 27 Sep 1813 - Gunboat No. 112 - Ran on 2 Nov 1813 at New York

Brown, William (2) - Seaman - Payroll 2 - Number: 1651 - Entry Date: 25 Feb 1815 - Gunboat No. 105 - Statement - Number: 704 - Entry Date: 27 Sep 1813 - Gunboat No. 105

Brush, George B. - Seaman - Payroll 2 - Number: 1043 - Entry Date: 7 Nov 1813 - Ran

Brush, John - Landsman - Payroll 2 - Number: 2165 - Entry Date: 2 Nov 1815 - Discharged to the U.S. Storeship Tom Bowline

Bryan, James - Ordinary Seaman - Payroll 1 - Number: 45 - Entry Date: 3 Oct 1813 - Gunboat No. 6 - Statement - Number: 45 - Entry Date: 3 Oct 1813 - Gunboat No. 6 - Discharged on 14 Jul 1814 - Discharged to the U.S. Frigate President - Payroll 2 - Number: 780 - Entry Date: 14 Jul 1814 - Discharged to the U.S. Frigate President

Bryant, John - Seaman - Statement - Number: 872 - Entry Date: 27 Sep 1813 - Gunboat No. 113 - Discharged on 10 Jun 1814 - Statement - Number: 1433 - Entry Date: 14 Jun 1814 - Gunboat No. 113

Bunker, James - Quarter Gunner - Statement - Number: 919 - Entry Date: 27 Sep 1813 - Gunboat No. 114

Bunsan, Charles - Master's Mate - Statement - Number: 856 - Entry Date: 27 Sep 1813 - Gunboat No. 112

Burke, James - Ordinary Seaman - Payroll 2 - Number: 234 - Entry Date: 9 Feb 1814 - Gunboat No. 40 - Statement - Number: 339 - Entry Date: 18 Oct 1813 - Gunboat No. 40 - Discharged to the U.S. Frigate John Adams

Burke, Joseph (1) - Ordinary Seaman - Payroll 1 - Number: 24 - Entry Date: 3 Oct 1813 - Gunboat No. 6 - Payroll 2 - Number: 748 - Entry Date: 4 Mar 1814 - Gunboat No. 6 - Statement - Number: 23 - Entry Date: 3 Oct 1813 - Gunboat No. 6 - Discharged on 4 Mar 1814 - Discharged to the U.S. Sloop-of-War Peacock

Burke, Joseph (2) - Seaman - Payroll 1 - Number: 44 - Entry Date: 3 Oct 1813 - Gunboat No. 6 - Statement - Number: 44 - Entry Date: 3 Oct 1813 - Gunboat No. 6

Burke, William - Seaman - Statement - Number: 693 - Entry Date: 27 Sep 1813 - Gunboat No. 103 - Discharged on 12 Jul 1814

Burnett, John - Landsman - Payroll 2 - Number: 952 - Entry Date: 12 Oct 1813 - Discharged

Burrell, John - Master's Mate - Payroll 1 - Number: 63 - Entry Date: 3 Oct 1813 - Gunboat No. 8 - Master's Mate - Statement - Number: 66 - Entry Date: 3 Oct 1813 - Gunboat No. 8

Burridge, James - Seaman - Payroll 1 - Number: 89 - Entry Date: 3 Oct 1813 - Gunboat No. 8 - Payroll 2 - Number: 887 - Entry Date: 25 Feb 1814 - Gunboat No. 8 - Statement - Number: 92 - Entry Date: 3 Oct 1813 - Gunboat No. 8 - Discharged on 25 Feb 1814

Bush, George B. - Seaman - Payroll 1 - Number: 144 - Entry Date: 26 Sep 1813 - Gunboat No. 30 - Ran on 7 Nov 1813 at New York - Statement - Entry Date: 27 Sep 1813 - Gunboat No. 30

Bush, Henry - Seaman - Payroll 2 - Number: 2317 - Entry Date: 7 Jul 1816 - Ran

Buss, George - Seaman - Statement - Number: 805 - Entry Date: 27 Sep 1813 - Gunboat No. 109 - Discharged on 12 Jul 1814 - Discharged to the U.S. Frigate John Adams

Butler, Fortune - Ordinary Seaman - Payroll 1 - Number: 41 - Entry Date: 3 Oct 1813 - Gunboat No. 6 - Discharged on 26 Jan 1814 at New York

Butler, Fortune - Ordinary Seaman - Statement - Number: 41 - Entry Date: 3 Oct 1813 - Gunboat No. 6

Caley, Joseph - Ordinary Seaman - Payroll 1 - Number: 65 - Entry Date: 3 Oct 1813 - Gunboat No. 8 - Ran on 30 Nov 1813 at Long Branch - Statement - Number: 68 - Entry Date: 3 Oct 1813 - Gunboat No. 8

Callis, David - Ordinary Seaman - Payroll 2 - Number: 224 - Entry Date: 9 Feb 1814 - Discharged to the U.S. Frigate John Adams

Callow, William - Seaman - Payroll 2 - Number: 1978 - Entry Date: 3 Jul 1815 - Died

Cameron, Alexander - Seaman - Statement - Number: 703 - Entry Date: 27 Sep 1813 - Gunboat No. 105 - Discharged on 6 Dec 1813

Camey, John - Seaman - Payroll 2 - Number: 1070 - Entry Date: 28 Apr 1814 - Ran

Camp, William - Seaman - Payroll 1 - Number: 149 - Entry Date: 26 Sep 1813 - Gunboat No. 30 - Ran on 2 Nov 1813 from New York - Payroll 2 - Number: 900 - Entry Date: 2 Nov 1813 - Gunboat No. 30 - Seaman - Statement - Number: 151 - Entry Date: 27 Sep 1813 - Gunboat No. 30

Campbell, John - Landsman - Payroll 2 - Number: 1707 - Entry Date: 1 Apr 1815 – Discharged

Cappy, George - Seaman - Payroll 2 - Number: 879 - Entry Date: 2 Mar 1814 - Discharged to the U.S. Frigate President

Carr, John H. - Seaman - Payroll 1 - Number: 2 - Entry Date: 3 Oct 1813 - Gunboat No. 6 - Statement - Number: 2 - Entry Date: 3 Oct 1813 - Gunboat No. 6 - Discharged on 12 Jul 1814 - BLW 3865-160-55

Carrington, Robert - Landsman - Payroll 2 - Number: 1822 - Entry Date: 1 Apr 1815 - Discharged

Carrol, James - Ordinary Seaman - Payroll 2 - Number: 239 - Entry Date: 9 Feb 1814 - Gunboat No. A - Statement - Number: 172 - Entry Date: 3 Oct 1813 - Gunboat No. A - Discharged on 9 Feb 1814 - Discharged to the U.S. Frigate John Adams

Carter, John - Seaman - Statement - Number: 720 - Entry Date: 27 Sep 1813 - Gunboat No. 105 - Discharged on 13 Jul 1814 - Statement - Number: 1149 - Entry Date: 17 Mar 1814 - Gunboat No. 105

Case, Joseph - Ordinary Seaman - Statement - Number: 207 - Entry Date: 3 Oct 1813 - Gunboat No. B

Case, Thomas - Ordinary Seaman - Statement - Number: 208 - Entry Date: 3 Oct 1813 - Gunboat No. B

Catheart, Robert - Seaman - Statement - Number: 847 - Entry Date: 27 Sep 1813 - Gunboat No. 112 - Discharged on 13 Jun 1814

Chapman, Lewis - Seaman - Payroll 2 - Number: 1665 - Entry Date: 20 Jan 1815 - Ran

Chapman, Stephen - Boatswain's Mate - Promotions - Entry Date: 25 Jun 1814 - Gunboat No. 30 - Promoted - BLW 5112-160-55 - Statement - Entry Date: 8 Mar 1814 - Gunboat No. 30

Chase, Benjamin - Seaman - Payroll 2 - Number: 1774 - Entry Date: 13 Feb 1815 - Ran

Chesnut, Adam - Seaman - Payroll 2 - Number: 217 - Entry Date: 9 Feb 1814 - Discharged to the U.S. Frigate John Adams

Clark, Charles - Seaman - Payroll 1 - Number: 18 - Entry Date: 3 Oct 1813 - Gunboat No. 6 - Payroll 2 - Number: 2064 - Entry Date: 29 Sep 1815 - Gunboat No. 6 - Statement - Number: 17 - Entry Date: 3 Oct 1813 - Gunboat No. 6 - Discharged on 28 Jul 1814

Clark, James - Boy - Payroll 1 - Number: 115 - Entry Date: 3 Oct 1813 - Gunboat No. 29 - Statement - Number: 119 - Entry Date: 3 Oct 1813 - Gunboat No. 29 - Ran on 3 Nov 1813 at New York

Clark, John - Seaman - Payroll 1 - Number: 25 - Entry Date: 3 Oct 1813 - Gunboat No. 6 - Statement - Number: 24 - Entry Date: 3 Oct 1813 - Gunboat No. 6 - Discharged on 19 Sep 1814

Clemmons, William - Ordinary Seaman - Payroll 2 - Number: 1791 - Entry Date: 1 Apr 1815 - Served from 13 Jun 1814 to 1 Apr 1815 - BLW 3863-160-55 - Pension: WO-14249, WC-10126

Cleveland, John R. - Seaman - Statement - Number: 715 - Entry Date: 27 Sep 1813 - Gunboat No. 105 - Discharged on 2 Dec 1813

Clinton, Thomas - Ordinary Seaman - Payroll 1 - Number: 81 - Entry Date: 3 Oct 1813 - Gunboat No. 8 - Ran on 30 Nov 1813 at New York - Statement - Number: 84 - Entry Date: 3 Oct 1813 - Gunboat No. 8

Clorson, John - Seaman - Statement - Number: 702 - Entry Date: 27 Sep 1813 - Gunboat No. 105 - Discharged on 17 Jun 1814 - Discharged to the U.S. Sloop-of-War Peacock

Clossey, John - Seaman - Payroll 2 - Number: 204 - Entry Date: 9 Feb 1814 - Discharged to the U.S. Frigate John Adams

Cloud, Caleb - Seaman - Payroll 1 - Number: 32 - Entry Date: 3 Oct 1813 - Gunboat No. 6 - Statement - Number: 32 - Entry Date: 3 Oct 1813 - Gunboat No. 6 - Discharged on 19 Sep 1814

Clough, John - Sailing Master - Statement - Number: 843 - Entry Date: 27 Sep 1813 - Gunboat No. 112

Coffin, Goerge - Seaman - Payroll 2 - Number: 984 - Entry Date: 28 Sep 1813 - Ran

Coleman, Benjamin - Seaman - Payroll 2 - Number: 1717 - Entry Date: 1 Apr 1815 - Discharged Payroll 2 - Number: 1917 - Entry Date: 21 Jul 1815 - Discharged to the U.S. Brig Boxer

Coles, Henry - Ordinary Seaman - Statement - Number: 689 - Entry Date: 27 Sep 1813 - Gunboat No. 103 - Discharged on 12 Jul 1814

Colkins, Samuel - Seaman - Payroll 1 - Number: 74 - Entry Date: 3 Oct 1813 - Gunboat No. 8 - Discharged on 25 Jan 1814 from New York - Statement - Number: 77 - Entry Date: 3 Oct 1813 - Gunboat No. 8

Colley, Thomas - Seaman - Payroll 2 - Number: 1015 - Entry Date: 16 Feb 1814

Collier, Hezekiah - Master's Mate - Payroll 2 - Number: 1653 - Entry Date: 6 Apr 1815 - Discharged

Collins, Joseph - Ordinary Seaman - Statement - Number: 196 - Entry Date: 3 Oct 1813 - Gunboat No. B - Discharged on 10 May 1814

Collins, Thomas - Boatswain's Mate - Statement - Number: 695 - Entry Date: 27 Sep 1813 - Gunboat No. 103 - Discharged on 16 Feb 1814 - Statement - Number: 1079 - Entry Date: 18 Feb 1814 - Gunboat No. 103

Collis, David - Ordinary Seaman - Payroll 1 - Number: 114 - Entry Date: 3 Oct 1813 - Gunboat No. 29 - Discharged on 9 Feb 1814 - Discharged to the U.S. Frigate John Adams - Statement - Number: 118 - Entry Date: 3 Oct 1813 - Gunboat No. 29 - Discharged on 9 Feb 1814

Colman, Thomas - Seaman - Payroll 2 - Number: 1019 - Entry Date: 14 Jul 1814 - Ran

Combs, Samuel - Ordinary Seaman - Payroll 2 - Number: 1686 - Entry Date: 20 Feb 1815 - Discharged

Comley, Pierson - Seaman - Payroll 1 - Number: 70 - Entry Date: 3 Oct 1813 - Gunboat No. 8 - Statement - Number: 73 - Entry Date: 3 Oct 1813 - Gunboat No. 8 - Discharged on 12 Jul 1814

Cone, Aaron W. - Master's Mate - Payroll 2 - Number: 2298 - Entry Date: 20 Jun 1816 - Discharged to Lake Erie

Conrad, John (1) - Landsman - New York Naval Yard Muster 1 Aug 1815 - Number: 1404 - Entry Date: 5 Jun 1814 - Gunboat No. 33 - Discharged on 6 Nov 1814

Conrad, John (2)- Quarter Gunner - Payroll 2 - Number: 1776 - Entry Date: 6 Nov 1814 - Ran

Cook, Ansel - Quartermaster - Payroll 2 - Number: 774 - Entry Date: 16 May 1814 - Discharged to the U.S. Frigate Guerriere

Cook, David - Quarter Gunner - Payroll 1 - Number: 49 - Entry Date: 3 Oct 1813 - Gunboat No. 6 - Statement - Number: 49 - Entry Date: 3 Oct 1813 - Gunboat No. 6

Cooper, Griffith M. - Sailing Master - Payroll 2 - Number: 1384 - Entry Date: 29 Mar 1815 - Served from 3 Oct 1813 to 28 Mar 1817

Cooper, James B. - Sailing Master - Payroll 2 - Number: 1334 - Entry Date: 3 Oct 1814 - Discharged to the U.S. Storeship Alert

Cooper, Lewis - Boy - Payroll 2 - Number: 954 - Entry Date: 28 Feb 1814 - Ran

Coppy, George - Seaman - Payroll 1 - Number: 59 - Entry Date: 11 Nov 1813 - Gunboat No. 6 - Statement - Number: 59 - Entry Date: 3 Nov 1813 - Gunboat No. 6 - Discharged on 2 Mar 1814

Cornish, Daniel - Ordinary Seaman - Payroll 1 - Number: 67 - Entry Date: 3 Oct 1813 - Gunboat No. 8 - Discharged on 9 Feb 1814 - Discharged to the U.S. Frigate John Adams - Statement - Number: 70 - Entry Date: 3 Oct 1813 - Gunboat No. 8

Cotter, Michael R. - Steward - Payroll 1 - Number: 167 - Entry Date: 3 Oct 1813 - Gunboat No. A - Payroll 2 - Number: 2325 - Entry Date: 21 Oct 1816 - Gunboat No. A - Statement - Number: 169 - Entry Date: 3 Oct 1813 - Gunboat No. A - Discharged on 19 Sep 1814- Steward - Statement - Number: 642 - Entry Date: 21 Sep 1813 - Gunboat No. A

Covington, John - Master's Mate - Payroll 2 - Number: 1953 - Entry Date: 14 Jul 1815 - Discharged to the U.S. Frigate John Adams

Cowan, James (or Cowen) - Boy - Payroll 2 - Number: 1063 - Entry Date: 29 Oct 1813 - Ran

Cowen, John R. - Master's Mate - Statement - Number: 183 - Entry Date: 3 Oct 1813 - Gunboat No. A - Discharged on 9 Jul 1814

Crandle, Silas - Seaman - Payroll 2 - Number: 200 - Entry Date: 9 Feb 1814 - Discharged to the U.S. Frigate John Adams

Crawford, George - Ordinary Seaman - Payroll 2 - Number: 1736 - Entry Date: 22 Jan 1815 - Discharged to the U.S. Sloop-of-War Peacock

Crocker, David - Boatswain's Mate - Payroll 2 - Number: 1782 - Entry Date: 1 Apr 1815 - Discharged

Cruise, Jacob - Seaman - Payroll 2 - Number: 219 - Entry Date: 9 Feb 1814 - Discharged to the U.S. Frigate John Adams

Cruston, John - Seaman - Payroll 2 - Number: 786 - Entry Date: 14 Jul 1814 - Discharged to the U.S. Frigate President

Cummings, Samuel - Ordinary Seaman - Payroll 2 - Number: 1974 - Entry Date: 4 Sep 1815 - Ran

Cunningham, Alexander - Sailing Master - Gunboat No. 47 - BLW 3157-160-55

Cupid, Jacob - Boy - Payroll 2 - Number: 2320 - Entry Date: 1 Apr 1816 - Ran

Curtiss, William - Seaman - Statement - Number: 213 - Entry Date: 3 Oct 1813 - Gunboat No. B - Discharged on 25 Feb 1814

Cutter, Abraham - Seaman - Payroll 2 - Number: 1685 - Entry Date: 3 Feb 1815 - Discharged to the U.S. Frigate Congress

Dailey, Henry - Seaman - Statement - Number: 317 - Entry Date: 3 Oct 1813 - Gunboat No. 40 - Discharged on 9 Nov 1813

Damony, Michael - Ordinary Seaman - Payroll 2 - Number: 1784 - Entry Date: 1 Apr 1815 – Discharged

Daniels, John - Seaman - Payroll 2 - Number: 1835 - Entry Date: 1 Apr 1815 - Gunboat No. 103 - Statement - Number: 685 - Entry Date: 27 Sep 1813 - Gunboat No. 103 - Discharged on 13 Jun 1814

Dasharoon, George W. - Ordinary Seaman - Payroll 1 - Number: 139 - Entry Date: 26 Sep 1813 - Gunboat No. 30 - Ran on 2 Nov 1813 from New York - Payroll 2 - Number: 895 - Entry Date: 2 Nov 1813 - Gunboat No. 30 - Statement - Number: 143 - Entry Date: 27 Sep 1813 - Gunboat No. 30

Dassantez, Antonio - Ordinary Seaman - Payroll 1 - Number: 15 - Entry Date: 3 Oct 1813 - Gunboat No. 6 - Payroll 2 - Number: 799 - Entry Date: 14 Jul 1814 - Gunboat No. 6 - Statement - Number: 14 - Entry Date: 3 Oct 1813 - Gunboat No. 6 - Discharged on 14 Jul 1814 - Discharged to the U.S. Frigate President

Davenport, John - Seaman - Statement - Number: 718 - Entry Date: 27 Sep 1813 - Gunboat No. 105 - Discharged on 27 Nov 1813

Davis, George - Ordinary Seaman - Statement - Number: 335 - Entry Date: 3 Oct 1813 - Gunboat No. 40

Davis, John - Boatswain's Mate - Statement - Number: 313 - Entry Date: 3 Oct 1813 - Gunboat No. 40 - Discharged on 17 Sep 1814

Davis, London - Seaman - Statement - Number: 321 - Entry Date: 3 Oct 1813 - Gunboat No. 40 - Discharged on 9 Nov 1813

Davis, Moses - Seaman - Payroll 2 - Number: 1704 - Entry Date: 25 Dec 1814 - Ran

Day, Charles - Landsman - Payroll 2 - Number: 1735 - Entry Date: 1 Apr 1815 - Discharged

Dean, Elias - Seaman - Payroll 1 - Number: 135 - Entry Date: 26 Sep 1813 - Gunboat No. 30 - Statement - Number: 139 - Entry Date: 27 Sep 1813 - Gunboat No. 30 - Discharged on 7 Jun 1814

Dean, John - Seaman - Payroll 2 - Number: 2175 - Entry Date: 4 Oct 1815 - Sent to Sackets Harbor

DeCruize, Andrew - Ordinary Seaman - Statement - Number: 179 - Entry Date: 3 Oct 1813 - Gunboat No. A

Delabar, Henry - Seaman - Statement - Number: 338 - Entry Date: 6 Oct 1813 - Gunboat No. 40

Delano, Bado - Ordinary Seaman - Statement - Number: 924 - Entry Date: 27 Sep 1813 - Gunboat No. 114 - Discharged on 2 Nov 1813

Delap, William - Boy - Statement - Number: 187 - Entry Date: 3 Oct 1813 - Gunboat No. A - Discharged on 14 Jul 1814 - Discharged to the U.S. Frigate President

Demelt, William - Seaman - New York Naval Yard Muster 1 Aug 1815 - Number: 1356 - Entry Date: 21 May 1814 - Gunboat No. 47 - Discharged on 2 Dec 1814 - Payroll 2 - Number: 1750 - Entry Date: 22 Dec 1814 - Gunboat No. 47 - Statement - Number: 1363 - Entry Date: 21 May 1814 - Gunboat No. 47

Dennis, Thomas (1) - Ordinary Seaman - Payroll 1 - Number: 76 - Entry Date: 3 Oct 1813 - Gunboat No. 8 - Statement - Number: 79 - Entry Date: 3 Oct 1813 - Gunboat No. 8

Dennis, Thomas (2) - Master's Mate - Payroll 1 - Number: 112 - Entry Date: 3 Oct 1813 - Gunboat No. 8 - Statement - Number: 115 - Entry Date: 3 Oct 1813 - Gunboat No. 8 - Statement - Number: 609 - Entry Date: 3 Oct 1813 - Gunboat No. 8 - Discharged on 24 Feb 1814 - Statement - Number: 1234 - Entry Date: 17 Mar 1814 - Gunboat No. 8

Dennison, George - Quarter Gunner - Payroll 2 - Number: 764 - Entry Date: 6 Dec 1813 - Transferred to naval yard

Derby, John - Ordinary Seaman - Payroll 2 - Number: 917 - Entry Date: 26 Feb 1814 - Died

Deshoit, Frederick - Seaman - Payroll 2 - Number: 787 - Entry Date: 14 Jul 1814 - Discharged to the U.S. Frigate President

Dick, Charles - Landsman - New York Naval Yard Muster 1 Aug 1815 - Number: 1312 - Entry Date: 2 May 1814 - Gunboat No. 41 - Discharged on 1 Apr 1815 - Payroll 2 - Number: 1732 - Entry Date: 1 Apr 1815 - Gunboat No.

41 - Statement - Number: 1321 - Entry Date: 2 May 1814 - Gunboat No. 41

Dixon, Alexander - Ordinary Seaman - Payroll 2 - Number: 1718 - Entry Date: 1 Apr 1815 - Discharged

Dotey, Elisha - Seaman - Payroll 2 - Number: 1880 - Entry Date: 15 Jan 1815 - Ran

Douglass, Angustus C. - Steward - Statement - Entry Date: 7 Sep 1813 - Gunboat No. 30

Douglass, Samuel M. - Steward - Payroll 2 - Number: 1658 - Entry Date: 20 Oct 1815 - Gunboat No. 113- Steward - Statement - Number: 887 - Entry Date: 27 Sep 1813 - Gunboat No. 113

Downing, William - Ordinary Seaman - Payroll 1 - Number: 103 - Entry Date: 3 Oct 1813 - Gunboat No. 8 - Ordinary Seaman - Statement - Number: 106 - Entry Date: 3 Oct 1813 - Gunboat No. 8 - Discharged on 24 Feb 1814 from New York

Downing, William - Seaman - Statement - Number: 1263 - Entry Date: 28 Mar 1814 - Gunboat No. 8

Downs, Shubal - Sailing Master - Payroll 2 - Number: 2167 - Entry Date: 2 Nov 1815

Doyle, William - Landsman - Payroll 1 - Number: 146 - Entry Date: 26 Sep 1813 - Gunboat No. 30 - Payroll 2 - Number: 222 - Entry Date: 9 Feb 1814 - Gunboat No. 30 - Statement - Number: 148 - Entry Date: 27 Sep 1813 - Gunboat No. 30 - Discharged on 9 Feb 1814 - Discharged to the U.S. Frigate John Adams

Drew, James - Ordinary Seaman - Payroll 2 - Number: 982 - Entry Date: 26 Dec 1813 - Ran

Duce, Caleb - Ordinary Seaman - Payroll 1 - Number: 83 - Entry Date: 3 Oct 1813 - Gunboat No. 8 - Discharged on 9 Feb 1814 - Discharged to the U.S. Frigate John Adams - Statement - Number: 86 - Entry Date: 3 Oct 1813 - Gunboat No. 8

Dudley, William - Boatswain's Mate - New York Naval Yard Muster 1 Aug 1815 - Number: 1385 - Entry Date: 1 Jun 1814 - Gunboat No. 111 - Discharged on 1 Apr 1815 - Payroll 2 - Number: 1766 - Entry Date: 1 Apr 1815 - Gunboat No. 111 - Statement - Number: 838 - Entry Date: 27 Sep 1813 - Gunboat No. 111 - Statement - Number: 1392 - Entry Date: 1 Jun 1814 - Gunboat No. 111

Duffy, James - Ordinary Seaman - Statement - Number: 189 - Entry Date: 3 Oct 1813 - Gunboat No. A - Discharged on 10 Dec 1813

Dunham, John - Seaman - Payroll 2 - Number: 1050 - Entry Date: 15 Mar 1814 - Ran

Dunn, Charles - Ordinary Seaman - Statement - Number: 184 - Entry Date: 3 Oct 1813 - Gunboat No. A - Discharged on 7 Dec 1813

Dupersnar, John - Boatswain's Mate - Statement - Entry Date: 5 Oct 1814 - Gunboat No. 30

Dwart, Nicholas - Ordinary Seaman - Statement - Number: 126 - Entry Date: 3 Oct 1813 - Gunboat No. 29

Easton, Samuel - Seaman - Payroll 2 - Number: 998 - Entry Date: 28 Sep 1813 - Gunboat No. 113 - Statement - Number: 875 - Entry Date: 27 Sep 1813 - Gunboat No. 113 - Ran on 28 Sep 1813 at New York

Edgar, John - Seaman - New York Naval Yard Muster 1 Aug 1815 - Number: 1309 - Entry Date: 30 Apr 1814 - Gunboat No. 57 - Discharged on 1 Apr 1815 - Payroll 2 - Number: 1731 - Entry Date: 1 Apr 1815 - Gunboat No. 57 - Statement - Number: 1318 - Entry Date: 30 Apr 1814 - Gunboat No. 57

Edwards, Peter - Ordinary Seaman - Payroll 2 - Number: 202 - Entry Date: 9 Feb 1814 - Gunboat No. 114 - Statement - Number: 916 - Entry Date: 27 Sep 1813 - Gunboat No. 114 - Discharged on 9 Feb 1814 - Discharged to the U.S. Frigate John Adams

Eleves, Charles - Seaman - Payroll 2 - Number: 1872 - Entry Date: 2 Oct 1814 - Died

Ellias, Charles - Armorer - Payroll 2 - Number: 1976 - Entry Date: 8 Jun 1815 - Ran

Elliott, John - Ordinary Seaman - Payroll 2 - Number: 1734 - Entry Date: 1 Apr 1815 - Discharged

Ellis, Abel - Seaman - Payroll 1 - Number: 38 - Entry Date: 3 Oct 1813 - Gunboat No. 6 - Payroll 2 - Number: 1907 - Entry Date: 3 Jan 1815 - Gunboat No. 6 - Statement - Number: 38 - Entry Date: 3 Oct 1813 - Gunboat No. 6 - Discharged on 11 Nov 1813 from New York

Ellison, Richard - Landsman - Statement - Number: 164 - Entry Date: 20 Apr 1814 - Gunboat No. 30 - Ran on 20 Jun 1814 at New York

Enfield, James - Seaman - Payroll 2 - Number: 1930 - Entry Date: 20 May 1815 - ran

Enis, James - Seaman - Statement - Number: 319 - Entry Date: 3 Oct 1813 - Gunboat No. 40 - Discharged on 9 Nov 1813

Espagny, Mathias - Ordinary Seaman - Payroll 2 - Number: 949 - Entry Date: 12 Oct 1813 - Ran

Evaleth, John - Master's Mate - Statement - Number: 210 - Entry Date: 3 Oct 1813 - Gunboat No. B

Evans, Peter - Seaman - Payroll 2 - Number: 765 - Entry Date: 21 Apr 1814 - Transferred to naval yard

Evans, William - Seaman - Statement - Number: 891 - Entry Date: 27 Sep 1813 - Gunboat No. 113 - Discharged on 9 Jul 1814

Ewing, James - Seaman - Payroll 1 - Number: 19 - Entry Date: 3 Oct 1813 - Gunboat No. 6 - Statement - Number: 18 - Entry Date: 3 Oct 1813 - Gunboat No. 6 - Discharged on 28 Jul 1814 - BLW 3432-160-55

Fabier, William - Ordinary Seaman - Payroll 2 - Number: 942 - Entry Date: 4 Jun 1814 - Discharged

Fagan, Samuel - Ordinary Seaman - Payroll 2 - Number: 1642 - Entry Date: 20 Oct 1814 - Ran

Farries, Henry - Landsman - Payroll 2 - Number: 985 - Entry Date: 3 Nov 1813 - Gunboat No. 109 - Statement - Number: 789 - Entry Date: 27 Sep 1813 - Gunboat No. 109 - Discharged on 3 Nov 1813 - Ran on 3 Nov 1813 at New York

Felton, Thomas (2) - Seaman - Payroll 2 - Number: 1763 - Entry Date: 1 Apr 1815 - Discharged

Fenchell, Ferinand - Seaman - Payroll 1 - Number: 136 - Entry Date: 26 Sep 1813 - Gunboat No. 30 - Discharged on 9 Feb 1814 - Discharged to the U.S. Frigate John Adams - Statement - Number: 140 - Entry Date: 27 Sep 1813 - Gunboat No. 30

Fennell, Richard - Seaman - Statement - Number: 888 - Entry Date: 27 Sep 1813 - Gunboat No. 113 - Discharged on 13 Jul 1814

Fennell, William - Seaman - Payroll 2 - Number: 999 - Entry Date: 24 Nov 1813 - Gunboat No. 113 - Statement - Number: 877 - Entry Date: 27 Sep 1813 - Gunboat No. 113 - Ran on 20 Nov 1813 at New York

Ferguson, Henry - Seaman - New York Naval Yard Muster 1 Aug 1815 - Number: 972 - Entry Date: 14 Jan 1814 - Gunboat No. 47 - Discharged on 3 Mar 1815 - Payroll 2 - Number: 1674 - Entry Date: 3 Mar 1815 - Gunboat No. 47 - Statement - Number: 991 - Entry Date: 14 Jan 1814 - Gunboat No. 47

Ferguson, James - Sailing Master - Statement - Number: 899 - Gunboat No. 113

Ferguson, John - Seaman - Payroll 2 - Number: 1820 - Entry Date: 1 Apr 1815 - Discharged

Ferris, William - Seaman - Payroll 1 - Number: 80 - Entry Date: 3 Oct 1813 - Gunboat No. 8 - Payroll 2 - Number: 1632 - Entry Date: 15 May 1814 - Gunboat No. 8 - Statement - Number: 83 - Entry Date: 3 Oct 1813 - Gunboat No. 8

Fetton, Thomas - Seaman - Statement - Number: 330 - Entry Date: 3 Oct 1813 - Gunboat No. 40 - Discharged on 25 Jan 1814

Fields, Simeon - Ordinary Seaman - Statement - Number: 326 - Entry Date: 3 Oct 1813 - Gunboat No. 40

Fletcher, Henry - Seaman - Payroll 2 - Number: 971 - Entry Date: 30 Nov 1813 - Ran

Fletcher, Peter - Seaman - Statement - Number: 679 - Entry Date: 27 Sep 1813 - Gunboat No. 103 - Statement 1 - Number: 1348 - Entry Date: 16 Jun 1814 - Gunboat No. 103 - Discharged on 14 Jul 1814 - Discharged to the U.S. Sloop-of-War Peacock

Flood, Samuel - Quarter Gunner - Promotions - Entry Date: 5 Oct 1813 - Gunboat No. 113 - Promoted - Statement - Number: 873 - Entry Date: 27 Sep 1813 - Gunboat No. 113 - Discharged on 9 Jun 1814 - Statement - Number: 1389 - Entry Date: 1 Jun 1814 - Gunboat No. 113

Foley, Jeremiah - Seaman - Payroll 2 - Number: 125 - Entry Date: 17 Jan 1814 - Discharged to the U.S. Sloop-of-War Peacock

Fortune, Julius - Ordinary Seaman - Statement - Number: 680 - Entry Date: 27 Sep 1813 - Gunboat No. 103 - Discharged on 13 Jun 1814

Foster, Nathan - Steward - Statement - Number: 198 - Entry Date: 3 Oct 1813 - Gunboat No. B - Discharged on 10 Oct 1813

Fountain, William - Seaman - Statement - Number: 859 - Entry Date: 27 Sep 1813 - Gunboat No. 112 - Discharged on 17 Jan 1814 - Discharged to the U.S. Sloop-of-War Peacock

Fox, Thomas - Landsman - Payroll 2 - Number: 1787 - Entry Date: 1 Apr 1815 - Discharged to navy yard

Francis, John (1) - Ordinary Seaman - Statement - Number: 674 - Entry Date: 27 Sep 1813 - Gunboat No. 103 - Discharged on 14 Jul 1814 - Seaman - Statement - Number: 1140 - Entry Date: 12 Mar 1814 - Gunboat No. 103 - Statement 1 - Number: 1337 - Entry Date: 14 Jun 1814 - Gunboat No. 103

Francis, John (2) - Seaman - Payroll 2 - Number: 1797 - Entry Date: 1 Apr 1815 - Discharged

Frandurup, William - Seaman - Payroll 2 - Number: 1635 - Entry Date: 22 Sep 1814 - Discharged

Frazer, James - Seaman - Statement - Number: 848 - Entry Date: 27 Sep 1813 - Gunboat No. 112 - Discharged on 13 Jun 1814

Freeman, John - Ordinary Seaman - Statement - Number: 180 - Entry Date: 3 Oct 1813 - Gunboat No. A - Discharged on 10 Oct 1813

Freeman, Lewis - Landsman - Payroll 2 - Number: 958 - Entry Date: 11 Mar 1814 - Ran

Frenchall, Frederick - Seaman - Payroll 2 - Number: 225 - Entry Date: 9 Feb 1814 - Discharged to the U.S. Frigate John Adams

Frost, John - Landsman - Payroll 2 - Number: 922 - Entry Date: 20 Nov 1813 - Ran

Fry, John - Seaman - Statement - Number: 160 - Entry Date: 27 Sep 1813 - Gunboat No. 30 - Discharged on 12 Jul 1814

Fryman, John - Boy - Statement - Number: 681 - Entry Date: 27 Sep 1813 - Gunboat No. 103 - Discharged on 13 Jun 1814

Gabriel, John - Ordinary Seaman - Payroll 2 - Number: 983 - Entry Date: 26 Dec 1813 - Ran

Gabriel, William - Landsman - Statement - Number: 682 - Entry Date: 27 Sep 1813 - Gunboat No. 103 - Discharged on 14 Jul 1814 - Seaman - Statement 1 - Number: 1359 - Entry Date: 18 Jun 1814 - Gunboat No. 103 - Payroll 2 - Number: 1804 - Entry Date: 1 Apr 1815 - Gunboat No. 103

Gains, Sylvester - Boy - Statement - Number: 858 - Entry Date: 27 Sep 1813 - Gunboat No. 112 - Discharged on 12 Jul 1814

Gale, Moses - Master's Mate - Payroll 2 - Number: 1646 - Entry Date: 1 Apr 1815 - Discharged

Gales, William - Seaman - Statement - Number: 920 - Entry Date: 27 Sep 1813 - Gunboat No. 114 - Discharged on 12 Jul 1814

Gardiner, Peter - Ordinary Seaman - Payroll 1 - Number: 64 - Entry Date: 3 Oct 1813 - Gunboat No. 8 - Discharged on 17 Dec 1813 at New York - Statement - Number: 67 - Entry Date: 3 Oct 1813 - Gunboat No. 8 - Discharged on 17 Dec 1813 - Seaman - Statement - Number: 995 - Entry Date: 26 Jan 1814 - Gunboat No. 8

Geomy, Marcella - Ordinary Seaman - Payroll 2 - Number: 1844 - Entry Date: 1 Apr 1815 - Discharged

George, Eliphalet - Ordinary Seaman - Payroll 1 - Number: 147 - Entry Date: 26 Sep 1813 - Gunboat No. 30 - Payroll 2 - Number: 898 - Entry Date: 1 Feb 1814 - Gunboat No. 30 - Statement - Number: 149 - Entry Date: 27 Sep 1813 - Gunboat No. 30 - Ran on 1 Feb 1814 at New York

George, Jacob - Ordinary Seaman - Statement - Number: 322 - Entry Date: 3 Oct 1813 - Gunboat No. 40 - Discharged on 9 Nov 1813

Gere, William - Sailing Master - Statement - Number: 671 - Number 2: 671b - Entry Date: 27 Sep 1813 - Gunboat No. 103

Gibbs, Samuel - Ordinary Seaman - Statement - Number: 922 - Entry Date: 27 Sep 1813 - Gunboat No. 114 - Discharged on 12 Jul 1814

Gilford, Moses - Seaman - Payroll 2 - Number: 1027 - Entry Date: 30 May 1814

Gillis, James - Seaman - Payroll 1 - Number: 42 - Entry Date: 3 Oct 1813 - Gunboat No. 6 - Discharged on 3 Feb 1814 at New York - Statement - Number: 42 - Entry Date: 3 Oct 1813 - Gunboat No. 6

Gilmore, Mathew - Ordinary Seaman - Payroll 2 - Number: 1778 - Entry Date: 1 Feb 1815 - Discharged

Girdler, Richard - Quarter Gunner - Statement - Number: 188 - Entry Date: 3 Oct 1813 - Gunboat No. A - Discharged on 25 Feb 1814 - Statement - Number: 1232 - Entry Date: 17 Mar 1814 - Gunboat No. A

Gistle, William - Ordinary Seaman - Payroll 2 - Number: 1066 - Entry Date: 11 Mar 1814 - Discharged

Glover, Robert - Quarter Gunner - Statement - Number: 857 - Entry Date: 27 Sep 1813 - Gunboat No. 112

Golden, Patrick - Seaman - Payroll 1 - Number: 48 - Entry Date: 3 Oct 1813 - Gunboat No. 6 - Statement - Number: 48 - Entry Date: 3 Oct 1813 - Gunboat No. 6

Goodman, Robert - Seaman - Statement - Number: 712 - Entry Date: 27 Sep 1813 - Gunboat No. 105 - Discharged on 12 Jul 1814

Gordon, George - Seaman - Payroll 2 - Number: 1831 - Entry Date: 4 Mar 1815 - Ran

Gordon, John - Ordinary Seaman - Payroll 2 - Number: 1768 - Entry Date: 25 Dec 1814 - Ran

Gordon, William L. - Lieutenant - Payroll 2 - Number: 2220 - Entry Date: 6 Nov 1815 - Discharged to the U.S. Ship-of-the-Line Independence

Goss, John - Landsman - Payroll 2 - Number: 798 - Entry Date: 14 Jul 1814 - Gunboat No. 105 - Statement - Number: 726 - Entry Date: 5 Jan 1814 - Gunboat No. 105 - Discharged on 14 Jul 1814 - Discharged to the U.S. Frigate President

Graham, Anson - Seaman - Payroll 2 - Number: 1666 - Entry Date: 22 Feb 1815 - Gunboat No. 40 - Statement - Number: 336 - Entry Date: 7 Oct 1813 - Gunboat No. 40

Graham, John H. - Midshipman - Payroll 2 - Number: 870 - Entry Date: 25 Jan 1814 - Navy yard

Graves, John - Ordinary Seaman - Statement - Number: 870 - Entry Date: 27 Sep 1813 - Gunboat No. 112 - Discharged on 12 Jul 1814

Gray, David - Ordinary Seaman - Payroll 2 - Number: 198 - Entry Date: 9 Feb 1814 - Gunboat No. 109 - Statement - Number: 790 - Entry Date: 27 Sep 1813 - Gunboat No. 109 - Discharged on 9 Feb 1814 - Discharged to the U.S. Frigate John Adams

Gready, Nicholas - Seaman - Statement - Number: 168 - Entry Date: 3 Oct 1813 - Gunboat No. A - Discharged on 18 Sep 1814

Green, Gideon - Ordinary Seaman - Payroll 2 - Number: 963 - Entry Date: 15 Mar 1814 - Ran

Green, James (1) - Landsman - Payroll 2 - Number: 925 - Entry Date: 11 Nov 1813 - Ran

Green, James (2) - Seaman - Payroll 1 - Number: 140 - Entry Date: 26 Sep 1813 - Gunboat No. 30 - Ran on 26 Oct 1813 from New York - Payroll 2 - Number: 896 - Entry Date: 26 Oct 1813 - Gunboat No. 30 - Statement - Number: 144 - Entry Date: 27 Sep 1813 - Gunboat No. 30

Green, Jesse - Ordinary Seaman - Payroll 2 - Number: 778 - Entry Date: 14 Jul 1814 - Discharged to the U.S. Frigate President

Green, Joseph - Ordinary Seaman - New York Naval Yard Muster 1 Aug 1815 - Number: 1305 - Entry Date: 27 Arp 1814 - Gunboat No. 57 - Discharged on 1 Apr 1815 - Payroll 2 - Number: 1729 - Entry Date: 1 Apr 1815 - Gunboat No. 57 - Statement - Number: 1314 - Entry Date: 27 Apr 1814 - Gunboat No. 57

Gregory, Samuel - Ordinary Seaman - Payroll 2 - Number: 1803 - Entry Date: 1 Apr 1815 - Discharged

Griffin, Allen - Midshipman - Payroll 2 - Number: 840 - Entry Date: 5 Dec 1813 - Navy yard

Griffiths, George - Quarter Gunner - Payroll 1 - Number: 28 - Entry Date: 3 Oct 1813 - Gunboat No. 6 - Statement - Number: 28 - Entry Date: 3 Oct 1813 - Gunboat No. 6

Grouse, Robert - Ordinary Seaman - Payroll 2 - Number: 1060 - Entry Date: 5 Oct 1813 - Ran

Grunyer, William - Quarter Gunner - Payroll 2 - Number: 203 - Entry Date: 9 Feb 1814 - Discharged to the U.S. Frigate John Adams

Gurner, Prince - Landsman - Payroll 2 - Number: 1640 - Entry Date: 25 Feb 1815 - Discharged

Haddock, Joseph P. - Master's Mate - Payroll 2 - Number: 1045 - Entry Date: 3 Oct 1814 - Discharged

Haight, James - Master's Mate - Statement - Number: 47 - Entry Date: 3 Oct 1813 - Gunboat No. 6 - Sailing Master - Promotions - Entry Date: 11 Apr 1814 - Gunboat No. 6 - Promoted

Hair, Robert - Ordinary Seaman - Payroll 2 - Number: 945 - Entry Date: 3 Nov 1813 - Ran

Haley, Joshua - Seaman - Statement - Number: 788 - Entry Date: 27 Sep 1813 - Gunboat No. 109 - Discharged on 6 Dec 1813

Hall, David - Landsman - Payroll 2 - Number: 1769 - Entry Date: 1 Apr 1815 - Discharged

Hall, James - Master's Mate - Statement - Number: 889 - Entry Date: 27 Sep 1813 - Gunboat No. 113 - Discharged on 16 Jun 1814

Hall, Lawrence - Boatswain's Mate - Payroll 1 - Number: 85 - Entry Date: 3 Oct 1813 - Gunboat No. 8 - Discharged on 22 Mar 1814 at New York - Statement - Number: 88 - Entry Date: 3 Oct 1813 - Gunboat No. 8

Hall, Reuben - Seaman - Statement - Number: 812 - Entry Date: 24 Apr 1814 - Gunboat No. 109

Hall, Samuel - Landsman - Payroll 2 - Number: 1020 - Entry Date: 29 Aug 1814 - Discharged

Halsey, David P. - Master's Mate - Payroll 1 - Number: 54 - Entry Date: 3 Oct 1813 - Gunboat No. 6 - Statement - Number: 54 - Entry Date: 3 Oct 1813 - Gunboat No. 6

Hamilton, Conway - Seaman - Payroll 1 - Number: 16 - Entry Date: 3 Oct 1813 - Gunboat No. 6 - Statement - Number: 15 - Entry Date: 3 Oct 1813 - Gunboat No. 6

Hamlan, Robert - Seaman - Statement - Number: 710 - Entry Date: 27 Sep 1813 - Gunboat No. 105 - Discharged on 25 Mar 1814

Hand, James - Landsman - New York Naval Yard Muster 1 Aug 1815 - Number: 1080 - Entry Date: 6 Mar 1814 - Gunboat No. 47 - Ran on 2 Dec 1814 - Payroll 2 - Number: 1696 - Entry Date: 2 Oct 1814 - Gunboat No. 47

Hannah, Thomas - Seaman - Payroll 2 - Number: 126 - Entry Date: 17 Jan 1814 - Discharged to the U.S. Sloop-of-War Peacock

Hanson, John - Seaman - Statement - Number: 174 - Entry Date: 3 Oct 1813 - Gunboat No. A

Hardwick, Thomas - Sailing Master - Payroll 2 - Number: 1331 - Entry Date: 8 Apr 1814 - Gunboat No. B - Discharged to the U.S. Frigate United States - Statement - Number: 194 - Entry Date: 3 Oct 1813 - Gunboat No. B

Harlan, Dennis - Seaman - Payroll 2 - Number: 1655 - Entry Date: 20 Oct 1814 - Ran

Harman, John - Landsman - Payroll 2 - Number: 2003 - Entry Date: 21 Jul 1815 - Discharged to the U.S. Brig Boxer

Harper, Thomas S. - Seaman - Payroll 2 - Number: 1860 - Entry Date: 13 Feb 1815 - Ran

Harris, John (1) - Ordinary Seaman - Payroll 2 - Number: 889 - Entry Date: 7 Oct 1813 - Gunboat No. 8 - Statement - Number: 113 - Entry Date: 3 Oct 1813 - Gunboat No. 8 - Ran on 7 Oct 1813 at New York

Harris, John (2) - Master's Mate - Statement - Number: 869 - Entry Date: 27 Sep 1813 - Gunboat No. 112 - Sailing Master - Promotions - Entry Date: 11 Apr 1814 - Gunboat No. 112 - Promoted

Harrison, George - Seaman - Payroll 2 - Number: 238 - Entry Date: 9 Feb 1814 - Discharged to the U.S. Frigate John Adams

Harrison, John - Ordinary Seaman - Payroll 2 - Number: 232 - Entry Date: 9 Feb 1814 - Discharged to the U.S. Frigate John Adams

Hartfield, Daniel - Surgeon - Payroll 2 - Number: 1882 - Entry Date: 13 May 1815 - Died

Harvey, Howard - Boatswain's Mate - Payroll 2 - Number: 1928 - Entry Date: 10 May 1815 - Ran

Harvey, Thomas - Sailing Master - Payroll 2 - Number: 834 - Entry Date: 5 Dec 1813 - Discharged to the U.S. Frigate President

Hatsley, Frederick - Seaman - Statement - Number: 343 - Entry Date: 4 Nov 1813 - Gunboat No. 40

Hauld, John - Seaman - Payroll 2 - Number: 789 - Entry Date: 14 Jul 1814 - Discharged to the U.S. Frigate President

Hays, Adam - Seaman - Payroll 1 - Number: 86 - Entry Date: 3 Oct 1813 - Gunboat No. 8 - Discharged on 12 Feb 1814 at New York - Statement - Number: 89 - Entry Date: 3 Oct 1813 - Gunboat No. 8

Hazard, Anthony - Ordinary Seaman - Payroll 2 - Number: 1630 - Entry Date: 10 Oct 1814 - Gunboat No. 8 - Statement - Number: 69 - Entry Date: 3 Oct 1813 - Gunboat No. 8

Hazard, Benedict A. - Ordinary Seaman - Statement - Number: 346 - Entry Date: 3 Dec 1813 - Gunboat No. 40

Heard, Nathaniel - Seaman - Payroll 2 - Number: 220 - Entry Date: 9 Feb 1814 - Discharged to the U.S. Frigate John Adams

Heart, John - Ordinary Seaman - Payroll 2 - Number: 1986 - Entry Date: 21 Jul 1815 - Discharged to the U.S. Brig Boxer

Heart, Peter - Seaman - Payroll 2 - Number: 1815 - Entry Date: 1 Apr 1815 - Discharged

Henderson, William - Seaman - Payroll 1 - Number: 30 - Entry Date: 3 Oct 1813 - Gunboat No. 6 - Statement - Number: 30 - Entry Date: 3 Oct 1813 - Gunboat No. 6

Henfield, Thomas - Seaman - Payroll 2 - Number: 1721 - Entry Date: 1 Apr 1815 - Discharged

Henry, William (1) - Ordinary Seaman - Payroll 2 - Number: 1725 - Entry Date: 17 Dec 1814 - Ran

Henry, William (2) - Boatswain's Mate - Statement - Number: 854 - Entry Date: 27 Sep 1813 - Gunboat No. 112 - Discharged on 19 Jul 1814

Herron, William - Seaman - Payroll 2 - Number: 1906 - Entry Date: 1 Jan 1815 - Ran

Hewlings, William - Seaman - Payroll 2 - Number: 1996 - Entry Date: 21 Jul 1815 - Discharged to the U.S. Brig Boxer

Heyniger, Lambert - Master's Mate - Statement - Number: 312 - Entry Date: 3 Oct 1813 - Gunboat No. 40

Hill, James - Seaman - Payroll 2 - Number: 214 - Entry Date: 9 Feb 1814 - Gunboat No. 113 - Statement - Number: 876 - Entry Date: 27 Sep 1813 - Gunboat No. 113 - Discharged on 9 Feb 1814 - Discharged to the U.S. Frigate John Adams

Hill, Richard - Ordinary Seaman - Payroll 1 - Number: 118 - Entry Date: 3 Oct 1813 - Gunboat No. 29 - Statement - Number: 122 - Entry Date: 3 Oct 1813 - Gunboat No. 29 - Discharged on 22 Jul 1814

Hiller, George (1) - Seaman - Statement - Number: 102 - Entry Date: 3 Oct 1813 - Gunboat No. 8 - Discharged on 27 Feb 1814

Hiller, George (2) - Ordinary Seaman - Statement - Number: 103 - Entry Date: 3 Oct 1813 - Gunboat No. 8 - Discharged on 9 Feb 1814 - Discharged to the U.S. Frigate John Adams

Hinson, William - Ordinary Seaman - Statement - Number: 325 - Entry Date: 3 Oct 1813 - Gunboat No. 40 - Discharged on 9 Nov 1813

Hogan, Joseph - Boy - Payroll 2 - Number: 1863 - Entry Date: 1 Apr 1815 - Navy yard

Hollows, Stephen - Ordinary Seaman - Payroll 2 - Number: 919 - Entry Date: 19 Oct 1813 - Died

Holst, Neils - Seaman - Payroll 2 - Number: 233 - Entry Date: 9 Feb 1814 - Discharged to the U.S. Frigate John Adams

Homan, John - Seaman - Payroll 1 - Number: 97 - Entry Date: 3 Oct 1813 - Gunboat No. 8 - Statement - Number: 100 - Entry Date: 3 Oct 1813 - Gunboat No. 8 - Discharged on 22 Mar 1814 at New York - Statement - Number: 1269 - Entry Date: 31 Mar 1814 - Gunboat No. 8

Homan, Samuel - Ordinary Seaman - Payroll 1 - Number: 102 - Entry Date: 3 Oct 1813 - Gunboat No. 8 - Discharged on 9 Feb 1814 - Discharged to the U.S. Frigate John Adams - Payroll 2 - Number: 210 - Entry Date: 9 Feb 1814 - Gunboat No. 8 - Statement - Number: 105 - Entry Date: 3 Oct 1813 - Gunboat No. 8

Honle, Lott - Unknown - Payroll 2 - Number: 1902 - Entry Date: 22 Jan 1815 - Died

Hopkins, Davis - Ordinary Seaman - Payroll 1 - Number: 75 - Entry Date: 3 Oct 1813 - Gunboat No. 8 - Ran on 13 Oct 1813 from New York

Hopkins, Davis - Ordinary Seaman - Statement - Number: 78 - Entry Date: 3 Oct 1813 - Gunboat No. 8

Hough, John - Master's Mate - Statement - Entry Date: 20 Sep 1814 - Gunboat No. 30

Howard, John - Seaman - Statement - Number: 808 - Entry Date: 27 Sep 1813 - Gunboat No. 109 - Discharged on 12 Jul 1814

Howard, William - Ordinary Seaman - Payroll 2 - Number: 980 - Entry Date: 26 Dec 1813 - Ran

Howell, Usher - Seaman - Statement - Number: 316 - Entry Date: 3 Oct 1813 - Gunboat No. 40 - Discharged on 9 Nov 1813

Howland, Rouse - Seaman - Statement - Number: 787 - Entry Date: 27 Sep 1813 - Gunboat No. 109 - Discharged on 23 May 1814

Hubbard, Amos - Seaman - Statement - Number: 212 - Entry Date: 3 Oct 1813 - Gunboat No. B - Discharged on 24 Feb 1814

Hudson, William - Master's Mate - Payroll 2 - Number: 1911 - Entry Date: 8 Apr 1815 - Discharged

Huff, Laurence - Master's Mate - Statement - Number: 696 - Entry Date: 27 Sep 1813 - Gunboat No. 103

Huntington, Joseph - Yeoman - Payroll 2 - Number: 1903 - Entry Date: 16 Nov 1814 - Ran

Hutchings, James - Ordinary Seaman - Payroll 1 - Number: 90 - Entry Date: 3 Oct 1813 - Gunboat No. 8 - Statement - Number: 93 - Entry Date: 3 Oct 1813 - Gunboat No. 8

Hutchinson, John - Seaman - Payroll 2 - Number: 186 - Entry Date: 9 Feb 1814 - Discharged to the U.S. Frigate John Adams

Hutton, James - Seaman - Statement - Number: 880 - Entry Date: 27 Sep 1813 - Gunboat No. 113 - Discharged on 29 Nov 1813

Isaacs, William - Ordinary Seaman - Payroll 2 - Number: 1836 - Entry Date: 1 Apr 1815 - Navy yard

Jackson, Daniel - Ordinary Seaman - New York Naval Yard Muster 1 Aug 1815 - Number: 1355 - Entry Date: 21 May 1814 - Gunboat No. 50 - Discharged on 1 Apr 1815 - Payroll 2 - Number: 1749 - Entry Date: 1 Apr 1815 - Gunboat No. 50 - Statement - Number: 1362 - Entry Date: 21 May 1814 - Gunboat No. 50

Jackson, Edward - Ordinary Seaman - Payroll 1 - Number: 152 - Entry Date: 26 Sep 1813 - Gunboat No. 30 - Statement - Number: 154 - Entry Date: 27 Sep 1813 - Gunboat No. 30 - Discharged on 12 Jul 1814

Jackson, George - Ordinary Seaman - Payroll 2 - Number: 2166 - Entry Date: 2 Nov 1815

Jackson, Henry - Ordinary Seaman - Payroll 2 - Number: 1001 - Entry Date: 25 Nov 1813 - Gunboat No. 113 - Statement - Number: 886 - Entry Date: 27 Sep 1813 - Gunboat No. 113 - Statement - Number: 1042 - Entry Date: 27 Mar 1814 - Gunboat No. 113 - Ran on 18 May 1814 at New York

Jackson, John (1) - Ordinary Seaman - Payroll 2 - Number: 1779 - Entry Date: 1 Apr 1815 - Navy yard

Jackson, John (2) - Landsman - Statement - Number: 688 - Entry Date: 27 Sep 1813 - Gunboat No. 103 - Discharged on 12 Jul 1814 - Statement - Number: 1296 - Entry Date: 16 Apr 1814 - Gunboat No. 103

Jackson, John (3) - Boy - Statement - Number: 116 - Entry Date: 13 Nov 1813 - Gunboat No. 8 - Ran on 15 Jul 1814

Jackson, Robert - Ordinary Seaman - New York Naval Yard Muster 1 Aug 1815 - Number: 1287 - Entry Date: 19 Apr 1814 - Gunboat No. 45 - Ran on 25 Dec 1814 - Payroll 2 - Number: 1723 - Entry Date: 25 Dec 1814 - Gunboat No. 45 - Statement - Number: 1300 - Entry Date: 19 Apr 1814 - Gunboat No. 45

Jackson, William (1) - Landsman - Payroll 1 - Number: 79 - Entry Date: 3 Oct 1813 - Gunboat No. 8 - Statement - Number: 82 - Entry Date: 3 Oct 1813 - Gunboat No. 8 - Discharged on 2 Jul 1814

Jackson, William (2) - Seaman - Payroll 1 - Number: 142 - Entry Date: 26 Sep 1813 - Gunboat No. 30 - Statement - Number: 146 - Entry Date: 27 Sep 1813 - Gunboat No. 30 - Discharged on 7 Jun 1814

Jacobs, Faca - Seaman - Statement - Number: 201 - Entry Date: 3 Oct 1813 - Gunboat No. B - Discharged on 17 Jan 1814 - Discharged to the U.S. Sloop-of-War Peacock

James, Joseph - Quarter Gunner - Statement - Number: 874 - Entry Date: 27 Sep 1813 - Gunboat No. 113 - Discharged on 10 Jun 1814

Jamison, James - Seaman - Payroll 1 - Number: 4 - Entry Date: 3 Oct 1813 - Gunboat No. 6 - Statement - Number: 4 - Entry Date: 3 Oct 1813 - Gunboat No. 6 - Discharged on 14 Jul 1814

Janes, Timothy - Seaman - Payroll 2 - Number: 231 - Entry Date: 9 Feb 1814 - Discharged to the U.S. Frigate John Adams

Jansen, Lawrence - Seaman - Payroll 1 - Number: 11 - Entry Date: 3 Oct 1813 - Gunboat No. 6 - Statement - Number: 10 - Entry Date: 3 Oct 1813 - Gunboat No. 6

January, John - Landsman - Payroll 2 - Number: 1811 - Entry Date: 1 Apr 1815 - Discharged

Jarvis, Timothy - Landsman - Payroll 1 - Number: 154 - Entry Date: 26 Sep 1813 - Gunboat No. 30 - Discharged on 9 Feb 1814 - Discharged to the U.S. Frigate John Adams - Payroll 2 - Number: 223 - Entry Date: 9 Feb 1814 - Gunboat No. 30 - Discharged to the U.S. Frigate John Adams - Statement - Number: 156 - Entry Date: 27 Sep 1813 - Gunboat No. 30

Jeffreys, Solomon - Seaman - Payroll 1 - Number: 165 - Entry Date: 3 Oct 1813 - Gunboat No. A - Statement - Number: 167 - Entry Date: 3 Oct 1813 - Gunboat No. A - Discharged on 13 Jun 1814 - Statement - Number: 1463 - Entry Date: 13 Jun 1814 - Gunboat No. A

Jenkins, James - Seaman - Payroll 2 - Number: 968 - Entry Date: 30 Nov 1813 - Ran

Jenkins, William - Landsman - Payroll 1 - Number: 8 - Entry Date: 3 Oct 1813 - Gunboat No. A - Statement - Number: 26 - Entry Date: 3 Oct 1813 - Gunboat No. A - BLW 47136-160-55

John, Peter - Ordinary Seaman - Payroll 2 - Number: 1843 - Entry Date: 1 Apr 1815 - Discharged

Johnson, James - Landsman - Payroll 2 - Number: 1024 - Entry Date: 15 Jul 1814 - Died - Ordinary Seaman - Payroll 2 - Number: 1679 - Entry Date: 15 Jul 1814 - Ran

Johnson, John - Ordinary Seaman - Payroll 2 - Number: 1828 - Entry Date: 3 Feb 1815 - Ran

Johnson, Moses - Ordinary Seaman - Payroll 2 - Number: 2219 - Entry Date: 20 Sep 1815 - Ran

Johnson, Perry - Ordinary Seaman - Payroll 1 - Number: 157 - Entry Date: 26 Sep 1813 - Gunboat No. 30 - Statement - Number: 159 - Entry Date: 27 Sep 1813 - Gunboat No. 30 - Discharged on 12 Jul 1814

Johnson, Peter - Ordinary Seaman - Miscellaneous - Entry Date: 5 Oct 1813 - Gunboat No. 30 - Statement - Number: 1422 - Entry Date: 10 Jun 1814 - Gunboat No. 30 - Statement - Number: 206 - Entry Date: 3 Oct 1813 - Gunboat No. B - Discharged on 29 Nov 1813

Johnson, Samuel - Ordinary Seaman - Payroll 2 - Number: 1746 - Entry Date: 25 Mar 1815 - Discharged

Johnson, Stephen - Ordinary Seaman - Statement - Number: 182 - Entry Date: 3 Oct 1813 - Gunboat No. A

Johnson, Thomas - Ordinary Seaman - Payroll 2 - Number: 2012 - Entry Date: 16 Aug 1815 - Ran

Johnson, Tobias - Ordinary Seaman - Payroll 2 - Number: 1800 - Entry Date: 1 Apr 1815 - Gunboat No. 30 - Statement - Number: 39 - Entry Date: 3 Oct 1813 - Gunboat No. 30 - Statement 1 - Number: 1352 - Entry Date: 18 Jun 1814 - Gunboat No. 30 - Discharged at naval yard

Johnson, William (1) - Ordinary Seaman - Payroll 2 - Number: 1036 - Entry Date: 10 Jun 1814 - Ran

Johnson, William (2) - Quarter Gunner - Statement - Number: 311 - Entry Date: 3 Oct 1813 - Gunboat No. 40 - Discharged on 19 Sep 1814

Jonas, Pomp - Boy - Payroll 2 - Number: 916 - Entry Date: 18 Oct 1813 - Ran

Jones, Henry (1) - Seaman - Payroll 2 - Number: 236 - Entry Date: 9 Feb 1814 - Gunboat No. 113 - Statement - Number: 582 - Entry Date: 24 Dec 1813 - Gunboat No. 113 - Statement - Number: 897 - Entry Date: 27 Sep 1813 - Gunboat No. 113 - Discharged on 9 Feb 1814 - Discharged to the U.S. Frigate John Adams

Jones, Henry (2) - Ordinary Seaman - Statement - Number: 690 - Entry Date: 27 Sep 1813 - Gunboat No. 103 - Discharged on 13 Jul 1814

Jones, James - Landsman - Payroll 2 - Number: 977 - Entry Date: 4 Nov 1814 - Gunboat No. 105 - Statement - Number: 705 - Entry Date: 27 Sep 1813 - Gunboat No. 105 - Ran on 4 Nov 1813 at New York

Jones, John - Landsman - Payroll 2 - Number: 1688 - Entry Date: 25 Feb 1814 - Gunboat No. 40 - Statement - Number: 1095 - Entry Date: 25 Feb 1814 - Gunboat No. 40 - Ordinary Seaman - Statement - Number: 626 - Entry Date: 27 Sep 1813 - Gunboat No. 40 - Seaman - Statement - Number: 310 - Entry Date: 3 Oct 1813 - Gunboat No. 40 - Discharged on 19 Sep 1814 - BLW 6103-160-55

Jones, Joshua - Ordinary Seaman - Payroll 2 - Number: 1716 - Entry Date: 1 Apr 1815 - Discharged

Jones, Peter - Boy - Payroll 2 - Number: 1964 - Entry Date: 31 Jul 1815 - Ran

Jones, Samuel - Boy - Payroll 1 - Number: 20 - Entry Date: 3 Oct 1813 - Gunboat No. 6 - Statement - Number: 19 - Entry Date: 3 Oct 1813 - Gunboat No. 6 - Discharged on 14 Jul 1814 - Seaman - Payroll 2 - Number: 1849 - Entry Date: 1 Apr 1815 - Gunboat No. 6 - Seaman - Statement 1 - Number: 1448 - Entry Date: 15 Jul 1814 - Gunboat No. 6

Jones, William - Boatswain's Mate - Statement - Number: 879 - Entry Date: 27 Sep 1813 - Gunboat No. 113 - Statement - Number: 1385 - Entry Date: 31 May 1814 - Gunboat No. 113 - Discharged on 31 May 1814 and enlisted in the U.S. Army

Joseph, Charles - Boy - Payroll 1 - Number: 12 - Entry Date: 3 Oct 1813 - Gunboat No. 6 - Statement - Number: 11 - Entry Date: 3 Oct 1813 - Gunboat No. 6 - Discharged on 12 Jul 1814 - Discharged to the U.S. Sloop-of-War Peacock - Ordinary Seaman - Payroll 2 - Number: 1848 - Entry Date: 22 Jan 1815 - Gunboat No. 6 - Statement 1 - Number: 1447 - Entry Date: 15 Jul 1814 - Gunboat No. 6

Joseph, John - Ordinary Seaman - Payroll 2 - Number: 1824 - Entry Date: 1 Apr 1815 - Discharged

Joseph, Lewis - Seaman - Payroll 2 - Number: 797 - Entry Date: 14 Jul 1814 - Discharged to the U.S. Frigate President

Josephes, Antonio - Ordinary Seaman - Payroll 2 - Number: 1874 - Entry Date: 20 Dec 1815 - Discharged to the U.S. Storeship Alert

Josey, Manuel - Boy - Statement - Number: 424 - Entry Date: 3 Oct 1813 - Gunboat No. 29 - Seaman - Payroll 1 - Number: 123 - Entry Date: 3 Oct 1813 - Gunboat No. 29 - Statement - Number: 127 - Entry Date: 3 Oct 1813 - Gunboat No. 29

Jourdan, Peter - Seaman - Payroll 2 - Number: 943 - Entry Date: 5 Nov 1813 – Ran

Judah, John - Ordinary Seaman - Payroll 2 - Number: 1659 - Entry Date: 25 Oct 1815 - Ran

Keen, John - Ordinary Seaman - Payroll 2 - Number: 1059 - Entry Date: 5 Oct 1813 - Ran

Keith, William - Seaman - Payroll 2 - Number: 211 - Entry Date: 9 Feb 1814 - Discharged to the U.S. Frigate John Adams

Kelly, Walter - Seaman - Payroll 2 - Number: 1701 - Entry Date: 10 Mar 1815 - Gunboat No. B - Statement -

Number: 218 - Entry Date: 3 Oct 1813 - Gunboat No. B - Discharged on 17 Jan 1814 - Discharged to the U.S. Sloop-of-War Peacock - Statement - Number: 1026 - Entry Date: 10 Mar 1814 - Gunboat No. B - Statement - Number: 1126 - Entry Date: 10 Mar 1814 - Gunboat No. B - Quarter Gunner - Promotions - Entry Date: 18 Sep 1814 - Gunboat No. B - Promoted

Killis, Joseph - Seaman - Statement - Number: 318 - Entry Date: 3 Oct 1813 - Gunboat No. 40 - Discharged on 9 Nov 1813

Kimball, John - Ordinary Seaman - Payroll 2 - Number: 803 - Entry Date: 14 Jul 1814 - Discharged to the U.S. Frigate President

King, Joseph - Sailing Master - Payroll 2 - Number: 2005 - Entry Date: 21 Jul 1815 - Discharged to the U.S. Brig Boxer

King, Joseph - Seaman - Payroll 2 - Number: 195 - Entry Date: 9 Feb 1814 - Gunboat No. 109 - Discharged on 9 Feb 1814 - Discharged to the U.S. Frigate John Adams - Statement - Number: 797 - Entry Date: 27 Sep 1813 - Gunboat No. 109

Kromhout, Barney - Seaman - Payroll 2 - Number: 1010 - Entry Date: 29 Jul 1814 - Died - Statement - Number: 957 - Entry Date: 12 Oct 1813 - Gunboat No. 8 - Died on 29 Jul 1814 at Sandy Hook, NJ - BLW 1266-160-55

Kruhl, Henry K. - Seaman - Payroll 2 - Number: 2161 - Entry Date: 16 Aug 1815 - Died

Lakeman, Joseph - Seaman - Statement - Number: 191 - Entry Date: 3 Oct 1813 - Gunboat No. A

Lang, Benjamin - Seaman - Payroll 2 - Number: 929 - Entry Date: 24 Nov 1813 - Ran

Larkin, Peter - Ordinary Seaman - Payroll 2 - Number: 1777 - Entry Date: 10 Dec 1814 - Ran

Lattimore, Joseph - Ordinary Seaman - Payroll 1 - Number: 120 - Entry Date: 3 Oct 1813 - Gunboat No. 29 - Statement - Number: 124 - Entry Date: 3 Oct 1813 - Gunboat No. 29

Lawrence, James - Seaman - Payroll 2 - Number: 973 - Entry Date: 12 Apr 1814 - Gunboat No. 103 - Statement - Number: 675 - Entry Date: 27 Sep 1813 - Gunboat No. 103 - Ran on 2 Apr 1814 at New York

Lawrence, John - Seaman - Statement - Number: 388 - Entry Date: 27 Sep 1813 - Gunboat No. 114 - Discharged on 11 Jun 1814 - Statement - Number: 910 - Entry Date: 27 Sep 1813 - Gunboat No. 114 - Discharged on 13 Jun 1814

Lawson, Matthew - Seaman - New York Naval Yard Muster 1 Aug 1815 - Number: 917 - Entry Date: 11 Oct 1813 - Gunboat No. 8 - Discharged on 22 Oct 1814n - Payroll 2 - Number: 1667 - Entry Date: 22 Oct 1815 - Gunboat No. 8 - Seaman - Statement - Number: 955 - Entry Date: 12 Oct 1813 - Gunboat No. 8

Layton, John - Seaman - Payroll 1 - Number: 55 - Entry Date: 3 Oct 1813 - Gunboat No. 6 - Ran on 4 Feb 1814 at New York - Statement - Number: 55 - Entry Date: 3 Oct 1813 - Gunboat No. 6

Leach, Thomas - Landsman - Statement - Number: 861 - Entry Date: 27 Sep 1813 - Gunboat No. 112 - Discharged on 17 Jan 1814 - Discharged to the U.S. Sloop-of-War Peacock

Learmy, Simon - Seaman - Statement - Number: 893 - Entry Date: 27 Sep 1813 - Gunboat No. 113 - Discharged on 12 Jul 1814

Leaycraft, John R. - Sailing Master - Statement - Number: 701 - Entry Date: 27 Sep 1813 - Gunboat No. 105

Leichfield, John - Seaman - Statement - Number: 199 - Entry Date: 3 Oct 1813 - Gunboat No. B - Discharged on 12 Jul 1814

Leonard, Joseph - Boy - Payroll 1 - Number: 168 - Entry Date: 3 Oct 1813 - Gunboat No. A - Statement - Number: 170 - Entry Date: 3 Oct 1813 - Gunboat No. A - Discharged on 16 Sep 1814 - BLW 45577-160-55

Leonard, Thomas - Seaman - Payroll 2 - Number: 988 - Entry Date: 12 Feb 1814 - Gunboat No. 109 - Statement - Number: 807 - Entry Date: 27 Sep 1813 - Gunboat No. 109 - Ran on 12 Feb 1814 at New York

Lewis, Alexander - Ordinary Seaman - Payroll 2 - Number: 1739 - Entry Date: 1 Apr 1815 - Discharged

Lewis, David - Boy - Payroll 2 - Number: 1714 - Entry Date: 1 Apr 1815 - Discharged

Lewis, Thomas - Ordinary Seaman - Statement - Number: 913 - Entry Date: 27 Sep 1813 - Gunboat No. 114 - Discharged on 13 Jun 1814

Light, John - Seaman - Payroll 2 - Number: 912 - Entry Date: 27 Nov 1813 - Ran

Liston, John - Seaman - Payroll 2 - Number: 924 - Entry Date: 9 Nov 1813 - Ran

Lloyd, James - Seaman - Payroll 2 - Number: 940 - Entry Date: 4 Apr 1814

Lockman, Abraham - Ordinary Seaman - Payroll 2 - Number: 2214 - Entry Date: 30 Dec 1815 - Ran

Loomis, James - Sailing Master - Payroll 2 - Number: 2179 - Entry Date: 23 Jul 1815 - Orleans

Lord, John - Seaman - Statement - Number: 793 - Entry Date: 27 Sep 1813 - Gunboat No. 109 - Ran on 2 Dec 1813 at New York

Lott, Karney - Sailing Master - Payroll 1 - Number: 113 - Entry Date: 3 Oct 1813 - Gunboat No. 29 - Statement - Number: 117 - Entry Date: 3 Oct 1813 - Gunboat No. 29

Louis, William - Ordinary Seaman - Payroll 2 - Number: 1771 - Entry Date: 1 Apr 1815 - Discharged

Love, John - Boy - Payroll 2 - Number: 1698 - Entry Date: 1 Apr 1815 - Discharged

Low, Gilbert - Steward - Payroll 1 - Number: 3 - Entry Date: 3 Oct 1813 - Gunboat No. 6 - Statement - Number: 3 - Entry Date: 3 Oct 1813 - Gunboat No. 6

Lowe, Robert - Seaman - Payroll 2 - Number: 1825 - Entry Date: 1 Apr 1815 – Discharged

Luce, Caleb - Ordinary Seaman - Payroll 2 - Number: 205 - Entry Date: 9 Feb 1814 - Discharged to the U.S. Frigate John Adams

Lutton, John - Seaman - Payroll 2 - Number: 1710 - Entry Date: 1 Apr 1815 - Discharged

Lyman, John - Seaman - Statement - Number: 806 - Entry Date: 27 Sep 1813 - Gunboat No. 109 - Discharged on 9 Feb 1814

Lynch, James - Boy - Payroll 2 - Number: 1973 - Entry Date: 29 Sep 1815 - Ran

Lynn, Henry - Landsman - New York Naval Yard Muster 1 Aug 1815 - Number: 1366 - Entry Date: 28 May 1814 - Gunboat No. 113 - Discharged on 15 Feb 1815 - Payroll 2 - Number: 1757 - Entry Date: 15 Feb 1815 - Gunboat No. 113 - Statement - Number: 1373 - Entry Date: 28 May 1814 - Gunboat No. 113

Lynnan, James - Seaman - Payroll 2 - Number: 196 - Entry Date: 9 Feb 1814 - Discharged to the U.S. Frigate John Adams

Manher, John - Boy - Payroll 2 - Number: 1002 - Entry Date: 1 Nov 1813 - Gunboat No. 113 - Statement - Number: 894 - Entry Date: 27 Sep 1813 - Gunboat No. 113 - Ran on 1 Nov 1813 at New York

Mann, Thomas - Ordinary Seaman - Payroll 2 - Number: 1842 - Entry Date: 27 Feb 1815 - Ran - BLW 8299-160-55

Manning, Samuel - Boy - Payroll 2 - Number: 1963 - Entry Date: 31 Jul 1815 - Ran

Manning, Willis - Seaman - Payroll 2 - Number: 1046 - Entry Date: 3 May 1814 - Discharged

Mansfield, Richard - Master's Mate - Statement - Number: 890 - Entry Date: 27 Sep 1813 - Gunboat No. 113

Marenick, Andrew - Seaman - Payroll 2 - Number: 176 - Entry Date: 9 Feb 1814 - Discharged to the U.S. Frigate John Adams

Markey, Matthew - Seaman - Payroll 2 - Number: 979 - Entry Date: 12 Jul 1814 - Gunboat No. 105 - Statement - Number: 722 - Entry Date: 27 Sep 1813 - Gunboat No. 105 - Died on 12 Ju; 1814 at New York

Markson, Nicholas - Seaman - Statement - Number: 340 - Entry Date: 6 Oct 1813 - Gunboat No. 40

Marsh, John - Landsman - Payroll 1 - Number: 53 - Entry Date: 3 Oct 1813 - Gunboat No. 6 - Ran on 21 Oct 1813 from New York - Statement - Number: 53 - Entry Date: 3 Oct 1813 - Gunboat No. 6

Marshall, Robert - Master's Mate - Payroll 1 - Number: 57 - Entry Date: 3 Oct 1813 - Gunboat No. 6 - Served from 17 Sep 1812 to 9 Jul 1813, and from27 Aug 1813 to 3 Oct 1813 - BLW 29800-160-55 - Pension: WO-11924,

WC-6832 - Statement - Number: 57 - Entry Date: 3 Oct 1813 - Gunboat No. 6 - Discharged to the U.S. Frigate John Adams

Marston, John - Steward - New York Naval Yard Muster 1 Aug 1815 - Number: 990 - Entry Date: 8 Feb 1814 - Gunboat No. 37 - Statement - Number: 1004 - Entry Date: 8 Feb 1814 - Gunboat No. 37

Martin, John - Quarter Gunner - Statement - Number: 727 - Entry Date: 27 Sep 1813 - Gunboat No. 105 - Discharged on 12 Aug 1814

Martin, Matthias - Ordinary Seaman - New York Naval Yard Muster 1 Aug 1815 - Number: 1541 - Entry Date: 8 Jul 1814 - Gunboat No. 105 - Discharged on 5 Nov 1814 - Payroll 2 - Number: 1838 - Entry Date: 5 Nov 1814 - Gunboat No. 105 - Statement 1 - Number: 1425 - Entry Date: 8 Jul 1814 - Gunboat No. 105

Mason, John - Seaman - Payroll 2 - Number: 806 - Entry Date: 14 Jul 1814 - Discharged to the U.S. Frigate President

Maxfield, John - Landsman - Payroll 2 - Number: 1994 - Entry Date: 21 Jul 1815 - Discharged to the U.S. Brig Boxer

May, George - Seaman - Statement - Number: 706 - Entry Date: 27 Sep 1813 - Gunboat No. 105 - Discharged on 12 Jul 1814

Mayo, Oliver - Seaman - Payroll 1 - Number: 161 - Entry Date: 26 Sep 1813 - Gunboat No. 30 - BLW 66595-160-55 - Statement - Number: 163 - Entry Date: 27 Sep 1813 - Gunboat No. 30 - Discharged on 7 Jun 1814

McAllister, John - Seaman - Payroll 1 - Number: 10 - Entry Date: 3 Oct 1813 - Gunboat No. 6 - Seaman - Statement - Number: 9 - Entry Date: 3 Oct 1813 - Gunboat No. 6

McArthur, Samuel - Seaman - Payroll 2 - Number: 967 - Entry Date: 30 Nov 1813 - Ran

McCabe, Henry - Ordinary Seaman - Statement - Number: 195 - Entry Date: 3 Oct 1813 - Gunboat No. B - Discharged on 23 Mar 1814

McCaddens, David - Landsman - Payroll 1 - Number: 35 - Entry Date: 3 Oct 1813 - Gunboat No. 6 - Payroll 2 - Number: 1044 - Entry Date: 25 Jan 1814 - Gunboat No. 6 - Statement - Number: 35 - Entry Date: 3 Oct 1813 - Gunboat No. 6 - Discharged on 25 Jan 1814

McClashey, William - Seaman - Payroll 2 - Number: 1890 - Entry Date: 14 Feb 1815 - Ran

McDermet, Daniel - Ordinary Seaman - Payroll 1 - Number: 61 - Entry Date: 3 Oct 1813 - Gunboat No. 8 - Discharged on 16 Oct 1813 at New York - Statement - Number: 64 - Entry Date: 3 Oct 1813 - Gunboat No. 8

McDonald, Martin - Seaman - Payroll 2 - Number: 127 - Entry Date: 17 Jan 1814 - Gunboat No. B - Statement - Number: 222 - Entry Date: 3 Oct 1813 - Gunboat No. B - Discharged on 17 Jan 1814 - Discharged to the U.S. Sloop-of-War Peacock

McGruder, Samuel - Seaman - Payroll 1 - Number: 26 - Entry Date: 3 Oct 1813 - Gunboat No. 6 - Statement - Number: 25 - Entry Date: 3 Oct 1813 - Gunboat No. 6 - Discharged on 14 Jul 1814

McKay, John S. - Seaman - Payroll 1 - Number: 6 - Entry Date: 3 Oct 1813 - Gunboat No. 6 - Statement - Number: 6 - Entry Date: 3 Oct 1813 - Gunboat No. 6

McKearny, Robert - Sailing Master - Statement - Number: 63 - Entry Date: 3 Oct 1813 - Gunboat No. 8

McLane, Nathaniel - Quartermaster - Payroll 1 - Number: 5 - Entry Date: 3 Oct 1813 - Gunboat No. 6 - Boatswain's Mate - Statement - Number: 5 - Entry Date: 3 Oct 1813 - Gunboat No. 6 - Discharged on 19 Sep 1814

McLane, Thomas - Seaman - Payroll 2 - Number: 192 - Entry Date: 9 Feb 1814 - Gunboat No. 109 - Statement - Number: 800 - Entry Date: 27 Sep 1813 - Gunboat No. 109 - Discharged on 9 Feb 1814 - Discharged to the U.S. Frigate John Adams

McMahoon, Jeremiah - Landsman - Payroll 1 - Number: 36 - Entry Date: 3 Oct 1813 - Gunboat No. 6 - Statement - Number: 36 - Entry Date: 3 Oct 1813 - Gunboat No. 6

McQuay, Joseph - Ordinary Seaman - Payroll 2 - Number: 950 - Entry Date: 12 Oct 1813 - Discharged

McWaine, Daniel - Seaman - Payroll 2 - Number: 2272 - Entry Date: 20 Jun 1816 - Discharged

Melzard, John - Seaman - Statement - Number: 217 - Entry Date: 3 Oct 1813 - Gunboat No. B - Discharged on 25 Feb 1814 - Statement - Number: 1240 - Entry Date: 19 Mar 1814 - Gunboat No. B - Payroll 2 - Number: 947 - Entry Date: 12 Dec 1813 - Ran

Mento, John - Seaman - Statement - Entry Date: 27 Sep 1813 - Gunboat No. 30 - Discharged on 7 Jun 1814 - Boatswain's Mate - Promotions - Entry Date: 12 Feb 1814 - Gunboat No. 30 - Promoted

Merritt, Samuel - Seaman - Payroll 1 - Number: 50 - Entry Date: 3 Oct 1813 - Gunboat No. 6 - Discharged on 24 Feb 1814 at New York - Statement - Number: 50 - Entry Date: 3 Oct 1813 - Gunboat No. 6

Michins, Moses - Ordinary Seaman - New York Naval Yard Muster 1 Aug 1815 - Number: 1097 - Entry Date: 8 Mar 1814 - Gunboat No. 45 - Deserted and apprehended on 18 May 1814 - Payroll 2 - Number: 1699 - Entry Date: 18 May 1814 - Gunboat No. 45 - Statement - Number: 495 - Entry Date: 7 Mar 1814 - Gunboat No. 45

Miden, John - Seaman - Statement - Number: 901 - Entry Date: 27 Sep 1813 - Gunboat No. 114 - Discharged on 13 Jun 1814

Milan, Jasper - Boatswain's Mate - Statement - Number: 724 - Entry Date: 27 Sep 1813 - Gunboat No. 105 - Discharged on 17 Jan 1814

Millen, Andrew - Quarter Gunner - Payroll 1 - Number: 134 - Entry Date: 26 Sep 1813 - Gunboat No. 30 - Statement - Number: 138 - Entry Date: 27 Sep 1813 - Gunboat No. 30 - Discharged on 7 Jun 1814

Miller, James - Landsman - Payroll 2 - Number: 1908 - Entry Date: 10 Mar 1815 - Ran

Miller, Mark - Ordinary Seaman - Payroll 2 - Number: 1856 - Entry Date: 1 Apr 1815 - Gunboat No. 114 - Statement - Number: 921 - Entry Date: 27 Sep 1813 - Gunboat No. 114 - Discharged on 12 Jul 1814 - Statement 1 - Number: 1458 - Entry Date: 16 Jul 1814 - Gunboat No. 114

Miller, Peter - Seaman - Statement - Number: 882 - Entry Date: 27 Sep 1813 - Gunboat No. 113 - Discharged on 15 Jun 1814

Miller, Thomas - Seaman - Statement - Number: 691 - Entry Date: 27 Sep 1813 - Gunboat No. 103 - Discharged on 14 Jul 1814

Milligan, Basil - Master's Mate - Statement - Number: 917 - Entry Date: 27 Sep 1813 - Gunboat No. 114

Mitchell, Benjamin - Seaman - Payroll 2 - Number: 959 - Entry Date: 10 Oct 1813 - Discharged

Mitchell, Henry - Seaman - Statement - Number: 192 - Entry Date: 3 Oct 1813 - Gunboat No. A

Mitchell, Solomon - Landsman - Statement - Number: 684 - Entry Date: 27 Sep 1813 - Gunboat No. 103 - Discharged on 12 Jul 1814

Mitchell, William - Seaman - Statement - Number: 600 - Entry Date: 3 Oct 1813 - Gunboat - Killed in action on 3 Nov 1813 at Sandy Hook, NJ

Monk, John - Seaman - Payroll 1 - Number: 27 - Entry Date: 3 Oct 1813 - Gunboat No. 6 - Statement - Number: 27 - Entry Date: 3 Oct 1813 - Gunboat No. 6 - Discharged on 28 Jul 1814

Monroe, Thomas - Seaman - Payroll 2 - Number: 1834 - Entry Date: 1 Jan 1815 - Discharged

Montello, Nicholas - Seaman - Statement - Number: 166 - Entry Date: 3 Oct 1813 - Gunboat No. A - Discharged on 12 Jul 1814 - Statement 1 - Number: 1449 - Entry Date: 15 Jul 1814 - Gunboat No. A

Mooberry, John - Ordinary Seaman - Promotions - Entry Date: 19 Mar 1814 - Gunboat No. 105 - Reduced - Steward - Statement - Number: 711 - Entry Date: 27 Sep 1813 - Gunboat No. 105

Moone, Richard - Ordinary Seaman - Payroll 2 - Number: 201 - Entry Date: 9 Feb 1814 - Discharged to the U.S. Frigate John Adams

Moore, Edward - Ordinary Seaman - Payroll 2 - Number: 1638 - Entry Date: 6 Feb 1814 - Ran

Moore, Isaac - Seaman - Payroll 1 - Number: 92 - Entry Date: 3 Oct 1813 - Gunboat No. 8 - Discharged on 10 Oct 1813 at New York - Statement - Number: 95 - Entry Date: 3 Oct 1813 - Gunboat No. 8

Moore, Thomas - Ordinary Seaman - New York Naval Yard Muster 1 Aug 1815 - Number: 1017 - Entry Date: 15 Feb 1814 - Gunboat No. 97 - Discharged on 30 Oct 1814 - Payroll 2 - Number: 1681 - Entry Date: 30 Oct 1814 - Gunboat No. 97 - Statement - Number: 1061 - Entry Date: 15 Feb 1814 - Gunboat No. 97

Morrison, Joseph - Seaman - Statement - Number: 677 - Entry Date: 27 Sep 1813 - Gunboat No. 103 - Discharged on 13 Jun 1814

Morrison, William - Master's Mate - Payroll 1 - Number: 156 - Entry Date: 26 Sep 1813 - Gunboat No. 30 - Discharged on 12 Feb 1814 at New York - Statement - Number: 158 - Entry Date: 27 Sep 1813 - Gunboat No. 30

Morse, Thomas - Seaman - Payroll 2 - Number: 1922 - Entry Date: 22 Jun 1815 - Ran

Moses, John - Ordinary Seaman - Payroll 2 - Number: 2168 - Entry Date: 2 Nov 1815 - Discharged to the U.S. Storeship Tom Bowline

Munroe, Thomas - Seaman - New York Naval Yard Muster 1 Aug 1815 - Number: 1532 - Entry Date: 6 Jul 1814 - Gunboat No. 6 - Discharged on 1 Jan 1815 - Statement 1 - Number: 1416 - Entry Date: 6 Jul 1814 - Gunboat No. 6

Murphy, Henry - Sailing Master - Payroll 2 - Number: 1072 - Entry Date: 29 Jul 1814 - Died

Murphy, John - Seaman - Payroll 2 - Number: 1830 - Entry Date: 1 Apr 1815 – Discharged

Murray, Thomas - Boy - Payroll 2 - Number: 1068 - Entry Date: 29 Oct 1813 - Ran

Murray, William - Seaman - Payroll 2 - Number: 244 - Entry Date: 9 Feb 1814 - Discharged to the U.S. Frigate John Adams

Myers, Henry - Quarter Gunner - Statement - Number: 333 - Entry Date: 3 Oct 1813 - Gunboat No. 40 - Discharged on 25 Jan 1814

Neary, Edward - Seaman - Payroll 2 - Number: 926 - Entry Date: 17 Nov 1813 - Ran

Needham, William - Seaman - Statement - Number: 683 - Entry Date: 27 Sep 1813 - Gunboat No. 103 - Discharged on 11 Jun 1814

New, Walter W. - Surgeon - Payroll 2 - Number: 1370 - Entry Date: 1 Apr 1815 - Discharged to the U.S. Frigate John Adams

Newman, Eli - Seaman - Statement - Number: 215 - Entry Date: 3 Oct 1813 - Gunboat No. B - Discharged on 2 Dec 1813

Newman, Jacob - Seaman - Payroll 2 - Number: 920 - Entry Date: 10 Nov 1813 - Ran

Nichels, John - Ordinary Seaman - Statement - Number: 849 - Entry Date: 27 Sep 1813 - Gunboat No. 112 - Discharged on 12 Jul 1814

Nicherson, James - Seaman - Payroll 2 - Number: 1042 - Entry Date: 14 Aug 1814 - Discharged - Steward - Promotions - Entry Date: 8 Aug 1814 - Gunboat No. 109 - Promoted - Ordinary Seaman - Promotions - Entry Date: 17 Dec 1813 - Gunboat No. 109 - Reduced - Ordinary Seaman - Statement - Number: 794 - Entry Date: 27 Sep 1813 - Gunboat No. 109

Nicholson, Peter - Ordinary Seaman - Payroll 2 - Number: 795 - Entry Date: 14 Jul 1814 - Discharged to the U.S. Frigate President

Nixon, Henry - Landsman - Payroll 2 - Number: 1639 - Entry Date: 2 Jan 1815 - Died

Nutter, Henry - Seaman - Payroll 2 - Number: 1003 - Entry Date: 2 Nov 1813 - Gunboat No. 114 - Statement - Number: 907 - Entry Date: 27 Sep 1813 - Gunboat No. 114 - Died on 2 Nov 1813 at Sandy Hook, NJ

Nutterville, Thomas - Seaman - Payroll 2 - Number: 729 - Entry Date: 9 Feb 1814 - Discharged to the U.S. Frigate John Adams

O'Donnell, James - Seaman - Payroll 1 - Number: 68 - Entry Date: 3 Oct 1813 - Gunboat No. 8 - Seaman - Payroll 2 - Number: 882 - Entry Date: 9 Oct 1813 - Gunboat No. 8 - Statement - Number: 71 - Entry Date: 3 Oct 1813 -

Gunboat No. 8 - Discharged on 9 Oct 1813 - Discharged to the U.S. Frigate President

Oliver, Thomas - Seaman - Payroll 2 - Number: 1901 - Entry Date: 20 Dec 1814 - Ran

Orr, John - Ordinary Seaman - Payroll 2 - Number: 2205 - Entry Date: 7 Nov 1815 - Died

Otter, James - Master's Mate - Statement - Number: 197 - Entry Date: 3 Oct 1813 - Gunboat No. B - Discharged on 24 Nov 1813 - BLW 78661-160-55

Page, Benjamin - Seaman - Statement - Number: 905 - Entry Date: 27 Sep 1813 - Gunboat No. 114 - Discharged on 13 Jun 1814

Page, Daniel - Ordinary Seaman - Payroll 2 - Number: 1894 - Entry Date: 10 Oct 1814 - Ran

Page, John - Seaman - Statement - Number: 345 - Entry Date: 23 Nov 1813 - Gunboat No. 40

Paid, Peter - Seaman - Payroll 2 - Number: 226 - Entry Date: 9 Feb 1814 - Gunboat No. 103 - Statement - Number: 676 - Entry Date: 27 Sep 1813 - Gunboat No. 103 - Discharged on 4 Feb 1814 - Discharged to the U.S. Frigate John Adams

Parker, Thomas - Seaman - Statement - Number: 721 - Entry Date: 27 Sep 1813 - Gunboat No. 105 - Discharged on 12 Jul 1814 - BLW 12650-160-55

Patton, John - Ordinary Seaman - Promotions - Entry Date: 21 Dec 1813 - Gunboat No. B - Promoted - Statement - Number: 203 - Entry Date: 3 Oct 1813 - Gunboat No. B

Patton, Robert - Seaman - Statement - Number: 908 - Entry Date: 27 Sep 1813 - Gunboat No. 114 - Discharged on 13 Jun 1814

Paul, Duncan - Ordinary Seaman - New York Naval Yard Muster 1 Aug 1815 - Number: 1337 - Entry Date: 11 May 1814 - Gunboat No. 33 - Discharged on 9 Dec 1814 - Payroll 2 - Number: 1742 - Entry Date: 9 Dec 1814 - Ran

Paul, Henry - Seaman - Payroll 2 - Number: 1055 - Entry Date: 6 Apr 1814 - Ran

Paulson, George - Sailing Master - Statement - Number: 900 - Entry Date: 3 Oct 1813 - Gunboat No. 114 - Discharged on 1 Apr 1814

Pennyeard, William J. (or Pennycad) - Seaman - Promotions - Entry Date: 2 Aug 1814 - Gunboat No. 112 - Promoted- Seaman - Statement - Number: 867 - Entry Date: 27 Sep 1813 - Gunboat No. 112 - Discharged on 12 Jul 1814 - Boatswain's Mate - Statement - Number: 1396 - Entry Date: 2 Jun 1814 - Gunboat No. 112 - BLW 72616-160-55

Percival, John - Sailing Master - Payroll 1 - Number: 1 - Entry Date: 3 Oct 1813 - Gunboat No. 6 - Statement - Number: 1 - Entry Date: 3 Oct 1813 - Gunboat No. 6 - Discharged on 8 Mar 1814 - Discharged to the U.S. Sloop-of-War Peacock

Peters, Henry - Landsman - Payroll 2 - Number: 1993 - Entry Date: 21 Jul 1815 - Discharged to the U.S. Brig Boxer

Peters, John - Ordinary Seaman - Statement - Number: 186 - Entry Date: 3 Oct 1813 - Gunboat No. A

Peters, William - Seaman - Statement - Number: 150 - Entry Date: 27 Sep 1813 - Gunboat No. 30 - Ran on 2 Nov 1813 at New York

Peterson, James - Seaman - Payroll 1 - Number: 31 - Entry Date: 3 Oct 1813 - Gunboat No. 6 - Statement - Number: 31 - Entry Date: 3 Oct 1813 - Gunboat No. 6

Peterson, John - Ordinary Seaman - Payroll 2 - Number: 1810 - Entry Date: 1 Apr 1815 - Gunboat No. 30 - Payroll 1 - Number: 141 - Entry Date: 26 Sep 1813 - Gunboat No. 30 - Ran on 7 Nov 1813 at New York - Payroll 2 - Number: 897 - Entry Date: 7 Nov 1813 - Gunboat No. 30 - Statement - Number: 145 - Entry Date: 27 Sep 1813 - Gunboat No. 30 - Statement 1 - Number: 1373 - Entry Date: 22 Jun 1814 - Gunboat No. 30

Peterson, Richard - Seaman - Payroll 2 - Number: 208 - Entry Date: 9 Feb 1814 - Gunboat No. A - Statement - Number: 177 - Entry Date: 26 Jan 1814 - Gunboat No. A - Discharged on 9 Feb 1814 - Discharged to the U.S. Frigate John Adams

Phillips, Jackson - Seaman - Statement - Number: 714 - Entry Date: 27 Sep 1813 - Gunboat No. 105 - Discharged on

12 Jul 1814

Phillips, John - Ordinary Seaman - Payroll 2 - Number: 2176 - Entry Date: 4 Oct 1815 - Sent to Sackets Harbor

Phillips, William - Seaman - Statement - Number: 881 - Entry Date: 27 Sep 1813 - Gunboat No. 113 - Discharged on 10 Jun 1814

Pickins, John - Sailing Master - Payroll 1 - Number: 95 - Entry Date: 3 Oct 1813 - Gunboat No. 8 - Statement - Number: 98 - Entry Date: 3 Oct 1813 - Gunboat No. 8

Pithick, Thomas - Steward - Payroll 2 - Number: 993 - Entry Date: 1 Dec 1813 - Ran

Pollard, Robert - Seaman - Statement - Number: 884 - Entry Date: 27 Sep 1813 - Gunboat No. 113 - Discharged on 17 Dec 1813

Porter, George W, - Steward - Payroll 1 - Number: 111 - Entry Date: 3 Oct 1813 - Gunboat No. 8 - Payroll 2 - Number: 1022 - Entry Date: 29 Jul 1814 - Gunboat No. 8 - Statement - Number: 114 - Entry Date: 3 Oct 1813 - Gunboat No. 8 - Statement - Number: 1137 - Entry Date: 12 Mar 1814 - Gunboat No. 8 - Discharged on 29 Jul 1814 - Ran on 29 Jul 1814 at New York

Porter, John C. - Seaman - Payroll 1 - Number: 91 - Entry Date: 3 Oct 1813 - Gunboat No. 8 - Payroll 2 - Number: 813 - Entry Date: 14 Jul 1814 - Gunboat No. 8 - Statement - Number: 94 - Entry Date: 3 Oct 1813 - Gunboat No. 8 - Discharged on 14 Jul 1814 - Discharged to the U.S. Frigate President

Potts, Joseph - Seaman - Statement - Number: 719 - Entry Date: 27 Sep 1813 - Gunboat No. 105 - Discharged on 13 Jul 1814

Powers, Lewis R. - Seaman - Payroll 2 - Number: 1680 - Entry Date: 14 Jul 1814 - Discharged

Powers, Martin - Ordinary Seaman - Payroll 2 - Number: 1807 - Entry Date: 3 Feb 1815 - Discharged

Powers, Thomas - Master's Mate - Statement - Number: 791 - Entry Date: 27 Sep 1813 - Gunboat No. 8 - Ran on 25 Feb 1814 at New York - Statement - Number: 1186 - Entry Date: 8 Mar 1814 - Gunboat No. 8

Prato, Lawrence - Seaman - Payroll 1 - Number: 34 - Entry Date: 3 Oct 1813 - Gunboat No. 6 - Statement - Number: 34 - Entry Date: 3 Oct 1813 - Gunboat No. 6 - Discharged on 4 Mar 1814 - Discharged to the U.S. Sloop-of-War Peacock

Pratt, George S. - Ordinary Seaman - Payroll 2 - Number: 2296 - Entry Date: 10 Jul 1816 - Ran

Price, Joseph - Gunner - Payroll 2 - Number: 763 - Entry Date: 21 Jan 1814 - Transferred to naval yard

Price, Richard - Seaman - Payroll 1 - Number: 96 - Entry Date: 3 Oct 1813 - Gunboat No. 8 - Statement - Number: 99 - Entry Date: 3 Oct 1813 - Gunboat No. 8

Prince, John - Ordinary Seaman - New York Naval Yard Muster 1 Aug 1815 - Number: 1238 - Entry Date: 28 Mar 1814 - Gunboat No. 42 - Discharged on 24 May 1815 - Statement - Number: 1172 - Entry Date: 28 Mar 1814 - Gunboat No. 42

Proctor, Thomas - Ordinary Seaman - Payroll 2 - Number: 1957 - Entry Date: 26 Jun 1815 - Ran

Proutz, Charles - Ordinary Seaman - Payroll 2 - Number: 970 - Entry Date: 15 Nov 1813

Quann, George - Seaman - Payroll 2 - Number: 1728 - Entry Date: 1 Apr 1815 - Ran

Radcliff, William J. - Seaman - Payroll 1 - Number: 117 - Entry Date: 3 Oct 1813 - Gunboat No. 29 - Statement - Number: 121 - Entry Date: 3 Oct 1813 - Gunboat No. 29 - Discharged on 13 Jul 1814

Randolph, Francis - Seaman - Statement - Number: 903 - Entry Date: 27 Sep 1813 - Gunboat No. 114 - Discharged on 15 Jun 1814

Randolph, Simeon F. - Master's Mate - Statement - Number: 728 - Entry Date: 27 Sep 1813 - Gunboat No. 105

Rattus, John - Ordinary Seaman - Statement - Number: 885 - Entry Date: 27 Sep 1813 - Gunboat No. 113 - Discharged on 21 Jul 1814

Ray, Henry - Landsman - Payroll 2 - Number: 1692 - Entry Date: 31 Mar 1814 - Discharged

Raymond, William - Ordinary Seaman - Payroll 2 - Number: 1719 - Entry Date: 1 Apr 1815 - Discharged

Read, Daniel - Ordinary Seaman - Payroll 2 - Number: 1857 - Entry Date: 1 Apr 1815 - Discharged - Payroll 2 - Number: 1914 - Entry Date: 30 Sep 1815 - Ran

Redman, William - Seaman - Payroll 2 - Number: 976 - Entry Date: 2 Mar 1814 - Gunboat No. 103 - Statement - Number: 698 - Entry Date: 27 Sep 1813 - Gunboat No. 103 - Discharged on 2 Mar 1814 - Ran on 2 Mar 1814 at New York

Reed, Abraham - Ordinary Seaman - Payroll 1 - Number: 13 - Entry Date: 3 Oct 1813 - Gunboat No. 6 - Ran on 18 Nov 1814 from New York - Statement - Number: 12 - Entry Date: 3 Oct 1813 - Gunboat No. 6

Reed, Daniel - Ordinary Seaman - Payroll 1 - Number: 153 - Entry Date: 26 Sep 1813 - Gunboat No. 30 - Statement - Number: 155 - Entry Date: 27 Sep 1813 - Gunboat No. 30 - Discharged on 12 Jul 1814

Reed, John C. - Landsman - Statement - Number: 864 - Entry Date: 27 Sep 1813 - Gunboat No. 112 - Discharged on 9 Feb 1814 - Discharged to the U.S. Frigate John Adams

Reese, John - Ordinary Seaman - Statement - Number: 855 - Entry Date: 27 Sep 1813 - Gunboat No. 112

Reily, Isaac - Boy - Payroll 2 - Number: 953 - Entry Date: 20 Nov 1813 - Ran

Reubin, Lewis - Landsman - Payroll 2 - Number: 2209 - Entry Date: 1 Nov 1815 - Ran

Reynolds, John - Seaman - Payroll 2 - Number: 216 - Entry Date: 9 Feb 1814 - Discharged to the U.S. Frigate John Adams

Rhuse, John - Ordinary Seaman - Payroll 2 - Number: 1657 - Entry Date: 1 Apr 1815 - Discharged

Riboubt, Thomas - Seaman - Payroll 2 - Number: 1923 - Entry Date: 15 May 1815 - Ran

Richardson, George - Seaman - Payroll 2 - Number: 975 - Entry Date: 27 Nov 1813 - Gunboat No. 103 - Statement - Number: 692 - Entry Date: 27 Sep 1813 - Gunboat No. 103 - Ran on 27 Nov 1813 at New York

Richardson, John - Landsman - Payroll 2 - Number: 914 - Entry Date: 5 Nov 1813 - Ran

Richardson, Samuel - Ordinary Seaman - Payroll 2 - Number: 961 - Entry Date: 4 Oct 1813 - Discharged

Ricks, Martin - Seaman - Statement - Number: 809 - Entry Date: 27 Sep 1813 - Gunboat No. 109 - Discharged on 12 Jul 1814

Riley, James - Ordinary Seaman - Payroll 2 - Number: 816 - Entry Date: 14 Oct 1813 - Discharged

Rindherd, John H. - Seaman - Payroll 2 - Number: 777 - Entry Date: 14 Jul 1814 - Discharged to the U.S. Frigate President

Robbins, William M. - Sailing Master - Payroll 2 - Number: 1064 - Entry Date: 6 Oct 1813 - Transferred to Lake Champlain

Robbs, William - Ordinary Seaman - Payroll 2 - Number: 187 - Entry Date: 9 Feb 1814 - Discharged to the U.S. Frigate John Adams

Roberson, Daniel - Ordinary Seaman - Payroll 2 - Number: 951 - Entry Date: 13 Oct 1813 - Ran

Roberson, Thomas - Seaman - Statement - Number: 914 - Entry Date: 27 Sep 1813 - Gunboat No. 114 - Discharged on 25 Feb 1814

Roberts, John - Ordinary Seaman - Payroll 2 - Number: 875 - Entry Date: 4 Feb 1814 - Gunboat No. 6 - Statement - Number: 13 - Entry Date: 3 Oct 1813 - Gunboat No. 6 - Discharged on 4 Feb 1814 at Naval Yard

Roberts, Robert - Boy - New York Naval Yard Muster 1 Aug 1815 - Number: 1062 - Entry Date: 28 Feb 1814 - Gunboat No. 113 - Discharged on 3 Feb 1815 - Statement - Number: 1101 - Entry Date: 28 Feb 1814 - Gunboat No. 113

Roberts, Thomas - Seaman - Statement - Number: 707 - Entry Date: 27 Sep 1813 - Gunboat No. 105 - Discharged on 18 Aug 1814

Robertson, Robert - Seaman - Statement - Number: 716 - Entry Date: 27 Sep 1813 - Gunboat No. 105 - Discharged on 17 Jun 1814 - Discharged to the U.S. Sloop-of-War Peacock

Robinson, George - Ordinary Seaman - Payroll 1 - Number: 69 - Entry Date: 3 Oct 1813 - Gunboat No. 8 - Statement - Number: 72 - Entry Date: 3 Oct 1813 - Gunboat No. 8 - Discharged on 15 Jul 1814

Robinson, Hall - Landsman - Payroll 2 - Number: 938 - Entry Date: 14 Jul 1814 - Ran

Rock, John - Seaman - Payroll 2 - Number: 1041 - Entry Date: 25 Aug 1814 - Died

Roders, Jason - Steward - Statement - Number: 61 - Entry Date: 2 May 1814 - Gunboat No. 6 - Discharged on 14 Jul 1814

Rodgers, James - Sailing Master - Statement - Number: 871 - Entry Date: 3 Oct 1813 - Gunboat No. 113 - Discharged on 14 Jul 1814

Rodgers, Laban - Seaman - Statement - Number: 211 - Entry Date: 3 Oct 1813 - Gunboat No. B - Discharged on 2 Dec 1813

Rogers, George - Landsman - Payroll 2 - Number: 923 - Entry Date: 20 Nov 1813 - Ran

Rogers, James - Sailing Master - Payroll 2 - Number: 832 - Entry Date: 5 Dec 1813 - Gunboat No. 6 - Discharged to the U.S. Frigate President - Statement - Number: 62 - Entry Date: 2 May 1814 - Gunboat No. 6

Rogers, Nathaniel - Boy - Payroll 2 - Number: 1904 - Entry Date: 2 Jan 1815 - Ran

Rose, Francis - Seaman - Payroll 2 - Number: 987 - Entry Date: 2 Nov 1813 - Gunboat No. 109 - Statement - Number: 804 - Entry Date: 27 Sep 1813 - Gunboat No. 109 - Discharged on 2 Nov 1813

Rosemond, William - Seaman - Payroll 2 - Number: 1924 - Entry Date: 22 Apr 1815 - Ran

Ross, Lewis - Landsman - Payroll 2 - Number: 1775 - Entry Date: 1 Apr 1815 - Discharged

Roundy, Francis - Seaman - Statement - Number: 107 - Entry Date: 3 Oct 1813 - Gunboat No. 8 - Discharged on 24 Feb 1814 - Boatswain's Mate - Statement - Number: 1230 - Entry Date: 16 Mar 1814 - Gunboat No. 8

Russell, Henry - Landsman - Payroll 2 - Number: 1754 - Entry Date: 1 Apr 1815 - Discharged

Russell, John A. - Ordinary Seaman - Payroll 1 - Number: 130 - Entry Date: 3 Oct 1813 - Gunboat No. 29 - Ran on 18 Nov 1813 from New York - BLW 73724-160-55 - Pension: WO-20144, WC-26712 - Statement - Number: 134 - Entry Date: 3 Oct 1813 - Gunboat No. 29 - Served from 12 Mar 1813 to 18 Nov 1813, and from 8 Mar 1814 to 1 Apr 1815 - Statement - Number: 1195 - Entry Date: 8 Mar 1814 - Gunboat No. 29

Russell, John H. - Ordinary Seaman - Payroll 2 - Number: 893 - Entry Date: 18 Nov 1813 - Ran

Russell, Samuel - Ordinary Seaman - Payroll 2 - Number: 807 - Entry Date: 14 Jul 1814 - Discharged to the U.S. Frigate President

Russell, Thomas - Master's Mate - Payroll 1 - Number: 129 - Entry Date: 3 Oct 1813 - Gunboat No. 29 - Died on 17 Oct 1813 at New York - Payroll 2 - Number: 892 - Entry Date: 17 Oct 1813 - Gunboat No. 29 - Statement - Number: 133 - Entry Date: 3 Oct 1813 - Gunboat No. 29

Rutley, James - Seaman - Payroll 2 - Number: 886 - Entry Date: 4 Oct 1813 - Gunboat No. 8 - Statement - Number: 85 - Entry Date: 3 Oct 1813 - Gunboat No. 8 - Ran on 4 Oct 1813 at New York

Rysom, Peter - Ordinary Seaman - Statement - Number: 323 - Entry Date: 3 Oct 1813 - Gunboat No. 40 - Discharged on 9 Nov 1813 - Statement - Number: 344 - Entry Date: 4 Nov 1813 - Gunboat No. 40

Rysom, Richard (Dick) - Seaman - Statement - Number: 329 - Entry Date: 3 Oct 1813 - Gunboat No. 40 - Discharged on 31 May 1814 - Statement 1 - Number: 1350 - Entry Date: 18 Jun 1814 - Gunboat No. 40

Sands, Michael - Ordinary Seaman - Payroll 2 - Number: 2207 - Entry Date: 18 Oct 1815 - Died

Sands, Samuel R. - Midshipman - Payroll 2 - Number: 1084 - Entry Date: 10 Jun 1814 - Transferred to Lake Ontario

Sanniher, Asa - Ordinary Seaman - Payroll 2 - Number: 1918 - Entry Date: 8 Jun 1815 - Ran

Saunderson, Joseph - Landsman - Statement - Number: 175 - Entry Date: 3 Oct 1813 - Gunboat No. A

Sayer, Benjamin - Seaman - Payroll 2 - Number: 927 - Entry Date: 17 Nov 1813 - Ran

Sayre, Isaac W. - Steward - Statement - Number: 332 - Entry Date: 3 Oct 1813 - Gunboat No. 40 - Discharged on 25 Jan 1814- Master's Mate - Promotions - Entry Date: 11 Nov 1814 - Gunboat No. 40 – Promoted

Schoonover, Moses - Landsman - Payroll 1 - Number: 7 - Entry Date: 3 Oct 1813 - Gunboat No. 6 - Landsman - Statement - Number: 7 - Entry Date: 3 Oct 1813 - Gunboat No. 6

Scott, Aaron - Ordinary Seaman - Payroll 2 - Number: 1854 - Entry Date: 1 Apr 1815 - Discharged

Scott, Benjamin - Ordinary Seaman - Payroll 1 - Number: 37 - Entry Date: 3 Oct 1813 - Gunboat No. 6 - Promotions - Entry Date: 21 Dec 1813 - Gunboat No. 6 - Promoted - Statement - Number: 37 - Entry Date: 3 Oct 1813 - Gunboat No. 6

Scott, James - Seaman - Payroll 2 - Number: 1981 - Entry Date: 9 Jul 1815 - Discharged to Nonsuch

Scott, Robert - Seaman - Payroll 2 - Number: 1851 - Entry Date: 1 Apr 1815 - Discharged

Seabury, John M. - Steward - Statement - Number: 1132 - Entry Date: 11 Mar 1814 - Gunboat No. 33 - Discharged from service, served from 11 Mar 1812 to 6 Oct 1814 - BLW 10035-160-55 - Pension: SO-941, SC-3449

Session, Richard - Ordinary Seaman - Payroll 2 - Number: 884 - Entry Date: 7 Oct 1813 - Ran

Sharper, Anthony (or Sharp) - Landsman - Payroll 2 - Number: 1650 - Entry Date: 1 Apr 1815 - Discharged

Shay, John - Ordinary Seaman - Payroll 2 - Number: 1897 - Entry Date: 2 May 1815 - Discharged

Shay, John W. - Ordinary Seaman - Payroll 1 - Number: 33 - Entry Date: 3 Oct 1813 - Gunboat No. 6- Ordinary Seaman - Statement - Number: 33 - Entry Date: 3 Oct 1813 - Gunboat No. 6

Sheales, George - Ordinary Seaman - Payroll 2 - Number: 981 - Entry Date: 26 Dec 1813 - Ran

Sheldon, Jesse - Landsman - Payroll 2 - Number: 2001 - Entry Date: 21 Jul 1815 - Discharged to the U.S. Brig Boxer

Sherlock, Edward - Steward - Statement - Number: 455 - Entry Date: 3 Oct 1813 - Gunboat No. 44 - Pension: Old War IF-1357

Shipang, Andrew - Seaman - Payroll 2 - Number: 1801 - Entry Date: 1 Apr 1815 - Discharged

Shipley, John - Seaman - Payroll 2 - Number: 174 - Entry Date: 9 Feb 1814 - Discharged to the U.S. Frigate John Adams

Shiris, Thomas - Landsman - Payroll 2 - Number: 1855 - Entry Date: 1 Feb 1815 - Ran

Shortes, James - Quarter Gunner - Statement - Number: 694 - Entry Date: 27 Sep 1813 - Gunboat No. 103 - Discharged on 17 Aug 1814

Shotten, Thomas - Ordinary Seaman - Payroll 2 - Number: 228 - Entry Date: 9 Feb 1814 - Gunboat No. B - Ordinary Seaman - Statement - Number: 209 - Entry Date: 3 Oct 1813 - Gunboat No. B - Discharged on 9 Feb 1814 - Discharged to the U.S. Frigate John Adams

Sibley, Samuel A. - Landsman - Payroll 2 - Number: 1949 - Entry Date: 21 Jul 1815 - Ran

Silden, William - Seaman - Statement - Number: 131 - Entry Date: 3 Oct 1813 - Gunboat No. 29

Simmons, William - Quarter Gunner - Payroll 1 - Number: 109 - Entry Date: 3 Oct 1813 - Gunboat No. 8 - Discharged on 3 Mar 1814 at New York - Statement - Number: 112 - Entry Date: 3 Oct 1813 - Gunboat No. 8 - Statement - Number: 1111 - Entry Date: 4 Mar 1814 - Gunboat No. 8

Simms, Joseph - Seaman - Payroll 2 - Number: 229 - Entry Date: 9 Feb 1814 - Discharged to the U.S. Frigate John Adams

Simpson, Thomas - Seaman - Payroll 2 - Number: 2210 - Entry Date: 11 Oct 1815 - Confined in jail

Simpson, William - Seaman - Statement - Number: 904 - Entry Date: 27 Sep 1813 - Gunboat No. 114 - Discharged on 13 Jun 1814

Singleton, James - Ordinary Seaman - Payroll 1 - Number: 77 - Entry Date: 3 Oct 1813 - Gunboat No. 8 - Payroll 2 - Number: 883 - Entry Date: 20 May 1814 - Gunboat No. 8 - Statement - Number: 80 - Entry Date: 3 Oct 1813 - Gunboat No. 8 - Ran on 20 May 1814 at New York

Sission, Robert - Ordinary Seaman - Payroll 1 - Number: 78 - Entry Date: 3 Oct 1813 - Gunboat No. 8 - Ran on 7 Oct 1813 at New York - Statement - Number: 81 - Entry Date: 3 Oct 1813 - Gunboat No. 8

Slocum, Peter - Landsman - Payroll 2 - Number: 1034 - Entry Date: 13 Jun 1814 - Ran

Smith, Alexander - Landsman - Payroll 2 - Number: 1984 - Entry Date: 21 Jul 1815 - Discharged to the U.S. Brig Boxer

Smith, Benjamin - Ordinary Seaman - Payroll 2 - Number: 1796 - Entry Date: 1 Apr 1815 - Discharged

Smith, Charles - Seaman - Statement - Number: 717 - Entry Date: 27 Sep 1813 - Gunboat No. 105 - Discharged on 2 Dec 1813

Smith, Edward S. - Seaman - Payroll 2 - Number: 1773 - Entry Date: 1 Apr 1815 - Discharged

Smith, George - Seaman - Payroll 2 - Number: 990 - Entry Date: 2 Nov 1813 - Ran

Smith, Gilbert - Ordinary Seaman - New York Naval Yard Muster 1 Aug 1815 - Number: 1297 - Entry Date: 23 Apr 1814 - Gunboat No. 31 - Discharged on 16 Feb 1815 - Payroll 2 - Number: 1726 - Entry Date: 16 Feb 1815 - Gunboat No. 31 - Statement - Number: 1307 - Entry Date: 23 Apr 1814 - Gunboat No. 31

Smith, Hendrich - Seaman - Payroll 2 - Number: 206 - Entry Date: 9 Feb 1814 - Gunboat No. A - Statement - Number: 173 - Entry Date: 3 Oct 1813 - Gunboat No. A - Discharged on 9 Feb 1814 - Discharged to the U.S. Frigate John Adams

Smith, Henry - Seaman - Payroll 2 - Number: 1074 - Entry Date: 5 Apr 1814 - Transferred to Lake Ontario

Smith, Humphrey - Ordinary Seaman - Payroll 2 - Number: 930 - Entry Date: 20 May 1814 - Ran

Smith, Isaac - Ordinary Seaman - Payroll 2 - Number: 941 - Entry Date: 2 Nov 1813 - Ran

Smith, James (1) - Seaman - Payroll 2 - Number: 915 - Entry Date: 17 Sep 1814 – Died

Smith, James (2) - Ordinary Seaman - Payroll 1 - Number: 121 - Entry Date: 3 Oct 1813 - Gunboat No. 29 - Statement - Number: 125 - Entry Date: 3 Oct 1813 - Gunboat No. 29

Smith, James (3) - Seaman - Payroll 2 - Number: 1761 - Entry Date: 1 Apr 1815 - Discharged - Statement - Number: 898 - Entry Date: 23 Oct 1813 - Gunboat No. 113 - Discharged on 12 Aug 1814 - Payroll 2 - Number: 1761 - Entry Date: 1 Apr 1815 - Discharged - Statement - Number: 898 - Entry Date: 23 Oct 1813 - Gunboat No. 113 - Discharged on 12 Aug 1814

Smith, John (1) - Ordinary Seaman - Payroll 2 - Number: 1846 - Entry Date: 1 Apr 1815 - Discharged

Smith, John (2) - Seaman - Payroll 2 - Number: 1874 - Entry Date: 3 May 1814 - Ran

Smith, John (3) - Quartermaster - Payroll 2 - Number: 2009 - Entry Date: 8 Sep 1815 - Ran

Smith, John (4) - Seaman - Payroll 2 - Number: 179 - Entry Date: 9 Feb 1814 - Gunboat No. 112 - Payroll 2 - Number: 182 - Entry Date: 9 Feb 1814 - Gunboat No. 112- Seaman - Statement - Number: 868 - Entry Date: 27 Sep 1813 - Gunboat No. 112 - Discharged on 9 Feb 1814 - Discharged to the U.S. Frigate John Adams

Smith, John (5) - Landsman - Payroll 1 - Number: 73 - Entry Date: 3 Oct 1813 - Gunboat No. 8 - Discharged on 6 Dec 1813 at New Yok- Landsman - Statement - Number: 76 - Entry Date: 3 Oct 1813 - Gunboat No. 8

Smith, Joseph (1) - Ordinary Seaman - Payroll 2 - Number: 749 - Entry Date: 4 Mar 1814 - Gunboat No. 6 - Discharged to the U.S. Sloop-of-War Peacock - Statement - Number: 40 - Entry Date: 3 Oct 1813 - Gunboat No. 6 - Discharged on 4 Mar 1814 - Discharged to the U.S. Sloop-of-War Peacock

Smith, Joseph (2) - Boy - Statement - Number: 1060 - Entry Date: 15 Feb 1814 - Gunboat No. 6

Smith, Leonard - Landsman - Payroll 1 - Number: 46 - Entry Date: 3 Oct 1813 - Gunboat No. 6 - Discharged on 27 Jan 1814 at New York - Statement - Number: 46 - Entry Date: 3 Oct 1813 - Gunboat No. 6 - Seaman - Statement - Number: 1003 - Entry Date: 28 Jan 1814 - Gunboat No. 6

Smith, Robert - Master's Mate - Payroll 2 - Number: 928 - Entry Date: 17 Oct 1813 - Discharged

Smith, Samuel - Seaman - Payroll 2 - Number: 1832 - Entry Date: 13 Feb 1815 - Ran

Smith, Thomas - Seaman - Payroll 2 - Number: 1898 - Entry Date: 10 Oct 1814 - Ran

Smith, William (1) - Seaman - Payroll 2 - Number: 794 - Entry Date: 14 Jul 1814 - Discharged to the U.S. Frigate President

Smith, William (2) - Ordinary Seaman - Payroll 2 - Number: 1748 - Entry Date: 1 Apr 1815 - Discharged - Seaman - Payroll 2 - Number: 1765 - Entry Date: 1 Apr 1815 - Discharged

Smothers, William - Ordinary Seaman - Payroll 1 - Number: 17 - Entry Date: 3 Oct 1813 - Gunboat No. 6 - Discharged on 4 Mar 1814 - Discharged to the U.S. Sloop-of-War Peacock - Payroll 2 - Number: 751 - Entry Date: 4 Mar 1814 - Gunboat No. 6 - Statement - Number: 16 - Entry Date: 3 Oct 1813 - Gunboat No. 6

Sparrowhawk, B. D. - Boatswain's Mate - Payroll 2 - Number: 773 - Entry Date: 3 Jun 1814 - Discharged to the U.S. Frigate Guerriere

Spencer, James - Ordinary Seaman - Payroll 2 - Number: 960 - Entry Date: 26 Feb 1814 – Ran

Spires, Samuel - Boy - Payroll 2 - Number: 1823 - Entry Date: 22 Feb 1815 - Ran

Spregere, Richard - Seaman - Statement - Number: 725 - Entry Date: 27 Sep 1813 - Gunboat No. 105 - Discharged on 12 Jul 1814

Stanford, Henry - Boatswain's Mate - Payroll 2 - Number: 199 - Entry Date: 9 Feb 1814 - Discharged to the U.S. Frigate John Adams

Stanton, Elisha - Master's Mate - Payroll 1 - Number: 62 - Entry Date: 3 Oct 1813 - Gunboat No. 8 - Statement - Number: 65 - Entry Date: 3 Oct 1813 - Gunboat No. 8 - Discharged on 12 Aug 1814

Stanton, William - Seaman - Payroll 2 - Number: 974 - Entry Date: 27 Oct 1813 - Gunboat No. 103 - Statement - Number: 678 - Entry Date: 27 Sep 1813 - Gunboat No. 103 - Ran on 27 Dec 1813 at New York

Stanwood, John - Seaman - Statement - Number: 863 - Entry Date: 27 Sep 1813 - Gunboat No. 112 - Discharged on 12 Jul 1814

Starbuck, James - Seaman - Payroll 2 - Number: 894 - Entry Date: 3 Nov 1813 - Gunboat No. 30 - Statement - Number: 142 - Entry Date: 27 Sep 1813 - Gunboat No. 30 - Ran on 3 Nov 1813 at New York

Starkey, James - Seaman - Payroll 1 - Number: 88 - Entry Date: 3 Oct 1813 - Gunboat No. 8 - Discharged on 22 Feb 1814 at New York - Statement - Number: 91 - Entry Date: 3 Oct 1813 - Gunboat No. 8 - Statement - Number: 1086 - Entry Date: 22 Feb 1814 - Gunboat No. 8

Stephens, Benjamin (Stevens) - Master's Mate - Statement - Number: 811 - Entry Date: 27 Sep 1813 - Gunboat No. 109 - Discharged on 27 Jun 1814 - BLW 18292-160-55

Stephenson, Henry - Boatswain's Mate - Payroll 2 - Number: 964 - Entry Date: 11 Jun 1814 - Ran

Stevens, Binnesley - Seaman - Payroll 1 - Number: 126 - Entry Date: 3 Oct 1813 - Gunboat No. 29 - Discharged on 23 Mar 1814 at New York - Seaman - Statement - Number: 130 - Entry Date: 3 Oct 1813 - Gunboat No. 29

Steward, James - Ordinary Seaman - Payroll 2 - Number: 1048 - Entry Date: 15 Jul 1814 - Transferred to Lake Champlain

Steward, John - Ordinary Seaman - Payroll 2 - Number: 1712 - Entry Date: 25 Dec 1814 - Ran

Steward, Thomas - Quarter Gunner - Statement - Number: 1394 - Entry Date: 1 Jun 1814 - Gunboat No. 112 - Statement - Number: 866 - Entry Date: 27 Sep 1813 - Gunboat No. 112 - Discharged on 2 Jul 1814 - BLW 39187-160-50

Stewart, William - Seaman - Payroll 2 - Number: 1837 - Entry Date: 1 Apr 1815 - Discharged to navy yard

Story, Thomas H. - Quartermaster - Statement - Entry Date: 24 Aug 1814 - Gunboat No. 30

Stowell, Peter - Seaman - Payroll 2 - Number: 793 - Entry Date: 14 Jul 1814 - Gunboat No. 112 Statement -

Number: 853 - Entry Date: 27 Sep 1813 - Gunboat No. 112 - Discharged on 14 Jul 1814 - Discharged to the U.S. Frigate President - Statement 1 - Number: 1338 - Entry Date: 14 Jun 1814 - Gunboat No. 112

Strawbridge, Benjamin - Landsman - Payroll 1 - Number: 93 - Entry Date: 3 Oct 1813 - Gunboat No. 8 - Seaman - Payroll 2 - Number: 888 - Entry Date: 9 Oct 1813 - Gunboat No. 8 - Statement - Number: 96 - Entry Date: 3 Oct 1813 - Gunboat No. 8 - Discharged on 10 Oct 1813

Summersville, Charles - Ordinary Seaman - Payroll 2 - Number: 779 - Entry Date: 14 Jul 1814 - Discharged to the U.S. Frigate President

Swain, Edward - Master's Mate - Statement - Number: 709 - Entry Date: 27 Sep 1813 - Gunboat No. 105 - Discharged on 28 Mar 1814

Swain, Henry - Ordinary Seaman - Payroll 2 - Number: 2178 - Entry Date: 4 Dec 1815 - Gunboat No. 103 - Landsman - Statement - Number: 687 - Entry Date: 27 Sep 1813 - Gunboat No. 103 - Discharged on 12 Jul 1814 - Ordinary Seaman - Statement 1 - Number: 1437 - Entry Date: 13 Jul 1814 - Gunboat No. 103

Swinton, Thomas - Seaman - Statement - Number: 337 - Entry Date: 5 Oct 1813 - Gunboat No. 40

Tandurrup, William - Seaman - Statement - Number: 190 - Entry Date: 3 Oct 1813 - Gunboat No. A

Taylor, Henry - Seaman - Payroll 2 - Number: 1076 - Entry Date: 23 Jul 1814 - Ran

Taylor, Jeremiah - Ordinary Seaman - Payroll 2 - Number: 213 - Entry Date: 9 Feb 1814 - Gunboat No. 113 - Statement - Number: 895 - Entry Date: 27 Sep 1813 - Gunboat No. 113 - Discharged on 9 Feb 1814 - Discharged to the U.S. Frigate John Adams

Taylor, John - Landsman - Payroll 2 - Number: 1738 - Entry Date: 11 Feb 1815 - Discharged

Teir, Mark - Ordinary Seaman - Statement - Number: 334 - Entry Date: 3 Oct 1813 - Gunboat No. 40 - Discharged on 4 Jan 1814

Terrill, John - Ordinary Seaman - Payroll 2 - Number: 1886 - Number 2: 1886b - Entry Date: 1 Aug 1815 - Discharged

Thomas, Abraham - Quarter Gunner - Statement - Number: 202 - Entry Date: 3 Oct 1813 - Gunboat No. B

Thomas, Caleb D. - Seaman - Payroll 1 - Number: 21 - Entry Date: 3 Oct 1813 - Gunboat No. 6 - Discharged on 2 Oct 1813 at New York - Statement - Number: 20 - Entry Date: 3 Oct 1813 - Gunboat No. 6

Thomas, Cuff - Ordinary Seaman - Payroll 2 - Number: 2215 - Entry Date: 25 Dec 1815 - Died

Thomas, James - Seaman - Payroll 2 - Number: 997 - Entry Date: 6 Nov 1813 - Ran - Statement - Number: 865 - Entry Date: 27 Sep 1813 - Gunboat No. 112 - Statement - Number: 896 - Entry Date: 27 Sep 1813 - Gunboat No. 113 - Discharged on 12 Jul 1814

Thomas, John - Ordinary Seaman - Payroll 2 - Number: 1724 - Entry Date: 1 Apr 1815 - Gunboat No. 114 - Statement - Number: 906 - Entry Date: 27 Sep 1813 - Gunboat No. 114 - Discharged on 13 Jun 1814 Ordinary Seaman - Statement - Number: 1303 - Entry Date: 20 Apr 1814 - Gunboat No. 114

Thomas, Titus - Seaman - Statement - Number: 320 - Entry Date: 3 Oct 1813 - Gunboat No. 40 - Discharged on 9 Nov 1813

Thomas, William - Seaman - Payroll 2 - Number: 1980 - Entry Date: 5 Jul 1815 – Ran

Thompson, John (1) - Ordinary Seaman - New York Naval Yard Muster 1 Aug 1815 - Number: 925 - Entry Date: 18 Oct 1813 - Gunboat No. 6 - Discharged on 22 Oct 1814Seaman - Payroll 2 - Number: 123 - Entry Date: 17 Jan 1814 - Discharged to the U.S. Sloop-of-War Peacock - Ordinary Seaman - Statement - Number: 960 - Entry Date: 18 Oct 1813 - Gunboat No. 6

Thompson, John (2) - Landsman - Payroll 2 - Number: 1643 - Entry Date: 20 Jan 1815 - Ran

Thompson, Joseph - Seaman - Payroll 2 - Number: 1730 - Entry Date: 1 Apr 1815 - Discharged

Thompson, Robert - Landsman - New York Naval Yard Muster 1 Aug 1815 - Number: 1521 - Entry Date: 4 Jul 1814 - Gunboat No. 113 - Discharged on 1 Mar 1815 - Payroll 2 - Number: 1826 - Entry Date: 1 Mar 1815 -

Gunboat No. 11 - Statement 1 - Number: 1405 - Entry Date: 4 Jul 1814 - Gunboat No. 11

Thompson, Samuel J. - Steward - Payroll 2 - Number: 2031 - Entry Date: 12 Aug 1815 - Nonsuch

Thurston, John C. - Seaman - Payroll 2 - Number: 2174 - Entry Date: 30 Sep 1815 - Discharged

Tieser, Jose - Seaman - Payroll 1 - Number: 43 - Entry Date: 3 Oct 1813 - Gunboat No. 6 - Statement - Number: 43 - Entry Date: 3 Oct 1813 - Gunboat No. 6

Tishuel, John - Sailing Master - Statement - Number: 785 - Entry Date: 27 Sep 1813 - Gunboat No. 109

Titus, William - Seaman - Payroll 2 - Number: 899 - Entry Date: 2 Nov 1813 - Ran

Tolton, Joshua - Ordinary Seaman - Payroll 2 - Number: 802 - Entry Date: 14 Jul 1814 - Discharged to the U.S. Frigate President

Tompson, John - Ordinary Seaman - Payroll 2 - Number: 1668 - Entry Date: 22 Oct 1815 - Ran

Topham, Thomas - Steward - Payroll 1 - Number: 125 - Entry Date: 3 Oct 1813 - Gunboat No. 29 - Statement - Number: 129 - Entry Date: 3 Oct 1813 - Gunboat No. 29 - Discharged on 12 May 1814

Townsend, Solomon - Seaman - Statement - Number: 221 - Entry Date: 3 Oct 1813 - Gunboat No. B - Discharged on 17 Jan 1814 - Discharged to the U.S. Sloop-of-War Peacock

Trainer, William - Seaman - Statement - Number: 708 - Entry Date: 27 Sep 1813 - Gunboat No. 105 - Discharged on 12 Jul 1814

Treadell, John - Ordinary Seaman - Payroll 2 - Number: 1645 - Entry Date: 10 Oct 1814 - Discharged

Trefry, John - Quarter Gunner - Statement - Number: 792 - Entry Date: 27 Sep 1813 - Gunboat No. 109 - Discharged on 24 Feb 1814 - Statement - Number: 1235 - Entry Date: 17 Mar 1814 - Gunboat No. 109

Triehtis, John - Ordinary Seaman - Payroll 2 - Number: 934 - Entry Date: 16 Nov 1813 - Ran

Trimble, Joseph - Steward - Statement - Number: 925 - Entry Date: 22 Oct 1813 - Gunboat No. 114

Triner, Frederick - Seaman - Statement - Number: 713 - Entry Date: 27 Sep 1813 - Gunboat No. 105 - Discharged on 17 Jun 1814 - Discharged to the U.S. Sloop-of-War Peacock

Trusty, John - Landsman - Payroll 2 - Number: 1983 - Entry Date: 21 Jul 1815 - Discharged to the U.S. Brig Boxer

Trutson, Andrew - Seaman - Payroll 1 - Number: 71 - Entry Date: 3 Oct 1813 - Gunboat No. 8 - Discharged on 9 Feb 1814 - Discharged to the U.S. Frigate John Adams - Payroll 2 - Number: 190 - Entry Date: 9 Feb 1814 - Gunboat No. 8 - Statement - Number: 74 - Entry Date: 3 Oct 1813 - Gunboat No. 8

Tuck, Henry - Quarter Gunner - Statement - Number: 123 - Entry Date: 3 Oct 1813 - Gunboat No. 29 - Discharged on 10 Sep 1814

Tunis, John - Seaman - Statement - Number: 799 - Entry Date: 27 Sep 1813 - Gunboat No. 109 - Discharged on 12 Jul 1814

Tuxen, William - Ordinary Seaman - Payroll 2 - Number: 1790 - Entry Date: 1 Apr 1815 - Discharged

Twin, Jerry - Seaman - Payroll 2 - Number: 1634 - Entry Date: 15 Mar 1814 - Gunboat No. A - Landsman - Statement - Number: 181 - Entry Date: 3 Oct 1813 - Gunboat No. A

Utt, Peter N. - Master's Mate - Payroll 1 - Number: 94 - Entry Date: 3 Oct 1813 - Gunboat No. 8 - Discharged on 16 Feb 1814 at New York - Statement - Number: 97 - Entry Date: 3 Oct 1813 - Gunboat No. 8

Valentine, Benjamin - Ordinary Seaman - Payroll 2 - Number: 1839 - Entry Date: 1 Apr 1815 - Discharged

Van Buren, James - Landsman - Payroll 2 - Number: 1783 - Entry Date: 1 Apr 1815 - Discharged

Van Honniger, Francis - Seaman - Statement - Number: 699 - Entry Date: 27 Sep 1813 - Gunboat No. 103 - Discharged on 12 Jul 1814

Vanderpool, Robert - Ordinary Seaman - Payroll 1 - Number: 151 - Entry Date: 26 Sep 1813 - Gunboat No. 30 - Ran on 3 Nov 1813 at New York - Payroll 2 - Number: 901 - Entry Date: 3 Nov 1813 - Gunboat No. 30 -

Statement - Number: 153 - Entry Date: 27 Sep 1813 - Gunboat No. 30

Varnum, Samiel - Landsman - Payroll 2 - Number: 788 - Entry Date: 14 Jul 1814 - Discharged to the U.S. Frigate President

Vase, Charles - Landsman - Statement - Number: 909 - Entry Date: 27 Sep 1813 - Gunboat No. 114 - Discharged on 13 Jun 1814

Venderbeck, Jacob - Landsman - Statement - Number: 324 - Entry Date: 3 Oct 1813 - Gunboat No. 40 - Discharged on 9 Nov 1813

Verry, William - Seaman - Statement - Number: 104 - Entry Date: 3 Oct 1813 - Gunboat No. 8 - Discharged on 22 Mar 1814

Vincent, Jacob - Ordinary Seaman - Payroll 2 - Number: 237 - Entry Date: 9 Feb 1814 - Discharged to the U.S. Frigate John Adams

Vinton, Ebenezer - Steward - Statement - Number: 223 - Entry Date: 20 Oct 1813 - Gunboat No. B - Discharged on 17 Jan 1814

Wagner, Henry - Boatswain's Mate - Payroll 1 - Number: 137 - Entry Date: 26 Sep 1813 - Gunboat No. 30 - Discharged on 4 Dec 1813 at New York - Statement - Number: 141 - Entry Date: 27 Sep 1813 - Gunboat No. 30

Waine, Daniel M. - Seaman - Payroll 2 - Number: 1756 - Entry Date: 1 Apr 1815 - Discharged to navy yard

Waite, John - Ordinary Seaman - Payroll 2 - Number: 209 - Entry Date: 9 Feb 1814 - Discharged to the U.S. Frigate John Adams

Walker, Francis - Master's Mate - Statement - Number: 697 - Entry Date: 27 Sep 1813 - Gunboat No. 103

Walker, Joseph - Seaman - Statement - Number: 860 - Entry Date: 27 Sep 1813 - Gunboat No. 112 - Discharged on 17 Jan 1814 - Discharged to the U.S. Sloop-of-War Peacock

Walker, Lemmon - Landsman - Payroll 2 - Number: 1812 - Entry Date: 1 Apr 1815 - Discharged

Walker, Richard - Seaman - Payroll 2 - Number: 1896 - Entry Date: 22 May 1814 - Died

Wallis, Jacob - Seaman - Payroll 1 - Number: 108 - Entry Date: 3 Oct 1813 - Gunboat No. 8 - Discharged on 25 Feb 1814 at New York - Statement - Number: 111 - Entry Date: 3 Oct 1813 - Gunboat No. 8

Walsh, Thomas - Seaman - Payroll 2 - Number: 221 - Entry Date: 9 Feb 1814 - Discharged to the U.S. Frigate John Adams

Walton, John - Seaman - Payroll 2 - Number: 124 - Entry Date: 17 Jan 1814 - Gunboat No. 105 - Statement - Number: 723 - Entry Date: 27 Sep 1813 - Gunboat No. 105 - Discharged on 17 Jan 1814 - Discharged to the U.S. Sloop-of-War Peacock

Ward, John - Seaman - Payroll 2 - Number: 197 - Entry Date: 9 Feb 1814 - Gunboat No. 109 - Statement - Number: 810 - Entry Date: 27 Sep 1813 - Gunboat No. 109 - Discharged on 9 Feb 1814 - Discharged to the U.S. Frigate John Adams

Ward, Michael - Seaman - Statement - Number: 341 - Entry Date: 25 Oct 1813 - Gunboat No. 40

Ward, Robert - Steward - Statement - Number: 700 - Entry Date: 27 Sep 1813 - Gunboat No. 103

Warden, John - Seaman - Statement - Number: 205 - Entry Date: 3 Oct 1813 - Gunboat No. B - Discharged on 17 Jan 1814 - Discharged to the U.S. Sloop-of-War Peacock

Wares, Samuel - Sailing Master - Payroll 1 - Number: 163 - Entry Date: 3 Oct 1813 - Gunboat No. A - Statement - Number: 165 - Entry Date: 3 Oct 1813 - Gunboat No. A

Warner, Henry - Seaman - Payroll 2 - Number: 188 - Entry Date: 9 Feb 1814 - Discharged to the U.S. Frigate John Adams

Warner, John W. - Seaman - Payroll 2 - Number: 1049 - Entry Date: 24 Oct 1813 - Ran

Warner, Samuel - Seaman - Payroll 2 - Number: 1664 - Entry Date: 10 Oct 1815 - Discharged

Warren, Thomas - Landsman - Statement - Number: 902 - Entry Date: 27 Sep 1813 - Gunboat No. 114 - Discharged on 13 Jun 1814

Washburn, Noah - Master's Mate - Statement - Number: 315 - Entry Date: 3 Oct 1813 - Gunboat No. 40 - BLW 6190-160-55

Waterbury, Ezra - Landsman - Payroll 2 - Number: 1920 - Entry Date: 21 Sep 1815 - Ran

Waters, Daniel - Seaman - New York Naval Yard Muster 1 Aug 1815 - Number: 1042 - Entry Date: 22 Feb 1814 - Gunboat No. 47 - Discharged on 5 Jan 1814 - Payroll 2 - Number: 1687 - Entry Date: 5 Jul 1814 - Gunboat No. 47 - Statement - Number: 1084 - Entry Date: 22 Feb 1814 - Gunboat No. 47

Watson, George - Quartermaster - Payroll 2 - Number: 2218 - Entry Date: 20 Sep 1815 - Ran

Watson, James - Ordinary Seaman - Payroll 2 - Number: 1927 - Entry Date: 13 May 1815 - Died

Watson, John - Boatswain's Mate - Payroll 2 - Number: 185 - Entry Date: 9 Feb 1814 - Discharged to the U.S. Frigate John Adams

Weeks, John - Ordinary Seaman - Payroll 2 - Number: 955 - Entry Date: 10 Oct 1813 - Ran

Weigle, Frederick - Ordinary Seaman - Statement - Number: 314 - Entry Date: 3 Oct 1813 - Gunboat No. 40 - Discharged on 19 Sep 1814

Welding, Charles - Seaman - Payroll 2 - Number: 796 - Entry Date: 14 Jul 1814 - Discharged to the U.S. Frigate President - Payroll 2 - Number: 183 - Entry Date: 9 Feb 1814 - Gunboat No. 112

Weyman, Charles - Seaman - Statement - Number: 850 - Entry Date: 27 Sep 1813 - Gunboat No. 112 - Discharged on 9 Feb 1814 - Discharged to the U.S. Frigate John Adams

Wheylin, John - Seaman - Payroll 2 - Number: 227 - Entry Date: 9 Feb 1814 - Gunboat No. B - Statement - Number: 204 - Entry Date: 3 Oct 1813 - Gunboat No. B - Discharged on 9 Feb 1814 - Discharged to the U.S. Frigate John Adams

Whitcher, Royal - Seaman - Payroll 2 - Number: 1762 - Entry Date: 1 Apr 1815 - Gunboat No. 40 - Ordinary Seaman - Statement - Number: 331 - Entry Date: 3 Oct 1813 - Gunboat No. 40 - Discharged on 25 Jan 1814 - Statement - Number: 1000 - Entry Date: 26 Jan 1814 - Gunboat No. 40 - Statement - Number: 1383 - Entry Date: 31 May 1814 - Gunboat No. 40

White, Charles - Steward - Statement - Number: 918 - Entry Date: 27 Sep 1813 - Gunboat No. 114 - Discharged on 25 Feb 1814

White, Francis - Seaman - Payroll 2 - Number: 1853 - Entry Date: 1 Apr 1815 - Gunboat No. 114 - Ordinary Seaman - Statement - Number: 923 - Entry Date: 27 Sep 1813 - Gunboat No. 114 - Discharged on 12 Jul 1814 Seaman - Statement 1 - Number: 1455 - Entry Date: 16 Jul 1814 - Gunboat No. 114

White, George William - Seaman - New York Naval Yard Muster 1 Aug 1815 - Number: 948 - Entry Date: 27 Nov 1813 - Gunboat No. 6 - Discharged on 25 Mar 1814 - Payroll 2 - Number: 1670 - Entry Date: 25 Mar 1815 - Gunboat No. 6

White, George William - Seaman - Statement - Number: 972 - Entry Date: 27 Nov 1813 - Gunboat No. 6

White, John - Landsman - Payroll 2 - Number: 1713 - Entry Date: 1 Apr 1815 - Discharged

White, Obediah - Seaman - Statement - Number: 852 - Entry Date: 27 Sep 1813 - Gunboat No. 112 - Discharged on 15 Jun 1814

White, Rowland H. - Master's Mate - Payroll 2 - Number: 904 - Entry Date: 16 Mar 1814 - Died

Whiting, William - Seaman - New York Naval Yard Muster 1 Aug 1815 - Number: 1138 - Entry Date: 10 Mar 1814 - Gunboat No. 44 - Discharged on 17 Dec 1814

Whiting, William - Seaman - Payroll 2 - Number: 1702 - Entry Date: 17 Dec 1814 - Gunboat No. 44 Statement - Number: 1128 - Entry Date: 10 Mar 1814 - Gunboat No. 44

Whitmore, William (Whittemore) - Ordinary Seaman - Payroll 1 - Number: 52 - Entry Date: 3 Oct 1813 - Gunboat

No. 6 - Discharged on 22 Mar 1814 at New York - Statement - Number: 52 - Entry Date: 3 Oct 1813 - Gunboat No. 6 - BLW 48297-160-55

Widger, Thomas (1) - Seaman - Payroll 1 - Number: 105 - Entry Date: 3 Oct 1813 - Gunboat No. 8 - Discharged on 22 Mar 1814 at New York - Statement - Number: 108 - Entry Date: 3 Oct 1813 - Gunboat No. 8 - Statement - Number: 1259 - Entry Date: 28 Mar 1814 - Gunboat No. 8

Widger, Thomas (2) - Ordinary Seaman - Payroll 1 - Number: 106 - Entry Date: 3 Oct 1813 - Gunboat No. 8 - Discharged on 27 Mar 1814 at New York - Statement - Number: 109 - Entry Date: 3 Oct 1813 - Gunboat No. 8 - Boy - Statement - Number: 1261 - Entry Date: 28 Mar 1814 - Gunboat No. 8

Wike, Samuel - Landsman - Payroll 2 - Number: 1684 - Entry Date: 25 Feb 1815 - Discharged

Williams, Bearl - Seaman - Payroll 1 - Number: 159 - Entry Date: 26 Sep 1813 - Gunboat No. 30 - Payroll 2 - Number: 902 - Entry Date: 10 Feb 1814 - Gunboat No. 30 - Statement - Number: 161 - Entry Date: 27 Sep 1813 - Gunboat No. 30 - Ran on 10 Feb 1814 at New York

Williams, George (1) - Ordinary Seaman - Statement - Number: 851 - Entry Date: 27 Sep 1813 - Gunboat No. 112 - Discharged on 12 Jul 1814

Williams, George (2) - Boatswain's Mate - Statement - Entry Date: 8 Sep 1814 - Gunboat No. 30

Williams, Isaac - Landsman - Payroll 2 - Number: 2000 - Entry Date: 21 Jul 1815 - Discharged to the U.S. Brig Boxer - Statement - Number: 911 - Entry Date: 27 Sep 1813 - Gunboat No. 114 - Discharged on 13 Jun 1814

Williams, James (1) - Seaman - New York Naval Yard Muster 1 Aug 1815 - Number: 995 - Entry Date: 11 Feb 1814 - Gunboat No. 30 - Discharged on 4 May 1814

Williams, James (2) - Seaman - New York Naval Yard Muster 1 Aug 1815 - Number: 1018 - Entry Date: 16 Feb 1814 - Gunboat No. 47 - Discharged on 7 May 1814

Williams, James (3) - Seaman - Payroll 2 - Number: 1678 - Entry Date: 3 May 1814 - Ran

Williams, James (4) - Ordinary Seaman - Payroll 2 - Number: 1706 - Entry Date: 1 Apr 1815 - Discharged

Williams, James (5) - Ordinary Seaman - Payroll 2 - Number: 1997 - Entry Date: 21 Jul 1815 - Discharged to the U.S. Brig Boxer

Williams, James (6) - Seaman - Statement - Number: 1008 - Entry Date: 11 Feb 1814 - Gunboat No. 30

Williams, James (7) - Seaman - Statement - Number: 1062 - Entry Date: 16 Feb 1814 - Gunboat No. 47

Williams, James (8) - Seaman - Payroll 2 - Number: 1682 - Entry Date: 7 May 1814 - Ran

Williams, John (1) - Seaman - Payroll 2 - Number: 175 - Entry Date: 9 Feb 1814 - Discharged to the U.S. Frigate John Adams

Williams, John (2) - Ordinary Seaman - Payroll 2 - Number: 1862 - Entry Date: 1 Apr 1815 - Gunboat No. 113 - Statement - Number: 878 - Entry Date: 27 Sep 1813 - Gunboat No. 113 - Discharged on 12 Jul 1814 - Statement - Number: 1447 - Entry Date: 2 Aug 1814 - Gunboat No. 113- Seaman - Statement - Number: 494 - Entry Date: 26 Sep 1813 - Gunboat No. 113

Williams, John (3) - Seaman - Payroll 2 - Number: 1073 - Entry Date: 20 Apr 1814 - Ran

Williams, John (4) - Seaman - Payroll 2 - Number: 1660 - Entry Date: 25 Oct 1815 - Ran

Williams, Joshua - Master's Mate - Payroll 2 - Number: 1821 - Entry Date: 1 Apr 1815 - Discharged

Williams, Peter - Seaman - Payroll 2 - Number: 1886 - Number 2: 1886a - Entry Date: 15 May 1815 - Ran - Payroll 2 - Number: 1912 - Entry Date: 6 Mar 1815 - Ran

Williams, Richard (Rick) - Seaman - Payroll 1 - Number: 160 - Entry Date: 26 Sep 1813 - Gunboat No. 30 - Statement - Number: 162 - Entry Date: 27 Sep 1813 - Gunboat No. 30 - Discharged on 13 Jul 1814

Williams, Rufus - Ordinary Seaman - Payroll 2 - Number: 1827 - Entry Date: 1 Apr 1815 - Discharged

Williams, Stephen - Sailing Master - Payroll 1 - Number: 133 - Entry Date: 26 Sep 1813 - Gunboat No. 30 -

Statement - Number: 137 - Entry Date: 3 Oct 1813 - Gunboat No. 30

Williams, Stephen - Sailing Master - Statement - Number: 60 - Entry Date: 14 Mar 1814 - Gunboat No. 6 - Discharged on 12 Apr 1814

Williams, Thomas - Ordinary Seaman - Payroll 2 - Number: 946 - Entry Date: 3 Nov 1813 - Ran

Williams, William (1) - Seaman - Statement - Number: 795 - Entry Date: 27 Sep 1813 - Gunboat No. 109 - Discharged on 18 Jul 1814

Williams, William (2) - Seaman - Statement - Number: 798 - Entry Date: 27 Sep 1813 - Gunboat No. 109 - Discharged on 17 Jan 1814

Williamson, John - Landsman - Payroll 2 - Number: 1817 - Entry Date: 1 Apr 1815 - Discharged

Willis, Jacob - Seaman - Payroll 2 - Number: 1814 - Entry Date: 1 Apr 1815 - Gunboat No. 112 - Ordinary Seaman - Statement - Number: 844 - Entry Date: 27 Sep 1813 - Gunboat No. 112 - Discharged on 9 Jul 1814 - Statement 1 - Number: 1384 - Entry Date: 25 Jun 1814 - Gunboat No. 112

Wilson, David - Landsman - Payroll 1 - Number: 132 - Entry Date: 3 Oct 1813 - Gunboat No. 29 - Boy - Payroll 2 - Number: 2285 - Entry Date: 9 Jul 1816 - Gunboat No. 29 - Landsman - Statement - Number: 136 - Entry Date: 3 Oct 1813 - Gunboat No. 29 - Discharged on 12 Aug 1814

Wilson, George M. - Sailing Master - Payroll 2 - Number: 1883 - Entry Date: 4 Aug 1814 - Discharged to Washington, DC

Wilson, Peter - Seaman - Statement - Number: 220 - Entry Date: 3 Oct 1813 - Gunboat No. B - Discharged on 17 Jan 1814 - Discharged to the U.S. Sloop-of-War Peacock

Wilson, Samuel (1) - Quarter Gunner - Statement - Number: 178 - Entry Date: 3 Oct 1813 - Gunboat No. A

Wilson, Samuel (2) - Ordinary Seaman - Payroll 1 - Number: 72 - Entry Date: 3 Oct 1813 - Gunboat No. 8 - Statement - Number: 75 - Entry Date: 3 Oct 1813 - Gunboat No. 8

Wilson, Sidney - Seaman - Payroll 2 - Number: 995 - Entry Date: 6 Nov 1813 - Gunboat No. 112 - Statement - Number: 846 - Entry Date: 27 Sep 1813 - Gunboat No. 112 - Ran on 6 Nov 1813 at New York

Winasset, James - Seaman - Payroll 1 - Number: 143 - Entry Date: 26 Sep 1813 - Gunboat No. 30 - Statement - Number: 147 - Entry Date: 27 Sep 1813 - Gunboat No. 30 - Discharged on 7 Jun 1814

Wood, George - Seaman - Statement - Number: 803 - Entry Date: 27 Sep 1813 - Gunboat No. 109 - Discharged on 12 Jul 1814

Wood, Thomas - Ordinary Seaman - Payroll 2 - Number: 2010 - Entry Date: 20 Aug 1815 - Ran

Woodfine, Richard - Seaman - Payroll 1 - Number: 107 - Entry Date: 3 Oct 1813 - Gunboat No. 8 - Discharged on 28 Feb 1814 at New York - Statement - Number: 110 - Entry Date: 3 Oct 1813 - Gunboat No. 8

Wormstead, John B. - Seaman - Statement - Number: 219 - Entry Date: 3 Oct 1813 - Gunboat No. B - Discharged on 17 Jan 1814 - Discharged to the U.S. Sloop-of-War Peacock

Wright, Darrel - Seaman - Statement - Number: 193 - Entry Date: 5 Oct 1813 - Gunboat No. A

Wright, James (1) - Seaman - Payroll 2 - Number: 986 - Entry Date: 2 Nov 1813 - Ran

Wright, James (2) - Seaman - Statement - Number: 801 - Entry Date: 27 Sep 1813 - Gunboat No. 109 - Discharged on 2 Nov 1813

Young, Thomas - Seaman - Payroll 2 - Number: 1810 - Entry Date: 1 Apr 1815 – Discharged

War of 1812 Naval Dictionary

Armorer
An armorer is a seaman who repairs the ship's small arms.

Barge – See Row Galley

Battery
All of the guns on one side of a ship is referred to as a battery. Each warship would have a starboard battery and a port battery.

Boatswain
A boatswain is a warrant officer who is in charge of the work of the seamen, the general oversight of the cleanliness of the ship, and of the work pertaining to the boats, spars, rigging, etc., anchoring and the mooring and unmooring of the ship.

Boatswain's Mate
A boatswain's mate is a petty officer who assists the boatswain in his duties. Then a boatswain is not assigned to a ship, then the boatswain's mate assumed all of the duties of a boatswain.

Boy
A minor (male) who served as a cabin boy, a powder monkey, and ship's boy on ships.

Brig
A brig is a two-mast vessel with square sails on both masts. All of the cannons are on the top deck.

Cannon – see Long Gun

Captain - U.S. Navy/U.S. Flotilla Service
The highest commissioned officer in the U.S. Navy during the War of 1812. A captain was above a master commandant.

Captain – U.S. Marine Corps
A captain is a U.S. Marine Corps officer who is above a first lieutenant and below a major.

Captain - Title
A captain was a title given to any naval officer commanding a warship regardless of his rank.

Carpenter
A carpenter is a warrant officer who is responsible for maintenance of the ship's hull, boats, and masts.

Carpenter's Mate
A carpenter's mate is a petty officer who assists the carpenter in his duties. He assumes all of the duties of a carpenter when a ship is too small to rate a carpenter's position.

Carronade
A carronade was a short barrel, smooth bore light weight cannon which fired a large caliber projectile. They were a short-range weapon which was used at close quarters.

Causality
A causality is any subtraction of manpower from a military unit or ship. These subtractions included deaths, men who were killed in action, men who have died from wounds, men who were captured by the enemy, hospital patients, and men who were assigned to temporary duty away from their unit or ship.

Chaplain
A chaplain was a warrant officers who provided pastoral, spiritual, and emotional support for the ship's personnel.

Commission
A commission is a certificate conferring military rank and authority upon naval officers who have been promoted to the rank of lieutenant and above. In the U.S. Marine Corps, commission were given to second lieutenants and above.

Commodore
A title in the U.S. Navy given by the Secretary of the Navy for senior captains who were in command of a naval base (which constructed ships), a squadron, or a flotilla. They had the rank of a commodore but they received a captain's pay. The rank of commodore would not be created by the U.S. Congress for the navy until 1862.

Commodore – Title
Commodore also was an unauthorized naval title given to officers who manned more than one vessel, regardless of their ranks or the number of vessels in their command. In most cases, these titles were self-conferred by the officers themselves.

Cook
A cook was a seaman who handled the preparation of food for the ship's personnel.

Cooper
A cooper was a seaman in charge of the barrels and casks of supplies on board a ship.

Coxswain

A coxswain is a seaman who was in charge of the crew of a captain's boat on a vessel of war. The coxswain steered the boat while the crew manned the oars.

First Lieutenant - U.S Marine Corps

First lieutenant is a U.S. Marine Corps officer's rank above second lieutenant and below captain.

Flotilla

A squadron of small boats, gunboats, or bateaux was called a flotilla.

Frigate

A three-mast sailing ship with square sails which had a gun deck. The number of guns varied from 28 to 44 and sometimes more guns. There were guns also placed on the spar deck. (See also Heavy Frigate)

Gunboat

A gunboat was the smallest warship in the U.S. Navy. They could be propelled by oars or sails, and they were usually designed for coastal waters and harbors. Gunboats had no decks, but they had one or two platforms on either end of the boat to accommodate cannons.

Gunboat – merchant ships

Merchant schooners and sloops which were converted to warships were called gunboats. They normally carried one or two heavy cannons.

Gunner

A gunner was a warrant officer who was responsible for the care and maintenance of the ship's guns and gunpowder.

Gunner's Mate

A gunner's mate who a petty officer who assisted the gunner in his duties. He also performed the duties of a gunner when a ship did not rate a gunner's position.

Landsman

A landsman was a naval recruit who was in training to became a seaman.

Lieutenant

A lieutenant was a commissioned naval officer who was below the rank of master commandant and above a sailing master.

Lieutenant Colonel Commandant

The commander of the U.S. Marine Corps had the rank of lieutenant colonel commandant. The rank was above the rank of major.

Long Gun

An artillery piece with a long smooth bore, which had a longer range than a carronade. These pieces were mounted within fortifications or on naval vessels.

Major

The rank of major in the U.S. Marine Corps was below the rank of lieutenant colonel commandant and above the rank of captain.

Marines

Naval soldiers who were used as guards aboard ships which provides musket support during naval battles. They also assisted in shore actions, and serve as the body guards for ship's captains.

Master - U.S. Navy

The master was the senior warrant officer on board a ship who was a qualified navigator and experienced seaman who set the sails, maintained the ship's log and advised the captain on the seaworthiness of the ship and crew. They were also called sailing masters.

Master - Merchant Vessel

The commander of a merchant vessel was called a master. Other terms used were sea captain, captain, and shipmaster.

Master Commandant

A commissioned naval officer's rank which was below a captain and above a lieutenant. The name of this rank was changed to 'commander' in 1838.

Master's Mate

A master's mate was a pretty officer who assisted the sailing master.

Masters-at-Arms

Masters-at-Arms were seaman who were in charge of keeping the swords, pistols, carbines and muskets in good working order.

Midshipman

Midshipmen were warrant officers who were in training to become commissioned officers. The rank was below a sailing master.

Muster Rolls

Muster rolls were a register of the men assigned to a ship which were completed every month.

Naval Forces

Naval forces are the U.S. Navy, U.S. Marine Corps, U.S. Flotilla Service, and the U.S. Revenue Marine.

Ordinary Seamen
Ordinary Seaman was an enlisted rank above a landsman and below an able seaman.

Pilot
A person having a special knowledge of a section of a coast, who holds a permit to offer his services to conduct vessels in and out of harbors and between coastwise points.

Privateer
An armed vessel, owned by private parties, licensed to prey on an enemy's commerce in time of war. In the war of 1812 a number of the merchant vessels of the United States, which were debarred from their usual trade, were fitted out as armed cruisers and created much havoc among British shipping.

Purser
The purser was a warrant officer responsible for supplies, provisions, and pay for the crew.

Quarter Gunner
A quarter gunner was a pretty officer who reported to the gunner. He was in charge of the care and maintenance of the cannons and gun equipment on board ship.

Quartermaster
A quartermaster was a seaman in charge of the care and maintenance of the navigation instruments and clocks.

Row Galley
Row galleys were enlarged gunboats with crew up to sixty men, which may have had a deck.

Sailmaker
A sailmaker is a warrant officer who makes and repairs the ship's sails.

Sailmaker's Mate
A sailmaker's mate is a pretty officer who assists the sailmaker in his duties.

Sailing Master – see Master

Schooner
A two-mast vessel with triangular sails before and after the mast is called a schooner.

Seaman
Seaman was the lowest skilled enlisted rank in the navy. They ranked above a landsman.

Second Lieutenant
A second lieutenant in the U.S. Marine Corps was the lowest commissioned officer rank in the corps. The rank was below a first lieutenant.

Ship
A sailing vessel with three masts and rigged with square sails. A captain normally commanded a ship. The ship did not have a gun deck and it was rated between a frigate and a brig. A sloop-of-war and a corvette were ships which performed a specialized duty.

Ship-of-the-Line
Ship-of-the-lines were the largest warship during the sailing era. They had either two- or three-gun decks and from 50 to 120 cannons.

Sloop
1) A small vessel with one mast equipped with triangular sails before and after the mast.

2) A naval vessel commanded by a master commandant. This vessel could be rigged as a schooner, a brig, or as a ship.

Sloop-of-War
A sloop-of-war was smaller than a frigate but larger that a brig. They were normally commanded by a master commandant.

Squadron
A squadron is a naval force consisting of more than one vessel with a commodore in command.

Steward
A steward organizes the mess (meals) aboard ship working with the cook and the purser.

Store Ship
A vessel attached to a navy and used to transport supplies to distant naval depots.

Surgeon
A surgeon was a warrant officer in charge of the medical department. On larger ships, the surgeon had one or more assistant surgeons, also called a surgeon's mate.

Surgeon's Mate
Surgeon's mates were warrant officers who were in charge of the patients, the medical supplies and instruments, and the medial records. They were normally medical training assistants but could be medical doctors or surgeons.

Swivel Gun
A small cannon mounted on a swivel.

Warrant Officer

Warrant officers were ship officers who received a warrant and not a commission. Warrants were issued for a specific trade, that is, a purser, a carpenter, a sailmaker, etc. These men were not line officers and could not command a ship. However, masters (sailing masters) could and did command small vessels for the navy.

Yeoman

A yeoman is a petty officer who performs a part of the clerical work on a ship.

Miscellaneous Records of the Department of the Navy
The U.S. Flotilla Service

The Chesapeake Bay Flotilla Squadron

Muster (U.S. Flotilla Service) - **6 Apr 1814**
Pay roll of the Chesapeake Flotilla under Captain Barney, Naval Records Collection of the Office of Naval Records and Library, Record Group 45.2.3, Roll 203, 6 April 1814, pp. 66-71; National Archives and Records Administration, Washington, D.C.

Payroll 1a (U.S. Flotilla Service) - **7 Apr 1814**
Pay roll of the Chesapeake Flotilla under Captain Barney, Naval Records Collection of the Office of Naval Records and Library, Record Group 45.2.3, Roll 112, 7 April 1814, pp. 86; National Archives and Records Administration, Washington, D.C.

Payroll 1 (U.S. Flotilla Service) - **6 Apr 1814**
Pay roll of the officers & seamen attached to the Chesapeake Flotilla, Joshua Barney commanding, Naval Records Collection of the Office of Naval Records and Library, Record Group 45.2.3, Roll 203, 6 April 1814, pp. 11-24; National Archives and Records Administration, Washington, D.C.

Payroll 2 (U.S. Flotilla Service) - **15 Apr 1815**
Pay roll of the officers & seamen attached to the Chesapeake Flotilla, Joshua Barney commanding, Naval Records Collection of the Office of Naval Records and Library, Record Group 45.2.3, Roll 203, 15 Apr 1815, pp. 25-65; National Archives and Records Administration, Washington, D.C.

Transfers (to U.S. Sloop-of-War Ontario) - **6 Dec 1814**
Pay roll of seamen & transfers from the U.S. Flotilla, Commodore Barney, to the Sloop of War Ontario, Naval Records Collection of the Office of Naval Records and Library, Record Group 45.2.3, Roll 14, 6 December 1814, pp. 342-343; National Archives and Records Administration, Washington, D.C.

U.S. Frigate Adams Muster - 10 Dec 1814
Muster roll of the U.S. Frigate Adams 1812-1813 (4 May 1814), Naval Records Collection of the Office of Naval Records and Library, Record Group 45.2.3, Roll 112, 10 December 1814, pp. 87-103; National Archives and Records Administration, Washington, D.C.

U.S. Frigate Adams Payroll - 4 May 1814
Pay roll of the U.S. Frigate Adams 1812-1813 (4 May 1814), Naval Records Collection of the Office of Naval Records and Library, Record Group 45.2.3, Roll 112, 4 May 1814, pp. 111-128; National Archives and Records Administration, Washington, D.C.

U.S. Frigate United States - 1 Apr 1815
Pay roll of the United States Frigate United States 1812-1814, Naval Records Collection of the Office of Naval Records and Library, Record Group 45.2.3, Roll 128, 1 April 1815, pp. 24-43; National Archives and Records Administration, Washington, D.C.

U.S. Gunboat 137 - 11 Apr 1814
Abstract pay roll of nineteen men transferred from the Potomac Flotilla to the Baltimore Station (U.S. Gunboat No. 137), Naval Records Collection of the Office of Naval Records and Library, Record Group 45.2.3, Roll 203, 11 April 1814, page 4; National Archives and Records Administration, Washington, D.C.

U.S. Gunboat 138 - 6 Apr 1814
Statement of the accounts of that part of the crew of Gun Boat No. 138 left on the Baltimore station, Naval Records Collection of the Office of Naval Records and Library, Record Group 45.2.3, Roll 138, 6 April 1814, page 7; National Archives and Records Administration, Washington, D.C.

U.S. Schooner Shark - 20 Apr 1814
Abstract pay roll of twenty-six men transferred from the Potomac to the Chesapeake Flotilla (U.S. Schooner Shark), Naval Records Collection of the Office of Naval Records and Library, Record Group 45.2.3, Roll 203, 20 April 1814, page 7; National Archives and Records Administration, Washington, D.C.

U.S. Sloop Asp - 26 May 1814

Abstract pay roll of ten men transferred from the Potomac to the Chesapeake Flotilla (U.S. Schooner Asp), Naval Records Collection of the Office of Naval Records and Library, Record Group 45.2.3, Roll 203, 26 May 1814, page 3; National Archives and Records Administration, Washington, D.C.

U.S. Sloop Scorpion 1 - 16 Mar 1814
Abstract pay roll of seven men transferred from the Potomac Flotilla to the Baltimore Station (U.S. Sloop Scorpion), Naval Records Collection of the Office of Naval Records and Library, Record Group 45.2.3, Roll 203, 16 March 1814, page 6; National Archives and Records Administration, Washington, D.C.

U.S. Sloop Scorpion 2 - 16 Mar 1814
Abstract pay roll of twenty-two men transferred from the Potomac Flotilla to the Baltimore Station (U.S. Sloop Scorpion), Naval Records Collection of the Office of Naval Records and Library, Record Group 45.2.3, Roll 203, 16 March 1814, page 5; National Archives and Records Administration, Washington, D.C.

U.S. Sloop-of-War Ontario - Mar 1815
Muster roll of the U.S. Sloop-of-War Ontario from January 1814 to Mar 1815, Naval Records Collection of the Office of Naval Records and Library, Record Group 45.2.3, Roll 203, January 1814-March 1815, pp. 1-10, 12; National Archives and Records Administration, Washington, D.C.

U.S. Frigate Adams Payroll (not transcribed yet) **- 10 Dec 1814**
Pay roll of the U.S. Frigate Adams 1812-1813, Naval Records Collection of the Office of Naval Records and Library, Record Group 45.2.3, Roll 116, 10 December 1814, pp. 24-56; National Archives and Records Administration, Washington, D.C.

POW Dartmoor
General Entry Book of American Prisoners of War, British Admiralty, Public Record Office, London, Great Britain (Series ADM 103 / Ledgers 87 through 91), General Entry Book of American prisoners of war at Dartmoor Prison.

POW Halifax
General Entry Book of American Prisoners of War, British Admiralty, Public Record Office, London, Great Britain (Series ADM 103 / Ledgers 167 and 168), General Entry Book of American prisoners of war at Halifax Prison.

The New York Flotilla Squadron

Pay roll of the U.S. Flotilla, Jacob Lewis, Esquire, Commanding, 3 October 1813, Naval Records Collection of the Office of Naval Records and Library, Record Group 45, Roll 202, 3 October 1813 to March 1814, pp. 160-166; National Archives and Records Administration, Washington, D.C.

Payroll 3 - 87-94 - No dates - No. 933-1156
Pay roll report of the U.S. Flotilla, no date, Naval Records Collection of the Office of Naval Records and Library, Record Group 45, Roll 154, pp. 87-94; National Archives and Records Administration, Washington, D.C.

Payroll 2 - 210-221 -7 Jan 1814 - 30 Sep 1814 - No. 123-2753 (many missing numbers)
Pay roll report of the U.S. Flotilla, 17 January 1814 through 30 September 1814, Naval Records Collection of the Office of Naval Records and Library, Record Group 45, Roll 194, 7 January 1814 - 30 September 1814, pp. 210-221; National Archives and Records Administration, Washington, D.C.

Promotion - 57-58 - Oct 1813-Dec 1814 - No numbers
List of petty officers, seaman, ordinary seaman, landsmen, and boys promoted and reduced by order of Jacob Lewis, Esquire, commanding U.S. Flotilla New York, 2 October 1813 through 16 December 1814, Naval Records Collection of the Office of Naval Records and Library, Record Group 45.2.3, Roll 154, pp. 57-58; National Archives and Records Administration, Washington, D.C.

Statement 1, 2, & 3 - 178-243 - 12 Dec 1814 - No. 1-1476
Statement of amount advanced to officers and men attached to the New York Station from 1 October 1813 to 30 September 1814 inclusive, Naval Records Collection of the Office of Naval Records and Library, Record Group 45.2.3, Roll 155, 12 December 1814, pp. 178-243 National Archives and Records Administration, Washington, D.C.

New York Naval Station Muster Roll 1815-1817, Naval Records Collection of the Office of Naval Records and Library, Record Group 45.2.3, Roll 154, 1 Jan 1818, pp. 125-144, National Archives and Records Administration, Washington, D.C.

Bibliography

American State Papers, Naval Affairs, volume 1, (Gales and Seaton: Washington, DC 1834).

Baker II, Harrison Scott, *American Prisoners of War Held at Halifax During the War of 1812*, (Heritage Books, Inc.: Westminster, MD, 2004), volumes 1 and 2.

Callahan, Edward W., *List of Officers of the Navy of the United States and of the Marine Corps from 1775 to 1900*, (New York, New York: L. R. Hamersley & Company, 1901).

Crawford, Michael J., *The Naval War of 1812: A Documentary History,* Volume 3, 1814-1815*, Chesapeake Bay, Northern Lakes, and Pacific Ocean.* (Washington, DC: Naval Historical Center, 2002).

The Debates and Proceedings in the Congress of the United States, Thirteenth Congress, Third Session 19 Sep 1814 to 3 March 1815, (Gales and Seaton: Washington, DC 1854).

Dudley, William S., *The Naval War of 1812, A Documentary History*, Volume 2, 1813, (Washington, DC: Naval Historical Center, Department of the Navy, 1992).

Gibson, Gary M., *The U.S. Brig Oneida: A Design & Operational History*, The War of 1812 Magazine, Issue 19, December 2012.

Guernsey, R. S., *New York City and Vicinity during the War of 1812-15*, 2 volumes, (Charles L. Woodward: New York, NY 1895).

Hughes, Christine F. and Charles E. Brodine, Jr., *The Naval War of 1812: A Documentary History,* Volume 4, 1814-1815*, Atlantic Ocean and Gulf of Mexico,* (Washington, DC: Naval Historical Center, 2023).

Johnson, Eric E., *American Prisoners of War Held at Dartmoor during the War of 1812*, (Heritage Books, Inc.: Berwyn Heights, MD, 2016).

Muster Rolls of the U.S. Marine Corps, 1798-1892; (National Archives Microfilm Publication T1118; Records of the U.S. Marine Corps, Record Group 127, National Archives and Records Administration, Washington, D.C.

National Archives and Records Administration, Record Group 52 Records of the Bureau of Medicine and Surgery, Field Records Case Files for Patients at Naval Hospitals and Registers, Entry 45, *The Register of Patients Naval Hospitals 1812 -1934* Volume 45, Washington Naval Hospital, Register of Patients from the Battle of Bladensburg entries 1-90.

Naval Records Collection of the Office of Naval Records and Library, General Records of the Office of the Secretary of the Navy, Record Group 45.2.1, National Archives and Records Administration, Washington, D.C.

Public Statutes at Large of the United States of America, volume II, Twelfth Congress, (Charles C. Little and James Brown: Boston 1845).

Public Statutes at Large of the United States of America, volume III, (Boston: Charles C. Little and James Brown, 1846).

Records relating to American Prisoners of War 1812-1815, British Admiralty, Microfilm BRRAM ADM 103 series, reel 5, volumes 167 through 173, Halifax Depot, Public Records Office, London, Great Britain.

Sheads, Scott S., *The Chesapeake Campaigns 1813-15*, (Osprey Publishing Ltd.: New York, NY 2014).

Shomette, Donald G., *Flotilla: The Patuxent Naval Campaign in the War of 1812*, (The Johns Hopkins University Press: Baltimore, MD 2009).

Silverstone, Paul H., *The Sailing Navy 1775-1854*, (Naval Institute Press: Annapolis, MD 2001).

Slavery in the United States: A Narrative of the Life and Adventures of Charles Ball, a Black Man, (John S. Taylor, publisher: New York, NY 1837).

Waterhouse, Charles H., *Marines in the Frigate Navy*, (History Division, U.S. Marine Corps: Washington, DC 2006).

Weller, M. I., *Commodore Joshua Barney: The Hero of the Battle of Bladensburg*, Records of the Columbia Historical Society (Washington, DC 1911).

www.ingramcontent.com/pod-product-compliance
Lightning Source LLC
LaVergne TN
LVHW061249100826
845148LV00008B/1069

* 9 7 8 0 7 8 8 4 4 6 4 4 3 *